ENGINEERING ECONOMIC

Engineering Economics and Costing

Sasmita Mishra

Faculty of Economics
Department of Mathematics and Humanities
College of Engineering and Technology (BPUT)
Bhubaneswar, Orissa

PHI Learning Private Limited

New Delhi-110001
2009

Rs. 225.00

ENGINEERING ECONOMICS AND COSTING
Sasmita Mishra

ISBN-978-81-203-3893-7

The export rights of this book are vested solely with the publisher.

Published by Asoke K. Ghosh, PHI Learning Private Limited, M-97, Connaught Circus, New Delhi-110001 and Printed by Jay Print Pack Private Limited, New Delhi-110015.

Contents

Preface .... *xi*

Part I Engineering Economics

1. Engineering Economics–An Overview **3–11**

    1.1   Introduction   *3*
    1.2   Engineering and Economics   *5*
    1.3   Economics: Brief Description   *5*
    1.4   Engineering Economy   *6*
    1.5   Definition and Scope of Engineering Economics   *6*
          1.5.1   Definition   *6*
          1.5.2   Scope   *6*
    1.6   Basic Economic Problems   *6*
    1.7   Subject Matter of Economics   *7*
    1.8   Interdependence of Firm, Households and Government   *9*
    1.9   Principles of Engineering Economics   *10*
    1.10 Engineering Design Process Activities   *11*
    Review Questions   *11*

2. Utility Analysis **12–33**

    2.1   Introduction   *12*
    2.2   Assumption of Marginal Utility Analysis   *12*
    2.3   Laws of Diminishing Marginal Utility Analysis   *13*
    2.4   Principle of Equi-Marginal Utility: Consumer's Equilibrium   *14*
    2.5   Derivation of Demand Curve and Law of Demand   *16*
    2.6   Demand   *19*
          2.6.1   Meaning of Demand   *19*
          2.6.2   Meaning of Demand Schedule   *19*
    2.7   Law of Demand   *22*
          2.7.1   Meaning   *22*

2.7.2   Assumptions of the Law   *23*

2.7.3   Limitations of the Law/Exception to Law of Demand   *24*

2.8   Elasticity of Demand   *24*

2.8.1   Introduction   *24*

2.8.2   Various Concepts of Demand Elasticity   *25*

2.8.3   Price Elasticity of Demand   *25*

2.8.4   Types of Price Elasticity   *26*

2.8.5   Factors Determining Price Elasticity of Demand   *28*

2.8.6   Price Elasticity and Changes in Total Expenditure   *29*

2.8.7   Measurement of Elasticity at a Point on the Demand Curve   *29*

2.8.8   Arc Elasticity of Demand   *30*

Review Questions   *32*

3. Theory of Production 34–62

3.1   Introduction   *34*

3.2   Importance of the Theory of Production   *34*

3.3   Equal Product Curves or Isoquants   *35*

3.4   Marginal Rate of Technical Substitution   *36*

3.5   Diminishing Marginal Rate of Technical Substitution   *37*

3.6   Properties of Isoquants or Equal Product Curves   *38*

3.7   Law of Variable Proportions   *38*

3.7.1   Three Stages of the Law of Variable Proportions   *40*

3.8   Returns to Scale   *41*

3.8.1   The Concept of Returns to Scale   *41*

3.8.2   Constant Returns to Scale   *42*

3.8.3   Increasing Returns to Scale   *43*

3.8.4   Decreasing Returns to Scale   *43*

3.8.5   Varying Returns to Scale in a Single Production Function   *44*

3.9   Cost of Production and Cost Curves   *44*

3.9.1   Short-Run Total Costs   *45*

3.9.2   The Short-Run Average Cost Curves   *47*

3.9.3   Relationship between the Average and Marginal Cost Curves   *50*

3.9.4   Long-Run Average Cost Curve   *51*

3.10   Law of Supply   *54*

3.10.1   Elasticity of Supply   *54*

3.11   Price Determination under Perfect Competition Market Structure   *57*

3.11.1   Pricing under Perfect Competition   *58*

3.11.2   Determination of Price   *59*

Review Questions   *62*

4. Time Value of Money 63–74

4.1   Introduction   *63*

4.2   Techniques for Adjusting Time Value of Money or Interest Formulas   *63*

4.2.1   Single-Payment Compound Amount/Future Value of an Amount   *64*

4.2.2   Single-Payment Present Worth Amount   *64*

4.2.3   Equal-Payment Series Compound Amount/Future Value of an Annuity   *65*

4.2.4   Equal-Payment Series Sinking Fund   *66*

4.2.5   Equal-Payment Series Present Worth Amount   *68*
4.2.6   Equal-Payment Series Capital Recovery Amount   *69*
4.3   Uniform Gradient Series Factor (*A/G, i, N*)   *70*
4.4   Annuity   *71*
4.4.1   What is an Annuity?   *71*
4.5   Annuity Due   *72*
4.6   Calculation of Deferred Annuity   *72*
Review Questions   *73*

5. Cash Flows for Investment Analysis: Concepts and Diagrams 75–81

5.1   Introduction   *75*
5.2   Types/Components of Cash Flows   *75*
5.3   Cash Flow Diagrams   *76*
5.4   Principles of Equivalence   *78*
5.4.1   Equivalence between Cash Flows   *78*
5.4.2   Equivalence at Any Common Point of Time   *79*
5.4.3   Equivalence Depends on Interest Rate   *79*
5.4.4   Equivalence between Receipts and Disbursements   *80*
5.5   Uses and Significance of Cash Flow Statement   *80*
5.6   Limitations of Cash Flow Statement   *81*
Review Questions   *81*

6. Evaluation of Engineering Alternatives 82–123

6.1   Introduction   *82*
6.2   Present Worth Method   *82*
6.2.1   Steps Needed for Present Worth Comparison   *82*
6.2.2   Revenue-based Cash Flow Diagram   *83*
6.2.3   Cost-based Cash Flow Diagram   *84*
6.3   Future Worth Method   *89*
6.3.1   Steps for Computing Future Worth Method   *89*
6.4   Equivalent Annual Worth Comparison   *94*
6.4.1   Steps for Computing EAW   *95*
6.5   Rate of Return Method   *100*
6.5.1   Minimum Acceptable Rate of Return   *101*
6.5.2   Internal Rate of Return (IRR)   *101*
6.6   Project Evaluation and Cost-Benefit Analysis   *110*
6.6.1   Cost-Benefit Analysis   *111*
Review Questions   *115*

7. Depreciation Analysis 124–136

7.1   Introduction   *124*
7.2   Causes of Depreciation   *124*
7.3   Depreciable Property   *125*
7.4   Depreciation Methods   *126*
7.4.1   Straight Line Depreciation Method   *126*
7.4.2   Declining Balance Method   *127*
7.4.3   Modified Accelerated Cost Recovery System   *130*

7.5   Sum of the Years-Digit Method   *133*
7.6   After Tax Economic Comparisons   *134*
Review Questions   *135*

8. **Break-Even Analysis** **137–149**

8.1   Introduction   *137*
  8.1.1   Break-Even Point   *137*
  8.1.2   Determination of Break-Even Point   *137*
  8.1.3   Break-Even Point in Terms of Quantity   *138*
  8.1.4   Break-Even Point in Terms of Sales Value   *139*
  8.1.5   Break-Even Point as a Percentage of Capacity   *140*
8.2   Break-Even Chart   *140*
8.3   Break-Even Analysis Assumptions   *142*
8.4   Managerial Uses of Break-Even Analysis   *142*
  8.4.1   Safety Margin   *142*
  8.4.2   Volume Needed to Attain Target Profit   *142*
  8.4.3   Change in Price   *143*
  8.4.4   Change in Costs   *143*
8.5   Limitations of Break-Even Analysis   *144*
8.6   Profit-Volume (P/V) Analysis   *145*
Review Questions   *148*

Part II   Financial System

9. **Commercial Banking** **153–164**

9.1   Introduction   *153*
9.2   Functions of Commercial Banks or Modern Banks   *154*
  9.2.1   Accepting Deposits   *154*
  9.2.2   Advancing of Loans   *154*
  9.2.3   Credit Creation   *155*
  9.2.4   Promoting Cheque System   *155*
  9.2.5   Agency Functions   *155*
  9.2.6   General Utility Function   *156*
9.3   Role of Commercial Bank in a Developing Economy   *157*
9.4   Sound Banking System for Underdeveloped Countries   *158*
9.5   Types of Banks   *159*
9.6   Balance Sheet of a Bank   *160*
  9.6.1   Liabilities of the Bank   *161*
  9.6.2   Assets of the Bank   *161*
  9.6.3   Importance of Balance Sheet of a Bank   *162*
9.7   New Developments in Commercial Banking System   *163*
Review Questions   *164*

10. **Reserve Bank of India** **165–173**

10.1   Introduction   *165*
10.2   Organization   *165*

10.3 Functions of Reserve Bank of India   *166*
   10.3.1   Note Issue   *166*
   10.3.2   Banker to Government   *166*
   10.3.3   Banker's Bank   *167*
   10.3.4   Custodian of Exchange Reserves   *167*
   10.3.5   Controller of Credit   *167*
   10.3.6   Ordinary Banking Functions   *168*
   10.3.7   Miscellaneous Functions   *168*
   10.3.8   Forbidden Business   *168*
   10.3.9   Promotional and Developmental Functions   *169*
10.4 Monetary Policy of RBI   *169*
10.5 Policy of Credit Expansion   *170*
10.6 Policy of Credit Control   *171*
Review Questions   *173*

11. Indian Money Market **174–193**
11.1 Introduction   *174*
11.2 Structure of Indian Money Market   *174*
11.3 Unorganized Sector of the Indian Money Market   *175*
11.4 Organized Sector of Indian Money Market   *176*
11.5 Drawbacks of the Indian Money Market   *178*
11.6 Shortcomings of Indian Money Market   *179*
11.7 Measures to Strengthen the Indian Money Market   *180*
11.8 Indian Capital Market   *181*
11.9 Structure of Development Banks of India   *181*
   11.9.1   Agricultural Development Banks   *181*
   11.9.2   Industrial Development Banks   *182*
Review Questions   *193*

Part III   Cost Accounting

12. Costing and Cost Concepts **197–204**
12.1 Introduction *197*
12.2 Costing and Cost Accounting   *197*
12.3 Objectives of Cost Accounting   *198*
12.4 Cost Concepts   *198*
   12.4.1   Behavioural Classification   *198*
   12.4.2   Direct Cost and Indirect Cost   *201*
   12.4.3   Relevant Cost and Irrelevant Cost   *201*
   12.4.4   Product Cost and Period Cost   *202*
   12.4.5   Real Cost of Production   *202*
   12.4.6   Opportunity Cost   *203*
12.5 Elements of Cost   *203*
Review Questions   *204*

13. Process Costing **205–210**

13.1   Meaning   *205*
13.2   Elements of Production Cost in Process Costing   *205*
13.3   Methods of Process Costing   *205*
13.4   Principles of Process Costing   *206*
13.5   Spoilage   *208*
Review Questions   *210*

14. Marginal Costing **211–213**

14.1   Introduction   *211*
14.2   Features of Marginal Costing   *211*
14.3   Assumptions   *211*
14.4   Profit under Marginal Costing   *212*
14.5   Significance of Marginal Costing   *212*
14.6   Break-Even Point   *212*
14.7   P/V Ratio   *213*
Review Questions   *213*

15. Standard Costing and Variance Analysis **214–221**

15.1   Concept of Standard Costing   *214*
15.2   Definition and Meaning   *215*
15.3   Standard Costing and Budgetary Control   *215*
15.4   Standard Cost and Estimated Cost   *217*
        15.4.1   Advantages of Standard Costing   *217*
        15.4.2   Limitations of Standard Costing   *218*
15.5   Computation and Analysis of Variances   *219*
        15.5.1   Favourable and Unfavourable Variance   *219*
        15.5.2   Controllable and Uncontrollable Variances   *220*
        15.5.3   Material Cost Variances   *220*
        15.5.4   Labour Cost Variances   *221*
Review Questions   *221*

16. Cost Control and Cost Reduction **222–225**

16.1   Cost Control   *222*
16.2   Features of Cost Control   *222*
16.3   Techniques of Cost Control   *223*
16.4   Cost Reduction   *223*
16.5   Cost Reduction Programme   *224*
16.6   Areas of Application   *224*
16.7   Distinction between Cost Control and Cost Reduction   *225*
Review Questions   *225*

Appendix: Interest Tables *227–298*

Bibliography *299*

Index *301–303*

Preface

This book *Engineering Economics and Costing* has been written primarily to meet the requirements of B.Tech. and MCA students of Biju Pattanaik University of Technology (BPUT), Orissa. It would also be useful to undergraduate students of engineering in other universities/institutes. The text aims at providing a clear understanding of the fundamentals of Economics, Engineering Economics, Money, Banking, Financial Markets, and Development Banking. I have taken special care to present a simple, systematic and analytical study to the students without involving them in the intricacies and unnecessary details of the subject. The book provides an exhaustive Appendix on Interest Tables for a wide range of interest rates (0.25–50%) and a period ranging from one year to 100 years. These tables, along with the topics discussed, will be of great help to the students of Engineering in the evaluation of engineering projects.

The book is organized into three parts: Part I Engineering Economics; Part II Financial System; and Part III Cost Accounting.

Part I consists of eight chapters with emphasis on demand and supply theory, evaluation of engineering projects, theory of production, time value of money, depreciation accounting, and break-even analysis. Chapter 1 introduces the subject matter of Economics and basic economic activities which represent a blend of subjects that build on the traditional engineering concern for operating economics. Chapters 2 and 3 explain elasticity of demand and supply, law of variable proportion, returns to scale, and their applications in different sectors. Chapters 4–6 present the conventional mathematics of money and comparisons of alternatives based on present worth method, future worth method, internal rate of return, equivalent annual worth, and cost-benefit analysis. Chapters 7 and 8 illustrate current depreciation and income tax consideration relevant to such operations. In Chapter 8, break-even analysis is also presented, which helps in examining the current conditions of a business.

Part II consists of three chapters. Chapter 9 discusses Commercial Banking. Commercial banks play a significant role in enlarging the productive potential of the economic system by mobilizing the available resources from the people and channelling those into productive activities. Chapter 10 deals with the Reserve Bank of India. Chapter 11 analyses the Indian Money Market which is formed to meet the ever increasing credit requirements of industry and trade.

Part III comprises five chapters and is devoted to a discussion on the techniques of cost ascertainment, classification of cost, division of cost and their application for planning, control, performance, evaluation and decision-making. Here, cost is classified and analysed on the basis of function, process, product, centres, etc. This can aid in the process of cost computation, cost saving and cost reduction. Cost accounting consists of certain principles and rules to which the technique of costing should be applied. Chapter 12 explains costing and cost concepts. Chapters 13 and 14 elucidate process costing and marginal costing. Chapter 15 investigates standard costing and variance analysis while Chapter 16 discusses cost control and cost reduction.

I am thankful to Prof. S.P. Mohanty, Head of the Department of Mathematics and Humanities, College of Engineering and Technology (CET) for giving me the opportunity to teach in CET and for his encouragement in preparing this text. I am indebted to Dr. S.K. Mishra for his support and cooperation. I am also grateful to my students and colleagues for their inspiration and valuable suggestions in preparing the text. I express my sincere gratitude to Prof. N.C. Sahu, Department of Economics, Berhampur University, for helping me in completing this project. Finally, I wish to thank the editorial, production and sales team of the Publishers, PHI Learning, in particular, K.C. Devasia, Senior Editor, and D.P. Tripathy, Sales Executive, for their assistance and careful processing of the manuscript.

Comments and suggestions for improvement of the text will be gratefully accepted.

Sasmita Mishra

Part I

ENGINEERING ECONOMICS

1

Engineering Economics–An Overview

1.1   INTRODUCTION

The word Economics has been derived from two Greek words, namely, *Oikus* and *Nemein*. *Oikus* means "household" and *Nemein* means "management". Economics, like engineering, has its roots deep in history. For example, the construction of the pyramids is considered an engineering marvel. Economics, as a science, deals with the problem of allocation of scarce resources among competing ends and giving maximum satisfaction at minimum cost.

Economics affects almost every aspect of human life; it makes its presence felt when consumers and nations make decisions. It gives us techniques founded in sound logic with which decisions can be assessed in relation to the pros and cons, advantages and disadvantages, and benefits and costs involved. Economics is closely related to the term 'money', the modern equivalent of the long sought after 'philosopher's stone'. For centuries, alchemists vainly sought the stone that could transform metals into gold. Now at present may has required that ability by mining fold. With money as the medium of exchange, we can convert one type of resource into another very easily. The worthiness of this transformation is a subtle aspect of the mission of engineering economists. Tell-tale analyses of alternatives reveal the innermost workings of a project and burden the analyst with ethical responsibilities. A prerequisite to bearing the burden is a thorough knowledge of accepted economic principles and practices. This knowledge facilitates putting a legitimate monetary value on the transformation of each resource, and allows an accurate and conscientious appraisal of worthiness when combined with technical expertise about the subject. Resource commitments monetized as cash flows set a quantitative framework for ensuring qualitative value considerations.

Engineers are planners and builders. They are also problem solvers, managers, and decision-makers. Engineering economics touches each of these activities. Much of the management function of an engineer is directed towards economic objectives and monitored by economic measures.

Engineering economics is closely aligned with conventional microeconomics, optimization and determination of equilibrium. It is devoted to problem-solving and decision-making at the operations level. Optimization is done at the micro level of decision-making, wherein the decision-maker's objective is to arrive at the best combination of goods to be consumed or produced, or of inputs to be employed.

An engineering economist draws on the accumulated knowledge of engineering and economics to identify the alternative uses of limited resources and select the preferred course of action. Evaluations rely mainly on mathematical models and cost data, but judgement and experience are vital inputs. Many accepted models are available for analyses of short-range projects when the time value of money is not relevant, and of long-range proposals when discounting is required for input data assumed to be known or subject to risk. Familiarity with these models, gained from studying the ensuring chapters of this text will guide your passage as a reader through the engineering economic decision.

An engineer might encounter a number of problems in his day-to-day working:

1. Which one of the several competing engineering designs should be selected?
2. Should the machine now in use be replaced with a new one?
3. With limited capital available, which investment alternative should be accepted?
4. Would it be preferable to pursue a safer conservative course of action or follow a riskier one that offers higher potential returns?
5. How many units of production have to be sold before a profit can be made?
6. Among several proposals for funding that yield substantially equivalent worthwhile results but have different cash flow patterns, which is preferable?
7. Are the benefits expected from a public service project large enough to make its implementation costs acceptable?

Two characteristics of the above-mentioned questions should be apparent: *first*, each deals with a choice among alternatives; *second*, all such questions involve economic considerations. The less obvious characteristics are the requirements of adequate data and an awareness of technological constraints to define the problem and identify legitimate solutions. These considerations are embodied in the decision-making role of engineering economists to

1. identify alternative uses for limited resources and obtain appropriate data; and
2. analyse the data to determine the better alternative.

The breadth of problems, depth of analysis, and scope of application, which practicing engineers encounter, vary widely. Newly graduated engineers are regularly assigned to cost reduction projects and are expected to be cost conscious in all their operations. As these engineers gain more experience, they may become specialists in certain application areas or may undertake more general responsibilities as managers. Moreover, beginners are usually restricted to short-range decisions for low-budget operations, whereas engineering managers are confronted with policy decisions that involve large sums of money and are influenced by many factors with long-range consequences. However, both the situations are served by the principles and practices of engineering economics.

Now let us be a little more specific with engineering economic problems than we were with the general questions already discussed. Economic decisions are required in the following typical situations:

1. When a manufacturing plant wishes to produce a part in its own production facility, knowing that major investment will be needed in buying a new equipment.
2. When a country has to decide between (i) immediately implementing a manually controlled irrigation system with a planned upgrading of an automated system in four years, and (ii) immediately implementing a more expensive automated control system.
3. When an electric utility is considering updating its computer networking capability and has to decide between upgrading its existing minicomputer file servers, and scrapping them for new IBM minicomputer systems. If it opts for the latter, then should it buy or lease?
4. If an oil refinery needs to enlarge its port facilities to allow more tankers to be serviced per week, then what are the potential gains associated with a dock expansion?

5. A manufacturing engineer is planning a high-speed production line that will use automated transfer mechanisms to move and position products from one automated workstation to the next. More complex workstations will allow more operations to be completed at a workstation at the expense of lower production rates per hour. However, such a situation could have the advantage of allowing fewer expensive transfer mechanisms. Given the forecast of product demand for the next six years, the engineer has to decide between a one-shift operation with a certain number of transfer mechanisms and a two-shift operation with fewer transfer mechanisms.

A decision is simply the selection of an option from two or more courses of action, whether it takes place in construction or production operations, service or manufacturing industries, private or public agencies. Most major decisions, even personal ones, have economic overtones. This makes the subject of engineering economics especially challenging and rewarding.

1.2 ENGINEERING AND ECONOMICS

Before 1940, engineers were mainly concerned with the design, construction, and operation of machines, structures and processes. They paid little attention to resources, human and natural, that produced the final products. Many factors have since contributed to the expansion of engineering responsibilities and concerns.

Besides the traditional work of transforming scientific discoveries into useful products, engineers are now also expected to generate novel technological solutions, along with making skillful financial analyses of the effects of the implementation. In today's close and tangled relations among the industry, public, and government, cost and value analyses are expected to be more detailed and inclusive (e.g. worker safety, environmental effects, consumer protection, resource conservation) than ever before. Without these analyses, project can easily become more of a burden than a benefit.

Most definitions of engineering suggest that the mission of the engineers is to transform natural resources for the benefit of the human race. The types of resources susceptible to engineering enrichment include everything from ores and crops to information and energy. A growing awareness of the finite limits of the earth's resources has added a pressing dimension to engineering evaluations. Thus, focus on scarce resources welds engineering to economics.

1.3 ECONOMICS: BRIEF DESCRIPTION

Thomas Malthus (1766–1834) in *Principles of Population* had conjectured about the causes of economic crisis, saying that population tends to increase geometrically and the means of subsistence increases only arithmetically; His forecast of misery for most of the population predisposed the 'dismal science' nickname for economics. John Stuart Mill (1806–1873), in his *Treatise on Political Economy*, was against Malthus pessimism and suggested that the laws of distribution are not as immutable as are the laws of production.

In *Das Kapital*, Karl Marx (1818–1883) had argued that capitalism would be superseded by socialism, which would then develop into communism. According to Marx, workers produce more value in comparison to the wages they receive. The surplus money generated takes the form of profit and allows capital accumulation. He contended that the capitalist system will eventually fail, owing to cyclic depression and other inherent weaknesses. However, recent dramatic changes in the political and geographical structure of eastern Europe show that many of the predictions of Marx did not come true as evidenced in the decline of many communist countries. Not may scholars agree with Marx's views today.

From the work of John Maynard Keynes (1883–1946) in the 1930s there emerged 'New economics'. In *The General Theory of Employment, Interest and Money*, Keynes clashed with classical economic theoriests by proclaiming that the interest rates and price-wage adjustments are not adequate mechanisms for controlling unemployment in capitalistic economies. Thus, Keynes and Marx theories deal with the entire economic system with respect to national income, flow of money, consumption, investment, wages, and general prices. This form of analysis, concerned with the economy as a whole, is called **macroeconomics**. It produces economy-wide statistical measures, such as national cost of living index and total employment figures. Engineering economics, with its focus on economic decision-making in an individual organizational unit, is closely aligned with microeconomics.

1.4 ENGINEERING ECONOMY

The development of the methodology of engineering economy which is now used in all engineering works is of relatively recent origin. In 1930, Eugene L. Grant (1897–1996), who is considered the father of engineering economy, published *Principles of Engineering Economy*, in which he discussed the importance of judgement factors and short-term investment evaluation along with conventional comparisons of long-run investments in capital goods based on compound interest calculations.

1.5 DEFINITION AND SCOPE OF ENGINEERING ECONOMICS

1.5.1 Definition

Engineering economics deals with the methods that enable one to make economic decisions towards evaluation of design and engineering alternatives. It helps in examining the relevancy of a project, estimating its value and justifying it from the engineering viewpoint.

1.5.2 Scope

In this text we have covered topics, such as law of demand and supply, demand and supply elasticity, concept of short-run and long-run cost, law of variable proportion, returns to scale, time value analysis, interest formulaes, bases for comparing engineering alternatives (e.g. present worth method, future worth method, annual equivalent method, rate of return method) and cost-benefit analysis.

The text also covers depreciation accounting, break-even analysis, variance analysis, process costing, standard costing, marginal costing, functions of commercial banks and the Reserve Bank of India (RBI), money market, and Export-Import (EXIM) policy.

1.6 BASIC ECONOMIC PROBLEMS

1. **Allocation of resources:**   The wants or requirements of an individual, business firm or the government far exceed the resources available to satisfy these needs. So with scarce resources, a choice has to be made regarding which all wants should be satisfied. Whether a country should have more of agriculture or industry, the government has to decide. The

choice involves allocation of scarce resources to different sectors so that the country can have the highest living standards. This allocation of resources has different objectives in different countries. For example, in a country, like India, the resources should be so utilized to increase the per capita income of people, reduce poverty and better the living standards of people.

2. **By what methods are goods purchased:**   Goods are produced, in various ways. For example, agricultural goods can be produced by using more of labour and less of capital or more capital and less of labour. When the former is used, it is known as **labour intensive method** while the latter is known as **capital intensive method**. Moreover, one may also have to decide between taking recourse to large-scale production and small-scale production. Another question is the technique of production. Will it be traditional or modern? These decisions are very crucial and, at the same time, controversial. But a country should make the decisions keeping in view the problems that are peculiar to it. India, for example, has got a vast labour force but less of capital. So here it would be better to adopt labour intensive methods of production.

3. **Distribution of goods:**   After the goods are produced, the question arises as to who is going to receive these and in what proportion. To put it in another way, how will the goods and services produced in a country he distributed among the owners of land, labour and capital? Can the Government by its policy change the distribution of income? If the Government changes the distribution of income, what will be the effects?

4. **Utilization of resources:**   The next question is: are the resources of the country, such as men, material and money, fully utilized or are they underutilized? This leads us to the question of employment of resources. We have discussed that resources are insufficient in relation to their use. But still we find that some men and machines remain unemployed or unutilized for years together. Non-application of resources is a basic economic problem. When resources remain unutilized, goods and services do not get produced. The cost of which is very huge for the society to bear. The resources should not only be put to use, but also efficient utilization of these is necessary. Efficient utilization means potential output rather than actual output. To achieve potential output, inefficiency should be reduced to the minimum at all levels.

1.7 SUBJECT MATTER OF ECONOMICS

The subject matter of any study is derived from its definition. The definition of Economics starts with the existence of *unlimited wants*. However, the resources to satisfy these wants are *limited*. Moreover, the same resource can be utilized for different purposes. Therefore, wants have to be satisfied in order of their importance.

All economic activities start because of the existence of human wants. Which must be satisfied so that man can live in this world. Wants can be satisfied with the help of resources only. Which can be earned by making efforts. More efforts mean more resources. With the help of resources, a person fulfils his wants and gets satisfaction. Hence, Economics is the study of wants, efforts and satisfaction as these constitute the very substance of its subject matter. It is a continuous circle of unending wants, efforts and satisfaction.

While in the primitive society, the link between wants, efforts and satisfaction was direct, today it has become indirect.

The prehistoric man when he felt hungry, collected fruits and roots and satisfied his hunger. But in the present modern and complex society of ours, there is no such direct link. A worker of a glass factory does not consume bottles that he makes. He works in the factory, gets his wages with the help of which he purchases his requirements of his life from the market. So in the modern economy, wants, efforts and satisfaction are linked through money.

As already mentioned, economics centres a round wants, efforts and satisfaction. The activities which are necessary to satisfy wants, increase efforts and maximize satisfaction are called *economic activities*. The study of economic activities is traditionally divided into several parts:

- Consumption
- Production
- Exchange and Distribution
- Money and Banking
- International Trade.

These are now briefly described.

Consumption

Consumption means the use of resources or wealth in order to satisfy one's needs. It also means destruction of resources by human beings. The study of consumption includes the study of human wants, their characteristics, and the laws which provide maximum satisfaction out of limited income.

Production

Consumption is only possible when there is production. As consumption is destruction of utilities, similarly production is creation of utilities to satisfy human wants. Production is possible by the combination of four factors: land, labour, capital, and organization. The process of production involves creation of three types of utilities that are form utility (e.g. making paddy rice), place utility (e.g. transporting rice from mill to shop) and time utility (e.g. rice stored in summer and sold in rainy season at a higher price). In this text, we study the methods, characteristics of factors of production, and the laws which teach us how to produce the maximum output with minimum resources.

Exchange and Distribution

Distribution means disp of national income among various factors of production. The land owners get rent, labourers get wages, suppliers of money get rate of interest, and organizers get profit. How much each of them should get constitutes the subject matter of distribution.

Money and Banking

Money is generally accepted by all as a means of payment, medium of exchange, standard of deferred payment, and store of all values. Modern economy is based on money. Economic activities are measured in terms of money. Things are purchased and factors are paid with the help of money. The institution that helps in keep in the money safe and at the same time generates it is the bank. So we have to study money and banking together. Bank is the financial institution that accepts money in the form of deposits and lends it for productive purposes.

International Trade

When nations trade among themselves, it is denoted as international trade. No country can produce all the commodities it requires. So in order to satisfy various needs a large number of items are imported from other countries. To pay for the imports, a few commodities are exported that are produces at low prices. Thus international trade is another field of economics.

1.8 INTERDEPENDENCE OF FIRM, HOUSEHOLDS AND GOVERNMENT

Firms are the production units. They produce goods, commodities and services. For this they require labour, factories and capital. Which in turn are provided by household units. By providing such factor services and labour, the household units get payment. These payments otherwise become the income of households. They then spend this income in purchasing commodities produced by the firms. The payments the households make become the income of the firms. These payments are made in terms of money. Therefore the transactions that take place between the households and the firms lead to flow of money from the firms to the households and back. Hence, we call this *circular flow of income*. This simple model of interdependence between firms and households is illustrated in Figure 1.1. It is to be remembered that here we have shown two flows. (i) the flow of goods, commodities, services, and factors (ii) the flow of money in terms of payment. The flow of goods, services and factors is known as *real flow*. The figure shows interdependence of the firm and the household sector in respect of providing services (firm) and payment for these services (households).

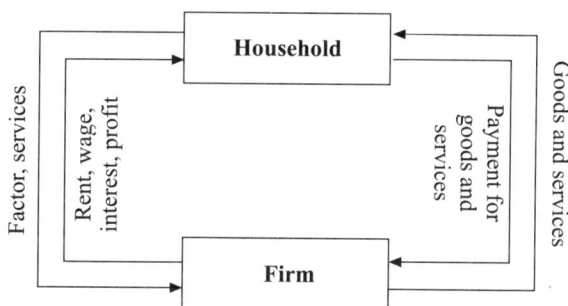

Figure 1.1   Interdependence between firm and household.

We need to remember two things here. *First*, it is not easy to distinguish between producers and consumers. A person can be both a producer and a consumer. For example, in the factory he is a producer and makes production decisions. At home, however, he is a consumer and makes consumption decisions. *Secondly*, a firm does not always sell to the household. There are different stages of production in which a firm sells to another firm which produces raw materials, e.g. steel, sells to another firm who makes grills and doors and, finally, sells the end product to the consumer. Therefore, a firm may not sell always to the household directly. It may first sell to other firms.

From the simplified circular flow of income, we can construct a complex flow of income where we can show three basic units of economics; *firms*, *households*, and *Government*. Firms purchase socially supplied goods and services from the Government and the latter takes from the former exports and revenue. Similarly, Government supplies general service to the households, and they in turn pay taxes. This is shown in Figure 1.2.

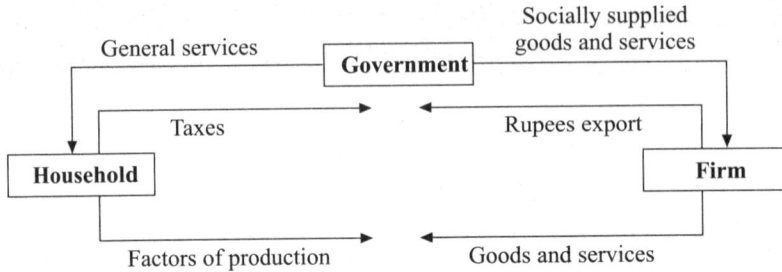

Figure 1.2   Interdependence among firm, household and government.

The entire network of economy is interdependent on each individual unit. Households pay Government taxes and the, Government sells general services to them. Firms receive from the Government socially supplied goods, such as electricity, transportation facilities like roads and railway, market facilities, and a host of other services. They in exchange supply the Government revenues and money in the form of exports. So the entire economic system is interdependent.

1.9   PRINCIPLES OF ENGINEERING ECONOMICS

The development, study and application of any discipline must begin with a basic foundation. The foundation for engineering economics is a set of seven principles or fundamental concepts that provide a comprehensive doctrine for developing the methodology.

PRINCIPLE 1:   *Develop the alternatives*

The choice (decision) is among the alternatives. The alternatives are to be identified and then defined for subsequent analysis. A decision situation involves making a choice among two or more alternatives. Developing and defining the alternatives for direct evaluation is important because of the resulting impact on the quality of the decision. Engineers and managers should place a high priority on these responsibilities.

PRINCIPLE 2:   *Focus on the differences*

Only the difference in expected future outcomes among the alternatives is relevant to their comparison and should be considered when making the decision. If all prospective outcomes of the feasible alternatives were exactly the same, then there would be no basis or need for comparison. We would be indifferent to the alternatives and make decision on the basis of random selection.

PRINCIPLE 3:   *Use a consistent viewpoint*

The prospective outcomes of the alternatives, economic and other, should be consistently developed from a defined viewpoint (perspective). It is important that the viewpoint for a particular decision be first defined and then used consistently in the description, analysis and comparison of the alternative.

PRINCIPLE 4:   *Use a common unit of measure*

Using a common unit of measurement to enumerate as many of the prospective outcomes as possible will make easier the analysis and comparison of alternatives.

PRINCIPLE 5:   *Consider all relevant criteria*

Selection of a preferred alternative (decision-making) requires the use of a criterion (or several criteria). The decision process should consider both the outcomes enumerated in the monetary unit and those expressed in some other unit of measurement made explicit in a descriptive manner.

PRINCIPLE 6: *Make uncertainty explicit*

Uncertainty is inherent in projecting (or estimating) the future outcomes of the alternative recognized in their analysis and comparison.

PRINCIPLE 7: *Revisit your decisions*

Improved decision-making results from an adoptive process. To the extent practicable, the initial projected outcomes of the selected alternative should be subsequently compared with the actual results achieved. A sound engineering economic analysis procedure incorporates the basic method and involves following:

1. Problem recognition, definition and evaluation
2. Development of feasible alternatives
3. Development of cash flow for each alternative
4. Selection of criteria
5. Analysis and comparison of the alternatives
6. Selection of the preferred alternative
7. Performance monitoring and post-evaluation results

There also six engineering design processes which provide information-related steps in the economic analysis procedure. They are discussed in the following section.

1.10 ENGINEERING DESIGN PROCESS ACTIVITIES

1. Problem / Need definition
2. Problem/Need formulation and evaluations
3. Synthesis of possible solutions, calculations
4. Analysis, optimization and evaluation
5. Specification of preferred alternative
6. Communication

REVIEW QUESTIONS

1. Who is the father of engineering economics?

2. What is the chief aim of economics?

3. Explain what is the main aim of engineering.

4. Name the earliest work of engineering economics.

5. How many procedures are there in engineering economics?

6. Why should engineers study economics? What is its applicability?

7. Explain about the origin and development of engineering economics.

8. What are the different principles of engineering economics?

CHAPTER 2

Utility Analysis

2.1 INTRODUCTION

Economists, like engineers, need a good set of tools to make decision. The most important tools for economists are *utility analysis, demand and supply analysis.*

The price of a product depends on the demand for and the supply of it. In this chapter, we are concerned with the theory of demand, which explains the need for a good and the factors determining it. An individual's demand for a product depends on the price of the product, income of the individual, and the prices of related goods. It can be put in the functional form as

$$D_A = f(P_A, I, P_B, P_C)$$

where D_A stands for the demand of good A, P_A for price of good A, I for individual's income, P_B, P_C, etc. for the prices of related goods. But among these determinants of demand, the economists single out the price of the good in question as the most important factor governing the demand for it. Indeed, the function of theory of demand is to establish a relationship between the quantity demanded of a good and its price, and provide an explanation for it. From time to time, different theories have been advanced to explain consumer's demand for a good and derive a valid demand theorem. Marginal utility analysis is the oldest theory of demand which provides an explanation of consumer's demand for a product. It derives the law of demand which establishes an inverse relationship between the price and the quantity demanded of the product.

2.2 ASSUMPTION OF MARGINAL UTILITY ANALYSIS

The marginal utility analysis of demand is based on certain important assumptions. Before enumerating how utility analysis explains a consumer's equilibrium with regard to the demand for goods, it is essential to describe those basic assumptions on which the whole utility analysis rests. The basic assumptions or premises of utility analysis are now discussed.

1. **The cardinal measurability of utility:** The exponents of marginal utility analysis regard utility to be a cardinal concept. According to them, utility is a measurable and quantifiable entity, and a person can express the utility or satisfaction he derives from the goods in

quantitative terms. Thus, he can say that he derives utility equal to 20 units from the consumption of a unit of good A, and 40 units from the consumption of a unit of good B. Moreover, the cardinal measurement of utility involves that the person can compare in respect of size how much one level of utility is greater than another, that is, a person can say that the utility he gets from the consumption of one unit of good B is double the utility he obtains from the consumption of one unit of good A.

2. **Constancy of the marginal utility of money:** Another important assumption of marginal utility analysis is the constancy of the marginal utility of money. Thus, while marginal utility analysis assumes that marginal utilities of commodities diminish as more of them are purchased or consumed, the marginal utility of money remains constant throughout when the individual is spending money on a good and due to which the amount of money with him varies. Alfred Marshall, (1842–1924), the famous exponent of marginal utility analysis, measured marginal utilities in terms of money. But the measurement of marginal utility of goods in terms of money is only possible if the marginal utility of money itself remains constant. It should be noted that the assumption of constant marginal utility of money is very crucial to the Marshallian analysis because, otherwise, Marshall could not have measured marginal utilities of goods in terms of money. If money, the unit of measurement, itself varies and one is measuring with it, then it cannot yield the correct measurement of the marginal utility of the good. Professor Tapas Majumdar in his book *Measurement of Utility* rightly says: "If money is supposed to provide the measuring rod of utility, then evidently as with all measuring rods, its unit must be invariant; it must measure the same amount of utility in all circumstances".

3. **Introspective method:** Another important hypothesis of the marginal utility analysis is the use of introspective method in judging the behaviour of marginal utility. Kauder in his book *A History of Marginal Utility Theory* says: "Introspection is the ability of the observer to reconstruct events which go on in the mind of another person with the help of self-observation". This form of comprehension may be just guess work, intuition or the result of long-lasting experience. Thus, economists reconstruct or build up with the help of their own experience the trend of feeling which goes on in other men's mind. An individual from his own response to certain forces, and by the experience and observation he has gained, tries to understand how other people's minds would work in similar situations. From his observation and experience along with the help of his imagination the individual tries to build up the trend of consciousness which goes on in other men's mind. This is known as introspective method. To sum up, in introspective method we attribute to another person what we know of our own mind. That is by looking into ourselves, we see inside the minds of other individuals. So the law of diminishing marginal utility is based on introspection. We know from our own mind that as we have more of a thing, the less utility we derive from an additional unit of it. We conclude from this that other individuals' mind will work in a similar fashion, that is, the marginal utility to them of a good will diminish as they have more units of it.

2.3 LAWS OF DIMINISHING MARGINAL UTILITY ANALYSIS

The founders of marginal utility analysis have developed two laws which occupy an important place in the economic theory. These two laws are: (i) *the law of diminishing marginal utility* and (ii) *the law of equimarginal utility*. It is with the help of these two laws about consumers' behaviour that the exponents of utility analysis have derived the law of demand.

Marshall stated the law of diminishing marginal utility as follows: "The additional benefit which a person derives from a given increase of his stock of thing diminishes with every increase in the stock that he already has".

This law is based on two important facts. *First*, while the total wants of a man are virtually unlimited, each single want is satiable. Therefore, as an individual consumes more and more units of a good, the intensity of his want for that good goes on falling and a point is reached where the individual no longer wants any more units of it. That is when the saturation point is reached and the marginal utility of a good becomes zero. The zero marginal utility of a good implies that the individual has all that he wants of the good in question. The *second* fact, on which the law of diminishing marginal utility is based, is that different goods are not perfect substitutes for each other in the satisfaction of various particular wants. When an individual consumes more and more units of a good, the intensity of his want for that good diminishes. However, if the units of that good could be devoted to the satisfaction of other wants and yielded as much satisfaction as they did initially in the satisfaction of the first want, the marginal utility of the good would not have diminished.

It is obvious from the above that the law of diminishing marginal utility describes a familiar and fundamental tendency of human nature. This law has been derived by introspection and by observing how people behave.

The significance of the diminishing marginal utility of a good for the theory of demand is that the quantity demanded of a good rises as the price falls and vice versa. Thus, it is because of the diminishing marginal utility that the demand curve slopes downward.

The law of diminishing marginal utility applies to all objects of desire, including money. But it is worth mentioning that marginal utility of money is generally never zero or negative. Money represents the purchasing power over all other goods, that is, a man can satisfy all his material wants if he possesses enough money. Since a man's total wants are practically unlimited, the marginal utility of money to him never falls to zero.

2.4 PRINCIPLE OF EQUI-MARGINAL UTILITY: CONSUMER'S EQUILIBRIUM

The principle of equi-marginal utility occupies an important place in the marginal utility analysis. A consumer has a fixed income which he has to spend on various goods he wants. Now the question is how he would allocate his money income between various goods. In other words, what would be his equilibrium position in respect of the purchases of the various goods? It may be mentioned here that the consumer is assumed to be 'rational', that is, he carefully calculates and substitutes goods for one another so as to maximize his utility or satisfaction.

Suppose there are only two goods X and Y on which a consumer has to spend a given income. The consumer's behaviour will be then governed by two factors: *first*, by the marginal utilities of the goods, and second, by the prices of the two goods. Suppose the prices of the goods are given for the consumer. The law of equi-marginal utility states that the consumer will distribute his money income between the goods in such a way that the utility derived from the last rupee spent on each good is equal. In other words, the consumer is in equilibrium position when the marginal utility of money expenditure on each good is the same. Now, the marginal utility of money expenditure on a good is equal to the marginal utility of a good divided by the price of the good. Mathematically,

$$MU_E = \frac{MU_X}{P_X}$$

where MU_E is the marginal utility of money expenditure, MU_x is the marginal utility of X, and P_x is the price of X. The law of equi-marginal utility can, therefore, be stated as: the consumer will spend his money income on different goods in such a way that the marginal utility of each good is proportional to its price. That is consumer is in equilibrium in respect of the purchases of the two goods X and Y when

$$\frac{MU_X}{P_X} = \frac{MU_Y}{P_Y}$$

Now, if MU_X/P_X and MU_Y/P_Y are not equal and MU_X/P_X is greater than MU_Y/P_Y, then the consumer will substitute good X for good Y. As a result of this substitution, the marginal utility of good X will fall and the marginal utility of good Y will rise. The consumer will continue substituting good X for good Y till MU_X/P_X becomes equal to MU_Y/P_Y. When both become equal, then the consumer will be in equilibrium.

The question is how far does a consumer go on purchasing the goods he wants. This is determined by the size of his money income. With a given income, a rupee has a certain utility for him. This utility is the marginal utility of money to him. Since the law of diminishing marginal utility applies to money income also, the greater the size of his money income, the smaller the marginal utility of money to him. Now the consumer will continue purchasing goods till the marginal utility of expenditure on each good becomes equal to the marginal utility of money to him.

The law can be explained with the help of a numerical example. Suppose, a consumer has Rs. 8 which he wants to spend on oranges and grapes so that he obtains the maximum total utility. Tables 2.1 and 2.2 show the marginal utility of spending successive rupees of income on oranges and grapes.

Table 2.1   Marginal Utility of Oranges

Units of money	Marginal utility of oranges
1	20
2	18
3	16
4	14
5	12
6	10
7	8
8	6

Table 2.2   Marginal Utility of Grapes

Units of money	Marginal utility of grapes
1	16
2	14
3	12
4	10
5	8
6	6
7	4
8	2

From the two tables we can easily observe that the consumer will start spending his first rupee on oranges because the highest marginal utility is 20 in oranges. The second rupee is also spent on oranges because the next highest utility is 18 here. The third rupee is spent on grapes, the fourth on oranges again. In this way, the consumer goes on spending rupee by rupee till he spends all the eight rupees with him. The last rupee spent on oranges gives the same marginal utility as the last rupee spent on grapes. Both give 12 utilities, of marginal utility to the consumer. The total utility for the consumer is 122 utilities, which is the highest with the expenditure of eight rupees. Any other allocation of the eight rupees will give less total utility to the consumer. Therefore, the consumer will be in equilibrium when he is spending five units of money on oranges and three units of money on grapes.

The consumer's equilibrium is graphically represented in Figure 2.1. Since the marginal utility curves of goods slope downward, the curves depicting MU_X/P_X and MU_Y/P_Y will also slope downward. Thus,

$$\frac{MU_X}{P_X} = \frac{MU_Y}{P_Y} = MU_M$$

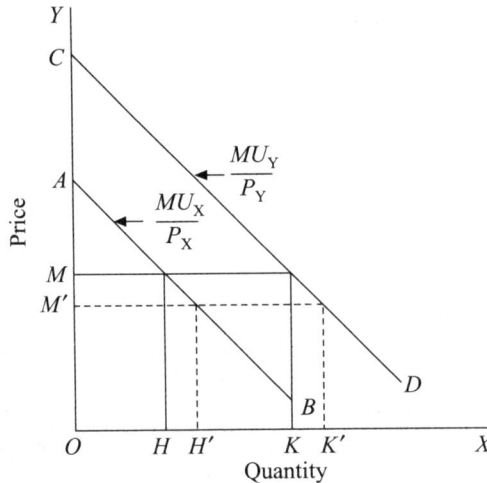

Figure 2.1   Consumer's equilibrium.

Therefore, the consumer is in equilibrium when he is buying *OH* of X and *OK* of Y. No other allocation of money expenditure will yield greater utility than when he is buying *OH* of X and *OK* of Y. If now the money income of the consumer increases, then his marginal utility of money will fall. Suppose the new marginal utility of money is equal to *OM'* then the consumer will increase the purchases of good X and Y to *OB'* and *OK'* respectively. The marginal utility on each good becomes equal to the marginal utility of money.

2.5   DERIVATION OF DEMAND CURVE AND LAW OF DEMAND

The demand curve or the law of demand shows the relationship between the price of a good and its quantity demanded. Marshall derived the demand curves for goods from their utility functions. The

Marshallian technique of deriving demand curves for the goods from their utility functions rests on the hypothesis of addititve utility functions. It means utility function of each good consumed by the consumer does not depend on the quantity consumed of any other good. As already mentioned, in the case of independent utilities or additive utility functions, the relations of substitution and complementarily between goods are ruled out. Further, in deriving the demand curve or law of demand, Marshall assumes the marginal utility of money expenditure (MU_m) to remain constant. The law of demand or the demand curve can be derived in two ways: *first*, with the aid of law of diminishing marginal utility; *second*, with the help of the law of equi-marginal utility. We shall explain below the two ways of deriving the demand curve and the law of demand in Figures 2.2 and 2.3, respectively.

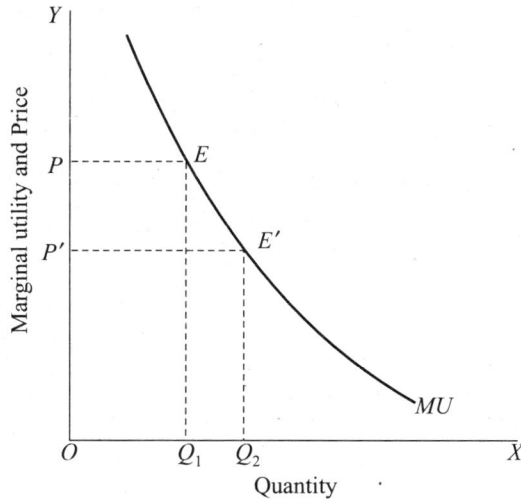

Figure 2.2   Demand curve.

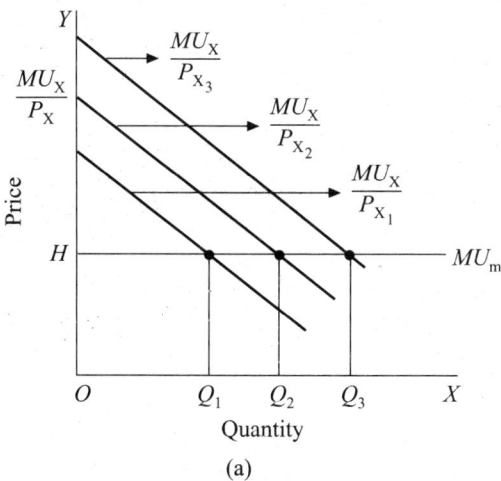

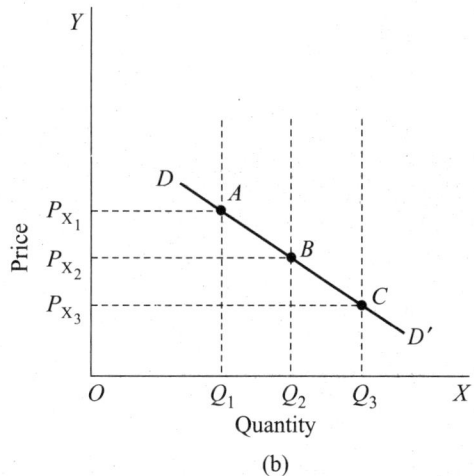

Figure 2.3   Law of demand through equi-marginal utility.

1. The law of marginal utility states that as the quantity of a good with a consumer increases, the marginal utility of the good to him expressed in terms of money falls. In other words, the marginal utility curve of a good is downward sloping. Now, a consumer will go on purchasing a good until its marginal utility equals the market price. His satisfaction will be maximum only when the marginal utility equals price. Thus, "marginal utility equals price" is the condition of equilibrium. When the price of the good falls, the downward sloping marginal utility curve implies that the consumer must buy more of the good so that its marginal utility falls and becomes equal to the new price. It therefore follows that the diminishing marginal utility curve implies the downward sloping demand curve, that is, as the price of a good falls, the more of it will be bought. The whole argument will be more clearly understood from Figure 2.2. In this figure, the curve *MU* represents the diminishing marginal utility of the good measured in terms of money. Suppose the price of the good is *OP*. At this price, the consumer will be in equilibrium when he purchases OQ_1 quantity of the good since at OQ_1 the marginal utility is equal to the given price *OP*. Now, if the price of the good falls to *OP′*, then the equality between the marginal utility and the price will be disturbed. The marginal utility Q_1E at the quantity OQ_1 will be greater than the new price *OP*. In order to equate the marginal utility with the lower price *OP′*, the consumer must buy more of the good. It is evident from Figure 2.2 that when the consumer increases the quantity purchased to OQ_2, the marginal utility of the good falls and becomes equal to the new price *OP′*.

2. According to the law of equi-marginal utility, the consumer is in equilibrium in regard to his purchases of various goods when the marginal utilities of the goods are proportional to their prices. Thus, the consumer is in equilibrium when he is buying the quantities of the two goods in such a way that the following proportionality rule is satisfied:

$$\frac{MU_X}{P_X} = \frac{MU_Y}{P_Y} = MU_m$$

where MU_m is the marginal utility of money income.

In Figure 2.3, on the *Y*-axis price is shown, and on the *X*-axis, the quantity demanded of the good. Given a certain income of the consumer, the marginal utility of money is equal to *OH*. The consumer is buying OQ_1 of good X when the price is P_{X_1} since at the quantity OQ_1 of X, the marginal utility of money *OH* is equal to MU_X/P_X. Now, when the price of good X falls, the curve will shift upwards to the new position MU_X/P_{X2}. In order to equate the marginal utility of money (*OH*) with the new MU_X/P_{X2}, the consumer increases the quantity demanded to OQ_2. Thus, with the fall in price of good X, the consumer buys more of it. It should be noted that no account is taken of the increase in real income of the consumer as a result of the fall in the price of good X. This is because if the change in real income is taken into account, then the marginal utility of money will also change. And this would have an effect on the purchases of goods.

In Figures 2.3(a) and 2.3(b), the demand curve for X is derived. In this figure, price is measured on the *Y*-axis and the *X*-axis represents quantity. When the price of good is P_{X_1} the relevant curve of marginal utility/price is MU_X/P_{X1}. With MU_X/P_{X1}, the consumer buys OQ_1 of good X. Now, in the lower portion [Figure 2.3(b)] this quantity, OQ_1 is directly shown to be demanded at the price P_{X_1}. When the price of X falls to P_{X_2} the curve of marginal utility/price shifts upwards to the new position MU_X/P_{X2}. With MU_X/P_{X2}, the consumer buys OQ_2 of X. This quantity OQ_2 is directly shown to be demanded at price P_{X_2} in the lower portion. Similarly, by varying the price further we can know the quantity demanded at other prices. By joining points *A*, *B* and *C*, we obtain the demand curve *DD'*. It slopes downward which shows that, as the price of the good falls, its quantity purchased rises.

2.6 DEMAND

2.6.1 Meaning of Demand

The demand for any commodity, at a given price, is the quantity of it, which will be bought per unit of time at that price. From this definition of demand, two things are quite clear. *First*, demand always refers to demand at a price. If the demand is not related to price, then it conveys no sense. To say that the demand for mangoes is 100 kg fails to convey any sense. It should always be related to price. Again, in the words of Shearman, "To speak of the demand of a commodity in the sense of the mere amount that will be purchased without reference to any price will be meaningless". *Second,* demand always means demand per unit of time. The time may be a day, a week or a month, etc. Therefore, according to G. L. Thirkettle "the demand for any commodity or service is the amount that will be bought at any given price per unit of time."

So, demand implies three things: (i) the desire to possess a thing, (ii) the means of purchasing it, and (iii) the willingness to use those means for purchasing it".

2.6.2 Meaning of Demand Schedule

The demand schedule depicts the various quantities of a commodity which will be demanded at different prices. The quantity demanded will be different at different prices because, with an increase in price, the demand falls and, with a fall in price, the demand rises. The demand schedule can be of the following two types:

1. Individual demand schedule
2. Market demand schedule

1. **Individual demand schedule:** It shows the various quantities demanded by one person at different prices. Individual demand schedule can be shown as in Table 2.3.

Table 2.3   Individual Demand Schedule

Price (Rs.)	Demand of mangoes (kg)
5	1
4	2
3	3
2	4
1	5

As is clear from the table, a consumer's demand for mangoes is 1 kg when the price is Rs. 5/kg. When the price falls to Rs. 4, the demand for mangoes goes upto 2 kg. Again, the demand for mangoes rises to 5 kg when the price is Rs. 1/kg. We can show the individual demand schedule with the help of Figure 2.4.

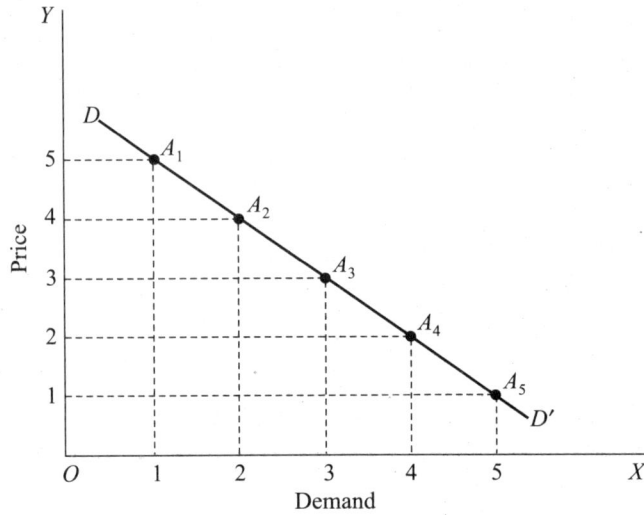

Figure 2.4   Individual demand schedule curve.

On the *OX*-axis, we measure the quantity demand while on the *Y*-axis we take the price of mangoes per kg. When the price is Rs. 5 per kg, the demand is 1 kg. Likewise, when the price is Rs. 4/kg, the demand is 2, etc. By combining points A_1, A_2, A_3, A_4, A_5, we get the demand curve *DD'*. This is called the *individual demand curves*.

2. **Market demand schedule:**   If we add up the demand at various prices of all consumers in the market, then we will get the market demand schedule. Let us suppose there are three consumers, A, B and C in the market. If we now add the quantity demanded by A, B and C at different prices, then we will get the market demand schedule (see Table 2.4).

Table 2.4   Market Demand Schedule

Price (Rs.)	Demand of A	Demand of B	Demand of C	Total Demand (A + B + C)
5	1	3	2	6
4	2	4	3	9
3	3	5	4	12
2	4	6	5	15
1	5	7	6	18

Market demand curve: It is presented in Figure 2.5a.

On the *OX*-axis, we take the total quantity demanded of the mangoes in the market. On the *Y*-axis, we measure the prices. When the price is Rs. 5, the total quantity demanded is 6. Again, when the price is Rs. 4, the total quantity demand goes up to 9, and as on. By combining the points *A*, *B*, *C*, *D* and *E*, we get *DD'*, the demand curve market as a whole. The market demand curve can also be known by adding up the individual demand curves. We assume that there are two consumers A and B. If we know the demand curve of A and B, we can find our market curve as depicted in Figure 2.5b.

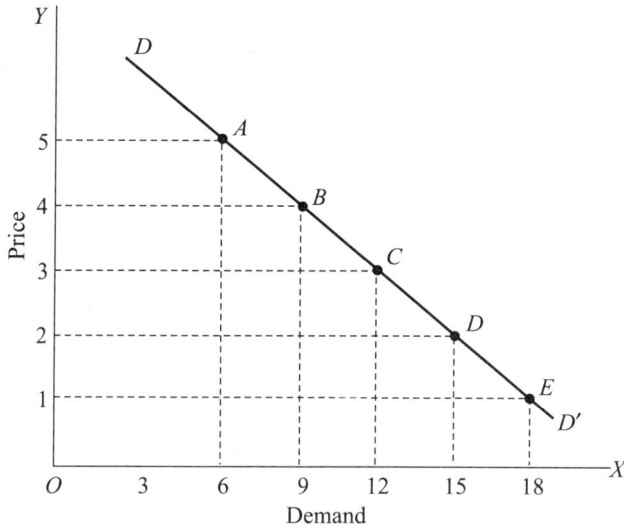

(a)

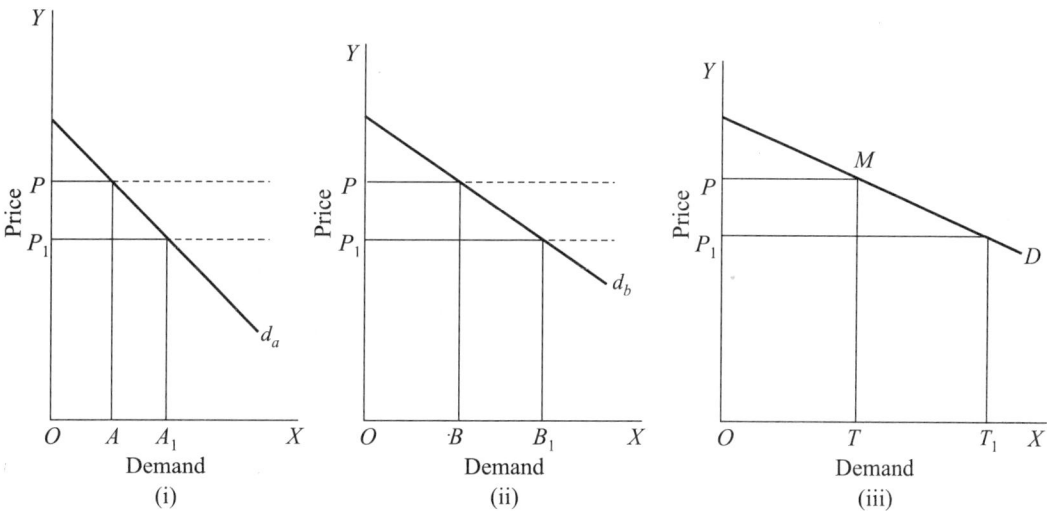

(b)

Figure 2.5 Market demand curve.

In Figures 2.5b(i)–2.5b(iii), we show the demand of consumer A, consumer B and the total demand, respectively. On the OX-axis, we measure demand, and the QY-axis we measure price. d_a shows the demand curve of consumer A and d_b shows the demand curve of consumer B. At price OP, the quantity demanded by consumer A is OA, while the quantity demanded by consumer B at this price is OB. The total demand of consumers A and B shall be $OA+OB$. In Figure 2.5b(iii), the total demand is OT at price OP. Here, $OT = OA + OB$. When the price falls to OP_1 the quantity demanded increases to OA_1 and OB_1 in the case of consumers A and B, respectively. Now the market demand at price OP_1 shall be equal to $OA_1 + OB_1$. In Figure 2.5b(iii), the total demand is OT_1

at price OP_1. Here, $OT_1 = OA_1 + OB_1$. By joining points M and N, we get D which is the market demand curve.

Demand schedule is important for the following reasons:

1. With the help of demand schedule, we can know the approximate changes in demand because of a change in price.
2. We can discuss the elasticity of demand with the help of demand/schedule.
3. The law of demand can also be discussed with the help of demand schedule.
4. The price in the market is also determined with the help of demand schedule and supply schedule.
5. The demand schedule is very useful for the business community. With its help, a businessman can know the extent of increase in demand because of a fall in price.

2.7 LAW OF DEMAND

2.7.1 Meaning

The law of demand establishes a relationship between the price and the quantity demanded of a commodity. Other things remaining the same, when the price of a commodity falls, its demand will go up. Likewise, when the price of a commodity rises, its demand will fall. Price and demand move in opposite directions. There is no proportionate relationship between the two. A 10 per cent fall in price will not necessarily lead to a 10 per cent increase in demand.

In the words of Marshall,

"The greater the amount to be sold, the smaller must be the price at which it is offered in order that it may find purchasers; or in other words, the amount demanded increases with a fall in price, and diminishes with a rise in price".

According to Paul Samuelson, "When the price of a good is raised, less of it will be demanded. People will buy more at lower price and buy less at higher prices".

According to Gerald M. Mayers, "People demand a larger quantity of goods and services only a it a lower price than at a higher price".

Simply stated, the law of demand says that other things being equal, more will be demanded at lower prices than at higher prices. The law of demand can be illustrated as in Table 2.5.

Table 2.5 Law of Demand

Price of apples (Paisa)	Demand for apples (Unit)
50	2
40	4
30	6
20	8
10	10

When the price is 30 paisa, the consumer demand is six apples. When the price falls to 20 paisa, he demands eight apples, and when the price rises to 40 paisa, he demands four apples. Thus, when the price falls, the demand increases and when the price rises, the demand falls.

The law of demand can also be illustrated with the help of Figure 2.6.

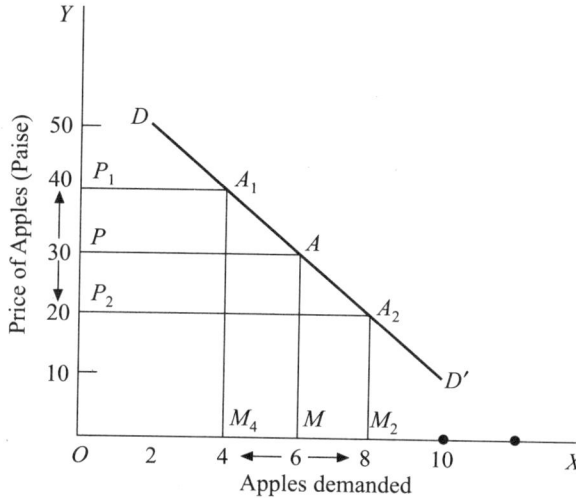

Figure 2.6 Diagrammatic representation of the law of demand.

The figure shows that at *OP*, the demand is *OM*. When the price increases to *OP*$_1$, the demand falls to *OM*$_1$. When the price falls to *OP*$_2$, the demand increases to *OM*$_2$.

The law of demand applies because of the following reasons:

1. **Law of diminishing marginal utility:** It is quite natural that when a person continues buying large number of units of the same commodity, its marginal utility will progressively fall. On the other hand, when the stock of a commodity goes on falling, its marginal utility will progressively rise. We also know that marginal utility is measured by price. When a person purchases less amount of a commodity, the marginal utility of that commodity will be high for him and he will be ready to pay more price and vice versa. So we come to the conclusion that people purchase more at a low price and less at a high price.

2. **Income effect:** When the price falls, the real income of the consumer rises. He is, therefore, in a position to purchase more units of the commodity. When the price rises, the real income of the consumer falls and he purchases less units of a commodity.

3. **Substitution effect:** When the price of one commodity falls, people purchase more of that commodity. When the price of one commodity rises, people purchase less of that commodity. The substitution effect of a price reduction is always positive and hence, larger quantities will be bought at lower prices.

2.7.2 Assumptions of the Law

The law of demand is based on the following assumptions:

1. The income of the buyer remains the same.
2. The taste of the buyer remains the same.
3. The prices of other goods—substitutes and complements—remain unchanged.
4. No close substitute is discovered.

2.7.3   Limitations of the Law/Exception to Law of Demand

1. **Change in habit, customs and income:**   The law of demand tells us that the demand for a commodity goes up with a fall in price and goes down with a rise in price. But an increase in price will bring down the demand if at the same time the income of the consumer has also increased.

2. **Necessities of life:**   The law of demand is not applicable in the case of necessities of life. For instance, an increase in the price of flour will not bring down its demand. Similarly, a fall in its price will not very much increase the demand for it.

3. **Fear of shortage in future:**   If there is a fear of shortage of a commodity in the near future, its demand in the present increases because people start storing it. But, according to the law of demand, the demand for a commodity should go up only when its price falls.

4. **Fear of a rise in prices in future:**   Similarly, if people think that the price of a particular, commodity will increase in future, then they will store it. In other words, the demand of that commodity will increase even at the same price. But the law of demand states that demand should go up only if the price goes down while an increase in the price will lower the demand.

5. **Articles of distinction:**   This law does not hold good in the case of those commodities which confer social distinction. When the price of such commodities goes up, their demand will also increase. For example, an increase in the price of diamond will raise its demand and a fall in price will lower the demand.

6. **Giffen goods:**   Sir Robert Giffen (1837–1910) observed that sometimes people buy less of a good at a lower price and more of a good at a higher price. These are called Giffen goods as their price elasticity of demand is positive. When price goesup, the quantity demanded also goes up, and vice versa. He cited the example of low-paid British wage earners. During the early period of the 19th century, a rise in the price of bread forced the poor labour class families to curtail their consumption of meat and the more expensive farinaceous foods. Since bread was still by far the cheapest food which they could get and would take, they consumed more of it and not less of it.

7. **Ignorance:**   It is possible that a consumer may not be aware of the previous price of a commodity. In this case, he might start purchasing more of a commodity when its price has actually gone up.

2.8   ELASTICITY OF DEMAND

2.8.1   Introduction

When the price of a good falls, its quantity demanded rises and when the price of a good rises, its quantity demanded falls. This is generally known as *law of demand*. This law of demand indicates only the direction of the change in quantity demanded in response to a change in price. This does not tell us by how much or to what extent the quantity demanded of a good will change in response to a change in its price. This information as to how much or to what extent the quantity demanded of a good will change as a result of a change in its price is provided by the concept of elasticity of demand. The concept of elasticity has great importance in economic theory and engineering economics.

2.8.2 Various Concepts of Demand Elasticity

The price elasticity of a demand is usually referred to as elasticity of demand. The concept of elasticity of demand refers to the degree of responsiveness of quantity demanded of a good to a change in its price, income or prices of related goods. There are three kinds of demand elasticity: price elasticity, income elasticity, and cross elasticity. **Price elasticity** of demand relates to the responsiveness of quantity demanded of a good to the change in its price. **Income elasticity** of demand refers to the sensitiveness of the quantity demanded to the change in income. **Cross elasticity** of demand means the degree of responsiveness of demand of a good to a change in the price of a related good, which may be either a substitute for it or a complementary with it. Besides these three kinds of elasticities, there is another type of elasticity of demand called **elasticity of substitution** which refers to the change in quantity demanded of a good in response to the change in its relative price alone, the real income of the individual remaining the same.

2.8.3 Price Elasticity of Demand

Price elasticity means the degree of responsiveness or sensitiveness of the quantity demanded of a good to changes in its prices. In other words, the price elasticity of demand is a measure of the relative change in quantity purchased of a good in response to a relative change in its price. Price elasticity can be precisely defined as "the proportionate change in quantity demanded in response to a small change in price, divided by the proportionate change in price". Thus,

$$\text{Price Elasticity} = \frac{\text{Proportionate change in quantity demanded}}{\text{Proportionate change in price}}$$

$$= \frac{\text{Change in quantity demanded}}{\text{Quantity demanded}} \bigg/ \frac{\text{Change in price}}{\text{Price}}$$

Or, mathematically,

$$e_p = \frac{(\Delta q/q)}{(\Delta p/p)} = \frac{\Delta q}{q} \bigg/ \frac{\Delta p}{p}$$

$$= \frac{\Delta q}{q} \times \frac{p}{\Delta p}$$

$$= \frac{\Delta q}{\Delta p} \times \frac{p}{q}$$

where

e_p = price elasticity of demand
q = quantity
p = price
Δ = infinitesimal change

Mathematically speaking, price elasticity of demand (e_p) is negative since the change in quantity demanded is in opposite direction to the change in price. When the price falls, the quantity demanded rises and vice versa. But, for the sake of convenience in understanding the magnitude of response of quantity demanded to the change in price, we ignore the negative sign and take into account only the numerical value of elasticity. Thus, if a 2 per cent change in price leads to an 8 per cent change in the quantity demanded of good A and a 16 per cent change in that of B, then the above formula of elasticity will give the price elasticity value of good A equal to 4 and of good B equal to 8. It indicates that the quantity demanded of good B changes much more than that of good A in response to a given change in price. But if we had written minus signs before the numerical values of elasticities of two goods, that is, if we had written the elasticities as -4 and -8 respectively, as strict mathematics would require us to do, then since -8 is smaller than -4, we would have been misled in concluding that price elasticitiy of demand of B is less than that of A.

2.8.4   Types of Price Elasticity

Different products react differently to price change. A price change for an essential product such as rice has little impact on its demand while the price change in other products may have huge impact on their demand. This gives rise to different types of price elasticities. They are generally classified into the following categories:

1. Perfectly elastic demand
2. Absolutely inelastic demand or perfectly inelastic demand
3. Unit elasticity of demand
4. Relatively elastic demand
5. Relatively inelastic demand

1. **Perfectly elastic demand** $(e_p = \infty)$:   Here there is no need for reduction in price to create an increase in demand. If this be the case, then a firm can sell all the quantity it wants at the prevailing price, but it can sell none at all at even a slightly higher price. Here the demand curve is horizontal as shown in Figure 2.7.

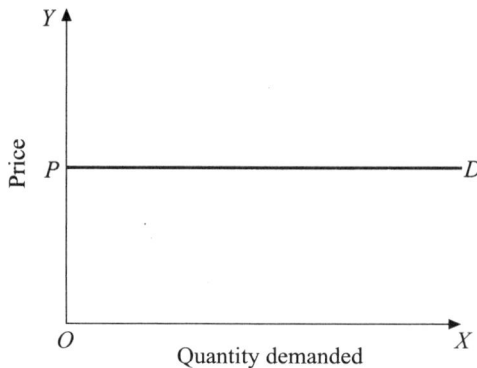

Figure 2.7   Perfectly elastic demand curve.

2. **Absolutely inelastic demand or perfectly inelastic demand** $(e_p = 0)$:   This is where a change in price, howsoever large, causes no change in the quantity demanded of a product. Here, the shape of the demand curve is vertical. Some examples of absolutely inelastic demand are the demand of essential commodities such as rice and wheat whose change in price does not affect the quantity demanded. This is illustrated in Figure 2.8.

3. **Unit elasticity of demand** $(e_p = 1)$:   See Figure 2.9. Unit elasticity of demand occurs where a given proportionate change in price causes an equally proportionate change in the quantity demanded of the product. The shape of the demand curve here is that of a rectangular hyperbola.

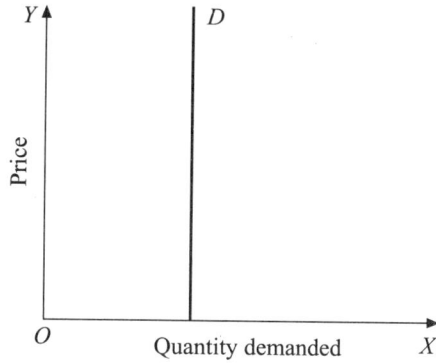

Figure 2.8   Absolutely inelastic demand.

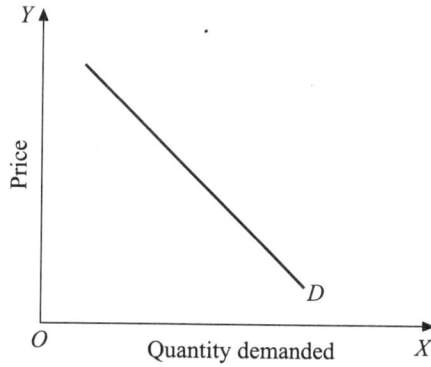

Figure 2.9   Unit elasticity of demand.

4. **Relatively elastic of demand** $(e_p > 1)$:   See Figure 2.10. It occurs when a reduction in price leads to more than proportionate change in demand. Here, the shape of the demand curve is flat.

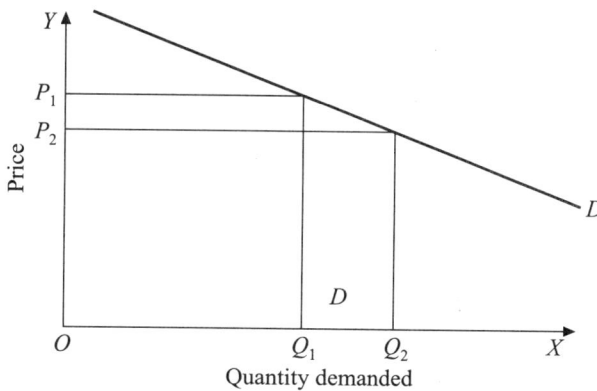

Figure 2.10   Relatively elastic of demand.

5. Relatively inelastic demand ($e_p < 1$):   See Figure 2.11. It is where a decline in price leads to less than proportionate increase in demand. Here the shape of the demand curve is steep.

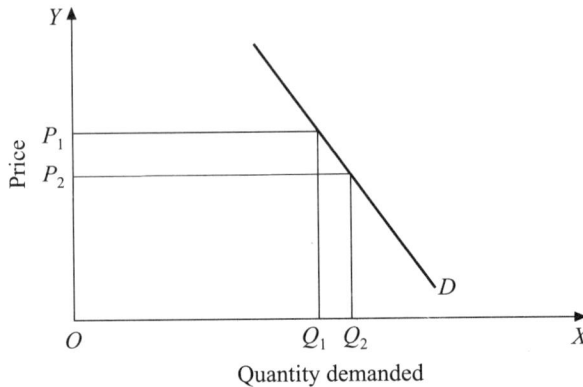

Figure 2.11   Relatively inelastic demand.

2.8.5   Factors Determining Price Elasticity of Demand

The elasticity of demand depends on the following factors:

1. Nature of the product
2. Extent of usage
3. Availability of substitutes
4. Income level of people
5. Proportion of the income spent on the product
6. Urgency of demand
7. Durability of a product

In the following paragraphs, we briefly explain the above-mentioned points.

1. **Nature of the product:**   The demand for products that fall in the category of necessities (e.g. rice, salt, wheat) is usually inelastic. This is because their demands do not change even when there is a change in price. On the other hand, the demand for luxuries (e.g. TVs, washing machines) is elastic where even a small change in price reflects a huge change in the demand of the product.

2. **Extent of usage:**   If a product has varied usage (e.g. steel, aluminum, wood) then it has comparatively elastic demand. For example, if the price of teak wood falls, then its demand will increase as it will be put to various uses. On the contrary, when the price rises, its use will be restricted in certain areas though in other areas its usage will not witness any change.

3. **Availability of substitutes:**   When a product has many substitutes, then its demand will be relatively elastic. This is because, if the price of one substitute goes down, then customers switch to it and vice versa. Products without substitutes or having weak substitutes have relatively inelastic demand.

4. **Income level of people:**   Individuals with high income are less affected by price changes in products while people with low income are more affected by price rise. People with high income will not change their buying habits because of the increase in price of either essential

commodities or luxuries. People with low incomes will cut back on purchase of certain commodities to compensate for essential commodities.

5. **Proportion of income spent on the commodity:** When a person spends only a very small part of his income on certain products (match boxes, salt, etc.) the price change in these products does not materially affect his demand for then. Here the demand is inelastic.

6. **Urgency of demand:** If a person requires buying a product immediately no matter what the price is or has no other way but to buy a product at that point of time, with no substitutes available, then the demand for that product becomes inelastic. For example, if one is building a house and is in urgent need of completing the construction, then any price change in cement, bricks or steel, etc. will have little impact on the demand of these products.

2.8.6 Price Elasticity and Changes in Total Expenditure

Let us now see what happens to the total expenditure by the consumers on a good when its price changes. Whether the total expenditure rises, falls or remains the same with the change in the price of the good depends on the price elasticity of demand. The total expenditure bears an important relationship with the price elasticity of demand, and this relationship is of great significance in the theory of price. The relationship between the changes in total expenditure and the price elasticity of demand leads to the following situation:

1. When the price elasticity of demand is equal to unity ($e_p = 1$), the total expenditure remains the same with the fall or rise in price.
2. When the price elasticity of demand is greater than one ($e_p > 1$), the total expenditure will increase with the fall in price and will decrease with the rise in price.
3. When the price elasticity of demand is less than one ($e_p < 1$), the total expenditure will decrease with the fall in price and will increase with the rise in price.

2.8.7 Measurement of Elasticity at a Point on the Demand Curve

Straight line demand curve *tT* is shown in Figure 2.12. It is required to measure elasticity at point *R* on this curve. In Figure 2.12, corresponding to point *R* on the demand curve *tT*, the price is *OP*, and the quantity demanded at it is *OQ*. With a small fall in price from *OP* to *OP'*, the quantity demanded rises from *OQ* to *OQ'*.

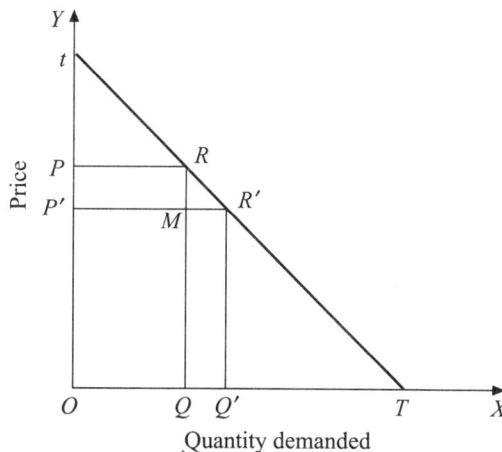

Figure 2.12 Point elasticity of demand.

$$\text{Price Elasticity } (e_p) = \frac{\text{Proportionate change in quantity demanded}}{\text{Proportionate change in price}}$$

In the figure, when the price falls from OP to OP', the quantity demanded rises from OQ to OQ'. This change in price by PP' causes change in quantity demanded by QQ'. In this Figure 2.13, $QQ' = MR'$ and $PP' = RM$ and $OP = QR$. Thus,

$$e_p = \frac{MR'}{RM} \times \frac{QR}{OQ}$$

Now, take triangles RMR' and RQT. Then

$$\angle MR'R = \angle QTR$$

$$\angle RMR' = \angle RQT$$

Third $\angle MRR'$ is common to both the triangles.

Therefore, the triangles RMR' and RQT are similar. A property of similar triangles is that their corresponding sides are proportional to each other. From this it follows that

$$\frac{MR'}{RM} = \frac{QT}{QR}$$

If we write (QT/QR) in place of (MR'/RM), then we get

$$e_p = \frac{QT}{QR} \times \frac{QR}{OQ} = \frac{QT}{QR}$$

Now, in the triangle OtT, QR is parallel to Ot. Therefore,

$$\frac{QT}{OQ} = \frac{RT}{Rt}$$

$$e_p = \frac{QT}{OQ} = \frac{RT}{Rt}$$

Hence, from the above we find that price elasticity at point R on the straight-line demand curve tT is

$$\frac{RT}{Rt} = \frac{\text{Lower segment}}{\text{Upper segment}}$$

2.8.8 Arc Elasticity of Demand

The point elasticity of demand refers to the price elasticity at a point or the demand curve In other words, it refers to the price elasticity when the changes in the price and the resultant changes in quantity demanded are infinitesimally small. In this case, if we take the original price or the subsequent price as the basis of measurement, then there will not be any significant difference in the elasticity figure. However, when the price change is somewhat large or we have to measure the elasticity over an arc of the demand curve rather than at a specific point on it, the measure of point elasticity, namely, $(\Delta q/\Delta p) \times (p/q)$, does not provide us the true and correct figure of price elasticity of demand.

Further, in such cases, the measure of price elasticity would depend on whether we choose original price and quantity, or the subsequent price and quantity demanded as the basis for measurement of price elasticity. There will be a significant difference in the two measures of elasticity obtained from using two bases. Consider the following example of changes in price and consequent changes in the quantity demanded:

Price (Rs.)	Quantity demanded (Units)
5 (P_1)	100 (q_1)
4 (P_2)	110 (q_2)

If we take Rs. 5 and the quantity demanded at it (100 units) as the basis of measuring the price elasticity with the point elasticity formula, then we get the following data for elasticity:

$$e_p = \frac{\Delta q}{\Delta p} \times \frac{p}{q} = \frac{10}{1} \times \frac{5}{100} = \frac{1}{2}$$

It we take Rs. 4 and the quantity demanded at it (110 units) as the basis of measuring the price elasticity with the point elasticity formula, then we get the following data for elasticity:

$$e_p = \frac{\Delta q}{\Delta p} \times \frac{p}{q} = \frac{10}{1} \times \frac{4}{110} = \frac{4}{11}$$

We thus see that when there is a change in the price point, the elasticity formula will yield two significantly different elasticity measures (as 1/2 and 4/11 in our above example) depending on whether we use the original price and quantity demanded, or the subsequent price and quantity demanded as the basis for measurement. The arc elasticity of demand is shown in Figure 2.13.

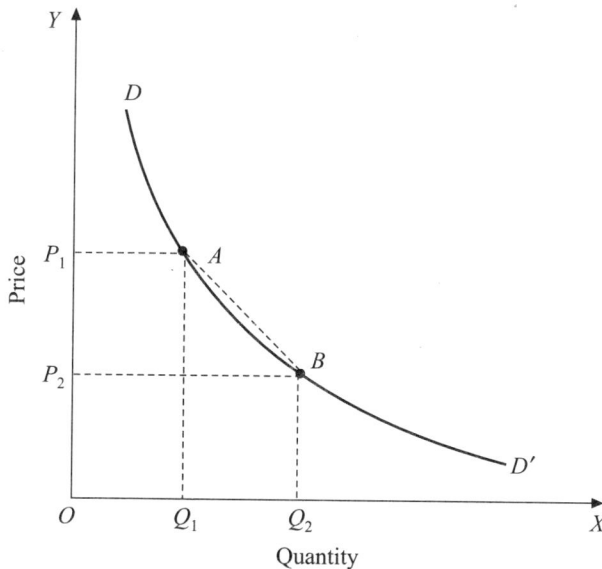

Figure 2.13   Arc elasticity.

In terms of demand curve, when we have to measure the price elasticity over an arc of the demand curve such as between points A and B on the demand curve DD' in the above figure, the point elasticity formula will not yield the true and correct measure of price elasticity. For measuring price elasticity in such cases, when the changes in price are somewhat large or the price elasticity over an arc of the demand curve (that is, between the two points on a demand curve, which lie close to each other) is to be measured, the concept of arc elasticity has been evolved. In the measurement of arc elasticity, we use the average of the two price figures (original and subsequent) and the average of the two quantity figures (original and subsequent). Thus, the formula for measuring the arc price elasticity of demand is:

$$e_p = \frac{\Delta q}{[(q_1 + q_2)/2]} \bigg/ \frac{\Delta p}{[(p_1 + p_2)/2]}$$

$$= \frac{\Delta q}{[(q_1 + q_2)/2]} \times \frac{[(p_1 + p_2)/2]}{\Delta p}$$

$$= \frac{\Delta q}{q_1 + q_2} \times \frac{p_1 + p_2}{\Delta p}$$

$$= \frac{\Delta q}{\Delta p} \times \frac{p_1 + p_2}{q_1 + q_2}$$

$$= \frac{\Delta q (p_1 + p_2)}{\Delta p (q_1 + q_2)}$$

If the arc elasticity is to be measured between points A and B on the demand curve DD', we will have to take the average of prices OP_1 and OP_2, and the average of quantities OQ_1 and OQ_2. It should be further noted that the arc elasticity formula given above measures the elasticity over a dashed line AB which is taken to be the approximation of the arc elasticity along the true arc (the demand curve from points A to B). Therefore, the greater the convexity of the demand curve between A and B, the greater is the divergence between the dashed line AB and the true demand curve and, therefore, the poorer the approximation of arc elasticity measure (of the dashed line AB) for the true curve between A and B. Moreover, the larger the distance between A and B on the demand curve, the greater will be the divergence between the dashed straight line AB and the true curve from A to B, and, consequently, the greater will be the discrepancy between the elasticity on the true curve and the elasticity on the dashed line AB measured by the arc elasticity formula given above. That is why the concept of arc elasticity is relevant even when the arc involved is small, that is, the two points A and B lie close to each other. Therefore, the arc elasticity formula should be used when the change in price is somewhat large but not very large. On the other hand, when the two points on the demand curve are very close, the arc (dashed straight line) becomes almost identical with the true curve and the arc elasticity measurement becomes almost identical with the point elasticity measurement on the demand curve.

REVIEW QUESTIONS

1. Define the law of demand. Explain the exceptions to the law of demand.
2. Explain the various elasticities of demand.

3. What do you mean by demand? Distinguish between individual and market demand schedules.

4. "Demand varies inversely to price". Is there any exception to the relationship between price and demand?

5. Why does demand curve always slope from left to right?

6. Define price elasticity of demand.

7. Define income elasticity of demand.

8. What are the factors determining the price elasticity of demand?

CHAPTER 3

Theory of Production

3.1 INTRODUCTION

The production function shows for a given state of technological knowledge and managerial ability, that maximum rates of output can be obtained from different combinations of productive factors. The word production in Economics is not only confined to effecting physical transformation in the matter, but involves it also involves rendering of services, such as transporting, financing, wholesailing and retailing. The laws of production or, in other words, generalizations regarding relations between inputs and outputs presented in this chapter will apply to all types of production.

The relation between inputs and outputs of a firm has been called 'production function'. Thus, the theory of production is the study of production function. The production function of a firm can be studied by holding the quantities of some factors fixed, while varying the amount of other factors. This is done when the law of variable proportions is derived. The production function of a firm can also be studied by varying the amounts of all factors. The behaviour of production when all factors are varied is the subject matter of the law of returns to scale. Thus, the theory of production is the study of: (i) the law of variable proportions, and (ii) the law of returns to scale.

3.2 IMPORTANCE OF THE THEORY OF PRODUCTION

The theory of production plays a dual role in the price theory. *First*, it provides a basis for the analysis of relation between costs and the amount of output. Costs govern supply of a product which, together with demand, determine the price of a product. The prices of inputs or factors of production influence the costs of production and, therefore, they play a part in determining the prices of products. *Second*, the theory of production provides a basis for the theory of a firm's demand for factors (inputs) of production. The demand for factors of production or inputs, together with the supply of them, determines their prices.

The theory of production is relevant to the macrotheory of distribution. The aggregate distributive shares of various factors, for instance, aggregative shares of wages and profits in national income, depend on the elasticity of substitution between factors, which is an important concept of the theory of production.

3.3   EQUAL PRODUCT CURVES OR ISOQUANTS

Equal product curves represent all those input combinations which are capable of producing the same level of output. These curves are contour lines which trace the loci of equal outputs. They are also known as *isoquants* (meaning "equal quantities") and *iso-product curves*. Since an equal product curves represent those combinations of inputs which are capable of producing an equal quantity of output, the producer would be indifferent between them. Therefore, another name given to equal product curves is *production-indifference curve'*.

The concept of equal product curves can be easily understood from Table 3.1. The resulting equal product curve is shown in Figure 3.1. It is presumed that two factors X and Y are being employed to produce a product.

Table 3.1   Various Factor Combinations to Produce a Given Level of Output

Factor combination	Factor X	Factor Y	Output (Units)
A	1	12	50
B	2	8	50
C	3	5	50
D	4	3	50
E	5	2	50

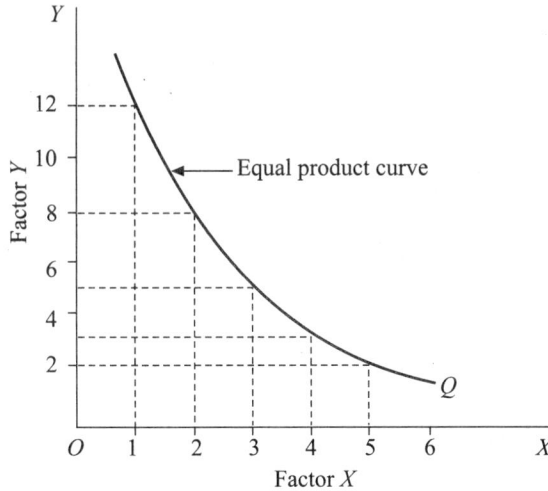

Figure 3.1   Equal product curve.

Each of the factor combinations A, B, C, D and E produces the same level of output, say, 50 units. To start with, factor combination A consisting of 1 unit of factor X and 12 units of factor Y produces the given 50 units of output. Similarly, factor combination B consisting of 2 units of X and 8 units of Y, factor combination C consisting of 3 units of X and 5 units of Y, combination D consisting of 4 units of X and 3 units of Y, and factor combination E consisting of 5 units of X and 2 units of Y are capable of producing the same amount of output. We have plotted all these combinations and by joining them we obtain the equal product curve showing that every combination represented on it can produce 50 units of output.

Though equal product curves are similar to the indifference curves of the theory of consumer behaviour, yet there is one important difference between the two: The indifference curves represent all those combinations of two goods which provide the same satisfaction or utility to a consumer but no attempt is made to specify the level of satisfaction or utility they stand for. This is so because the measurement of satisfaction or utility in unambiguous terms is not possible. That is why we usually label indifference curves by ordinal numbers I, II, III, etc. indicating that a higher indifference curve represents a higher level of satisfaction than a lower one. But the information as to by how much one level of satisfaction is greater than another is not provided. On the other hand, we can label the equal product curves in the physical units of output without any difficulty. The production of a good, being a physical phenomenon, lends itself easily to absolute measurement in physical units. Since each equal product curve represents the specified level of production, it is possible to say by how much one equal product curve indicates greater or less production than another. In Figure 3.2, we have drawn an equal product map or isoquant map with a set of four equal product curves which represent 50 units, 100 units, 150 units and 200 units of output, respectively. Then, from this set of equal product curves, it is very easy to judge by how much production level of one equal product curve is greater or less than on another.

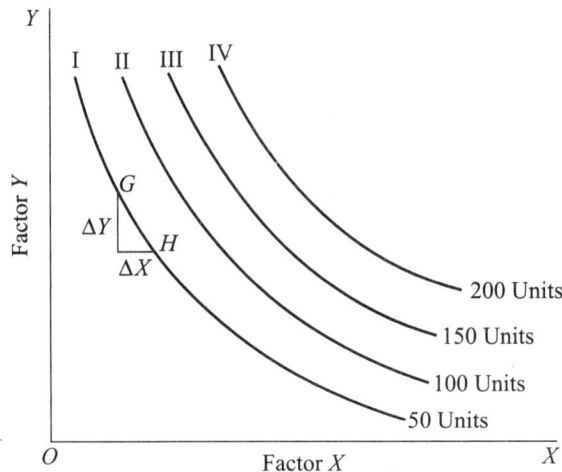

Figure 3.2 Isoquant map.

3.4 MARGINAL RATE OF TECHNICAL SUBSTITUTION

Marginal Rate of Technical Substitution (MRTS) in the theory of production is similar to the concept of marginal rate of substitution in the indifference curve analysis of consumer's demand. It indicates the rate at which factors can be substituted at the margin without changing the level of output. More precisely, the marginal rate of technical substitution of factor X for factor Y may be defined as the amount of factor Y which can be replaced by one unit of factor X, the level of output remaining unchanged. The concept of MRTS can be easily understood from Table 3.2. We have assumed 50 units of output here.

Each of the input combinations A, B, C, D and E yields the same level of output. Moving down the table from combination A to combination B, four units of Y are replaced by one unit of X in the production process without any change in the level of output.

Table 3.2 Marginal Rate of Technical Substitution

Factor combinations	Factor X	Factor Y	MRTS of X for Y
A	1	16	....
B	2	12	4:1
C	3	9	3:1
D	4	7	2:1
E	5	6	1:1

Therefore, MRTS is 4. At this stage, switching from input combination B to input combination C involves the replacement of three units of factor Y by an additional unit of factor X, the output remaining the same. Thus, MRTS is now three. Similarly, the MRTS between factor combinations C and D is 2, and between factor combinations D and E, it is 1.

The MRTS at a point on the equal product curve can be known from the slope of the equal product curve at that point. As shown in Figure 3.3, a small movement down the equal product curve P_1, from G to H, where a small amount of factor Y, say ΔY, is replaced by an amount of factor X, say ΔX, without any loss of output. The slope of the iso-product curve P_1, at point G is, therefore, equal to $(\Delta Y/\Delta X)$. Thus, MRTS = Slope = $(\Delta Y/\Delta X)$.

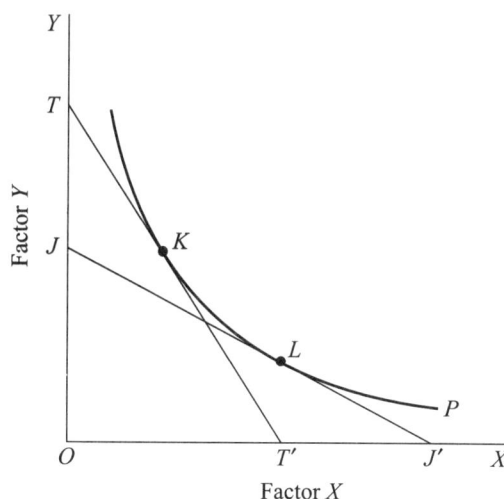

Figure 3.3 Diagrammatic representation of marginal rate of technical substitution.

The slope of the equal product curve at a point and, hence, the MRTS can also be known by the slope of the tangent drawn on the equal product curve at that point. In Figure 3.3, the tangent TT' is drawn at point K on the given equal product curve P. The slope of the tangent TT' is equal to (OT/OT'). Therefore, the MRTS at point K on the equal product curve P is equal to (OT/OT'). JJ' is the tangent to point L on the equal product curve P. Therefore, the MRTS at point L is equal to OJ/OJ'.

3.5 DIMINISHING MARGINAL RATE OF TECHNICAL SUBSTITUTION

An important characteristic of MRTS is that it diminishes as more and more of factor Y is substituted by factor X. In other words, as the quantity of factor X is increased and the quantity of factory Y is reduced, the amount of factor Y that is required to be replaced by an additional unit of factor X, so as to keep the output constant, will diminish. This is known as *Principle of diminishing marginal rate of technical substitution* and is merely an extension of the *law of diminishing returns* to the relation between the marginal physical productivities of the two factors. Along an equal product curve, as the quantity of factor X is increased and the quantity of factor Y is reduced, the marginal physical productivity of X diminishes and the marginal physical productivity of Y increases. Therefore, less and less of factor Y is required to be substituted by an additional unit of X so as to maintain the same level of output.

It may also be noted that the rate at which MRTS diminishes is a measure of the extent to which the two factors can be substituted for each other. The smaller the rate at which the MRTS diminishes, the greater the substitutability between the two factors. If the marginal rate of substitution between any two factors does not diminish and remains constant, the two factors are perfect substitutes of each other.

3.6   PROPERTIES OF ISOQUANTS OR EQUAL PRODUCT CURVES

The following are the important properties of equal product curves.

1. *Isoquants, like indifference curves, slope downwards from left to right,* i.e. they have a negative slope. This is so because when the quantity of factor X is increased, the quantity of factor Y must be reduced so as to keep the output constant.

2. *No two equal product curves can intersect each other.* If the two equal product curves, one corresponding to 20 units of output and the other to 30 units of output intersect each other, there will then be a common factor combination corresponding to the point of intersection. Thus means that the same factor combination which can produce 20 units of output according to one equal product curve can produce 30 units of output according to the other equal product curve. But this is quite absurd. How can the same factor combination produce two different levels of output, the techniques of production remaining unchanged.

3. *Isoquants, like indifference curves, are convex to the origin.* The convexity of equal product curves means that, as we move down the curve, less and less of factor Y is required to be substituted by a given increment of factor X so as to keep the level of output unchanged. Thus, the convexity of equal product curves is due to the diminishing MRTS. If the equal product curves were concave to the origin, it would mean that MRTS increased as more and more of factor Y was replaced by factor X. This could be valid if the law of increasing returns is applied. Since in the real world it is the law of diminishing returns which is more true the principle of diminishing MRTS generally holds good and it makes the equal product curves convex to the origin.

3.7   LAW OF VARIABLE PROPORTIONS

The law of variable proportions occupies an important place in economic theory. This law examines the production function with one factor variable, keeping the quantities of other factors fixed. In other words, it refers to the input-output relation when the output is increased by varying the quantity of one input. When the quantity of one factor is varied, keeping the quantity of the other factors constant, the proportion between the variable factor and the fixed factor is changed; the ratio of employment of the variable factor to that of the fixed factor goes on increasing as the quantity of the variable factor is increased. Since under this law we study the effects on output of variations in factor proportions, it is known as the *law of variable proportions*. It is also referred to as *law of diminishing returns*. This law has played a vital role in the history of economic thought and occupies an equally important place in modern economic theory. It has been supported by empirical evidence about the real world. Various economists have stated the law of variable proportions or diminishing returns in the following manner:

"As equal increments of one input are added, the inputs of other productive services being held constant, beyond a certain point the resulting increments of product will decrease, i.e. the marginal products will diminish".

– (G.J. Stigler).

As the proportion of one factor in a combination of factors is increased, after a point, first the marginal and then the average product of that factor will diminish.

– (F. Benham).

An increase in some inputs relative to other fixed inputs will, in a given state of technology, cause output to increase; but after a point the extra output resulting from the same additions of extra inputs will become less and less.

– (P.A. Samuelson).

Marshall explained the law of diminishing returns in relation to agriculture. He defined the law as follows:

An increase in the capital and labour applied in the cultivation of land causes in general a less than proportionate increase in the amount of product raised unless it happens to coincide with an improvement in the arts of agriculture.

Assumptions of the law of variable proportions

The law of variable proportions (or diminishing returns), as stated above, holds good under the following conditions:

1. The state of technology is assumed to be given and unchanged. If there is improvement in technology, then the marginal and average product may rise instead of diminishing.

2. There must be some inputs whose quantity is kept fixed. It is only in this way that we can change the factor proportions and know its effects on output. This law does not apply in case all factors are proportionately varied. The behaviour of the output as a result of the variations in all inputs is discussed under returns to scale.

3. The law is based on the possibility of varying the proportions in which the various factors can be combined to produce a product. The law does not apply to those cases where the factors must be used in fixed proportions to yield a product. When various factors are required to be used in rigidly fixed proportions, then the increase in one factor would not lead to any increase in output, that is, the marginal product of the factor will then be zero and not diminishing. It may, however, be pointed out that products requiring fixed proportions of factors are quite uncommon. Thus, the law of variable proportions applies to most of the cases of production.

4. The law specially operates in the short run because here some factors are fixed while the proportion of others vary.

3.7.1   Three Stages of the Law of Variable Proportions

The varying quantity of one factor combined with a fixed quantity of the other can be divided into three distinct stages. In order to understand these three stages, we can graphically illustrate the production function with one factor variable as in Figure 3.4. In this figure, on the *X*-axis is the quantity of variable factor and on the *Y*-axis the total, the average and the marginal products. How the total product, the average product and the marginal product of the variable factor change as a result of the increase in its quantity, that is, by increasing the quantity of one factor to a fixed quantity of the others can be seen in Figure 3.4. The total product curve *TP* goes on increasing to a point and after that it starts declining. The average and marginal product curves also rise and then decline; the marginal product curve starts declining earlier than the average product curve. The behaviour of these total, average and marginal products of the variable factor consequent on the increase in its amount is generally divided into three stages which are explained below.

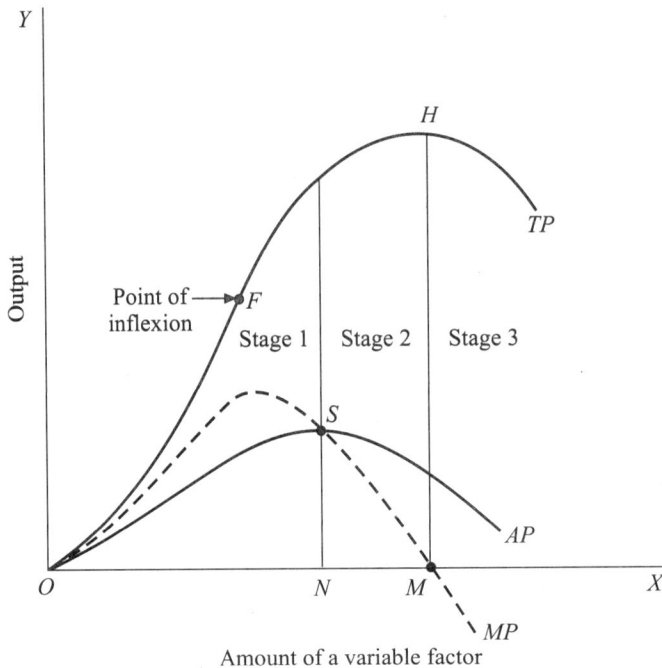

Figure 3.4   Three stages of law of variable proportion.

Stage 1:   In this stage, the total product to a point *increases at an increasing rate*. In Figure 3.4, from the origin to point *F*, the slope of the total product curve *TP* is increasing, that is, up to point *F*, the total product increases at an increasing rate (the total product curve *TP* is concave upwards up to point *F*), This means that the marginal product *MP* rises. From point *F* onwards during stage 1, the total product curve goes on rising but its slope is declining. It means that from point *F* onwards the total product increases at a diminishing rate (the total product curve is concave downwards), i.e. marginal product falls but is positive. The point where the total product stops increasing at an increasing rate and starts increasing at the diminishing rate is called the *point of inflexion*. Corresponding vertically to this point of inflexion the marginal product is maximum, after which it slopes downward.

Stage 1 ends where the average product curve reaches its highest point. During stage 1, when the marginal product of the variable factor is falling, it still exceeds its average product and so continues to cause the average product curve to rise. Thus, during this stage, whereas the marginal product curve rises in part and then falls, the average product curve rises throughout. Also during this stage, the quantity of the fixed factor is too much relative to the quantity of the variable factor so that if some of the fixed factor are withdrawn, the total product would increase. Thus, in the first stage, the marginal product of the fixed factor is *negative*.

Stage 2: *The stage of diminishing returns.* In this stage, the total product continues to increase at a diminishing rate until it reaches its maximum point *H* where the stage ends. Here, both the marginal product and the average product of the variable factor are diminishing but are positive. At the end of this stage, that is, at point *M*, the marginal product of the variable factor is zero. Stage 2 is very crucial and important because the firm will seek to produce in its range. It is known as the *stage of diminishing returns* as, during this state, both the average and the marginal products of the variable factor continuously fall.

Stage 3: *The Stage of negative returns.* In this stage, the total product declines and therefore, the total product curve *TP* slopes downward. As a result, the marginal product of the variable factor is negative and the marginal product curve MP goes below the *X*-axis. In this stage, the variable factor is too much relative to the fixed factor. It is also called the stage of negative returns, since, during this stage, the marginal product of the variable factor is negative.

It may be noted that stages 1 and 3 are completely symmetrical. In stage 1, the fixed factor is too much relative to the variable factor. Therefore, in stage 1, the marginal product of the fixed factor is negative. On the other hand, in stage 3, the variable factor is too much relative to the fixed factor. Therefore, in stage 3, the marginal product of the variable factor is negative. Stage 2 represents the range of rational production decisions.

3.8 RETURNS TO SCALE

The responsiveness of output to a given proportionate change in the quantities of all inputs is called returns to scale. Factor proportions are changed by keeping the quantity of one or some factors fixed and varying the quantity of the other. The changes in output as a result of the variation in factor proportions, as seen before, form the subject matter of the 'law of variable proportions'. We shall now undertake the study of changes in output when all factors or inputs in a particular production function are increased together. In other words, we shall study the behaviour of output in response to the changes in the scale. An increase in the scale means that all inputs or factors are increased in the same proportion. The increase in the scale, thus, occurs when all the factors or inputs are increased, keeping factor proportions unchanged. The study of changes in output as a consequence of changes in the scale forms the subject matter of returns to scale.

3.8.1 The Concept of Returns to Scale

Depending on whether the proportionate change in output equals, exceeds or falls short of the proportionate change in both inputs, a production function is classified as showing constant, increasing or decreasing returns to scale. In this section, we discuss how the returns vary with the changes in scale, that is, when all the factors are increased in the same proportion. But some economists have challenged the concept of returns to scale on the ground that all factors cannot be increased and, therefore, the proportions between factors cannot be kept constant. For instance, it has been pointed out that entrepreneurship is a factor of production which cannot be varied (in the single firm), though all other factors can be increased. The entrepreneur and his decision-making are indivisible and incapable of being increased. Thus, the entrepreneur is a fixed factor in all production functions. If labour and capital could produce a product with no one to supervise and make decisions, then the returns to scale in the sense of returns to all factors could be visualized. But the idea that labour and capital can produce goods without an entrepreneur is quite unrealistic. Thus, the concept of returns to scale is a puzzle for the economists and still remains unsolved. However, this puzzle can be solved by assuming entrepreneurship to be variable in the sense that the greater the other inputs or factors, the greater the entrepreneurial work to be performed.

In the following paragraph we shall explain the concept of returns to scale by assuming that only two factors, *labour* and *capital*, are needed for production.

3.8.2 Constant Returns to Scale

Returns to scale may be constant, increasing or decreasing. If we increase all factors (i.e. scale) in a given proportion and the output increases in the same proportion, then the returns to scale are said to be constant. Thus, if inputs are increased 50% and output is also increased by 50%, then the production function of a firm is said to be one having constant returns to scale. But, if the increase in all the factors leads to a more than proportionate increase in output, then the returns to scale are said to be increasing. Thus, if all factors are doubled and the output increases by more than a double, then the returns to scale are increasing. On the other hand, if the increase in all factors leads to a less than proportionate increase in the output, the returns to scale are decreasing. We shall explain in the following paragraphs these various types of returns to scale.

As discussed earlier, the constant returns to scale means that with the increase in the scale or the amounts of all factors leads to a proportionate increase in output, that is, doubling of all inputs doubles the output. In mathematics, the case of constant returns to scale is called *linear and homogeneous production function* or *homogeneous production function of the first degree*. Production function exhibiting constant returns to scale possesses very convenient mathematical properties which make it very useful for theoretical analysis. There are a number of special theorems which apply when production function exhibits constant returns to scale. Empirical evidence suggests that production function for the economy as a whole is not too far from being homogeneous of the first degree. It also suggests that, in production function, for an individual firm there is a long phase of constant returns to scale.

Let us illustrate diagrammatically the constant returns to scale with the help of an equal product map (Figure 3.5). It is assumed that in the production of the good only two factors, *labour* and *capital*, are used. In order to analyse whether or not the returns to scale are constant, we draw some straight lines through the origin. As shown in the figure, the straight lines passing through the origin indicate the increase in scale as we move upwards. It will be seen from the figure that successive equal product curves are equidistant from each other along each straight line drawn from the origin. Thus, along the line *OP*, $AB = BC = CD$; along the line *OQ*, $A'B' = B'C' = C'D'$; and along the line *OR*, $A''B'' = B''C'' = C''D''$. The distance between the successive equal product curves being the same along any straight line through the origin means that, if both labour and capital are increased in a given proportion, the output expands by the same proportion.

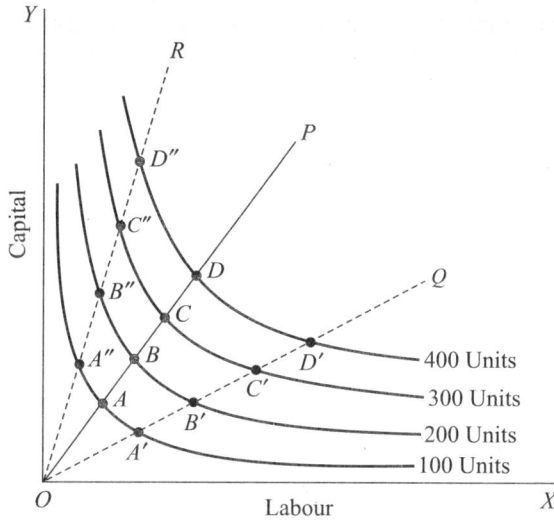

Figure 3.5 Illustration of Constant returns to scale.

3.8.3 Increasing Returns to Scale

As already mentioned increasing returns to scale means that output increases in a greater proportion than the increase in inputs. If, for instance, all inputs are increased by 40 per cent, and the output increases by 90 per cent, then, we have increasing returns to scale.

As already stated, Professor E.H. Chamberlin contends that returns to scale increase because of greater possibilities of specialization of labour and machinery. According to him, even if the factors were perfectly divisible, with the increase in the scale, the returns can increase because the firm can introduce a greater degree of specialization of labour and machinery (because now greater resources or amounts of factors are available) and also because it can install technologically more efficient machinery.

The increasing returns to scale can be shown in the equal product map. When the increasing returns to scale occur, the successive equal product curves will lie at decreasingly smaller distances along a straight line through the origin. In Figure 3.6 up to point *D* or equal product curve P_4, increasing returns to scale occur since *BC < AB, CD < BC*. This means that equal increases in the output are obtained by smaller and smaller increments in inputs.

3.8.4 Decreasing Returns to Scale

As already stated, when the output increases in a smaller proportion than the increase in all the inputs, the decreasing returns to scale are said to prevail. When a firm goes on expanding by increasing all its inputs, then eventually diminishing returns to scale will occur. But among the economists there is no agreement on a cause or causes of diminishing returns to scale. Some economists are of the view that the entrepreneur is a fixed factor of production; while all other inputs may be increased, he cannot be. According to this view, the decreasing returns to scale is therefore actually a special case of the law of variable proportions. In this case, they say, we get diminishing returns beyond a point because varying quantities of all other inputs are combined with a fixed entrepreneur. Thus, this view maintains that, the decreasing returns to scale is a special case of the law of variable proportions with the entrepreneur as the fixed factor. Other economists do not treat decreasing returns to scale as the special case of the law of variable proportions. They argue that decreasing returns to scale eventually occur because of the increasing difficulties of management, coordination and control. When the firm has expanded to a gigantic size, it is difficult to manage it with the same efficiency as was done earlier.

The case of decreasing returns to scale can be shown on an equal product map. When successive equal product curves lie at progressively larger and larger distance on a straight line passing through the origin, the returns to scale will be decreasing. In Figure 3.6, beyond point F upwards the decreasing returns to scale occur since $FG > EF$, $GH > FG$. This means that more and more of inputs (labour and capital) are required to obtain equal increments in output.

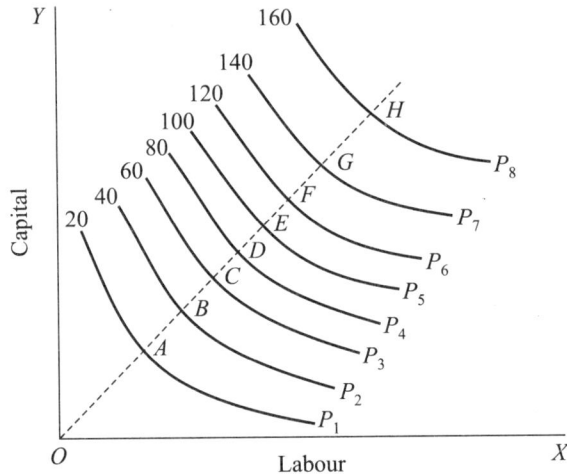

Figure 3.6   Increasing and decreasing returns to scale.

3.8.5   Varying Returns to Scale in a Single Production Function

It should be noted that it is not always the case that different production functions should exhibit separate types of returns to scale. It generally happens that there are three phases of increasing, constant and diminishing returns to scale in a single production function. In the beginning, when the scale increases, the increasing returns to scale are obtained because of greater possibilities of specialization of labour and machinery. After a point, there is a phase of constant returns to scale where the output increases in the same proportion as inputs. Empirical evidence suggests that the phase of constant returns to scale is quite long. If the firm continues to expand, then eventually a point will be reached beyond which decreasing returns to scale will occur due to mounting difficulties of coordination and control.

3.9   COST OF PRODUCTION AND COST CURVES

The relation between cost and output is called 'cost function'. The cost function of a firm depends on the production function and the prices of the factors used for production. How much costs the firm will incur on production will depend on the level of output. Moreover, the quantity of a product that will be offered by the firm for supply in the market will depend to a great degree on the costs of production incurred on the various possible levels of output. The cost of production is the most important force governing the supply of a product. It should be pointed out here that it is assumed that for each level of output, the firm chooses the least-cost combination of factors. In other words, the firm chooses a factor combination which lies on the expansion path corresponding to a given level of output. It is thus assumed that whatever the level of output a firm produces, it is produced at the minimum cost possible and, accordingly, the least-cost factor combination problem has already been solved by it.

In price theory, economists are generally interested in two types of cost functions, the *short-run cost function* and the *long-run cost function* and, accordingly, derive the short-run and long-run cost curves.

3.9.1 Short-Run Total Costs

Total fixed and variable costs

There are some inputs or factors which can be readily adjusted with the changes in the output level. Thus, a firm can readily employ more workers if it has to increase output. Likewise, it can secure and use more raw materials, more chemicals without much delay if it has to expand production. Thus, labour, raw materials, chemicals, etc. are the factors which can be readily varied with the change in output. Such factors are called *variable factors*. On the other hand, there are factors, such as capital equipment, building, top management personnel, which cannot be so readily varied. It requires a comparatively long time to make variations in them. For instances, it takes time to expand a factory building or build a new factory building with larger area or capacity. Similarly, it also takes time to order and install new machinery. The factors, such as raw materials, labour, which can be readily varied with the change in the output level, are known as *variable factors*, and the factors, such as capital equipment, building, which cannot be readily varied and require comparatively a longer time to make adjustment in them, are called *fixed factors*.

Corresponding to this distinction between variable factors and fixed factors, economists distinguish between the short run and the long run. The short run is a period of time in which the output can be increased or decreased by changing only the amount of variable factors such as labour, raw materials, and chemicals. In the short run, the quantities of the fixed factors such as capital, equipment, and factory building cannot be varied to make changes in the output. Thus, in the short run, the firm cannot build a new plant or abandon an old one. If the firm wants to increase the output in the short run, it can only do so by using more labour and more raw materials. It cannot increase the output in the short run by expanding the capacity of its existing plant or by building a new one with a larger capacity. Thus, the short run is the period of time in which only the quantities of variable factors can be varied, while the quantities of the fixed factors remain unchanged.

On the other hand, the long run is defined as the period of time in which the quantities of all factors may be varied. All factors being variable in the long run, the fixed and variable factors' dichotomy holds good only in the short run. In the long run, the output can be increased not only by using more quantities of labour and raw materials, but also by expanding the size of the existing plant or by building a new plant with a larger productive capacity. It may be noted that the word 'plant' in economics stands for a collection of fixed factors, such as factory building, machinery installed, the organization represented by the manager and other essential skilled personnel.

Having explained the difference between the fixed factors and the variable factors, and also between the short run and the long run, we are in a position to distinguish between the fixed costs and the variable costs which, when added together, make up the total costs of a business. *Fixed costs* are those that are independent output, which means they do not change with the changes in the output. These costs are a 'fixed' amount which must be incurred by a firm in the short run, whether the output is small or large. Even if the firm closes down for some time in the short run but remains in business in the long run, these costs have to be borne by it. The fixed costs are also known as *overhead costs* and include charges, such as contractual rent, insurance fee, maintenance costs, property taxes, interest on the capital invested, and minimum administrative expenses such as managers' salary, watchman's wages. Thus, fixed costs are those which are incurred in hiring the fixed factors of production whose amount cannot be changed in the short run.

The *variable costs*, on the other hand, are those costs which are incurred on the employment of variable factors of production whose amount can be changed in the short run. Thus, the total variable costs change with changes in the output in the short run, i.e. they increase or decrease when the output rises or falls. These costs include payments such as wages of labour employed, the price of the raw material, fuel and power used, the expenses incurred on transporting and the like. If a firm shuts down for some time in the short run, then it will not use the variable factors of production and will not, therefore, incur any variable costs. Moreover, variable costs are made only when some amount of output is produced and the total variable costs increase with the increase in the level of production. Variable costs are also called *prime costs* or *direct costs*. The total cost of a business is the sum of its Total Variable Cost (*TVC*) and Total Fixed Cost (*TFC*). Thus,

$$TC = TFC + TVC$$

Since one component, namely by, *TVC*, varies with the change in output, the total cost of production will also respond to the changes in the level of output. The total cost increases as the level of output rises. The total fixed cost and the total variable cost are shown in Figure 3.7 where the output is measured on the *X*-axis and the cost on the *Y*-axis.

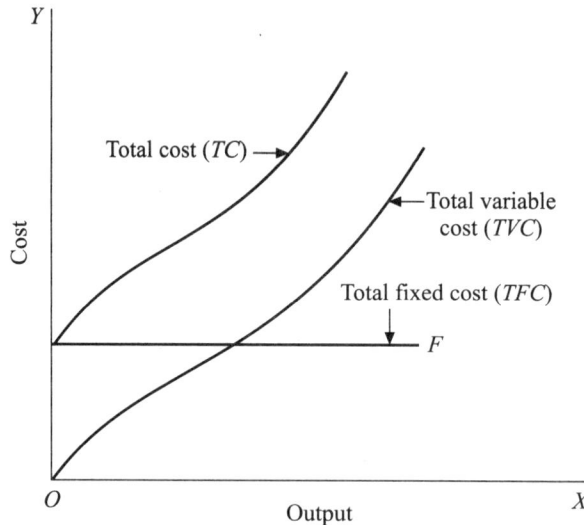

Figure 3.7 Short-run total cost curves.

Since the total fixed cost remains constant whatever the level of output, the *TFC* curve is parallel to the *X*-axis. It will be seen in Figure 3.7 that the *TFC* curve starts from a point on the *Y*-axis, meaning thereby that the *TFC* will be incurred even if the output is zero. On the other hand, the *TVC* rises upwards showing thereby that, as the output is increased, the total variable cost also increases. The Total variable cost (*TVC*) curve starts from the origin which shows that when the output is zero, the variable costs are also nil.

It should be noted that *TC* is a function of the total output q; the greater the output, the greater will be the *TC*. Mathematically,

$$TC = f(q)$$

$$TC = TFC + TVC$$

The Total cost (*TC*) curve has been obtained by adding up vertically *TFC* curve and *TVC* curve because the total cost is the sum of total fixed cost and total variable cost. It will be seen that the vertical distance between the *TVC* curve and *TC* curve is constant throughout. This is because the vertical distance between *TVC* and *TC* curves represents the amount of total fixed costs which remains unchanged as the output is increased in the short run. It should also be noted that the vertical distance between the *TC* curve and the *TFC* curve represents the amount of total variable costs which increase with the increase in output. The shape of the *TC* curve is exactly the same as that of the *TVC* curve because the same vertical distance always separates the two curves.

3.9.2 The Short-Run Average Cost Curves

We have explained in Section 3.9.1 the short-run total cost curves. However, both businessmen and economists use the cost concept more frequently in the form of cost per unit, or average costs rather than as totals. We, therefore, pass on to the study of short-run average cost curves.

Average fixed cost

Average Fixed Cost (*AFC*) is the total fixed costs divided by the number of units of output produced. Therefore,

$$AFC = \frac{TFC}{q}$$

where q represents the number of units of output produced.

Suppose for a firm TFC is Rs. 4000 when the output is 100 units, (*AFC*) will be Rs. 4000/100 = Rs. 40 and, when the output is 200 units, *AFC* will be Rs. 4000/200 = Rs. 20. Since *TFC* is a constant quantity, *AFC* will steadily fall as output increases. Therefore, *AFC* curve slopes downwards throughout its length. As output increases, *TFC* spreads over more and more units and, therefore, *AFC* becomes less and less. When output becomes very large, AFC as shown in Figure 3.8 approaches zero. It can be seen that AFC curve continuously falls throughout. Mathematically speaking, *AFC* curve approaches both axes asymptotically. In other words, *AFC* curve gets nearer to but never touches either of the axes.

The average fixed cost curve, *AFC*, possesses another important property. If we pick up any point on the *AFC* curve and multiply it at that point with the corresponding quantity of output produced then the product is always the same. This is because the product of the *AFC* and the corresponding quantity of output will yield the total fixed cost which remains constant throughout. A curve with such a property is called *rectangular hyperbola*.

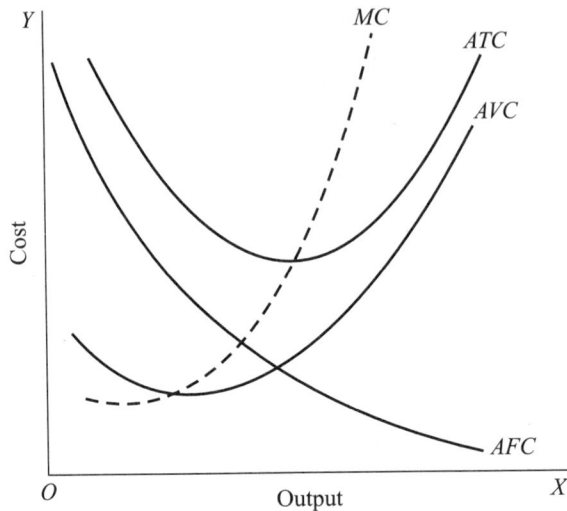

Figure 3.8   Short-run average and marginal cost curves.

Average variable cost

The average variable cost (AVC) is the total variable cost divided by the number of units of output produced. Therefore,

$$AVC = \frac{TVC}{q}$$

where q represents the total output produced.

Thus AVC is the variable costs per unit of output. The AVC will generally fall as the output increases from zero to the normal capacity output due to the occurrence of increasing returns. But beyond the normal capacity output, the average variable cost will rise steeply because of the operation of diminishing returns. The AVC curve is shown in Figure 3.8. The curve AVC which first falls, reaches a minimum and then rises.

The Average Total Cost (ATC) is the sum of the average variable cost and the average fixed cost. Therefore, as the output increases and the average fixed cost becomes smaller and smaller, the vertical distance between the average total cost curve, ATC and then average variable cost curve, AVC goes on declining. When the average fixed cost curve, AFC approaches the X-axis, the average variable cost curve approaches the average total cost curve, ATC.

Average total cost

The Average Total Cost (ATC) or, what is called simply average cost, is the total cost divided by the number of units of output produced. Thus,

$$\text{Average Total Cost} = \frac{\text{Total cost}}{\text{Output}}$$

or

$$ATC = \frac{TC}{q}$$

Since the total cost is the sum of total variable cost and total fixed cost, the average total cost is also the sum of average variable cost and average fixed cost. This can be proved as follows:

$$ATC = \frac{TC}{q}$$

Since

$$TC = TVC + TFC$$

We have

$$ATC = \frac{TVC + TFC}{q}$$

$$= \frac{TVC}{q} + \frac{TFC}{q}$$

$$= AVC + AFC$$

The average total cost is also known as the *unit cost* since it is cost per unit of output produced.

It follows from the above that the behaviour of the *ATC* curve will depend on the behaviour of the *AVC* curve and the *AFC* curve. In the beginning, both *AVC* and *AFC* curves fall, the *ATC* curve, therefore, falls sharply in the beginning. When the *AVC* curve begins to rise, but the *AFC* curve is falling steeply, the *ATC* curve continues to fall. This is because during this stage, the fall in the *AFC* curve is more than the rise in the *AVC* curve. But as the output increases further, there is a sharp rise in the *AVC* which more than offsets the fall in *AFC*. Therefore, the *ATC* curve rises after a point. Therefore, the *ATC* curve like the *AVC* curve first falls, reaches its minimum value and then rises. The *ATC* curve is, therefore, almost of a 'U' shape.

Marginal cost

The marginal cost (*MC*) is addition to the total cost caused by producing one more unit of output. In other words, *MC* is the addition to the total cost of producing n units instead of $n - 1$ units (i.e. one less), where n is any given number. Mathematically,

$$MC_n = TC_n - TC_{n-1}$$

Suppose production of five units of a product involves the total cost of Rs. 206. If the increase in production to six units raises the total cost to Rs. 236, then the marginal cost of the sixth unit of output is Rs. 30 ($236 - 206 = 30$). Let us illustrate the computation of marginal cost from a table of total cost and output.

In Table 3.3, when the output is one in the short run, the producer is incurring a total cost of Rs. 10 which represents the total fixed cost of production. When two units of output is produced, the total cost rises to Rs. 18. The marginal cost of the first unit of output is, therefore, Rs. 8 (Rs. $18 - 10 = 8$). When the output is increased to 3 units, the total cost goes up to Rs. 24. Therefore, the marginal cost is now Rs. 6 ($24 - 18 = 6$). In this way, the marginal cost can be found for further units of output.

Since the marginal cost is a change in the total cost as a result of unit change in the output, it can also be written as

$$MC = \frac{\Delta TC}{\Delta q}$$

where ΔTC represents a change in the total cost and Δq represents a small change in the output or total product.

Table 3.3   Computation of Marginal Cost

Output	Total cost	Marginal cost
1	10	10
2	18	8
3	24	6
4	28	4
5	35	7
6	48	13
7	63	15
8	80	17

The independence of marginal cost from the fixed cost can be proved algebraically as follows:

$$MC_n = TC_n - TC_{n-1}$$
$$= (TVC_n + TFC) - (TVC_{n-1} - TFC)$$
$$= TVC_n + TFC - TVC_{n-1} - TFC$$
$$= TVC_n - TVC_{n-1}$$

3.9.3   Relationship between the Average and Marginal Cost Curves

The relationship between the marginal cost and the average cost is the same as that between any other marginal-average quantities. When marginal cost is less than average cost, the latter falls and when marginal cost is greater than average cost, the latter rises. This marginal-average relationship is a matter of mathematical truism and can be easily understood by a simple example. Suppose that a cricket player's batting average is 45. If in the next innings he scores less than 45, say 40, then his average score will fall because his marginal (additional) score is less than his average score. If instead of 40, he had scored more than 45, say 50, then his average score will increase because now the marginal score is greater than his previous average score. Again, with his present average runs as 45, if he scored 45, then his average score will remain the same, i.e. 45, since his marginal score is just equal to the average score. Similarly, suppose a manufacturer is producing a certain number of units of a product and his average cost is Rs. 20. Now, if he produces one unit more, his average cost falls. It means that the additional unit must have cost him less than Rs. 20. On the other hand, if the production of the additional unit raises his average cost, then the marginal unit must have cost him more than Rs. 20. And, finally, if as a result of the production of an additional unit, the average cost remains the same, then the marginal unit must have cost him exactly Rs. 20, that is, the marginal cost and the average cost would be equal in this case.

The relationship between the average and marginal cost can be easily understood with the help of Figure 3.9. It is illustrated in this figure that when MC is above Average Cost (AC), the average cost rises. That is, MC pulls AC upwards. On the other hand, if MC is below AC, the average cost falls, that is, the marginal cost pulls the average cost downwards. When MC stands equal to AC, the latter remains the same, that is, MC pulls the AC horizontally. The relationship between AC and MC is shown in Figure 3.9.

Now again take Figure 3.9 where the short-run average cost curve *AC*, is drawn. As long as the short-run marginal cost curve, *MC*, lies below the short-run average cost curve, *AC*, the average cost curve, *AC* is failing. When *MC* lies above *AC*, *AC* is rising. At the point of intersection *L* where *MC* is equal to *AC*, the latter is neither falling nor rising. It follows that point *L*, where the *MC* curve crosses the *AC* curve to lie above the *AC* curve, is the minimum point on the *AC* curve. If the average cost curve is U-shaped, then its corresponding marginal cost curve will cut it at its lowest point (at the point *L* as shown in the Figure 3.9).

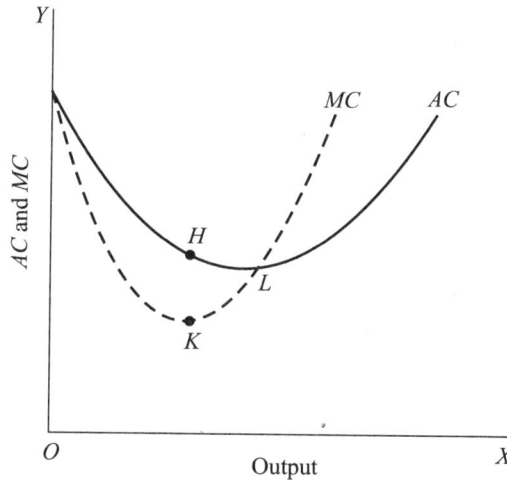

Figure 3.9 Relationship between *AC* and *MC* curves.

3.9.4 Long-Run Average Cost Curve

The long run, as already discussed, is a period of time during which the firm can vary all its inputs. In the short run, some inputs are fixed while others are varied to increase the level of output. In the long run, none of the factors is fixed and all can be varied to expand, the output. The long-run production function has, therefore, no fixed factors, and the firm has no fixed costs in the long run. It is conventional to regard the size or scale of a plant as a typical fixed input. The term 'plant' is here to be understood as consisting of capital equipment, machinery, land, etc. In the short run, the size of the plant is fixed and cannot be increased or reduced. That is to say, one cannot change the amount of capital equipment in the short run if one has to increase or decrease the output. On the other hand, the long-run as the name suggests, is a period of time sufficiently long to permit the changes required in plant, that is, in capital equipment, machinery, land, etc. in order to expand or contract the output. Thus, whereas in the short-run the firm is tied with a given plant, in the long run the firm moves from one plant to another; the firm can build a larger plant if it has to increase its output or a smaller plant if it has to reduce its output. The long-run cost of production is the least possible cost of production for producing any given level of output when all the inputs are variable, including, of course, the size of the plant. A long-run cost curve depicts the functional relationship between the output and the long-run cost of production as just defiend. The three short-run cost curves are shown in Figure 3.10.

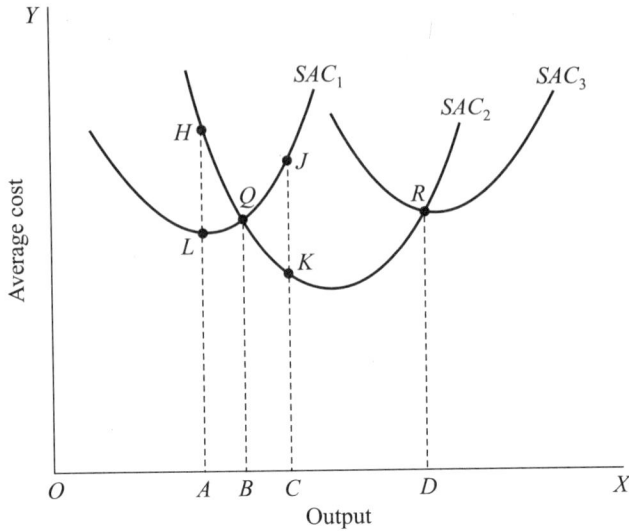

Figure 3.10 Plant curves.

The long-run average cost is the long-run total cost divided by the level of output. The long-run average cost curve depicts the least possible average cost for producing all possible levels of output. In order to understand how the long-run average cost curve is derived, consider the three short-run average cost curves as shown in the figure. These short-run average cost curves are also called *plant curves* since, in the short-run, the plant is fixed and each of the short-run average cost curve corresponds to a particular plant. In the short run, the firm can be operating on any short-run average cost curve, given the size of the plant. Suppose that only these three are technically possible sizes of the plants and that no other size of the plant can be built. Given the size of the plant or the short-run average cost curve, the firm will increase or decrease its output by varying the amount of the variable inputs. But, in the long run, the firm can choose among the three possible sizes of plant as depicted by the short-run average cost curves. In the long run, the firm will examine that with which size of the plant or on which short-run average cost curve it should operate to produce a given level of output at the minimum possible cost.

It will be seen from Figure 3.10 that up to *OB* amount of output, the firm will operate on the shot-run average cost curve SAC_1, though it could also produce with short-run average cost curve SAC_2. This is because up to *OB* amount of output, the production on SAC_1 curve entails lower cost than on SAC_2. For instance, if the level of output *OA* is produced with SAC_1.

It is thus clear that in the long run, the firm has a choice in the employment of a plant, and it will employ that plant which yields the possible minimum unit cost for producing a given output. The long-run average cost curve depicts the least possible average cost for producing various levels of output when all the factors, including the size of the plant, have been adjusted. Given that only three sizes of plants as shown in the figure are technically possible, then the long-run average cost curve is the curve which has scallops in it. This heavily scalloped long-run average cost curve consists of some segments of all the short-run average cost curves as explained above.

Suppose now that the size of the plant can be varied by infinitely small gradations so that there are infinite number of plants corresponding to which there will be numerous short-run average cost curves. In that case, the long-run average cost curve will be a smooth and continuous line without any scallops. Such a smooth long-run average cost curve has been shown in Figure 3.11 and labelled as *LAC*. In such a case, there will be infinite short-run average cost curves though only seven have been shown in the figure. This long-run average cost curve *LAC* is so drawn as to be tangent to each of the short-run average cost curves. Since an infinite number of short-run average cost curves are assumed, every point on the long-run average cost curve will be a tangency point with some short-run average cost curve. In fact, the long-run average cost curve is nothing but the locus of all these tangency points. It is again worth noting that the long-run average cost curve shows the least possible average cost of producing any output when all productive factors are variable. If a firm desires to produce a particular output in the long run, it will pick a point on the long-run average cost curve corresponding to that output and will then build a relevant plant and operate on the corresponding short-run average cost curve.

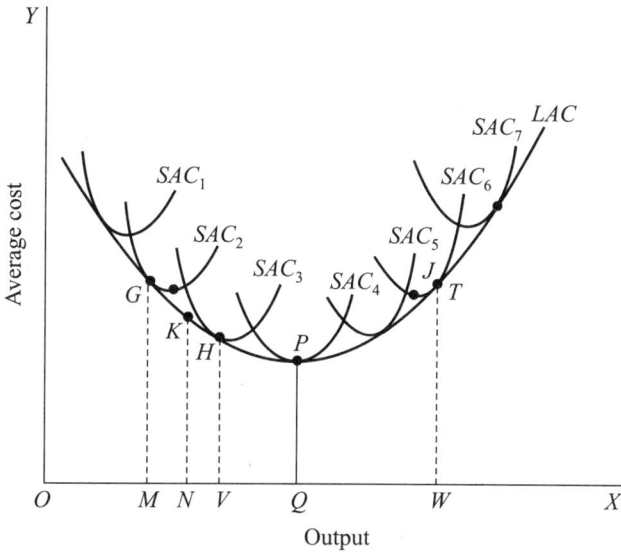

Figure 3.11 Long-run average cost curves.

In the situation as depicted in the figure for producing output *OM*, the corresponding point on the long-run average cost curve *LAC* is *G* at which the short-run average cost curve SAC_2 is tangent to the long-run average cost curve *LAC*. Thus, if a firm desires to produce the output *OM*, it will construct a plant corresponding to SAC_2 and operate on this curve at point G. Similar would be the case for all other outputs in the long run. Further, consider that the firm plans to produce output *ON*, which corresponds to the point *K* on the long-run average cost curve *LAC*. As already noted, every point on the long-run average cost curve is a tangency point with some short-run average cost curve and that there are infinite number of short-run average cost curves, So there will be a short-run average cost curve (not shown in the figure) which will be tangent to the long-run average cost curve, *LAC*, at the point *K* corresponding to the *ON* output. Thus, for producing the output *ON*, the firm will build a plant which will correspond to that short-run average cost curve which is tangent to the long-run average cost curve, *LAC*, at the point *K* corresponding to the *ON* output. The long-run average cost curve, *LAC*, is also called 'envelope' since it envelops or supports a family of short-run average cost curves.

It is evident from Figure 3.11 that larger outputs can be produced at the lowest cost with the larger plants, whereas smaller outputs can be produced at the lowest cost with the smaller plants.

3.10   LAW OF SUPPLY

The law of supply is an important law in economic theory in contrast to the law of demand. The law of supply is "other factor remaining the same, as the price of a commodity rises, its supply increases and, as the price of a commodity falls, its supply declines". Thus, the quantity supplied is directly proportional to the price.

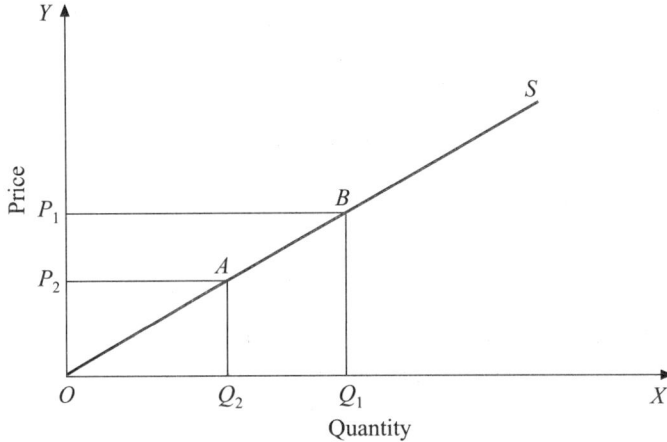

Figure 3.12   The supply curve.

The supply curve is the graphical representation of the supply schedule. See Figure 3.12. The movement along the supply curve, such as the one from *A* to *B*, shown in this figure, is called *change in quantity supplied*. So the supply curve reveals that when the price rises, the supply also rises, when the price declines, the supply also decreases.

3.10.1   Elasticity of Supply

The concept of elasticity of supply occupies an important place in the price theory. The elasticity of supply is the degree of responsiveness of supply to changes in the price of a good. In otherwords, the elasticity of supply can be defined as a relative change in the quantity supplied of a good in response to a relative change in the price of the good. Therefore,

$$e_s = \frac{\text{Proportionate change in quantity supplied}}{\text{Proportionate change in price}}$$

$$= \frac{\text{Change in quantity supplied}}{\text{Original quantity supplied}} \Big/ \frac{\text{Change in price}}{\text{Original price}}$$

In terms of symbols, we can write

$$e_s = \frac{\Delta q}{\Delta p} \Big/ \frac{\Delta p}{p} = \frac{\Delta q}{q} \times \frac{p}{\Delta p}$$

$$= \frac{\Delta q}{\Delta q} \times \frac{p}{q}$$

If the price of a machine rises from Rs. 4,000 per unit to Rs. 4100 per unit and, in response to this increase in price, the quantity supplied rises from 5,000 units to 5,500 units, the elasticity of supply will be

$$e_s = \frac{500}{100} \times \frac{4000}{5000} = 4$$

where

e_s = Elasticity of supply
q = Quantity supplied
Δq = Change in quantity supplied
P = Price
Δp = Change in price

The elasticity of supply depends on the case with which the output of the industry can be expanded and the behaviour of the marginal costs. Since there is greater scope for an increase in the output in the long run than in the short run, the supply of a good is more elastic in the long run than in the short run.

The elasticity of supply at a point on the supply curve can be easily measured by a formula. In what follows, we shall derive this formula

In Figure 3.13 the supply curve SS' is given and the elasticity of supply at point Q is required to be measured. At price OP, the quantity supplied is OM. With the rise in price from OP to OP', the quantity supplied rises from OM to OM'. Extend the supply curve SS' downward so that it meets the X-axis at T.

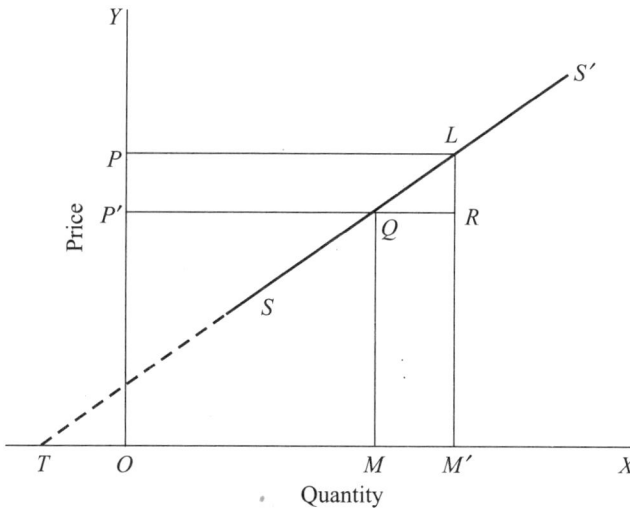

Figure 3.13 Measurement of point elasticity of supply, $e_s > 1$.

Then, the elasticity of supply at points

$$Q = \frac{\Delta q}{q} \Big/ \frac{\Delta p}{p}$$

$$= \frac{MM'}{OM} \div \frac{PP'}{OP} = \frac{MM'}{OM} \times \frac{OP}{PP'}$$

$$= \frac{MM'}{PP'} \times \frac{OP}{OM}$$

Substituting QR for MM', RL for PP' and MQ for OP_1, we get e_s at

$$Q = \frac{QR}{RL} \times \frac{MQ}{OM} \qquad\qquad (i)$$

Now, in triangles QRL and QMT

$$\angle LQR = \angle QTM \qquad \text{(Corresponding angles)}$$
$$\angle QRL = \angle QMT \qquad \text{(Right angles)}$$
$$\angle RLQ = \angle MQT \qquad \text{(Corresponding angles)}$$

Therefore, triangles QRL and QMT are similar. Hence,

$$\frac{QR}{RL} = \frac{MT}{MQ} \qquad\qquad (ii)$$

Substituting (MT/MQ) for (QR/RL) in (i) above, we obtain

$$e_s \text{ at } Q = \frac{MT}{MQ} \times \frac{MQ}{OM}$$
$$= \frac{MT}{OM}$$

Thus, we can get the value of elasticity of supply by dividing MT by OM. Since in the figure MT is greater than OM, the supply elasticity (MT/OM) will be greater than one. In Figure 3.14 the supply curve when extended meets the X-axis to the right of the point of origin so that MT is smaller than OM. In Figure 3.15, when extended, the supply curve SS' meets the X-axis exactly at the point of origin so that the MT is equal to OM. Therefore, in the figure the elasticity of supply will be equal to 1. In Figure 3.13, the elasticity of supply was greater than 1 at every point of the curve, but it will differ from point to point.

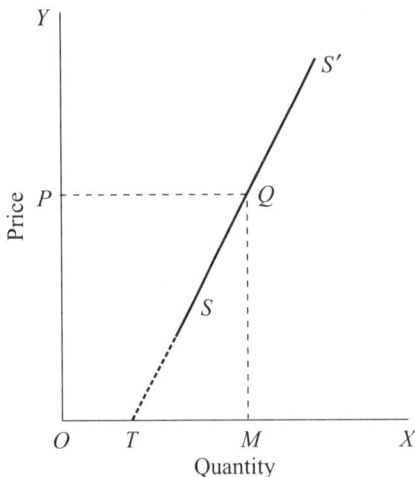

Figure 3.14   Elasticity of supply, $e_s < 1$.   **Figure 3.15   Elasticity of supply, $e_s = 1$.**

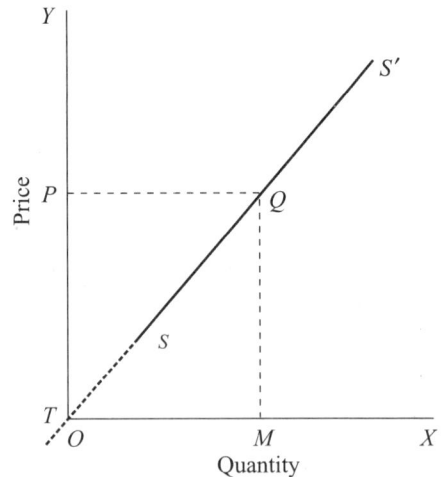

Similarly, in Figure 3.14 the supply elasticity is less than 1 at every point of the curve, but it will differ from point to point. However, Figure 3.15 shows that elasticity of supply will be equal to 1 at every point of the curve.

A perfectly elastic supply is one in which the supply is present only at one price. Any decrease in the price amounts to nothing being supplied in the market is shown in Figure 3.16.

Figure 3.16   Perfectly elastic supply, $e_s = \infty$.

Perfectly inelastic supply is shown in Figure 3.17. It is one in which the quantity supplied does not change as the price changes. The elasticity of supply of a commodity depends on the case with which increases in output can be obtained without bringing about a rise in the cost of production. If, with the increase in production, the marginal cost of production goes up, to that extent the elasticity of supply would be less. In the short run, with some factors of production being fixed, the increase in the amount of variable factor eventually causes diminishing marginal returns and, as a result, with the expansion of the output, the marginal cost of production rises. However, in the long-run, the firm can increase the output by varying all factors and also new firms can enter the industry, and thereby add to the supply. The long-run supply curve of a commodity is more elastic than that in the short-run.

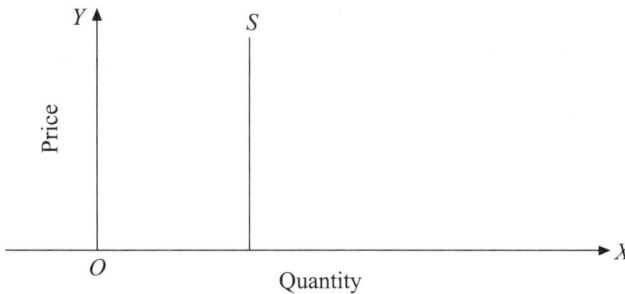

Figure 3.17   Perfectly inelastic supply, $e_s = 0$.

3.11   PRICE DETERMINATION UNDER PERFECT COMPETITION MARKET STRUCTURE

Perfect competition is a form of market in which there is a large number of buyers and sellers producing a homogeneous product. Every pricing situation is unique and must be explored in its own right. In business organizations, pricing decisions result from balancing a number of factors which are both related to the business organization and sometimes not related to the business organization. Pricing is a matter of judgement. If a judgement is to be effective, then it should be based on sound principles with full information possible and with common sense. Pricing always starts as a matter of trial and error. In fact, a price is always a trial in the market. No matter how logical the price may seem to be, if it does not attract the customers and does not bring in the necessary profits, then it is a wrong pricing policy.

Various types of market structures are based on four basic models:

1. Perfect competition
2. Monopoly
3. Monopolistic competition
4. Oligopoly market

3.11.1 Pricing under Perfect Competition

There are some necessary conditions for perfect competition which must be satisfied if the market is perfectly elastic. These are as follows.

1. **There are large number of undifferentiated buyers and sellers, each of when is 'small' relative to the market:** Each seller being small means the quantity supplied by any one of the sellers must be so insignificant that any increase or decrease in his output cannot appreciably affect the total supply and the market price. So also each buyer is small, meaning thereby that the quantity bought by any of the buyer should be so insignificant that any increase or decrease in his purchase cannot appreciably affect the total demand and the price. As a result, each seller will accept the market price as it is. So also each buyer will regard the price as determined by forces beyond his control and accept it as it is. The firm in perfect competition is essentially a price taker.

2. **Each firm in the market produces a homogeneous (identical) product:** And each competitor offers or seeks exactly a similar product as do the others. There is nothing to distinguish one product from the other so that one product can be substituted for the other.

3. **Buyers and sellers have perfect information:** The market in which the commodity is bought and sold must be well organized, trading must be continuous, and buyers and sellers must be so well informed that every unit bought or sold at any particular time will sell at the same price.

4. **There are no transaction costs.**

5. **Many competitors exist (whether sellers or buyers), each acting independently:** There are no restraints on the independence of the buyer or seller, either by custom, contract collusion, and fear of reprisal from the competitors or by any government control.

6. **The market price must be flexible:** That is it, must rise and fall in response to the changing conditions of demand and supply.

7. **There are no entry or exit barriers for any of the firms in the market.**

In perfect competition situation, all firms have equal access to technology and innovation. All the firms fix the same price. If a firm lowers its price, then everybody reduces the price, thus eliminating the competitive advantage gained by that firm. Hence, essentially all firms have the same price. As it is now clear, perfect competition is an extreme case and is rarely to be found.

Actual competition is always different from perfect competition—which is the ideal. Perfect competition may be considered as a conceptual base on which varying degrees of imperfect competition are measured.

3.11.2   Determination of Price

No single firm operating in a perfectly competitive market exerts any influence on price. The market price is determined by the interaction of all the buyers and sellers in the market. The price under perfect competition is determined by the forces of supply and demand. Prices will be fixed at the point *E* where supply and demand are at equilibrium, see Figure 3.18. The equilibrium changes if the forces of demand and supply change.

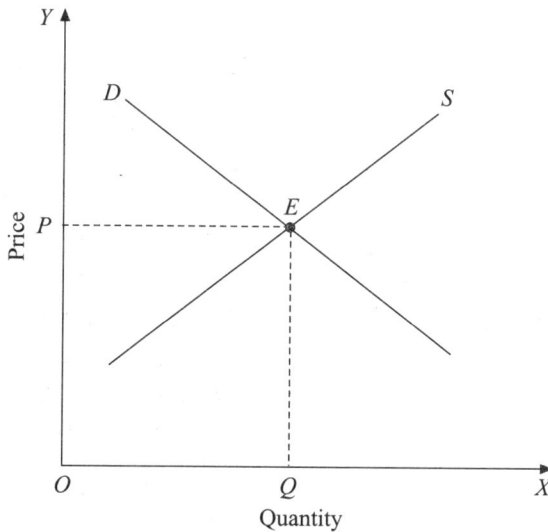

Figure 3.18   Price in perfect competition (market equilibrium).

We have seen that the price in the perfect competition is at the place where demand and supply meet. The firm must charge this 'market price'; otherwise, consumers will purchase from a firm charging a lower price. Thus, at this market price a firm can sell as much as it wishes, and this is shown as a horizontal curve in Figure 3.20.

Figures 3.19 and 3.20 illustrate the distinction between market demand and firm demand. In a perfect competitive situation, as far as the market price structure is considered, the price is fixed at the intersection of demand and supply. When it comes to the firm, it has to adhere to this price fixed by the market. If it fixes its product price above 'P', it cannot sell any of its products. If it fixes its price below price 'P', all other competitors will respond to that, and hence the *P* will come down.

The price determination and equilibrium of the firm under perfect competition is shown in Figure 3.20. As seen from Figure 3.20, the firm's demand curve (*D'*) is horizontal at the price determined in the market by the intersection of the demand and supply curves. The demand curve is also the firm's Average Revenue (*AR*) curve. This is so because, if the firm sells all its output units of a commodity at the same price, the revenue brought in by an average unit must be its price. We also know that when the *AR* curve is neither rising nor falling, then it will be the same as the Marginal Revenue (*MR*) curve.

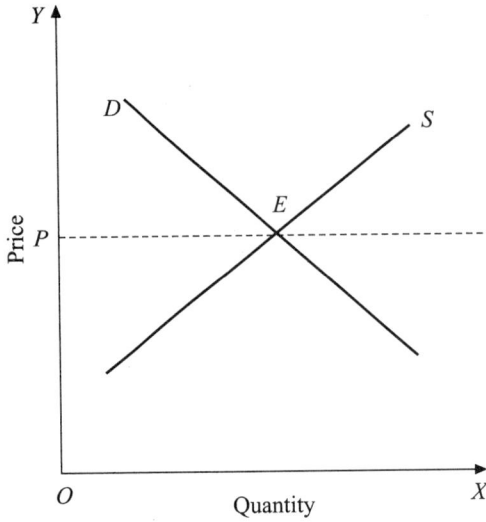

Figure 3.19 Demand for Market.

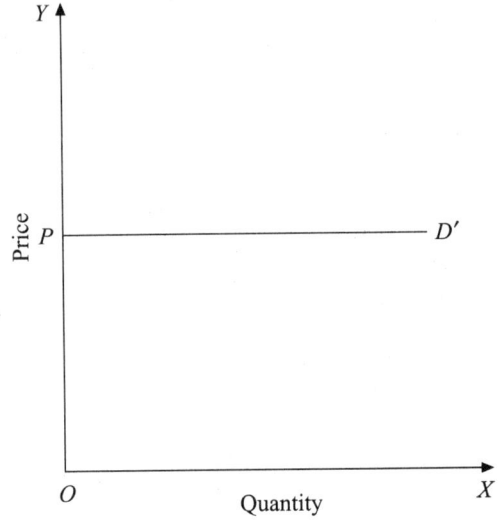

Figure 3.20 Demand for Firm.

The profit of the firm is given by the rectangle *DABC* in Figure 3.21! In the short run, a firm can just break even (no loss no profit), depending on its cost function and market conditions. In the long run, no firm makes profit or loss under perfect competition. This is because of the characteristics of perfect competition of free entry and exit of firms.

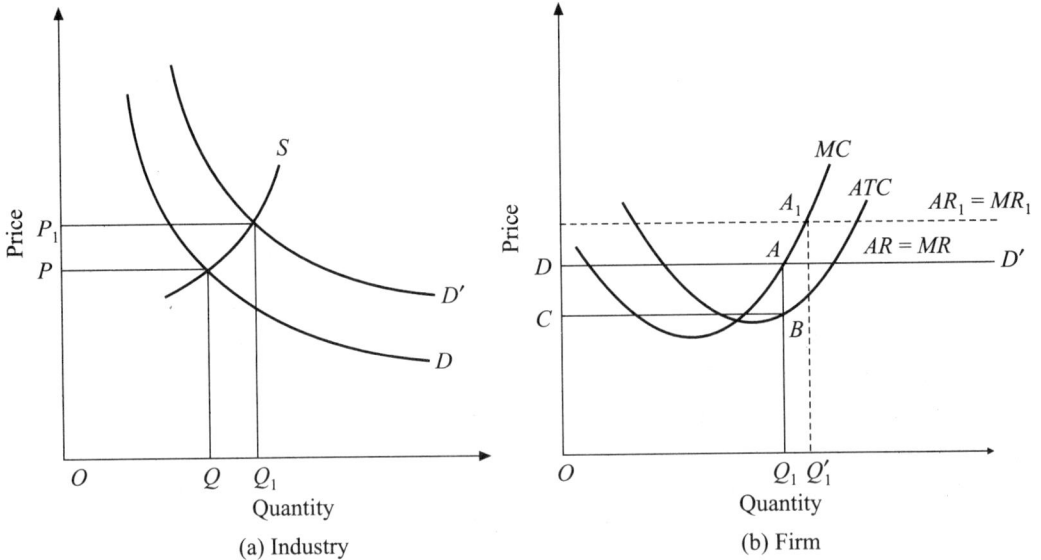

(a) Industry

(b) Firm

Figure 3.21   Pricing under perfect competition.

A change in the market demand or a change in the market supply can cause a change in the market price. This is explained here. Responses to a change in demand in the market or a change in supply in the market may be primarily in price or in quantity. If the demand is highly elastic, then consumers will respond readily to price changes by dropping out of the market when the prices are raised a little and by coming in and increasing purchases when the prices are lowered a little. As a result, most of the adjustments to changes in supply will be adjustments in quantity purchased if the demand is highly elastic. If the demand is inelastic, then the adjustments will take place primarily in price.

Similarly, sellers respond readily by greatly increasing their supply to the market on a slight increase in price. The adjustments to changes in demand will be largely in quantity exchanged. If the suppliers do not respond to the price change (if the supply is inelastic), then the adjustments to changes in demand will take place largely through shifts in price. In view of the above said phenomena, the following points may be derived:

1. If demand rises, then prices go up and vice versa. In Figure 3.22, the demand rises (i.e. the demand curve shifts to the right) from D to D_1, whereas the supply remains the same. As a result, the price goes up from P to P_1. So also the sales increases from Q to Q_1.

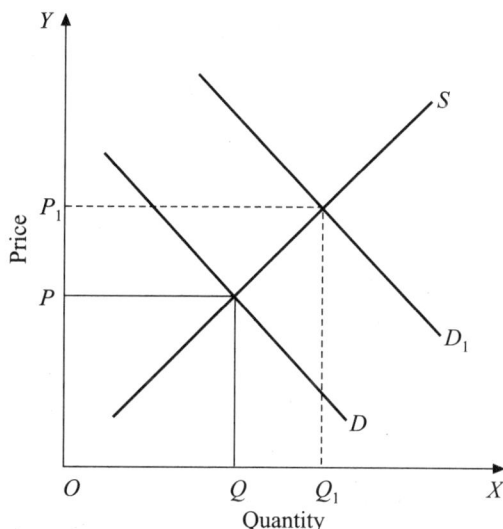

Figure 3.22   Change in market demand.

2. If supply rises, prices go down and vice versa. This is illustrated in Figure 3.23. Here, the supply quantity increases (i.e. the supply curve shifts to the right) from S to S_1 while the demand curve remains unchanged. The result is that the price falls from P to P_1 but the sales increases from Q to Q_1.

3. Given a shift in the demand curve, the price will rise less if the supply curve is elastic (flat). Price will rise more or fall more if the supply curve is inelastic (steep). If the rise in price is more, then the rise in sales will be less. If the rise in price is less, then the rise in sales will be more.

4. If both demand and supply increase, then sales are bound to increase but the price may or may not rise.

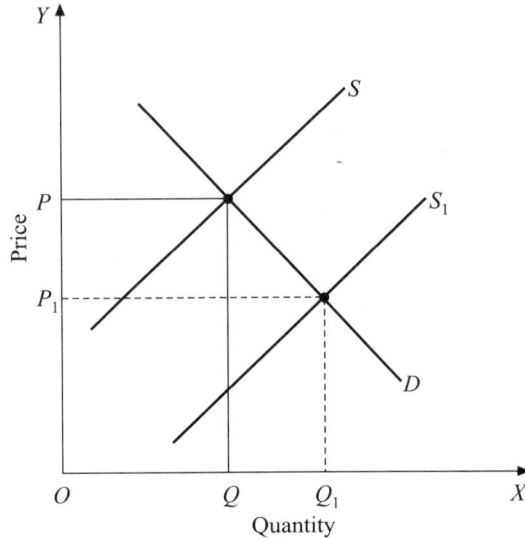

Figure 3.23 Change in market supply.

5. An increase in demand with a simultaneous decrease in supply will raise the price and increase the sales if the new demand price for the old equilibrium amount is higher than its new supply price. Similarly, the price will rise and the sales will diminish if the new supply price for the old amount is higher than its new demand price.

REVIEW QUESTIONS

1. Discuss the law of variable proportion and explain the conditions of its applicability.

2. Make a comparison between law of increasing and diminishing returns.

3. Describe the concept of returns to scale.

4. Explain the concept of elasticity of supply.

5. What do you mean by cost of production? Distinguish between fixed cost and variable cost.

6. Explain and illustrate the concept of *TC*, *AC* and *MC*.

7. Describe and illustrate short-run cost curves of a firm.

8. Explain and illustrate cost curves of a firm in the long-run.

9. State and explain the essential conditions of perfect competition.

CHAPTER 4

Time Value of Money

4.1 INTRODUCTION

The value/purchasing power of money at a particular time is called *time value of money*. A rupee today is worth more than a rupee that will be received tomorrow. The income expected at a future date will have lower value than the money held today. For example, suppose you have deposited Rs. 200 in a bank with a 10 per cent rate of interest. After one year, the interest would be Rs. 20 and, consequently, the amount will become Rs. 220 at the end of the year. It follows that Rs. 220 expected one year hence is worth only Rs. 200 today.

The value of money is more today because

1. it gives liquidity, and an opportunity to invest and earn returns (interest);
2. individuals, in general, prefer current consumption to future consumption because the future is always uncertain and involves risk;
3. capital can be employed productivily to generate positive returns; and
4. in inflationary period, a rupee represents a greater real purchasing power than a rupee a year hence.

Thus, as money has earning and purchasing power, it has *time value*.

4.2 TECHNIQUES FOR ADJUSTING TIME VALUE OF MONEY OR INTEREST FORMULAS

While making investment decisions, computations are done in many ways. To simplify all these computations, it is extremely important to know how to use interest formulas more effectively. Before discussing the effective application of interest formulas for making decisions on investments we shall describe the various interest formulas.

Interest rate can be classified into *simple interest rate* and *compound interest* rate. In the simple interest rate, the interest is calculated based on the initial deposit for every interest period. In the compound interest rate, the interest for the current period is computed based on the amount (principal plus interest up to the end of the previous period) at the beginning of the current period.

The notations used in various interest formulas are as follows:

P = Principal amount
n = No. of interest periods
i = Interest rate (it may be compounded monthly, quarterly, semi-annually or annually)
F = Future amount at the end of year n
A = Equal amount deposited at the end of every interest period
G = Uniform amount which will be added/subtracted, period after period to/from the amount of deposit A_1 at the end of period 1

4.2.1 Single-Payment Compound Amount/Future Value of an Amount

In this section the objective is to find the single future sum (F) of the initial payment (P) made at time 0 after n periods, at an interest rate i compounded every period. See Figure 4.1.

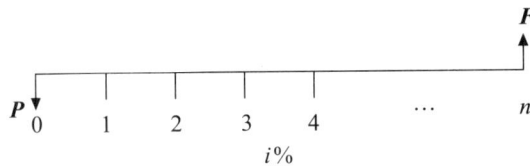

Figure 4.1   Cash flow diagram for single-payment compound amount.

The formula to obtain the single-payment compound amount is

$$F = P(1+ i)^n$$

Or

$$F = P(F/P, i, n)$$

where
$(F/P, i, n)$ is called as single-payment compound amount factor.

EXAMPLE 4.1

A person deposits a sum of Rs. 20,000 at the interest rate 18% compounded annually for 10 years. Find the maturity value after 10 year.

Solution

P = Rs. 20,000
i = 18% compounded annually
n = 10 years
F = $P(1 + i)^n = P(F/P, i, n)$
   = 20,000 $(F/P, 18\%, 10)$
   = 20,000 × 5.234 = Rs. 104,680

The maturity value of Rs. 20,000 invested now at 18 per cent compounded yearly is equal to Rs. 104,680 after 10 years.

4.2.2 Single-Payment Present Worth Amount

Here the objective is to find the present worth amount (P) of a single future (F) which will be received after n periods at an interest rate compound at the end of every interest period.

The corresponding cash flow diagram is shown in Figure 4.2.

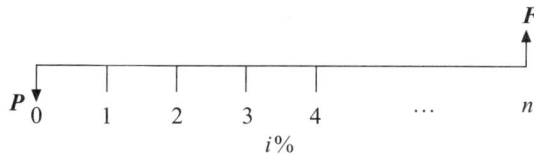

Figure 4.2 Cash flow diagram of single-payment present worth amount.

The formula to obtain the present worth is

$$P = \frac{F}{(1+i)^n} = F(P/F, i, n)$$

EXAMPLE 4.2

A person wishes to have a future sum of Rs. 100,000 for his son's education after 10 years from now. What is the single-payment that he has to deposit now so that he gets the desired amount after 10 years? The bank gives 15 per cent interest rate, compounded annually.

Solution

F = Rs. 100,000
i = 15%, compounded annually
n = 10 years
p = $F(P/F, i, n)$
   = $100,000 (P/F, 15\%, 10)$
   = $100,000 \times 0.2472$
   = Rs. 24,720

The person has to invest Rs. 24,720 now so that he will get a sum of Rs. 10,000 after 10 years at 15 per cent interest rate, compounded annually.

4.2.3 Equal-Payment Series Compound Amount/Future Value of an Annuity

The objective is to find the future worth of n equal payments which are made at the end of every interest period till the end of nth interest period at an interest rate compounded at the end of each period. The corresponding cash flow diagram is shown in Figure 4.3.

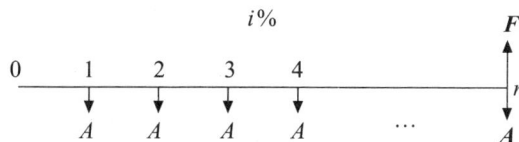

Figure 4.3 Cash flow diagram of equal-payment series compound amount.

The equal amount deposited at the end of each interest period = A
No. of interest periods = n

Rate of interest = i
Single future amount = F
The formula to obtain F is

$$F = A\left[\frac{(1+i)^n - 1}{i}\right] = A(F/A, i, n)$$

Where $(F/A, i, n)$ is termed as equal-payment series compound amount factor.

EXAMPLE 4.3

A person who is now 35 years is planning for his retired life. He plans to invest an equal sum of Rs. 10,000 at the end of every year for the next 25 years starting from the end of the next year. The bank gives 20 per cent interest rate, compounded annually. Find the maturity value of his account when he is 60 years..

Solution

$A =$ Rs. 10,000
$n =$ 25 years
$i =$ 20%
$F =$?

The corresponding cash flow diagram is shown in Figure E4.3.1.

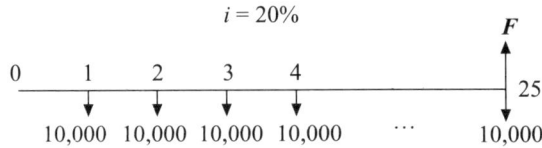

Figure E4.3.1

$$F = A\left[\frac{(1+i)^n - 1}{i}\right]$$
$$= A(F/A, i, n)$$
$$= 10,000\,(F/A, 20\%, 25)$$
$$= 10,000 \times 471.981$$
$$= \text{Rs. } 4,719,810$$

The future sum of the annual equal payments after 25 years is equal to Rs. 4,719,810.

4.2.4 Equal-Payment Series Sinking Fund

In this type of investment mode, the objective is to find the equivalent amount (A) that should be deposited at the end of every interest period for n interest periods to realize a future sum (F) at the end of nth interest period at an interest rate of i. See Figure 4.4.

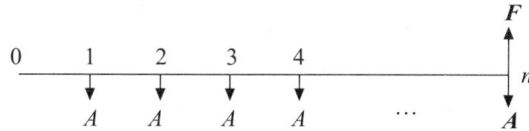

Figure 4.4 Cash flow diagram of equal-payment series sinking fund.

A = Equal amount to be deposited at the end of each interest period
n = No. of interest periods
i = Rate of interest
F = Single future amount at the end of the nth period

The formula to get F is

$$A = F\left[\frac{i}{(1+i)^n - 1}\right] = F(A/F, i, n)$$

where $(A/F, i, n)$ is called as equal-payment series sinking fund factor.

EXAMPLE 4.4

A company has to replace a present facility after 15 years at an outlay of Rs. 500,000. It plans to deposit an equal amount at the end of every year for the next 15 years at an interest rate of 18 per cent, compounded annually. Find the equivalent amount that must be deposited at the end of every year for the next 15 years.

Solution

$F =$ Rs. 500,000
$n =$ 15 years
$i =$ 18%
$A =$?

The corresponding cash flow diagram is shown in Figure E4.4.1.

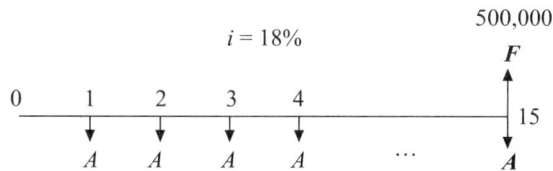

Figure E4.4.1

$$A = F\left[\frac{i}{(1+i)^n - 1}\right] = F(A/F, i, n)$$

$$= 500,000\,(A/F,\ 18\%,\ 15)$$

$$= 500,000 \times 0.0164$$

$$= \text{Rs. } 8200$$

The annual equal amount which must be deposited for 15 years is Rs. 8200.

4.2.5 Equal-Payment Series Present Worth Amount

The objective of this mode of investment is to find the present worth of an equal payment made at the end of every interest period for n interest periods at an interest rate i, compounded at the end of every interest period. The corresponding cash flow diagram is shown in Figure 4.5.

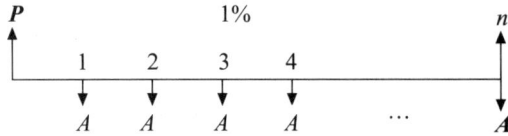

Figure 4.5 Cash flow diagram for equal-payment series present worth amount.

Here,

P = Present worth
A = Annual equivalent payment
i = Interest rate
n = No. of interest periods

The formula to compute P is

$$P = A\left[\frac{(1+i)^n - 1}{i(1+i)^n}\right] = A(P/A, i, n)$$

where $(P/A, i, n)$ is called *equal-payment series present worth factor*.

EXAMPLE 4.5

A company wants to set up a reserve which will help it to have an annual equivalent amount of Rs. 1,000,000 for the next year towards its employees welfare measures. The reserve is assumed to grow at the rate of 15 per cent annually. Find the single payment that must be made now to the reserve amount.

Solution

A = Rs. 1,000,000
i = 15%
n = 20 years
P = ?

The corresponding cash flow diagram is illustrated in Figure E4.5.1.

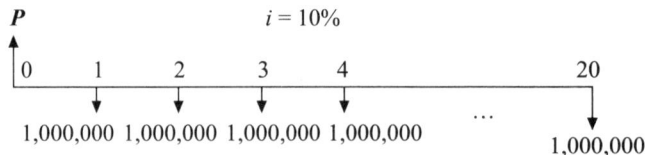

Figure E4.5.1

$$P = A\left[\frac{(1-i)^n - 1}{i\,(1+i)^n}\right] = A(P/A, i, n)$$

$$= 1{,}000{,}000 \times (P/A,\ 15\%,\ 20)$$

$$= 1{,}000{,}000 \times 6.2593$$

$$= \text{Rs. } 6{,}259{,}300$$

The amount of reserve which must be set up now is equal to Rs. 6,259,300.

4.2.6 Equal-Payment Series Capital Recovery Amount

The objective of this mode of investment is to find the annual equivalent amount (A) to be recovered at the end of every interest period for n interest periods for a loan P which is sanctioned now at an interest rate of i, compounded at the end of every interest period. See Figure 4.6.

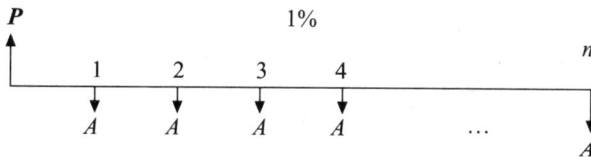

Figure 4.6   Cash flow diagram for equal-payment series capital recovery amount.

$P =$ Present worth (loan amount)
$A =$ Annual equivalent payment (recovery amount)
$i =$ Interest rate
$n =$ No. of interest periods

The formula to compute P is

$$A = P\left[\frac{i(1+i)^n}{(1-i)^n - 1}\right] = P(A/P, i, n)$$

where $(A/P, i, n)$ is called *equal-payment series capital recovery factor.*

EXAMPLE 4.6

A bank gives a loan to a company to purchase an equipment worth Rs. 1,000,000 at an interest rate of 18 per cent, compounded annually. This amount should be repaid in 15 yearly equal instalments. Find the instalment amount that the company has to pay to the bank.

Solution

$P =$ Rs. 1,000,000
$i =$ 18%
$n =$ 15 years
$A =$?

The corresponding cash flow diagram is shown in Figure E4.6.1.

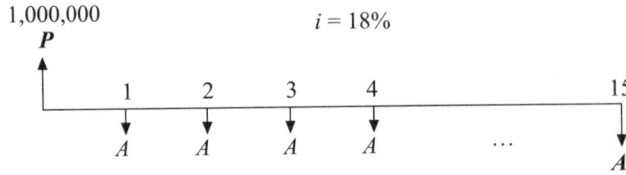

Figure E4.6.1

$$A = P\left[\frac{i(1+i)^n}{(1+i)^n - 1}\right] = P(A/P, i, n)$$

$$= 1,000,000 \times (A/P, 18\%, 15)$$

$$= 1,000,000 \times (0.1964)$$

$$= \text{Rs. } 196,400$$

The annual equivalent instalment to be paid by the company to the bank is Rs. 196,400.

4.3   UNIFORM GRADIENT SERIES FACTOR (*A/G, i, N*)

There are cases, where the periodic payments do not occur at an equal series. These payments may increase or decrease by a constant amount. For example, a series of payments would be uniformly increasing in Rs. 200, Rs. 250, Rs. 300 and Rs. 350 occurring at the end of the first, second, third and fourth years respectively. Similarly, a uniformly decreasing series will be Rs. 200, Rs. 150, Rs. 100, Rs. 50 occurring at the end of first, second, third and fourth years, respectively. In each case, an equal-payment series provides the base with a constant annual increase or decrease at the end of second year. See Figure 4.7.

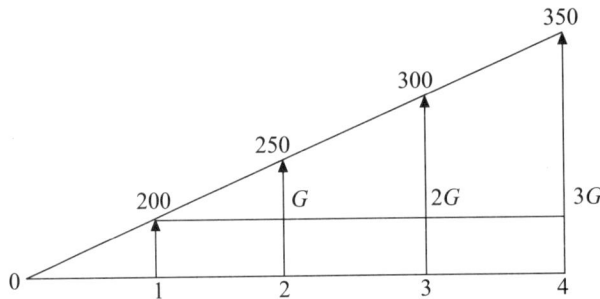

Figure 4.7   Gradient series cash flow diagram.

A series of payments that increases at a rate of Rs. 50 per year can be illustrated. The pattern of an arithmetic gradient is, then,

$$A', A' + G, A' + 2G, \dots A' + (N-1)^G$$

where N is the duration of the series ($N = 4$). A uniform series can be evaluated by calculating F or P for each individual payment, and the result should be added. In another method, the calculation can be made simple by converting the series to an equivalent annuity of equal payments *A*. The formula for the translation is developed by separating the series in two parts:

1. Base annually designated *A*
2. An arithmetic gradient series increasing by *G* each period. See Table 4.1

Table 4.1   Gradient Series and Equivalent Set of Series

End of year (1)	Gradient series (2)	Set of series equivalent to gradient series (3)	Annual series (4)
0	0	0	0
1	0	0	A
2	G	G	A
3	2G	G + G	A
4	3G	G + G + G	⋮
⋮	⋮	⋮	⋮
⋮	⋮	⋮	⋮
n − 1	(n − 2) G	G + G + G ... + G	A
n	(n − 1) G	G + G + G ... + G + G	A

$$F = G(F/A, i, n - 1) + (F/A, i, n - 2) + G(F/A, i, 2) + (F/A, i, 1)$$

$$= G\left[\frac{(1+i)^{n-1}-1}{i}\right] + G\left[\frac{(1+i)^{n-2}-1}{i}\right] + \cdots + G\left[\frac{(1+i)^2-1}{i}\right]$$

$$+ G\left[\frac{(1+i)^2-1}{i}\right] + G\left[\frac{(1+i)^1-1}{i}\right]$$

$$= \frac{G}{i}\left[(1+i)^{n-1} + (1+i)^{n-2} + \cdots + (1+i)^2 + (1+i) - (n-1)\right]$$

$$= \frac{G}{i}\left[(1+i)^{n-1} + (1+i)^{n-2} + \cdots + (1+i)^2 + (1+i) + 1\right] - \frac{nG}{i}$$

The terms inside the parentheses constitute the equal-payment series compound amount factor for *n* years. Therefore,

$$F = \frac{G}{i}\left[\frac{(1+i)^n-1}{i}\right] - \frac{nG}{i}$$

4.4   ANNUITY

4.4.1   What is an Annuity?

Annuity is characterized by: (i) equal payments (*A*) (ii) equal periods between payments *N*, and (iii) the first payment occurring at the end of the first period.

4.5 ANNUITY DUE

A series of payments made at the beginning instead at the end of each period is referred to as *annuity due*. In this case, calculation will be slightly different from general annuity It will differ in the following ways:

1. The series should be divided into two equal parts.
2. The first payment should be treated separately.
3. The remaining payments should follow the rule of general annuity calculation.

The present worth is the sum of first payment plus the product of annuity, and the series of present worth factor. N will be the number of payments minus 1. The formula for annuity due = $A + A'$ $(P/A, i, N)$.

EXAMPLE 4.7

What is the present worth of a series of 10 year-end payments of Rs. 1000 each, when the first payment is due today and the interest rate is 5 per cent.

Solution

See Figure E4.7.1.

$$A = \text{Rs. } 1000$$
$$P = A + A(P/A, 5, 9)$$
$$= 1000 + 1000\ (7.1078)$$
$$= 1000 + 7107.8$$
$$= \text{Rs. } 8107.8$$

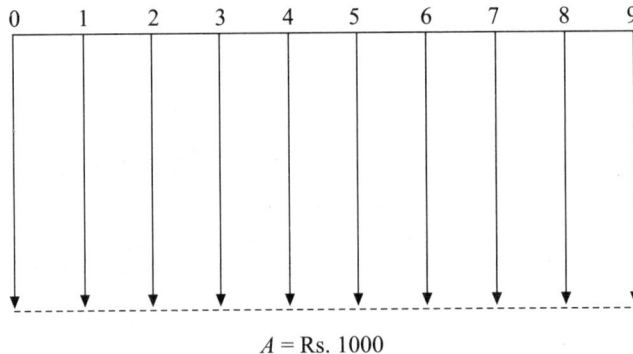

$$A = \text{Rs. } 1000$$

Figure E4.7.1

4.6 CALCULATION OF DEFERRED ANNUITY

In the case of deferred annuity, the first payment does not begin until some date later than the end of the first period. Deferred annuity can be calculated by dividing the series into two equal parts.

- The first part is the number of payments paid, which follows the general annuity calculation.

- The second part is the number of periods.
- Find out the present worth of annuity, then discount this value through the pre-annuity period. Hence, we get the deferred annuity.

REVIEW QUESTIONS

1.   Explain the time value of money.

2.   Give practical applications of various interest formulas.

3.   A person deposits a sum of Rs. 2,00,000 in a bank for the education of his son who will be admitted to a professional course after eight years. The bank pays 15 per cent interest rate, compounded annually. Find the future amount of the deposited money at the time of admitting his son in the professional course.

4.   A person needs a sum of Rs. 5,00,000 for his daughter's marriage which will take place 25 years from now. Find the amount of money that the person should deposit now in a bank if the bank gives 18 per cent interest, compounded annually.

5.   A person who is 20 years old is planning for his retired life. He plans to invest an equal sum of Rs. 20,000 at the end of every year for the next 20 years starting from the end of next year. The bank gives 15 per cent interest rate, compounded annually. Find the maturity value of his account when he is 50 years old.

6.   A company is planning to expand its business after four years from now. The expected money required for the expansion programme is Rs. 150,000,000. The company can invest Rs. 60,00,000 at the end of every year for the next five years. If the assured rate of return of investment is 18 per cent for the company, check whether the accumulated sum in the account would be sufficient to meet the fund for the expansion programme. If not, find the difference in amounts for which the company should make some other arrangement after four years.

7.   A financial institution introduces a plan to pay a sum of Rs. 2,500,000 after 20 years at the rate of 18 per cent, compounded annually. Find the annual equivalent amount that a person should invest at the end of every year for the next 20 years to receive Rs. 2,500,000 after 20 years from the institution.

8.   A company is planning to expand its business after eight years from now. The money required for the expansion programme is Rs. 90,000,000. What annual equivalent amount should the company deposit at the end of every year at an interest rate of 15 per cent compounded annually to get Rs. 90,000,000 after eight years from now?

9.   A company wants to set up a reserve which will help it to have an annual equivalent amount of Rs. 2,500,000 for the next 20 years towards its employees welfare measures. The reserve is assumed to grow at the rate of 15 per cent annually. Find the single payment that must be made as the reserve amount now.

10.   An automobile company recently advertised its car for a down payment of Rs. 350,000. Alternatively, the car can be taken home by customers without making any payment, but they have to pay an equal yearly amount of Rs. 25,000 for 15 years at an interest rate of 18 per cent, compounded annually. Suggest the best alternative to the customers.

11.   A company takes a loan of Rs. 4000,000 to modernize its boiler section. The loan is to be repaid in 30 equal instalments at 12 per cent interest rate, compounded annually. Find the equal instalment amount that should be paid for the next 30 years.

12. A bank gives a loan to a company to purchase an equipment which is worth Rs. 1,500,000, at an interest rate of 18 per cent compounded annually. This amount should be repaid in 25 yearly equal instalments. Find the instalment amount that the company has to pay to the bank.

13. A working woman is planning for her retired life. She has 30 more years of service. She would like to deposit 10 per cent of her salary which is Rs. 5000 at the end of the first year, and, thereafter, she wishes to deposit the same amount (Rs. 5000) with an annual increase of Rs. 2000 for the next 14 years with an interest rate of 18 per cent. Find the total amount at the end of the fifteenth year of the above series.

14. A person is planning for his retired life. He has 20 more years of service. He would like to deposit 20 per cent of his salary, which is Rs. 20,000 at the end of the first year and, thereafter, he wishes to deposit the same amount (Rs. 20,000) with an annual increase of Rs. 2000 for the next nine years with an interest rate of 20 per cent. Find the total amount at the end of the tenth year of the above series.

15. A person invests a sum of Rs. 60,000 in a bank at a nominal interest rate of 18 per cent for 15 years. The compounding is monthly. Find the maturity amount of the deposit after 15 years.

CHAPTER 5

Cash Flows for Investment Analysis: Concepts and Diagrams

5.1 INTRODUCTION

A *cash flow statement* describes the inflows (sources) and outflows (uses) of cash and cash equivalents in an enterprise during a specified period of time. Such a statement enumerates the net effects of various business transactions on cash and its equivalents, and takes into account the receipt and disbursement of cash. A cash flow statement summarizes the causes of change in the cash position of a business enterprise. An enterprise should prepare a cash flow statement and present it for each period for which the financial statements are prepared. The terms 'cash', 'cash equivalents' and 'cash flows' have the following meanings:

- **Cash:** It comprises cash on hand and demand deposits with banks.
- **Cash equivalents:** They are short-term, highly liquid investments that are readily convertible into known amounts of cash, e.g. preference shares of a company acquired shortly before their specified redemption date.
- **Cash flows:** These are inflows and outflows of cash and cash equivalents. The flow of cash is said to have taken place when any transaction makes changes in the amount of cash and cash equivalents available before it takes place.

5.2 TYPES/COMPONENTS OF CASH FLOWS

A typical investment decision, usually, involves three different types of cash flows:

1. Initial investment or cash outlay
2. Operating cash flow or net annual cash
3. Terminal cash flow

Initial investment (Outlays made in the beginning)

Initial investment is an outlay of cash that takes place in the initial period. It comprises primarily the cost of the new asset in terms of purchase of land, building, machinery, etc. including expenses on loading and unloading, installation cost and expenses on modification and repairs, etc. before it is put to use.

Operating cash flows (Cash flows arising out of operations of the project)

Every investment in capital assets is expected to generate future benefits in the form of net annual cash flows from operations. In simple words the net annual cash flows refer to the annual net earnings (profits) before depreciation and after taxes. These can be determined as follows:

$$NCF = \text{Cash revenues} - \text{Cash expenses} - \text{Tax}$$

or

$$NCF = \text{Net earning after tax} + \text{Depreciation} - \text{Tax}$$

Terminal cash flows (Cash flows resulting from winding up of a project)

At the end of the economic life of a capital asset, i.e. the last year when the asset is terminated, there is usually some value in point of time as scrap or it may fetch some salvage value. This inflow to a firm in the last (terminal) year is called terminal cash flow. Similarly, in the case of replacement decision where an old existing asset is replaced with a new asset, the reduction in cost of the new asset, i.e. the sale value of the old asset is the terminal cash flow of the asset replaced.

5.3   CASH FLOW DIAGRAMS

Cash flow diagrams are tools to help the decision-maker understand and solve problems in the process of engineering decision-making. They are visual representations of cash inflows and outflows along a time line. Before making cash flow diagrams, it is usually advantageous to first define the time frame over which the cash flows occur. This establishes the horizontal scale, which is divided into time periods, often in years. Cash inflows and outflows are then located on the time line in adherence to problem specification. Individual inflows or outflows are designated by vertical lines; the relative magnitude can be represented by the heights of lines, but exact scaling is not necessary. Usually, cash inflows are shown by vertical lines above the axis and cash outflows below the axis. The obvious requirements for cash flow diagramming are completeness, accuracy, and legibility.

We can classify cash flow transactions into five categories:

1. Single-payment cash flow
2. uniform-payment series
3. linear gradient series
4. geometric gradient series
5. Irregular-payment series

1. *Single-payment cash flow* this involves a single present or future cash flow. The cash flow diagram of this cash flow pattern is shown in Figure 5.1.

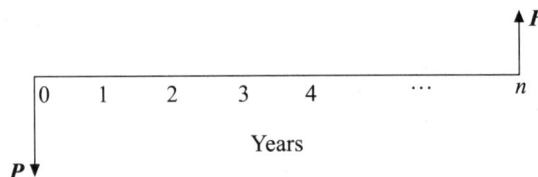

Figure 5.1   Single-payment cash flow diagram.

2. *Uniform payment series* cash flow involves a series of flows of equal amounts at regular intervals. The relevant cash flow diagrams are as illustrated in Figure 5.2.

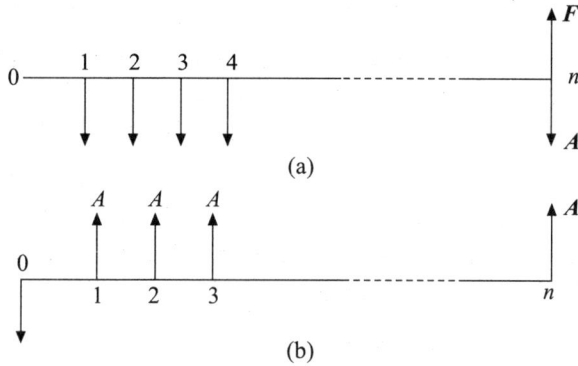

(a)

(b)

Figure 5.2   Uniform-payment series cash flow diagram.

3. *Linear gradient series* cash flow is a series of flows increasing or decreasing by a fixed amount at regular intervals. We call this type of cash flow pattern, a linear gradient series because its cash flow diagram produces an ascending (or descending) straight line as depicted in Figure 5.3.

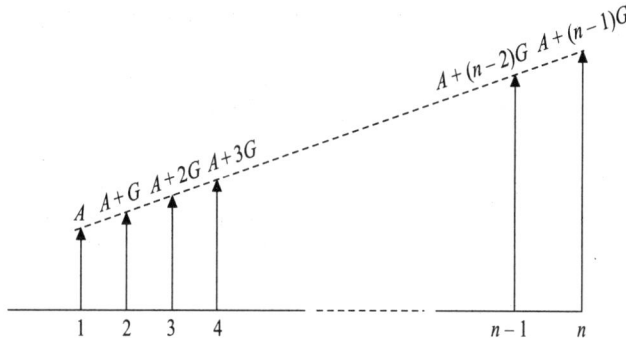

Figure 5.3   Linear gradient series cash flow diagram.

4. *Geometric gradient series* cash flow is a series of flows increasing or decreasing by a fixed percentage at regular intervals. The relevant cash flow diagram for this type of cash flow stream is given in Figure 5.4.

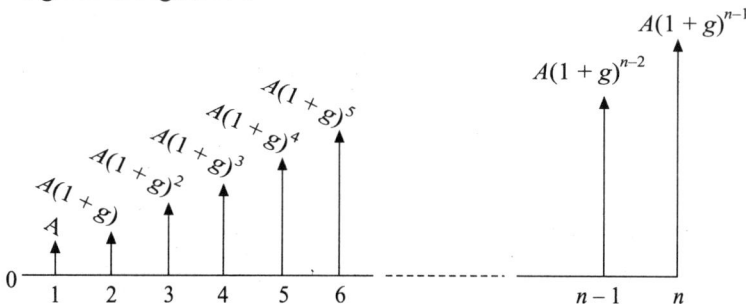

Figure 5.4   Geometric gradient series diagram.

5. *Irregular-payment series* is one that exhibits no regular overall pattern of cash flow. The cash flow diagram for such a series is as shown in Figure 5.5.

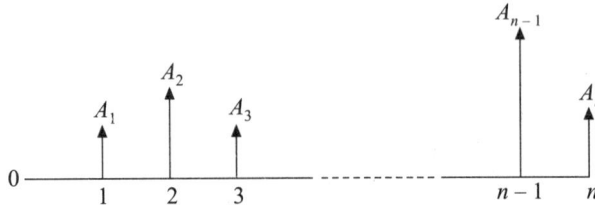

Figure 5.5   Irregular payment series.

5.4   PRINCIPLES OF EQUIVALENCE

5.4.1   Equivalence between Cash Flows

Equivalent cash flows are those that have the same value. The calculated expression of equivalence can be used as a basis for choice. For example, a present amount of Rs. 300 is equivalent to Rs. 798 if the amount is loaned for seven years and if the interest rate is 15 per cent. This is so because a person who considers 15 per cent to be a satisfactory rate of interest would be indifferent to receiving Rs. 300 now or Rs. 798 seven years from now. This equivalence between the two cash flows may be illustrated by the use of the single-payment formulas. A sum of Rs. 300 in the present is equivalent to Rs. 798 seven years hence. That is,

That is, $$F = \text{Rs. } 300(F/P, 15, 7)$$

$$= \text{Rs. } 300(10.15)^7 = \text{Rs. } 798.$$

Similarly, Rs. 798 to be received seven years from now is equivalent to Rs. 300 at present. These two situations are illustrated in Figures 5.6(a) and 5.6(b).

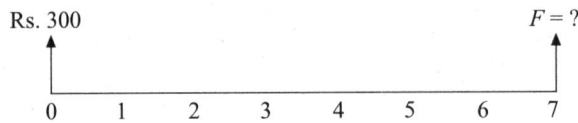

(a)

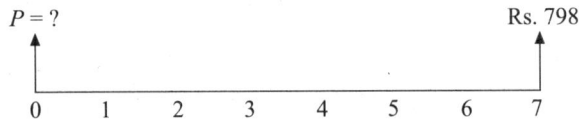

(b)

Figure 5.6   Equivalence between two cash flows.

$$P = \text{Rs. } 798(P/F, 15\%, 7)$$

$$= \text{Rs. } 798\left[\frac{1}{(1 + 0.15)^7}\right] = \text{Rs. } 300$$

Thus, the above two cash flows are equivalent.

5.4.2 Equivalence at Any Common Point of Time

This principle states that equivalent cash flows are equal at any common point of time. This principle can be explained with the help of Figure 5.7.

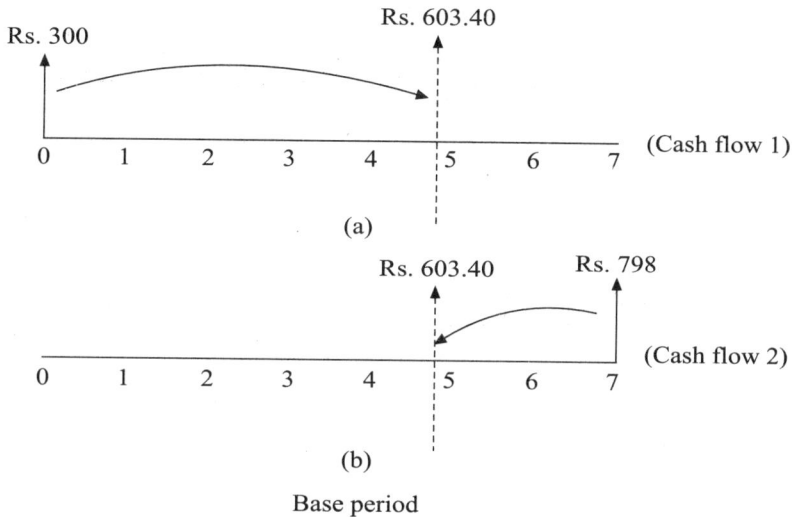

Figure 5.7 Equivalence at a common point.

Given an interest rate of 15 per cent per year, receiving Rs. 300 today is equivalent to receiving Rs. 798 in seven years. Are these cash flows also equivalent at the end of the fifth year? The solution can be followed from Figure 5.7.

The equivalent worth of cash flow 1 at the end of year 5 is

$$\text{Rs.}300(F/P, 15\%, 5) = \text{Rs. } 300(1 + 0.15)^5$$
$$= \text{Rs. } 603.40$$

Similarly, for cash flow 2, the equivalent worth at $n = 5$ is

$$\text{Rs. } 798(P/F, 15\%, 2) = \text{Rs. } 798\left[\frac{1}{(1 + 0.15)^2}\right]$$
$$= \text{Rs. } 603.40$$

Therefore, the two equivalent cash flows are equal at any common point of time.

5.4.3 Equivalence Depends on Interest Rate

This principle states that any change in the interest rate will destroy the equivalence between the two cash flows. The following example may clarify this point:

Given an interest rate of 15 per cent per year, receiving Rs. 300 today is equivalent to receiving Rs. 798 in seven years. Are these cash flows equivalent at an interest rate of 10 per cent?

Here, $P = $ Rs. 300, $i = 10\%$, $n = 7$ years. Is 'F' equal to Rs. 798?

Therefore, $\qquad\qquad\qquad F = \text{Rs. } 300(F/P, 10\%, 7)$

$$= \text{Rs. } 300 (1 + 0.10) \, 7$$
$$= \text{Rs. } 584.60$$

Since this amount is less than Rs. 798, the change in interest rate destroys the equivalence between the two cash flows.

5.4.4 Equivalence between Receipts and Disbursements

In engineering economies, calculations are often required to determine an unknown interest rate that brings about equivalence between the known receipts and disbursements. The principle of equivalence states that the rate earned on an investment is the one that sets the equivalent receipts equal to the equivalent disbursement.

The cash flow pattern given in Figure 5.8 can illustrates this principle.

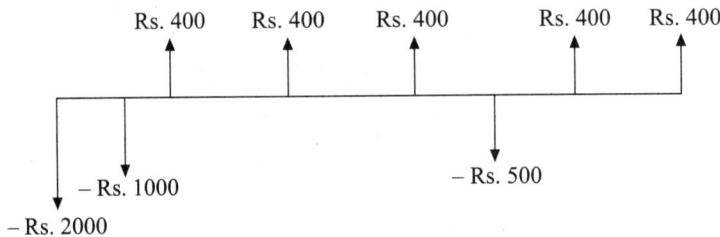

Figure 5.8 Equivalence between receipt and disbursement.

The objective is to find the interest rate that sets the receipt equivalent to disbursement.

$$\text{Rs. } 2000 + \text{Rs. } 1000 \, (P/F, i, 1) + \text{Rs. } 500 \, (P/F, i, 5) = \text{Rs. } 400 \, (P/A, i, 3) \, (P/F, i, 1)$$
$$+ \text{Rs. } 400 \, (P/A, i, 2), \, (P/F, i, 5)$$

By trial and error, 20 per cent is found to be the value for i that sets the receipt identified as positive value equal to the disbursement designated by negative value at present.

5.5 USES AND SIGNIFICANCE OF CASH FLOW STATEMENT

A cash flow statement is of vital importance to the financial management. It is an essential tool of financial analysis for short-term planning. The chief advantages of a cash flow statement are as follows:

1. Since a cash flow statement is based on the cash basis of accounting, it is very useful in the evaluation of the cash position of a firm.
2. A projected cash flow statement can be prepared in order to know the future cash position of a concern so as to enable a firm to plan and coordinate its financial operation properly.
3. A cash flow statement enables the firm to take immediate and effective action.
4. A series of intra-firm and inter-firm cash flow statements reveal whether the firm's liquidity (short-term paying capacity) is improving or deteriorating over a period of time and in comparison to other firm's over a given period of time.

5.6 LIMITATIONS OF CASH FLOW STATEMENT

Despite a number of uses/merits, the cash flow statement suffers from the following limitations:

- It is difficult to define precisely the term 'cash'. There are controversies over a number of items, such as cheques, stamps, postal order, that is whether these are to be considered as cash or not.
- A cash flow statement reveals the inflows and outflows of cash only. But it does not include the near cash items. Therefore, the true position of the liquidity is not revealed through this.

REVIEW QUESTIONS

1. What do you mean by cash flow diagram?
2. Why are cash flow diagrams significant?
3. How can you draw a cash flow diagram?
4. Classify cash flow transaction.
5. Explain the merits and demerits of a cash flow statement.

6

Evaluation of Engineering Alternatives

6.1 INTRODUCTION

In all engineering problems, engineers encounter one important question, i.e. which project to select. To select among the different alternatives, various methods have been evolved. There are several bases for comparing the worthiness of projects which as follows:

1. Present worth method
2. Future worth method
3. Annual equivalent method
4. Rate of return method
5. Cost-benefit analysis.

6.2 PRESENT WORTH METHOD

Many economists prefer the present worth method because it reveals the sum in today's rupee that is equivalent to a future cash flow stream. For example, Rs. 110 expected one year hence is worth only Rs. 100 today, if the rate of interest is 10 per cent, compounded annually. This means that Rs. 100 is the present value of Rs. 110 to be earned one year hence.

In the present worth method, the present worth of all cash inflows (revenues) is compared against the present worth of all cash outflows (costs) associated with an investment project. In this method of comparison, the cash flow of each alternative will be reduced to time zero by assuming an interest rate i. Then, depending on the type of decision, the best alternative will be selected by comparing the present worth amounts of the alternatives. The difference between the present worth of the cash flows (inflows – outflows) is referred to as the Net Present Worth (NPW) which determines whether or not the project is a feasible investment.

6.2.1 Steps Needed for Present Worth Comparison

The following are the steps involved in present worth comparison:

1. Estimate the interest rate that the firm wishes to earn on its investment.
2. Determine the service life of the project.

3. Ascertain the cash inflows over each service life.
4. Find out the cash overflows over each service period.
5. Calculate the net cash flows (inflows – outflows).

If there is a single investment proposal, then the decision whether a project will be selected or rejected can be made accordingly.

- If $PW > 0$, then the proposal will be selected. A positive NPW means that the equivalent worth of the inflows is greater than the equivalent worth of the outflows. So, the project will make profit.
- If $PW < 0$, then the investment project should be rejected. A negative NPW means the equivalent worth of the inflows is less than the equivalent worth of the outflows.
- If $PW = 0$, then one should remain indifferent to the investment.

In case there are mutually exclusive alternatives, then the present worth cash flows can be calculated by two prominent methods:

- Revenue-based present worth
- Cost-based present worth

In a revenue/profit-based cash flow diagram, the profit, revenue, salvage value (all inflows to an organization) will be assigned with a positive sign. The costs (outflows) will be assigned with a negative sign. In a cost-based cash flow diagram, on the other hand, the costs (outflows) will be assigned a positive sign and the profit, revenue, salvage value (all inflows), etc. will be assigned a negative sign. In revenue-based cases, the decision is to select the alternative with the maximum profit. Thus, the alternative with the maximum present worth will be selected. In cost bases cases, if the decision is to select the alternative with the minimum cost, then the alternative with the least present worth amount will be selected.

6.2.2 Revenue-based Cash Flow Diagram

See Figure 6.1.

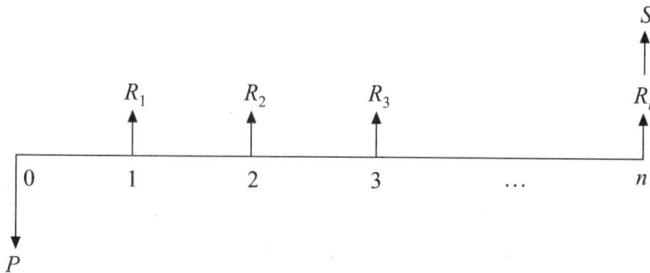

Figure 6.1 Revenue-based cash flow diagram.

Here, P is the initial investment, R_n is the net revenue at the end of nth year, i is the interest rate compounded annually, and S is the salvage value at the end of nth year.

To find the present worth of the cash flow from Figure 6.1 for a given interest rate, the required formula is

$$PW(i) = -P + \frac{R_1}{(1+i)^1} + \frac{R_2}{(1+i)^2} + \cdots + \frac{R_n}{(1+i)^n} + \frac{S}{(1+i)^n}$$

or

$$PW(i) = -P + R_1(P/F, i, 1) + R_2(P/F, i, 2) + \cdots + R_n(P/F, i, n) + S(P/F, i, n)$$

If it is a uniform series or equal-payment series, then the formula will be

$$PW(i) = -P + R(P/A, i, n) + S(P/F, i, n)$$

6.2.3   Cost-based Cash Flow Diagram

See Figure 6.2.

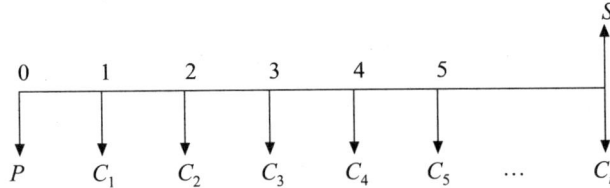

Figure 6.2   Cost-based cash flow diagram.

Here P is the initial investment, C_n is the net cost of operation and maintenance at the end of nth year, S is the salvage value at the end of nth year, and C_i is the discounted rate of interest.

Thus, the present worth expression is

$$PW(i) = P + \frac{C_1}{(1+i)^1} + \frac{C_2}{(1+i)^2} + \cdots + \frac{C_n}{(1+i)^n} - \frac{S}{(1+i)^n}$$

or

$$PW(i) = P + C_1(P/F, i, 1) + C_2(P/F, i, 2) + \cdots + C_n(P/F, i, n) - S(P/F, i, n)$$

If it is a uniform series or equal-payment series, then the formula will be

$$PW(i) = P + C(P/A, i, n) - S(P/F, i, n)$$

EXAMPLE 6.1

The following table summarizes a cash flow stream of an investment project:

Year (n)	Net cash flow (Rs.)
0	– 650,000
1	162,500
2	162,500
3	162,500
4	
5	
6	$\vdots$
7	
8	162,500

If the firm's rate of interest is 15 per cent, compute the NPW of this project. Moreover, this project acceptable?

Solution

The cash flow diagram for the given project is shown in Figure E6.1.1.

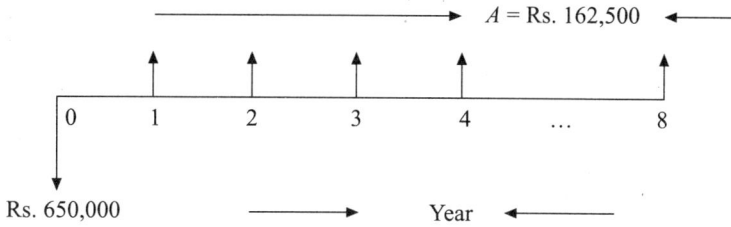

Figure E6.1.1

This is a uniform cash flow stream. Since the project requires an initial investment of Rs. 650,000 at present ($n = 0$) followed by eight equal annual receipts of Rs. 162,500, we can easily determine the NPW as follows:

$$NPW = -P + R(P/A, i, n)$$
$$= -\text{Rs. } 650,000 + \text{Rs. } 162,500(P/A, 15\%, 8)$$
$$= -\text{Rs. } 650,000 + \text{Rs. } 162,500(4.4873)$$
$$= -\text{Rs. } 650,000 + \text{Rs. } 729,186$$
$$= \text{Rs. } 79,186$$

Since $PW(15\%) > 0$, the project can be accepted.

EXAMPLE 6.2

The project cash flows of an investment proposal is given here

End of year (n)	Net cash flow (Rs.)
0	– 50,000
1	20,400
2	25,200
3	45,750

Evaluate the economic desirability of this project for $i = 10\%$.

Solution

The cash flow diagram for the given project is shown in Figure E6.2.1.

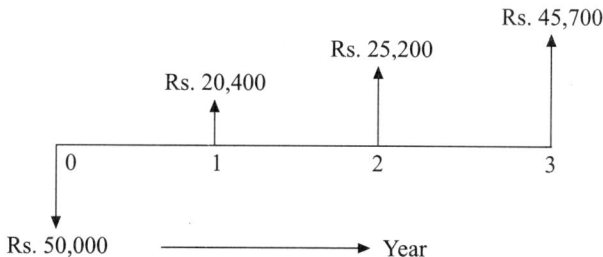

Figure E6.2.1

The present worth of this cash flow is

$$PW(10\%) = -50{,}000 + 20{,}400\,(P/F,\ 10\%,\ 1) + 25{,}200\,(P/F,\ 10\%,\ 2) + 45{,}750\,(P/F,\ 10\%,\ 3)$$

$$= -50{,}000 + 20{,}400\,(0.9091) + 25{,}200\,(0.8264) + 45{,}750\,(0.7513)$$

$$= \text{Rs. } 23{,}742.89$$

Since $PW(10\%) > 0$, the project can be accepted.

EXAMPLE 6.3

Given the following information, suggest the best alternative which is to be implemented based on the present worth method, assuming 20 per cent interest rate, compounded annually:

Alternative	Initial cost	Annual revenue	Life
A	Rs. 1,500,000	Rs. 800,000	15 years
B	Rs. 2,000,000	Rs. 600,000	15 years
C	Rs. 1,600,000	Rs. 400,000	15 years

Solution

The cash flow diagram for alternative A is given in Figure E6.3.1.

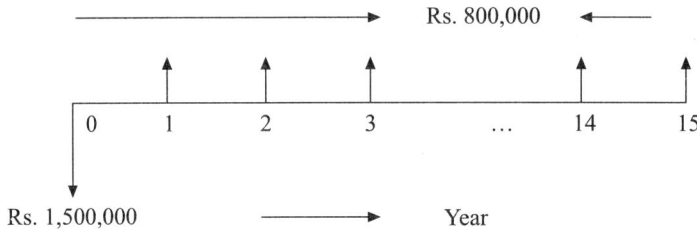

Figure E6.3.1

The present worth for this cash flow is

$$PW(20\%)_A = -\text{Rs. } 1{,}500{,}000 + \text{Rs. } 800{,}000\,(P/A,\ 20\%,\ 15)$$

$$= -\text{Rs. } 1{,}500{,}000 + \text{Rs. } 800{,}000\,(4.6755)$$

$$= \text{Rs. } 2{,}240{,}400$$

The cash flow diagram for alternative B is given in Figure E6.3.2.

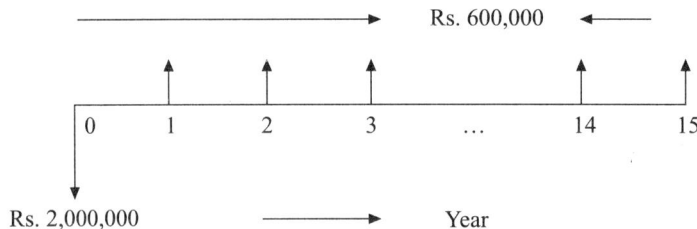

Figure E6.3.2

$$PW(20\%)_B = -\text{Rs. } 2,000,000 + \text{Rs. } 600,000(P/A, 20\%, 15)$$
$$= -\text{Rs. } 2,000,000 + \text{Rs. } 600,000(4.6755)$$
$$= \text{Rs. } 805,300$$

The cash flow diagram for alternative C is given in Figure E6.3.3.

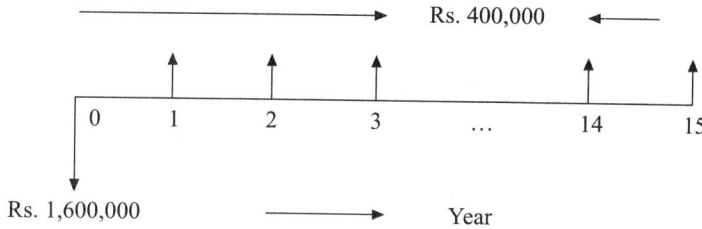

Figure E6.3.3

$$PW(20\%)_C = -\text{Rs. } 1,600,000 + \text{Rs. } 400,000(P/A, 20\%, 15)$$
$$= -\text{Rs. } 1,600,000 + \text{Rs. } 400,000(4.6755)$$
$$= \text{Rs. } 270,200$$

Since the present worth of alternative A is the highest among all the alternatives, so it is recommended for implementation.

EXAMPLE 6.4

Given the following information, suggest which technology should be selected based on the present worth method, assuming 15 per cent interest rate compounded annually.

Technology	Initial cost (Rs.)	Service life	Annual operational and management cost
A	400,000	15 years	25,000
B	500,000	15 years	29,000

Solution

The cash flow diagram for technology A is given in Figure E6.4.1.

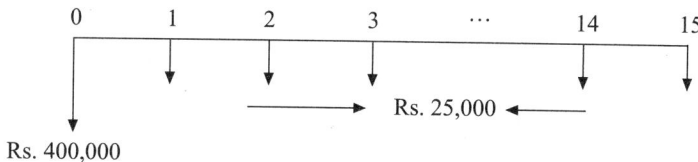

Figure E6.4.1

The present worth amount of this cash flow stream is

$$PW(15\%)_A = \text{Rs. } 400,000 + \text{Rs. } 25,000(P/A, 15\%, 15)$$
$$= \text{Rs. } 400,000 + \text{Rs. } 25,000(5.8474)$$

$$= \text{Rs. } 400{,}000 + \text{Rs. } 146{,}185$$
$$= \text{Rs. } 546{,}185$$

The cash flow diagram for technology B is given in Figure E6.4.2.

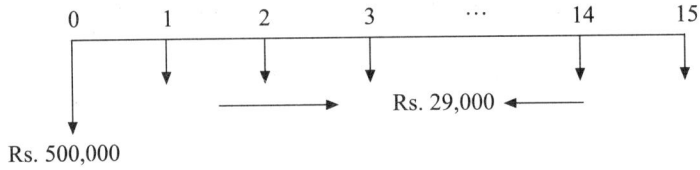

Figure E6.4.2

$$PW(15\%)_B = \text{Rs. } 500{,}000 + \text{Rs. } 29{,}000(P/A, 15\%, 15)$$
$$= \text{Rs. } 500{,}000 + \text{Rs. } 29{,}000(5.8474)$$
$$= \text{Rs. } 500{,}000 + \text{Rs. } 169{,}574.6$$
$$= \text{Rs. } 669{,}574.6$$

Since *PW* amount of technology A is lower, it should be selected.

EXAMPLE 6.5

A finance company advertises two investment plans. In plan 1, the company pays Rs. 22,000 after 15 years for every Rs. 1000 invested now. In plan 2, for every Rs. 1000 invested the company pays Rs. 4000 at the end of the tenth year and Rs. 4000 at the end of the fifteenth year. Select the best investment plan at $i = 10$ per cent compounded annually.

Solution

The cash flow diagram for plan 1 is given in Figure E6.5.1.

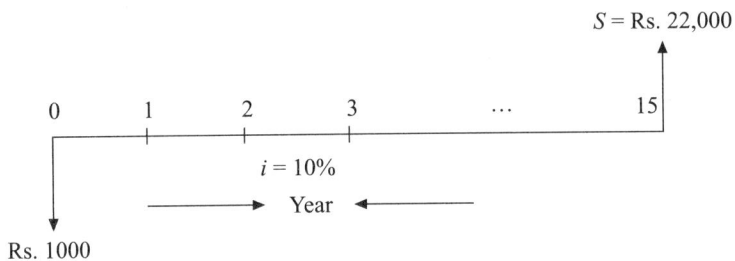

Figure E6.5.1

The present worth of the cash flow diagram is calculated as

$$PW(10\%)_1 = -\text{Rs. } 1000 + \text{Rs. } 22{,}000(P/F, 10\%, 15)$$
$$= -\text{Rs. } 1000 + \text{Rs. } 22{,}000(0.2394)$$
$$= \text{Rs. } 4266.8$$

The cash flow diagram for plan 2 is given in Figure E6.5.2.

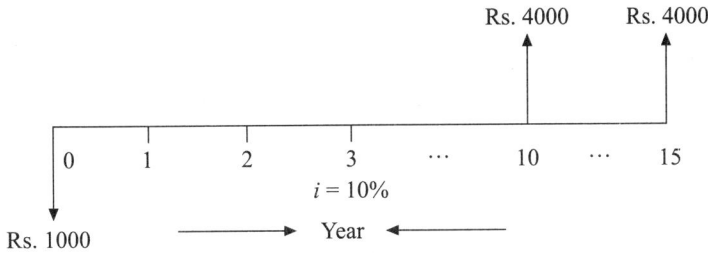

Figure E6.5.2

The present worth of the above cash flow diagram is computed as

$$PW(10\%)_2 = -\text{Rs. } 1000 + \text{Rs. } 4000\,(P/F,\ 10\%,\ 10) + \text{Rs. } 4000\,(P/F,\ 10\%,\ 15)$$

$$= -\text{Rs. } 1000 + \text{Rs. } 4000\,(0.3855) + \text{Rs. } 4000\,(0.2394)$$

$$= -\text{Rs. } 1000 + \text{Rs. } 11{,}118$$

$$= \text{Rs. } 10{,}118$$

The present worth of plan 1 is more than that of plan 2. So, plan 1 is the best plan from the investors' point of view.

6.3 FUTURE WORTH METHOD

Future worth method is particularly useful in an investment situation where we need to compute the equivalent worth of a project at the end of its investment period rather than at its beginning.

6.3.1 Steps for Computing Future Worth Method

The following are the steps for computing future worth method.

1. Determine the interest rate.
2. Estimate the service life of the project.
3. Calculate the cash inflows for each period over the service life.
4. Ascertain the cash outflows over each service period.
5. Find out the net cash flows (inflows – outflows).

For a single project evaluation, if

1. $FW > 0$, then the project will be accepted;
2. $FW < 0$, then the investment proposal will be rejected; and
3. $FW = 0$, then one will remain indifferent to the investment.

For a mutually exclusive alternative, the future worth cash flows can be calculated by the following:

1. Revenue-based future worth
2. Cost-based future worth

In revenue-based future worth, the alternative with the maximum future worth amount will be selected. In cost-based future worth, the alternative with the least future worth amount will be accepted. The formula for the future worth for a given interest rate i is

$$FW(i) = -P(1 + i)^n + R_1(1 + i)^{n-1} + R_2(1 + i)^{n-2} + \cdots + R_n + S$$

or

$$FW(i) = -P(F/P, i, n) + R_1(F/P, i, n - 1) + R_2(F/P, i, n - 2) + \cdots + R_n + S$$

If it is equal-payment series, then the formula will be

$$FW(i) = -P(F/P, i, n) + R(F/A, i, n) + S$$

In this case, the alternative with the maximum future worth amount should be selected as the best alternative.

If the cash flow stream is cost based, then the future worth is given by

$$FW(i) = P(1 + i)^n + C_1(1 + i)^{n-1} + C_2(1 + i)^{n-2} + \cdots + C_n - S$$

or

$$FW(i) = P(F/P, i, n) + C_1(F/P, i, n - 1) + C_2(F/P, i, n - 2) + \cdots + C_n - S$$

In equal-payment series, the formula will be

$$FW(i) = P(F/P, i, n) + C(F/A, i, n) - S$$

In this case, the alternative with the minimum future worth amount should be selected as the best alternative.

EXAMPLE 6.6

The project cash flow of an investment proposal is given in the following tabular form

Year (n)	Net cash flow (Rs.)
0	− 50,000
1	20,400
2	25,200
3	52,740

Compute the NFW at the end of year 3 at $i = 15$ per cent. Is this project acceptable?

Solution

The cash flow diagram for the project is given in Figure E6.6.1.

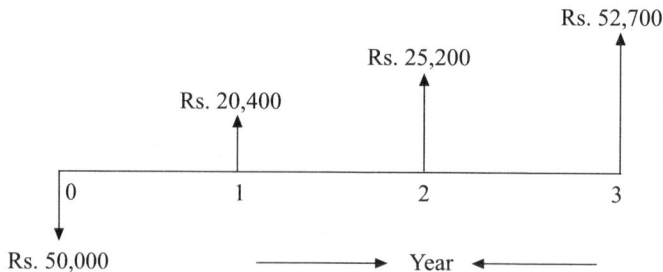

Figure E6.6.1

The future worth of the project is

$$FW(15\%) = -P(F/P, i, n) + R_1(F/P, i, n-1) + R_2(F/P, i, n-2) + R_3(F/P, i, n-3)$$

$$= -\text{Rs. } 50{,}000(F/P, 15\%, 3) + \text{Rs. } 20{,}400(F/P, 15\%, 2)$$

$$+ \text{Rs. } 25{,}200(F/P, 15\%, 1) + \text{Rs. } 52{,}740$$

$$= -\text{Rs. } 50{,}000(1.521) + \text{Rs. } 20{,}400(1.323) + \text{Rs. } 25{,}200(1.150) + \text{Rs. } 52{,}740$$

$$= \text{Rs. } 32{,}659.2$$

Since $FW(15\%) > 0$, the project is acceptable.

EXAMPLE 6.7

Given the following two mutually exclusive alternatives, select the best one based on future worth method of comparison assuming $i = 12$ per cent.

Alternative	Cash flow at the end of year (Rs.)				
	0	1	2	3	4
A	−4,000,000	1,000,000	1,000,000	1,000,000	1,000,000
B	−4,500,000	800,000	800,000	800,000	800,000

Solution

The cash flow diagram for alternative A is given in Figure E6.7.1.

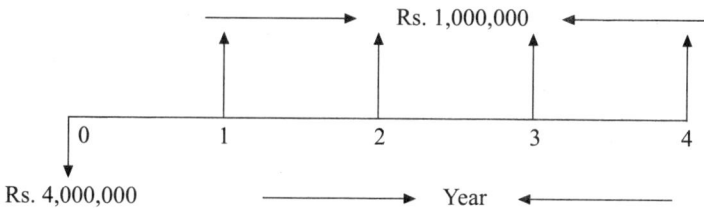

Figure E6.7.1

$$FW(12\%)_A = -\text{Rs. } 4{,}000{,}000(F/P, 12\%, 4) + \text{Rs. } 1{,}000{,}000(F/A, 12\%, 4)$$

$$= -\text{Rs. } 4{,}000{,}000(1.574) + \text{Rs. } 1{,}000{,}000(4.779)$$

$$= -\text{Rs. } 15{,}17{,}000$$

The cash flow diagram for alternative B is given in Figure E6.7.2.

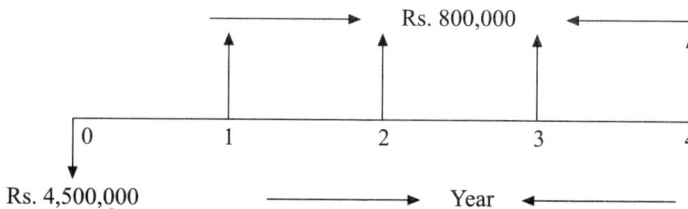

Figure E6.7.2

$$FW(12\%)_B = -\text{Rs. } 4,500,000(F/P, 12\%, 4) + \text{Rs. } 800,000(F/A, 12\%, 4)$$
$$= -\text{Rs. } 4,500,000(1.574) + \text{Rs. } 800,000(4.779)$$
$$= -\text{Rs. } 3,259,800$$

Since $FW(A) > FW(B)$, alternative A should be selected.

EXAMPLE 6.8

Given the following particulars, which machine should be selected based on future worth method, assuming 20 per cent interest rate, compounded annually.

Particulars	Machine A	Machine B
Initial cost (Rs.)	8,000,000	7,000,000
Life (years)	12	12
Annual operational and maintenance cost (Rs.)	800,000	900,000
Salvage value (Rs.)	500,000	400,000

Solution

The cash flow diagram for machine A is given in Figure E6.8.1.

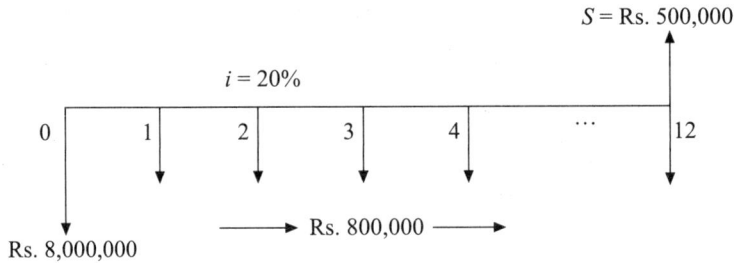

Figure E6.8.1

The future worth amount of machine A is computed as

$$FW(20\%)_A = \text{Rs. } 8,000,000(F/P, 20\%, 12) + \text{Rs. } 800,000(F/A, 20\%, 12) - \text{Rs. } 500,000$$
$$= \text{Rs. } 102,492,800$$

The cash flow diagram for machine B is given in Figure E6.8.2.

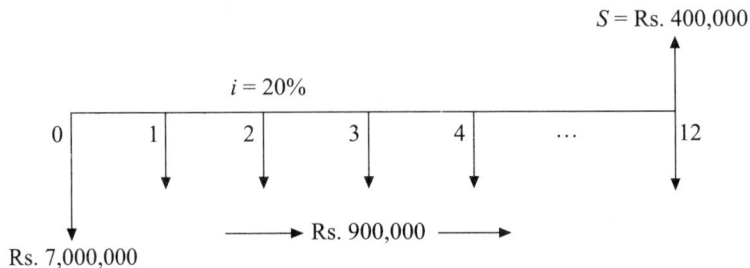

Figure E6.8.2

The future worth amount of machine B is computed as

$$FW(20\%)_B = \text{Rs. } 7,000,000(F/P, 20\%, 12) + \text{Rs. } 900,000(F/A, 20\%, 12) - \text{Rs. } 400,000$$
$$= \text{Rs. } 97,634,900$$

The future worth cost of machine B is less than that of machine A. So, machine B should be selected.

EXAMPLE 6.9

Which alternative from the following should be selected based on the future worth method of comparison assuming 12 per cent interest rate, compounded annually.

Particulars	Alternative A	Alternative B
Initial cost (Rs.)	400,000	800,000
Useful life (year)	4	4
Salvage value (Rs.)	200,000	550,000
Annual cost (Rs.)	40,000	Nil

Solution

The cash flow diagram of alternative A is shown in Figure E6.9.1.

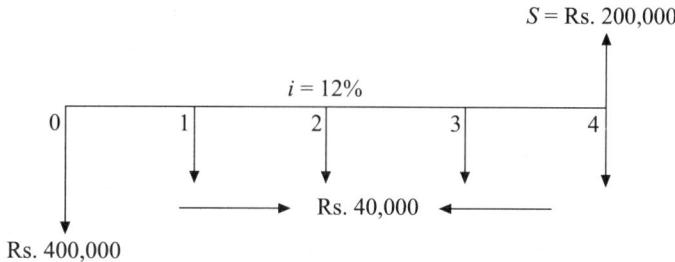

Figure E6.9.1

The future worth amount of alternative A is computed as

$$FW(12\%)_A = \text{Rs. } 400,000(F/P, 12\%, 4) + \text{Rs. } 40,000(F/A, 12\%, 4) - \text{Rs. } 200,000$$
$$= \text{Rs. } 620,760$$

The cash flow diagram for alternative B is given in Figure E6.9.2.

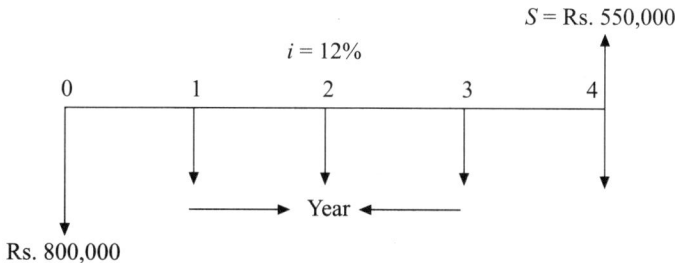

Figure E6.9.2

The future worth amount of alternative B is computed as

$$FW(12\%)_B = \text{Rs. } 800,000(F/P, 12\%, 4) - \text{Rs. } 550,000$$
$$= \text{Rs. } 800,000(1.574) - \text{Rs. } 550,000$$
$$= \text{Rs. } 709,200$$

The future worth cost of alternative A is less than that of alternative B. Therefore, alternative A should be selected.

6.4 EQUIVALENT ANNUAL WORTH COMPARISON

There are various alternatives for comparing the worthiness of a project. Equivalent Annual Worth (EAW) is one important method for comparing engineering alternatives. In an annual worth method, all the receipts and disbursements occurring over a period are converted to an equivalent uniform yearly amount. EAW is a popular method because a year's profit and loss are taken into account. A large number of engineering economic decisions are based on annual comparison and hence the term 'equivalent uniform yearly amount' is often used. For example, cost accounting procedures, depreciation charges, tax calculations. These yearly cost tabulations generally make the annual worth method easier.

Equivalent Annual Cost (EAC) indicates that the equivalent value of negative cash flow for disbursement is greater than the corresponding positive flow of receipts.

We will use the term EAW when costs and receipts are both present. See Figure 6.3.

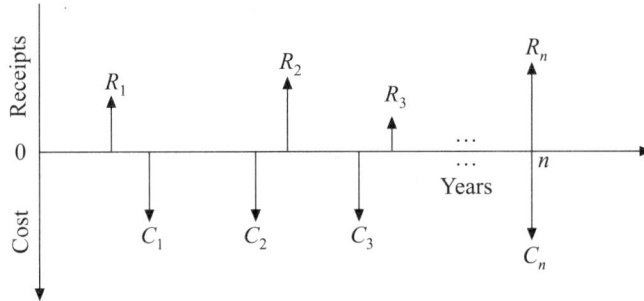

Figure 6.3 Equivalent annual worth diagram.

We will use the term EAC to designate comparison involving only costs. See Figure 6.4.

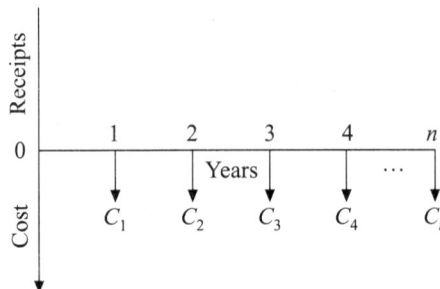

Figure 6.4 Equivalent annual cost diagram.

6.4.1　Steps for Computing EAW

The following are the steps for computing EAW.

1. Estimate the cash flows (inflows, outflows) over each service period.
2. Calculate the service life of the project.
3. Determine the interest rate.
4. Compare with before tax cash flows.
5. Do not include intangible considerations for EAW comparisons.

For single alternatives, if

1. $EAW > 0$, then the investment proposal will be accepted;
2. $EAW < 0$, then the investment proposal will be rejected; and
3. $EAW = 0$, then one should remain indifferent to the investment.

For multiple alternatives or mutually exclusive alternatives, if all the alternatives are revenue dominated, then the alternative with the higher EAW will be selected. If all the alternatives are cost based, then the alternative with the least EAW will be accepted.

Equivalent annual worth consists of the following steps:

1. Compute the net present worth.
2. Multiply the amount of present worth by the capital recovery factor, i.e. $EAW = PW(i)$ $(A/P, i, n)$, where $(A/P, i, n)$ is called *equal-payment series capital recovery factor*.

The annual equivalent worth can be computed by using the general formula,

$$EAW = PW(i) \frac{i(1+i)^n}{(1+i)^n - 1}$$

EXAMPLE 6.10

Consider a machine that costs Rs. 40,000 and a 10 year useful life. At the end of tenth year, it can be sold for Rs. 5,000 after tax adjustment. If the firm could earn an after tax revenue of Rs. 10,000 per year with this machine, should it be purchased at an interest rate of 15 per cent, compounded annually.

Solution

Initial cost (P)　　= Rs. 40,000
Useful life (n)　　= 10 years
Salvage value (S)　= Rs. 5,000
Revenue　　　　= Rs. 10,000
$i = 15$ per cent, compounded annually

The cash flow diagram for the given project is shown in Figure E6.10.1.

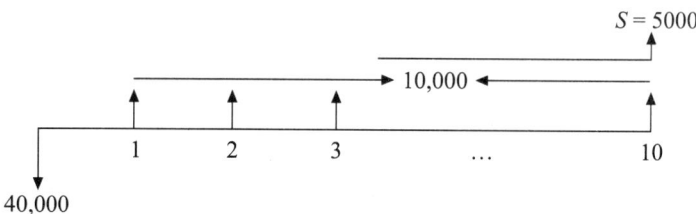

Figure E6.10.1

Step 1: To find $NPW(15\%)$

$$NPW(15\%) = -P + R(P/A, i, n) + S(P/F, i, n)$$
$$= -40,000 + 10,000(5.0188) + 5000(0.2472)$$
$$= \text{Rs. } 11,424$$

Step 2: To find $EAW(15\%)$

$$EAW(15\%) = PW(i)\ (A/P, i, n)$$
$$= \text{Rs. } 11,424\ (A/P, 15\%, 10)$$
$$= \text{Rs. } 11,424\ (0.1993)$$
$$= \text{Rs. } 2276.80$$

Since $EAW(15\%) > 0$, so the project can be accepted.

There will be an equivalent profit of Rs. 2276.8 per year over the machine life.

EXAMPLE 6.11

A company invests in one of the two mutually exclusive alternatives. The life period of both the alternatives is estimated to be 15 years with the following investments, annual equal returns and salvage values:

Particulars	Alternative 1	Alternative 2
First cost	Rs. 100,000	Rs. 110,000
Annual equal returns	Rs. 70,000	Rs. 80,000
Salvage value	Rs. 10,000	Rs. 20,000

Determine the better alternative based on the annual equivalent method by assuming $i = 20$ per cent, compounded annually.

Solution

Alternative 1

First cost (P) = Rs. 100,000
Annual equal return = Rs. 70,000
Salvage value (S) = Rs. 10,000
Interest rate, (i) = 20%

The cash flow diagram for alternative 1 is given in Figure E6.11.1.

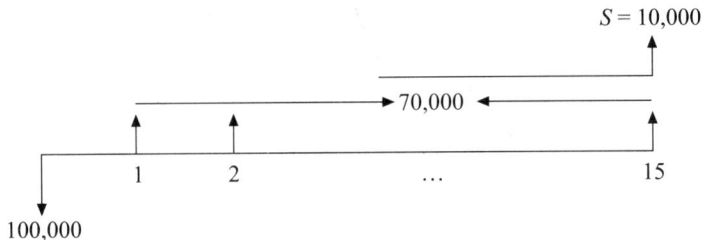

Figure E6.11.1

$$NPW(20\%) = -P + R(P/A, i, n) + S(P/F, i, n)$$
$$= -100,000 + 70,000\,(4.6755) + 10,000\,(0.0649)$$
$$= \text{Rs. } 227,934$$

$$EAW(20\%)_1 = NPW(A/P, i, n)$$
$$= \text{Rs. } 227,934(A/P, 20\%, 15)$$
$$= \text{Rs. } 227,934(0.2139)$$
$$= \text{Rs. } 48,755,082$$

Alternative 2

First cost(P) = Rs. 110,000
Annual equal return = Rs. 80,000
Salvage value(S) = Rs. 20,000
Interest rate(i) = 20%

The cash flow diagram for alternative 2 is given in Figure E6.11.2.

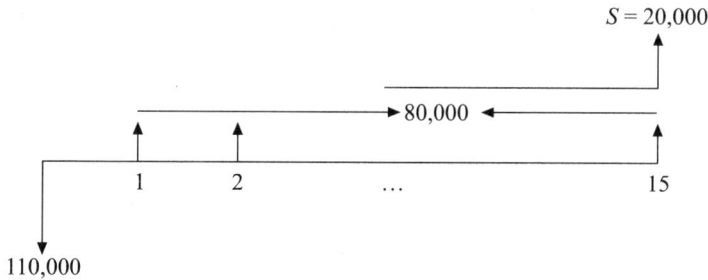

Figure E6.11.2

$$NPW(20\%)_2 = -P + R(P/A, i, n) + S(P/F, i, n)$$
$$= \text{Rs. } 110,000 + \text{Rs. } 80,000\,(4.6755) + \text{Rs. } 20,000\,(0.0649)$$
$$= \text{Rs. } 485,338$$

$$EAW(20\%)_2 = NPW(A/P, i, n)$$
$$= \text{Rs. } 485,338(A/P, 20\%, 15)$$
$$= \text{Rs. } 485,338(0.2139)$$
$$= \text{Rs. } 103,813.79$$

Since EAW of alternative 2 is higher than that of alternative 1, the former should be accepted.

EXAMPLE 6.12

Particulars	Machine A	Machine B
Initial investment	Rs. 150,000	Rs. 240,000
Estimated life	12 years	12 years
Salvage value	Rs. 0	Rs. 6000
Annual operational and maintenance cost	Rs. 0	Rs. 4500

Suggest which machine should be selected based on annual equivalent cost by assuming 15 per cent, interest rate, compounded annually.

Solution

Machine A

Initial investment (P)	= Rs. 150,000
Life period (n)	= 12 years
Salvage value (S)	= Rs. 0
Annual operational and management cost (A)	= Rs. 0
Interest (i)	= 15 per cent compounded annually

The cash flow diagram for machine A is given in Figure E6.12.1.

Figure E6.12.1

The annual equivalent cost of the above cash flow diagram is

$$AEC(15\%) = \text{Rs. } 150,000(A/P, i, n)$$
$$= \text{Rs. } 150,000(0.1845)$$
$$= \text{Rs. } 27,675$$

Machine B

Initial investment (P)	= Rs. 240,000
Life period (n)	= 12 years
Salvage value (S)	= Rs. 6000
Annual operational and management cost (A)	= Rs. 4500
Interest rate (i)	= 15%

The cash flow diagram for machine B is given in Figure E6.12.2.

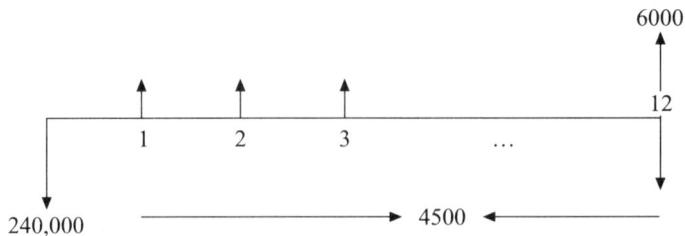

Figure E6.12.2

$$NPW_B(15\%) = P + C(P/A, i, n) - S(P/F, i, n)$$
$$= 240{,}000 + 4500\,(5.4206) - 6000\,(0.1869)$$
$$= \text{Rs. } 263{,}271.3$$
$$= EAC_B(15\%)$$
$$= NPW(A/P, i, n)$$
$$= NPW(A/P, 15\%, 12)$$
$$= \text{Rs. } 263{,}271.3\,(0.1845)$$
$$= \text{Rs. } 48{,}573.55$$

The annual equivalent cost of machine A is less than that of machine B. So machine A is a more cost-effective machine.

EXAMPLE 6.13

Particulars	Machine A	Machine B
First cost	Rs. 300,000	Rs. 600,000
Life period	4	4
Salvage value	Rs. 200,000	Rs. 300,000
Operational and management cost	Rs. 30,000	Rs. 0

Suggest which machine should be purchased at 15 per cent interest rate based on annual equivalent worth method.

Solution

Machine *A*

First cost (P)	= Rs. 300,000
Life period (n)	= 4 years
Salvage value (S)	= Rs. 200,000
Operational and management cost (A)	= Rs. 30,000
Interest rate (i)	= 15 per cent, compounded annually.

The cash flow diagram for machine A is shown in Figure E6.13.1.

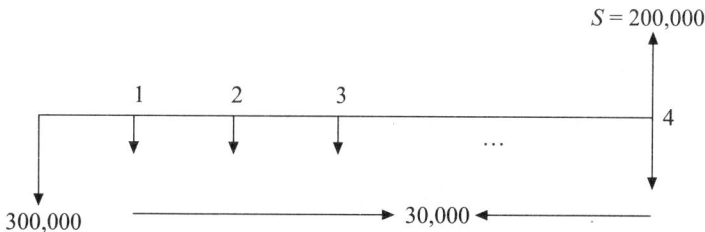

Figure E6.13.1

$$NPW(15\%)_A = P + C(P/A,\, i,\, n) - S(P/F,\, i,\, n)$$
$$= 300,000 + 30,000\,(P/A,\, i,\, n) - 200,000\,(P/F,\, i,\, n)$$
$$= 300,000 + 30,000\,(2.8550) - 200,000\,(0.5718)$$
$$= \text{Rs. }271,290$$

$$EAW(15\%)_A = NPW \times A/P,\, i,\, n$$
$$= \text{Rs. }271,290\,(A/P,\, 15\%,\, 4)$$
$$= \text{Rs. }271,290\,(0.3503)$$
$$= \text{Rs. }95,032.887$$

Machine B

First cost(P)	= Rs.6,00,000
Life period(n)	= 4 years
Salvage value(S)	= Rs. 300,000
Operational and management cost(A)	= Rs. 0
Interest rate(i)	= 15 per cent, compounded annually.

The cash flow diagram for machine B is shown in Figure E6.13.2.

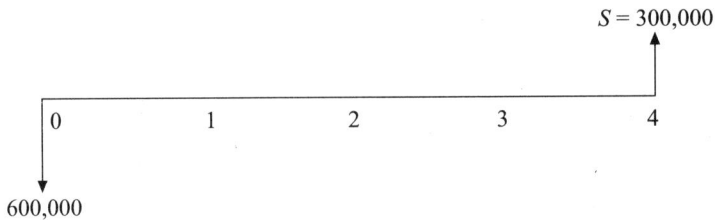

Figure E6.13.2

$$NPW(15\%)_B = P - S(P/F,\, i,\, n)$$
$$= 600,000 - 300,000\,(0.5718)$$
$$= \text{Rs. }600,000 - 171,540$$
$$= \text{Rs. }428,460.$$

$$EAW(15\%)_B = NPW \times A/P,\, i,\, n$$
$$= \text{Rs. }428,460 \times 0.3503$$
$$= \text{Rs. }150,089.53$$

Since the annual equivalent cost of machine A is less than that of machine B, it is advisable to purchase machine A.

6.5 RATE OF RETURN METHOD

The rate of return is a percentage that indicates the relative yield on different uses of capital. The following three rates of return appear frequently in engineering economics studies:

1. The **Minimum Acceptable Rate of Return (MARR)** is the rate set by an organization to designate the lowest level of return that makes an investment acceptable.

2. The **Internal Rate of Return (IRR)** is the rate on the unrecovered balance of the investment in a situation where the terminal balance is zero. It is a discount rate at which NPW equals to zero.

3. The **External Rate of Return (ERR)** is the rate of return that is possible to obtain for an investment under the current economic conditions. For example, suppose the analysis of an investment shows that it will realize an IRR of 50 per cent. Rationally, it is not reasonable to expect that we can invest in the external market and get that high a rate. In engineering economics studies, the external interest rate most often will be set to the MARR.

6.5.1 Minimum Acceptable Rate of Return

The (MARR) also known as minimum attractive rate of return, is a lower limit for investment acceptability set by organizations or individuals. It is a method designed to make the best possible use of a limited resource, i.e. money. Rates vary widely according to the type of organization. They even vary within the organization. Historically, government agencies and regulated public utilities have utilized lower required rates of return than have competitive industrial enterprises. Within a given enterprise, the required rate may be different for various divisions or activities. These variations usually reflect the risks involved. For instance, the rate of return required for cost reduction proposals may be lower than that required for research and development projects where there are less certainty about the prospective cash flows.

6.5.2 Internal Rate of Return (IRR)

The IRR is the best known and most widely used rate of return method. It is also known as the **true rate of return method** and the **discounted cash flow method**. The IRR represented by i in the traditional interpretation of interest rates, is the rate of interest earned by an alternative investment on the unrecovered balance of an investment.

The IRR can be calculated by equating the annual, present, or future worth of cash flow to zero, and solving for the interest rate (IRR) that allows equality. It should be added that solving for the interest rate in this manner results in a polynomial equation, a function of i, which may result in multiple roots of the equation. In such cases, the IRR may or may not be one of the equation roots.

Although both the EAW and the FW approaches are legitimate, the rate of return is often defined in terms of present worth, under the constraints of possible i^* roots, where IRR is

- the interest rate at which the present worth of the cash flow of a project is zero, or,
- to restate this in another way the rate which when employed in computing the present worth of all costs and present worths of all returns will make both equal.

As the rate of return computations usually begin with a problem expressed in terms of present worth or annual worth, it is necessary to pay attention to the guidelines for EAW and PW methods. In particular, mutually exclusive alternatives (where selection of one precludes the selection of another) must be compared on the basis of equivalent outcomes. In the case of independent alternatives (the choice of one does not affect the choice of another, except for limited capital availability), all costs and benefits must be explicitly stated.

Calculation of IRR

The IRR should be determined based on the type of investment (simple, pure, and mixed) and the characteristics of the alternatives (mutually exclusive or independent). If we have independent projects, we may fund combinations of the projects since an independent project does not affect the funding of another project (except for capital availability limitations which are very real in most situations analysed by the engineering economist). The cash flows of several independent alternatives that are being considered as a group may be summed to form the group's composite cash flow. The analysis can then be performed on this composite cash flow. Where capital limitations are apparent in a department and several independent alternatives are competing for funding, the combinations of alternatives may be formed where each combinations first cost has to be equal to or less than the capital available. In this case, mutually exclusive combination's will usually be realized, where selection of one group of independent alternatives will preclude the selection of another. This can be due to alternatives being in more than one group and/or capital limitations.

We will see that the ranking alternatives according to their IRR values are not consistent with PW, FW, or AW rankings. Mutually exclusive alternatives may be analysed by incremental IRR analysis, and the results will be found to be completely consistent with PW, FW, and AW methods. Incremental analysis assumes that we start with a satisfactory low investment alternative. Analysis of a higher investment alternative is then based on the differences between the cash flows of the second alternative and the acceptable alternative. These differences in cash flows are incremental cash flows. The cash flow of the second alternative is equal to the cash flow of the first alternative plus the incremental cash flow. Thus, if the incremental cash flow is acceptable when compared to MARR, then the higher investment has to be a better investment than the first alternative, which was also acceptable. Otherwise, do not consider the higher investment. This type of evaluation is continued until all alternatives have been evaluated; one of the mutually exclusive alternatives is then determined to be the best investment. As mentioned earlier, there is a possibility that the PW equation may be a polynomial in terms of i such that multiple roots i^* of polynomial PW(i') may result. Often, multiple i^*s are assumed to be multiple IRR values. This is misleading since there is really only one true IRR for an investment, and so we will need to determine which i^*, if any, is the investment IRR. Classifying investments into simple and non-simple investments will tell us if just one i^* exists. Thus, in turn, tells us that we have found the IRR when we have found i^*. An investment is simple if there is only one cash flow sign change (minus to plus) from period to period. A simple investment is given in Table 6.1.

Table 6.1   Simple Investment

Time period	Cash flow (Rs.)	Sign change
0	−2000	
1	−200	
2	500	Yes (− to +)
3	500	
4	500	

There will only be one i^* if the investment is simple. A non-simple investment will have more than one sign change in the cash flow sequence, as given in Table 6.2.

Table 6.2 Non-simple Investment

Time period	Cash flow (Rs.)	Sign change
0	−2000	Yes (− to +)
1	200	Yes (+ to −)
2	−500	Yes (− to +)
3	500	
4	500	

There may be multiple i^* values if the investment is non-simple.

Finally, if we have multiple i^* values (non-simple investment), we will need to determine the true IRR. First, we determine whether the investment is pure or mixed. A pure investment occurs if the project cash flow balances, evaluated at i^*, are all less than or equal to zero. We should now realize that a simple investment has to be a pure investment as exemplified in the following paragraph. If any of the project cash balances are positive (and some are negative), then we have a need to use an external interest rate for reinvestment. This is called a **mixed investment** since we will 'externally' reinvest at the external rate (MARR) when balances are positive and 'internally' invest at the IRR rate when balances are negative or zero.

Single, simple investment

The rate of return for a single, simple investment is determined by setting the present worth (or EAW) of receipts equal to the present worth (or EAW) of disbursements. Then an interest rate is sought that makes the discounted cash flows conform to equality.
Find i so that

$$PW(\text{receipts}) = PW(\text{disbursements})$$

The same relation obviously occurs when the discounted flows are subtracted from each other to equal zero.
Find i so that

$$PW(\text{receipts}) - PW(\text{disbursements}) = \text{Net } PW = 0$$

For either PW formulation, the manual calculation of i is usually a trial and error procedure. When a single proposal is for a cost reduction project, the receipts take the form of net savings from the method of operation used before the cost reduction investment. In effect, we get an incremental investment that is the difference between do-nothing case and single investment.

The rate of return of a cash flow pattern is the interest rate at which the present worth of that cash flow pattern reduces to zero. In this method of comparison, the rate of return for each alternative is computed. Then the alternative which has the highest rate of return is selected as the best alternative.

EXAMPLE 6.14

A person is planning a new business. The initial outlay and cash flow pattern for the new business are as given in the tabular representation.

Period	Cash flow (Rs.)
0	-100,000
1	30,000
2	30,000
3	30,000
4	30,000
5	30,000

The expected life of the business is five years. Find the rate of return for the new business.

Solution

Initial investment   = Rs. 100,000
Annual equal revenue = Rs. 30,000
Life   = 5 years

The cash flow diagram for this situation is given in Figure E6.14.1.

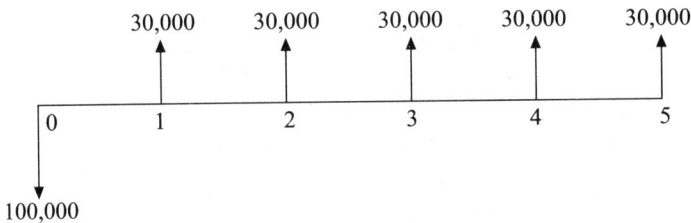

Figure E6.14.1

The present worth function for the business is

$$PW(i) = -100,000 + 30,000(P/A, i, 5)$$

When $i = 10\%$

$$PW(10\%) = -100,000 + 30,000(P/A, 10\%, 5)$$
$$= -100,000 + 30,000(3.7908)$$
$$= \text{Rs. } 13,724$$

When $i = 15\%$

$$PW(15\%) = -100,000 + 30,000(P/A, 15\%, 5)$$
$$= -100,000 + 30,000(3.3522)$$
$$= \text{Rs. } 566$$

When $i = 18\%$

$$PW(18\%) = -100,000 + 30,000(P/A, 18\%, 5)$$
$$= -100,000 + 30,000(3.1272)$$
$$= \text{Rs. } -6,184$$

$$i = 15\% + \frac{566 - 0}{566 - (-6184)} \times (3\%)$$

$$= 15\% + 0.252\%$$
$$= 15.252\%$$

Therefore, the rate of return for the new business is 15.252 per cent.

EXAMPLE 6.15

A company is trying to diversify its business in a new product line. The life of the project is 10 years with no salvage value at the end of its life. The initial outlay of the project is Rs. 2,000,000. The annual net profit is Rs. 350,000. Find the rate of return for the new business.

Solution

Life of the product line(n) = 10 years
Initial outlay = Rs. 2,000,000
Annual net profit = Rs. 350,000
Scrap value after 10 years = 0

The cash flow diagram for this situation is shown in Figure E6.15.1.

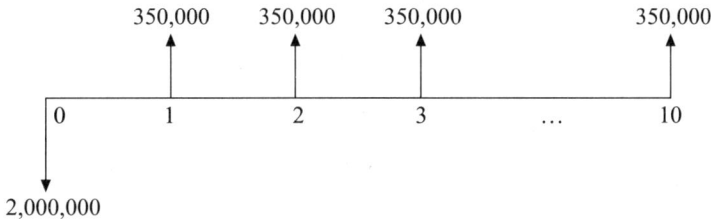

Figure E6.15.1

The formula for the net present worth function of the situation is

$$PW(i) = -2,000,000 + 350,000 (P/A, i, 10)$$

When $i = 10\%$,

$$PW(10\%) = -2,000,000 + 350,000 (P/A, 10\%, 10)$$
$$= -2,000,000 + 350,000 (6.1446)$$
$$= \text{Rs. } 150,610.$$

When $i = 12\%$

$$PW(12\%) = -2,000,000 + 350,000 (P/A, 12\%, 10)$$
$$= -2,000,000 + 350,000 (5.6502)$$
$$= \text{Rs. } -22,430$$

$$i = 10\% + \frac{150,610 - 0}{150,610 - 22,430} \times (2\%)$$

$$= 11.74\%$$

Therefore, the rate of return of the new product line is 11.74 per cent.

EXAMPLE 6.16

A firm has identified three mutually exclusive investment proposals whose details are given below. The life of all the three alternatives is estimated to be five years with negligible salvage value. The minimum attractive rate of return for the firm is 12 per cent.

	Alternative		
	A_1	A_2	A_3
Investment	Rs. 150,000	Rs. 210,000	Rs. 255,000
Annual net income	Rs. 45,570	Rs. 58,260	Rs. 69,000

Find the best alternative based on the rate of return method of comparison.

Solution

Calculation of rate of return for alternative A_1:

    Initial outlay   = Rs. 150,000
    Annual profit = Rs. 45,570
    Life   = 5 years

The cash flow diagram for alternative A_1 is shown in Figure E6.16.1.

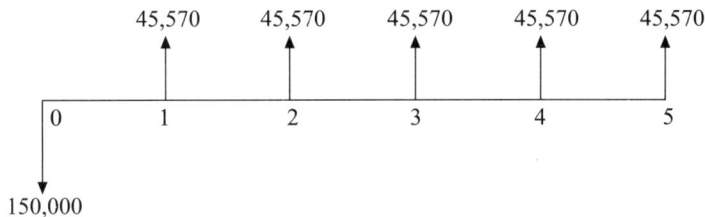

Figure E6.16.1

The formula for the net present worth for alternative A_1 is given as

$$PW(i) = -150,000 + 45,570 (P/A, i, 5)$$

When $i = 10\%$

$$PW(10\%) = -150,000 + 45,570 (P/A, 10\%, 5)$$
$$= -150,000 + 45,570 (3.7908)$$
$$= \text{Rs. } 22,746.76$$

When $i = 12\%$

$$PW(12\%) = -150,000 + 45,570 (P/A, 12\%, 5)$$
$$= -150,000 + 45,570 (3.6048)$$
$$= \text{Rs. } 14,270.74$$

When $i = 15\%$

$$PW(15\%) = -150,000 + 45,570 (P/A, 15\%, 5)$$
$$= -150,000 + 45,570 (3.3522)$$
$$= \text{Rs. } 2759.75$$

When $i = 18\%$

$$PW(18\%) = -150,000 + 45,570 \, (P/A, \, 18\%, \, 5)$$
$$= -150,000 + 45,570 \, (3.1272)$$
$$= \text{Rs.} \, -7493.50$$

Therefore, the rate of return for alternative A_1 is

$$i = 15\% + \frac{2759.75 - 0}{2759.75 - (-7493.50)} \times (3\%)$$
$$= 15\% + 0.81\%$$
$$= 15.81\%$$

Calculation of the rate of return for alternative A_2:

    Initial outlay   = Rs. 210,000
    Annual profit   = Rs. 58,260
    Life of alternative A_2 = 5 years

The cash flow diagram for alternative A_2 is shown in Figure E6.16.2.

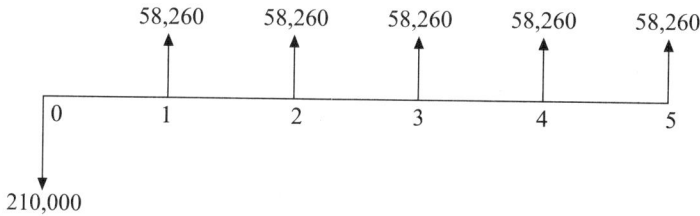

Figure E6.16.2

The formula for the net present worth of this alternative is

$$PW(i) = -210,000 + 58,260 \, (P/A, \, i, \, 5)$$

When $i = 12\%$

$$PW(12\%) = -210,000 + 58,260 \, (P/A, \, 12\%, \, 5)$$
$$= -210,000 + 58,260 \, (3.6048)$$
$$= \text{Rs.} \, 15.65$$

When $i = 13\%$

$$PW(13\%) = -210,000 + 58,260 \, (P/A, \, 13\%, \, 5)$$
$$= -210,000 + 58,260 \, (3.5172)$$
$$= \text{Rs.} \, -5087.93$$

Therefore, the rate of return for alternative A_2 is

$$i = 12\% + \frac{15.65 - 0}{15.65 - (-5087.93)} \times (1\%)$$
$$= 12\% + 0\%$$
$$= 12\%$$

Calculation of the rate of return for alternative A_3:

Initial outlay   = Rs. 255,000
Annual profit   = Rs. 69,000
Life of alternative A_3 = 5 years

The cash flow diagram for alternative A_3 is depicted in Figure E6.16.3.

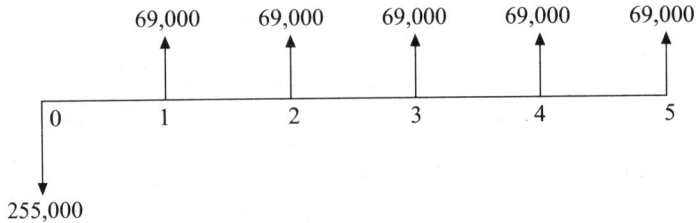

Figure E6.16.3

The formula for the net present worth for this alternative A_3 is

$$PW(i) = -255,000 + 69,000(P/A, i, 5)$$

When $i = 11\%$

$$PW(11\%) = -255,000 + 69,000(P/A, 11\%, 5)$$
$$= -255,000 + 69,000(3.6959)$$
$$= \text{Rs. } 17.1$$

When $i = 12\%$

$$PW(12\%) = -255,000 + 69,000(P/A, 12\%, 5)$$
$$= -255,000 + 69,000(3.6048)$$
$$= \text{Rs. } -6268.80$$

Therefore, the rate of return for alternative A_3 is

$$i = 11\% + \frac{17.1 - 0}{17.1 - (-6268.80)} \times (1\%)$$

$$= 11\%$$

The rates of returns for the three alternatives are tabulated here.

Alternative	Rate of return
A_1	15.81%
A_2	12%
A_3	11%

From the data, it is clear that the rate of return for alternative A_3 is less than the minimum attractive rate of return of 12 per cent. So, it should not be considered for comparison. The remaining two alternatives qualify for consideration. Among alternatives A_1 and A_2, the rate of return of alternative A_1 is greater than that of alternative A_2. Hence, alternative A_1 should be selected.

EXAMPLE 6.17

A company is planning to expand its present business activity. It has two alternatives for the expansion programme and the corresponding cash flows are tabulated below. Each alternative has a life of five years and a negligible salvage value. The minimum attractive rate of return for the company is 12 per cent. Suggest the best alternative to the company.

	Initial investment (Rs.)	Yearly revenue (Rs.)
Alternative 1	500,000	170,000
Alternative 2	800,000	270,000

Solution

Alternative 1

Initial outlay   = Rs. 500,000
Annual revenue   = Rs. 170,000
Life of alternative 1 = 5 years

The cash flow diagram for alternative 1 is illustrated in Figure E6.17.1.

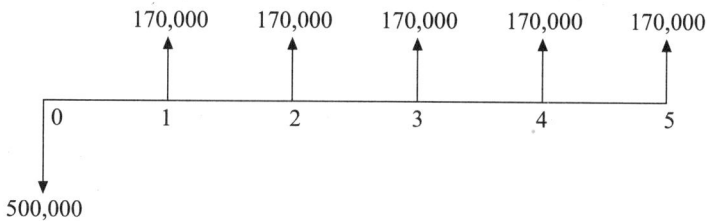

Figure E6.17.1

The formulas for the net present worth for alternative 1 are as follows:

$$PW_1(i) = -500,000 + 170,000(P/A, i, 5)$$
$$PW_1(15\%) = -500,000 + 170,000(P/A, 15\%, 5)$$
$$= -500,000 + 170,000(3.3522)$$
$$= \text{Rs. } 69,874$$
$$PW_1(17\%) = -500,000 + 170,000(P/A, 17\%, 5)$$
$$= -500,000 + 170,000(3.1993)$$
$$= \text{Rs. } 43,881$$
$$PW_1(20\%) = -500,000 + 170,000(P/A, 20\%, 5)$$
$$= -500,000 + 170,000(2.9906)$$
$$= \text{Rs. } 8402$$
$$PW_1(22\%) = -500,000 + 170,000(P/A, 22\%, 5)$$
$$= -500,000 + 170,000(2.8636)$$
$$= \text{Rs. } -13,188$$

Therefore, the rate of return for alternative 1 is

$$i = 20\% + \frac{8402 - 0}{8402 - (-13,188)} \times (2\%)$$

$$= 20.78\%$$

Alternative 2

Initial outlay	= Rs. 800,000
Annual revenue	= Rs. 270,000
Life	= 5 years

The cash flow diagram for alternative 2 is depicted in Figure E6.17.2.

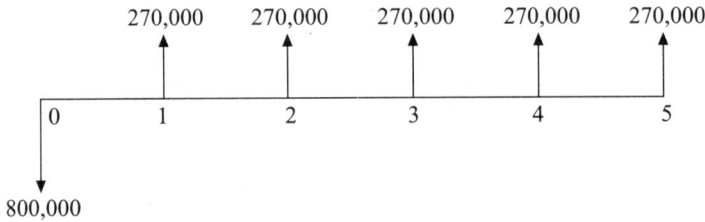

Figure E6.17.2

The formula for the net present worth for alternative 2 is

$$PW_2(i) = -800,000 + 270,000\,(P/A, i, 5)$$

$$PW_2(20\%) = -800,000 + 270,000\,(P/A, 20\%, 5)$$

$$= -800,000 + 270,000\,(2.9906)$$

$$= \text{Rs. } 7462$$

$$PW_2(22\%) = -800,000 + 270,000\,(P/A, 22\%, 5)$$

$$= -800,000 + 270,000\,(2.8636)$$

$$= \text{Rs. } -26,828$$

Thus, the rate of return for alternative 2 is

$$i = 20\% + \frac{7462 - 0}{7462 - (-26,828)} \times (2\%)$$

$$= 20.435\%$$

Since the rate of return of alternative 1 is greater than that of select it.

6.6   PROJECT EVALUATION AND COST-BENEFIT ANALYSIS

Project evaluation, as a technique of development planning, has grown rapidly in application in recent years. In fact, it has on its own become a method of economic planning. The public investment analysis involves the treatment of a number of important aspects of which appraisal of the economic costs and benefits of the project are perhaps the most important.

The preparation of a report on a project is a complex task which requires the services of both engineers and economists. Prior to the preparation of a project report, a 'pre-feasibility study' is carried out by the appropriate authority. The pre-feasibility study states, in broad terms, the objectives, and defines the alternative means (sizes, designs, location, etc.) which the report appraisal team is expected to examine. The project report is generally known as 'feasibility report'. It has now become the main basis on which authorities decide whether a particular project is to be accepted, modified or rejected. Project reports are not prepared on uniform lines and often differ considerably in their presentation. However, one can identify the following six main components of these reports:

1. **Terms of reference:**   They are based on the pre-feasibility study and provide guidelines for the project appraisal team. These include the definition of the objectives of the study, outline of the project alternatives, etc.

2. **Engineering study:**   Its purpose is to determine the technical feasibility of the project. Engineering study covers the physical characteristics of the project, the design of construction and plant, the technical aspect of output, time schedule for the project execution, etc.

3. **Financial study:**   It provides cost estimates of the project in budgetary terms. Financial study examines the direct costs of construction of a plant at market prices and presents financial evaluation on an accounting basis.

4. **Cost-benefit analysis:**   This analysis includes appraisal of the economic costs and benefits of the project and alternatives, and its impact on the economy and on the welfare of the people who are directly or indirectly affected by it. This analysis, thus, provides the basis on which the project should be accepted, modified or rejected.

5. **Implementation:**   It examines the social and environmental implications of the project.

6. **Recommendation:**   It presents a brief summary of the project with specific recommendations for consideration at the decision-making level. This report is usually submitted to the planning authority, the relevant ministry and also to the project financing agency. If the project is accepted, it may be undertaken. It will usually pass through the three main stages: viz. the *design stage*, the *construction* and the *entry into the operation*.

6.6.1 Cost-Benefit Analysis

The question to which cost-benefit analysis addresses itself is whether it is socially desirable to undertake a number of investment projects A, B, C, D, etc. and if investible funds are limited, then how many of these should be selected. Since the choice involves maximization, we have to discuss what it is that investment planners wish to maximize. In general terms, an investment planner wants to maximize the present value of all benefits less that of all costs, subject to specific constraints. This general formulation raises the following specific questions, the answers to which provide the general principles of cost-benefit analysis:

- In project appraisal which costs and which benefits are to be considered?
- How are these costs and benefits to be valued?
- How can profitability of a project be measured?
- What is the relevance of uncertainty in project appraisal?
- What are the relevant constraints?

There is certainly some arbitrariness in the choice of these questions. In evaluating alternatives of private organizations, the criterion is to select the alternative with the maximum profit. Profit maximization is the main goal of private organizations besides providing goods/services as per specifications to their customers. But the same criterion cannot be used while evaluating public alternatives. Examples of some public alternatives are: constructing bridges, roads, dams, establishing public utilities.

The main objective of any public alternative is to provide goods/services to the public at the minimum cost. In this process, one should see whether the benefits of the public activity are at least equal to its costs. If yes, then the public activity can be undertaken for implementation. Otherwise, it can be cancelled. This is nothing but making a decision based on Benefit-Cost ratio (BC) given by

$$\text{BC ratio} = \frac{\text{Equivalent benefits}}{\text{Equivalent costs}}$$

The benefits may occur at different time periods of the public activity. For the purpose of comparison, these are to be converted into a common time base (present worth, future worth or annual equivalent). Similarly, the costs consist of initial investment, yearly operation and maintenance cost. These are to be converted to a common time base as done in the equivalent benefits. Now, the ratio between the equivalent benefits and the equivalent costs is known as the'benefit-cost ratio'. If this ratio is at least one, the public activity is justified; otherwise, it is not justified. Let

B_P = Present worth of the total benefits
B_F = Future worth of the total benefits
B_A = Annual equivalent of the total benefits
P = Initial investment
P_F = Future worth of the initial investment
P_A = Annual equivalent of the initial investment
C = Yearly cost of operation and maintenance
C_P = Present worth of yearly cost of operation and maintenance
C_F = Future worth of yearly cost of operation and maintenance

$$\text{BC ratio} = \frac{B_P}{P + C_P} + \frac{B_F}{P_F + C_F} + \frac{B_A}{P_A + C}$$

EXAMPLE 6.18

In a particular locality of a state, the vehicle users take a roundabout route to reach certain places because of the presence of a river. This results in excessive travel time and increased fuel cost. So, the state government is planning to construct a bridge across the river. The estimated initial investment for constructing the bridge is Rs. 4,000,000. The estimated life of the bridge is 15 years. The annual operation and maintenance cost is Rs. 150,000. The value of fuel savings due to construction of the bridge is Rs. 600,000 in the first year and it increases by Rs. 50,000 every year thereafter till the end of the life of the bridge. Check whether the project is justified based on BC ratio by assuming an interest rate of 12 per cent, compounded annually.

Solution

Initial investment	= Rs. 4,000,000
Annual operation and maintenance	= Rs. 150,000
Annual fuel savings during the first year	= Rs. 600,000
Equal increment in fuel savings in the following years	= Rs. 50,000

Life of the project   = 15 years
Interest rate   = 12%

The cash flow diagram for the project is shown in Figure E6.18.1.

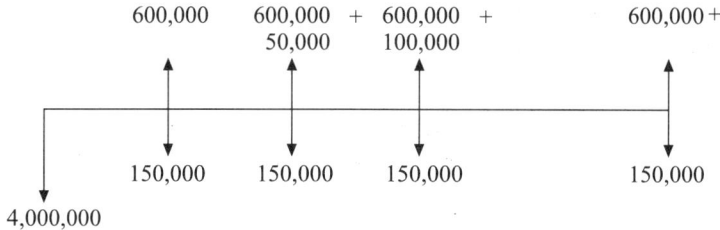

Figure E6.18.1

Total present worth of costs = Initial investment (P)
           + Present worth of annual operating and maintenance cost (C_P)

$$= P + C_P$$

$$= \text{Rs. } 4,000,000 + 150,000 \times (P/A, \ 12\%, \ 15)$$

$$= \text{Rs. } 4,000,000 + 150,000 \times 6.8109$$

$$= \text{Rs. } 5,021,635$$

Total present worth of fuel savings (B_P):

A_1 = Rs. 600,000
G = Rs. 50,000
N = 15 years
i = 12 per cent

Annual equivalent fuel savings $(A) = A_1 + G(A/G, \ 12\%, \ 15)$

$$= 600,000 + 50,000 \ (4.9803)$$

$$= \text{Rs. } 849,015$$

Present worth of the fuel savings $(B_P) = A(P/A, \ 12\%, \ 15)$

$$= 849,015 \ (6.8109)$$

$$= \text{Rs. } 5,782,556$$

$$\text{BC ratio} = \frac{B_P}{P + C_P} + \frac{5,782,556}{5,021,635} = 1.1515$$

Since the BC ratio is more than 1, the construction of the bridge across the river is justified.

EXAMPLE 6.19

A state government is planning a hydroelectric project for a river basin. In addition to the production of electric power, this project will provide flood control, irrigation and recreation benefits. The estimated benefits and costs that are expected to be derived from this project are as follows:

Initial cost	= Rs. 80,000,000
Annual power sales	= Rs. 6,000,000
Annual flood control savings	= Rs. 3,000,000
Annual irrigation benefits	= Rs. 5,000,000
Annual recreation benefits	= Rs. 2,000,000
Annual operating and maintenance costs	= Rs. 3,000,000
Life of the project	= 50 years

Check whether the state government should implement the project (assume $i = 12\%$).

Solution

Initial cost	= Rs. 80,000,000
Annual power sales	= Rs. 6,000,000
Annual flood control savings	= Rs. 3,000,000
Annual irrigation benefits	= Rs. 5,000,000
Annual recreation benefits	= Rs. 2,000,000
Annual operating and maintenance costs	= Rs. 3,000,000
Life of the project = 50 years, and i	= 12%

Total annual benefits

$$= \text{Flood control savings} + \text{Irrigation benefits} + \text{Recreation benefits}$$

$$= \text{Rs. } 3,000,000 + \text{Rs. } 5,000,000 + \text{Rs. } 2,000,000$$

$$= \text{Rs. } 10,000,000$$

$$\text{Present worth of the benefits} = \text{Total annual benefits} \times (P/A, 12\%, 50)$$

$$= 10,000,000 \times (8.3045)$$

$$= \text{Rs. } 83,045,000$$

Present worth of costs = Initial cost + Present worth of annual operation and maintenance cost − Present worth of power sales

$$= \text{Rs. } 80,000,000 + 3,000,000 \times (P/A, 12\%, 50) - 6,000,000 (P/A, 12\%, 50)$$

$$= \text{Rs. } 80,000,000 + 3,000,000 \times 8.3045 - 6,000,000 \times 8.3045$$

$$= \text{Rs. } 55,086,500$$

$$\text{BC ratio} = \frac{\text{Present worth of benefits}}{\text{Present worth of costs}} = \frac{83,045,000}{55,086,500} = 1.508$$

Since the BC ratio is more than 1, the state government can implement the hydroelectric project.

EXAMPLE 6.20

Two mutually exclusive projects are being considered for investment. Project A_1 requires an initial outlay of Rs. 3,000,000 with the net receipts estimated as Rs. 900,000 per year for the next five years. The initial outlay for project A_2 is Rs. 6,000,000, and the net receipts have been estimated at Rs. 1,500,000 per year for the next seven years. There is no salvage value associated with either of the projects. Using the benefit-cost ratio, which project would you select? Assume an interest rate of 10 per cent.

Solution

Alternative A₁

Initial cost(P) = Rs. 3,000,000
Net benefits/year(B) = Rs. 900,000
Life(n) = 5 years

Annual equivalent of initial cost $= P \times (A/P, 10\%, 5)$

$$= 3,000,000 \times 0.2638$$

$$= \text{Rs. } 791,400$$

$$\text{Benefit-cost ratio} = \frac{\text{Annual equivalent benefit}}{\text{Annual equivalent cost}}$$

$$= \frac{900,000}{791,400}$$

$$= 1.137$$

Alternative A₂

Initial cost(P) = Rs. 6,000,000
Net benefits/year(B) = Rs. 1,500,000
Life(n) = 7 years

Annual equivalent of initial cost $= P \times (A/P, 10\%, 7)$

$$= 6,000,000 \times 0.2054$$

$$= \text{Rs. } 1,232,400$$

$$\text{BC ratio} = \frac{\text{Annual equivalent benefit}}{\text{Annual equivalent cost}}$$

$$= \frac{1,500,000}{1,232,400}$$

$$= 1.217$$

The benefit-cost ratio of alternative A₁ is more than that of alternative A₂. Hence, alternative A₁ is to be selected. The comparison is made on a 35-year period which is the minimum common multiple of the lives of alternatives 1 and 2.

REVIEW QUESTIONS

1. A project involves an initial outlay of Rs. 2,000,000, with the following transactions for the next five years.

End of the year (n)	Maintenance and operating expense (Rs.)	Revenue (Rs.)
1	200,000	900,000
2	250,000	1,000,000

(Contd.)

(*Contd.*)

End of the year (*n*)	Maintenance and operating expense (Rs.)	Revenue (Rs.)
3	300,000	1,200,000
4	300,000	1,300,000
5	400,000	1,200,000

The salvage value at the end of the life of the project after five years is Rs. 300,000. Draw a cash flow diagram of the project and find its present worth by assuming $i = 15$ per cent, compounded annually.

2. Find the present worth of the following cash flow series, assuming $i = 15$ per cent, compounded annually:

End of the year (*n*)	Cash flow (Rs.)
0	−20,000
1	40,000
2	40,000
3	40,000
4	40,000
5	40,000

3. Consider the following cash flow series over a 20-year period. Assuming the interest rate as 18 per cent compounded annually, compute the present worth of the series. Give your comments.

End of the year (*n*)	Cash flow (Rs.)
0	−4,000,000
1	600,000
2	600,000
.	.
.	.
20	600,000

4. The cost of erecting an oil well is Rs. 250,000. The annual equivalent yield from the oil well is Rs. 3,000,000. The salvage value after its useful life of 10 years is Rs. 300,000. Assuming an interest rate of 18 per cent, compounded annually, find out whether the erection of the oil well is financially feasible, based on the present worth method.

5. The details of the feasibility report of a project are given here. Check the feasibility of the project based on the present worth method, using $i = 20\%$.

Initial outlay   = Rs. 3,000,000
Life of the project   = 20 years
Annual equivalent revenue   = Rs. 2,500,000
Modernizing cost at the end of the tenth year = Rs. 400,000
Salvage value at the end of the project life   = Rs. 400,000.

6. Consider the following cash flow diagram.

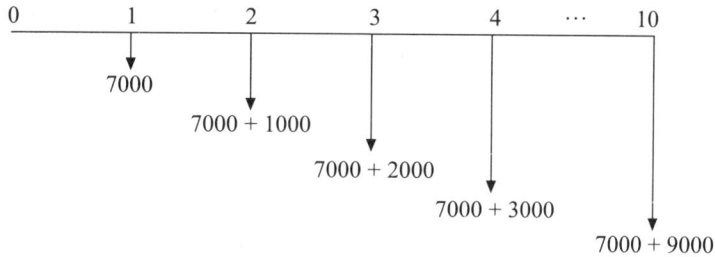

0   1   2   3   4   ...   10

7000

7000 + 1000

7000 + 2000

7000 + 3000

7000 + 9000

Find the present worth using an interest rate of 15%, compounded annually.

7. An automobile company recently advertised its car for a down payment of Rs. 450,000. Alternatively, the car can be taken home by customers without making any payment, but they have to pay an equal yearly amount of Rs. 20,000 for 15 years at an interest rate of 18 per cent, compounded annually. You are asked to advise the best alternative for the customers based on the present worth method of comparison.

8. The cash flows of two project proposals are given in the tabular representation. Each of the project has an expected life of 10 years. Select the best project based on the present worth method of comparison using an interest rate of 18 per cent, compounded annually.

	Initial outlay (Rs.)	Annual equivalent revenue (Rs.)	Salvage value after 10 years (Rs.)
Project 1	−750,000	400,000	50,000
Project 2	−950,000	325,000	200,000

9. A suburban taxi company is considering buying taxis with diesel engines instead of petrol engines. The cars average 30,000 km a year, with a useful life of three years for the taxi running on petrol and four years for the taxi running on diesel. Other comparative information are as follows:

	Diesel	Petrol
Vehicle cost	Rs. 300,000	Rs. 200,000
Fuel cost per litre	Rs. 9.00	Rs. 24.00
Mileage (km/litre)	30	20
Annual insurance premium	Rs. 300	Rs. 300
Salvage value at the end of vehicle life	Rs. 70,000	Rs. 100,000

Determine the more economical choice based on the future worth method of comparison if the interest rate is 15 per cent, compounded annually.

10. A motor cycle is sold for Rs. 40,000. The motor cycle dealer is willing to sell the motorcycle on the following terms:

(a) Make no down payments but pay Rs. 2,500 at the end of each of the first four months and Rs. 2,000 at the end of each month. After that for 18 continuous months.

(b) Make no down payment but pay a total amount of Rs. 50,000 at the end of the twenty second month; till that time the buyer should mortgage property worth Rs. 20,000 at present. Based on these terms and a 12 per cent annual interest rate compounded monthly, find the best alternative for the buyer based on the future worth method of comparison.

11.   Consider the following two mutually exclusive alternatives.

	A	B
Cost	Rs. 2000	Rs. 4000
Uniform annual benefit	Rs. 640	Rs. 960
Useful life (years)	30	30

Using a 15 per cent interest rate, determine which alternative should be selected based on the future worth method of comparison.

12.   A company must decide whether to buy machine A or machine B :

	Machine A	Machine B
Initial cost	Rs. 300,000	Rs. 500,000
Useful life (years)	5.0	5.0
Salvage value at the end of machine life	Rs. 100,000	Rs. 250,000
Annula maintenance cost	Rs. 20,000	Rs. 0

At 15 per cent interest rate, which machine should be selected? (Use the future worth method of comparison.)

13.   Due to increasing awareness of customers, two different television manufacturing companies started a marketing war. The details of the advertisements of the companies are as follows:

	Brand X	Brand Y
Selling price of a television set	Rs. 25,000	Rs. 20,000
Amount returned to buyer after five years	Rs. 18,000	...

Select the most economical brand from the customers' point of view using the future worth method of comparison, assuming an interest rate of 15 per cent, compounded annually.

14.   Alpha finance company is coming with an option of accepting Rs. 20,000 now and paying a sum of Rs. 260,000 after 20 years. Beta finance company is coming with a similar option of accepting Rs. 20,000 now and paying a sum of Rs. 300,000 after 25 years. Compare and select the best alternative based on the future worth method of comparison with 15 per cent interest rate, compounded annually.

15.   An insurance company gives an endowment policy for a person aged 40 years. The yearly premium for an insured sum of Rs. 200,000 is Rs. 8,000. The policy will mature after 20 years. Also the person is entitled for a bonus of Rs. 70 per thousand per year at the end of the policy. If a person survives till the end of the twentieth year:

(a) What will be the total sum that he will get from the insurance company at that time?

(b) Instead of paying the premium for the insurance policy, if the person invests an equal sum of Rs. 8,000 at the end of each year for the next 20 years in some other scheme which is having similar tax benefit, find the future worth of the investment at 15 per cent interest rate, compounded annually.

(c) Rate the above alternatives assuming that the person is sure of living for the next 20 years.

16. A company has three proposals for expanding its business operations. The details are as follows:

Alternative	Initial cost (Rs.)	Annual revenue (Rs.)	Life (Years)
A_1	2,000,000	1,800,000	10
A_2	2,000,000	1,600,000	10
A_3	4,000,000	1,000,000	10

Each alternative has insignificant salvage value at the end of its life. Assuming an interest rate of 15 per cent, compounded annually, find the best alternative for expanding the business operations of the company using the annual equivalent method.

17. An automobile dealer has recently advertised for its new car. There are three alternatives for purchasing the car which are explained here.

Alternative 1: The customer can take delivery of a car after making a down payment of Rs. 35,000. The remaining money should be paid in 30 equal monthly instalments of Rs. 10,000 each.

Alternative 2: The customer can take delivery of the car after making a down payment of Rs. 100,000. The remaining money should be paid in 30 equal monthly instalments of Rs. 7,000 each.

Alternative 3: The customer can take delivery of the car by making full payment of Rs. 300,000.

Suggest the best alternative of buying cars for customers by assuming an interest rate of 30 per cent, compounded annually. Use the annual equivalent method.

18. A small-scale industry is in the process of buying a milling machine. The purchase value of the milling machine is Rs. 50,000. It has identified two banks for loan to purchase the milling machine. The banks can give only 80 per cent of the purchase value of the milling machine as loan. In Urban Bank, the loan is to be repaid in 50 equal monthly instalments of Rs. 2500 each. In State Bank, the loan is to be repaid in 40 equal monthly instalments of Rs. 4500 each. Suggest the most economical loan scheme for the company, based on the annual equivalent method of comparison. Assume a nominal rate of 20 per cent, compounded monthly.

19. There are two alternatives of replacing a machine. The details of the alternatives are as follows:

Alternative 1

Purchase value of the new machine	= Rs. 300,000
Life of the machine	= 10 years
Salvage value of the new machine at the end of its life	= Rs. 10,000
Annual operation and maintenance cost	= Rs. 40,000
Buyback price of the existing machine	= Rs. 20,000

Alternative 2

Purchase value of the new machine	= Rs. 300,000
Life of the machine	= 10 years

Salvage value of the new machine at
the end of its life   = Rs. 15,000
Annual operation and maintenance cost = Rs. 35,000
Buyback price of the existing machine   = Rs. 8,000

Suggest the best replacement option for the company using the annual equivalent cost method of comparison by assuming 10 per cent interest rate, compounded annually.

20. A company receives two options for purchasing a copier machine for its office.

    Option 1:   Make a down payment of Rs. 30,000 and take delivery of the copier machine. The remaining money is to be paid in 24 equal monthly instalments of Rs. 4500 each.

    Option 2:   Make a full payment of Rs. 100,000 and take delivery of the copier machine.

    Suggest the best option for the company to buy the copier machine based on the annual equivalent method of comparison by assuming 15 per cent interest rate, compounded annually.

21. Find the best alternative using the annual equivalent method of comparison. Assume an interest rate of 10 per cent compounded annually.

Alternative	A	B	C
Initial cost (Rs.)	500,000	800,000	600,000
Annual receipt (Rs.)	200,000	150,000	120,000
Life (years)	10	10	10
Salvage value (Rs.)	100,000	50,000	30,000

22. Consider the following cash flow of a project:

Year	Cash flow
0	−10,000
1	3000
2	4500
3	6000
4	8500
5	5000

Find the rate of return of the project.

23. A person invests a sum of Rs. 200,000 in a business and receives equal net revenue of Rs. 50,000 for the next 10 years. At the end of the tenth year, the salvage value of the business is Rs. 25,000. Find the rate of return of the business.

24. A company is in the process of selecting the best alternative among the following three mutually exclusive alternatives:

Alternative	Initial investment (Rs.)	Annual revenue (Rs.)	Life (Years)
A_1	Rs. 500,000	100,000	10
A_2	Rs. 800,000	140,000	10
A_3	Rs. 300,000	70,000	10

Find the best alternative based on the rate of return method of comparison.

25. A shipping firm is considering the purchase of a materials handling system for unloading ships at a dock. The firm has reduced its choice to three different systems, all of which are expected to provide the same unloading speed. The initial costs and the operating costs estimated for each system are tabulated here.

System	Initial cost	Annual operating expenses
S_1	Rs. 650,000	Rs. 91,810
S_2	Rs. 780,000	Rs. 52,600
S_3	Rs. 750,000	Rs. 68,417

The life of each system is estimated to be five years and the firm's minimum attractive rate of return is 15 per cent. If the firm must select one of the materials handling systems, which one is the most desirable?

26. A firm has identified three mutually exclusive alternatives. The life of all three alternatives is estimated to be five years. The minimum attractive rate of return is 12 per cent. Find the best alternative based on the rate of return method.

Alternative	Initial investment (Rs.)	Annual income (Rs.)
A_1	300,000	50,000
A_2	380,000	70,000
A_3	360,000	100,000

27. An automobile company is planning to buy a robot for its forging unit. It has identified two different companies for the supply of the robot. The details of cost and incremental revenue of using robots are summarized in the following tabular representation.

	Brand	
	Speedex	**Giant**
Initial cost (Rs.)	500,000	900,000
Annual incremental revenue (Rs.)	80,000	250,000
Life (years)	4	4
Life-end slavage value (Rs.)	40,000	60,000

The minimum attractive return for the company is 10 per cent. Suggest the best brand of robot to the company based on the rate of return method.

28. A bank introduces two different investment schemes whose details are as follows:

	Alpha bank	**Beta bank**
Deposit amount (Rs.)	100,000	200,000
Period of deposit (years)	5 years	3 years
Maturity amount (Rs.)	300,000	450,000

Find the best investment alternative from the investor's point of view.

29. A company is planning for its expansion programme which will take place after five years. The expansion requires an equal sum of Rs. 500,000 for consecutive three years. Gamma bank has recently introduced a scheme in this line. If the company invests Rs. 700,000 now with this bank, it will make equal repayments of Rs. 500,000 for three consecutive years starting from the end of the fifth year from now. The minimum attractive rate of return for the company is 12 per cent. Suggest whether the company should invest with Gamma Bank for its expansion programme.

30. Consider the following table which summarizes the data of two alternatives:

	First cost	Annual return	Life
Alternative 1	Rs. 500,000	Rs. 150,000	10 years
Alternative 2	Rs. 800,000	Rs. 250,000	10 years

Find the best alternative based on the rate of return method of comparison.

31. A company is planning to expand its present business activity. It has two alternatives for the expansion programme and the corresponding cash flows are given in the tabular representation below. Each alternative has a life of five years and a negligible salvage value. The minimum attractive rate of return for the company is 15 per cent. Suggest the best alternative to the company.

	Initial investment (Rs.)	Yearly revenue (Rs.)
Alternative 1	450,000	150,000
Alternative 2	750,000	250,000

32. A governmental agency is considering four independent projects, each having 30-year projected useful lives. The current budget for this agency allows not more than 35,000,000 to be spent, in terms of initial investment, and the nominal interest rate 10 per cent per year. Using the BC ratio method, which of the projects shown below should be selected?

Project	Initial investment (Rs.)	Annual cost (Rs.)	Annual benefit (Rs.)
A	10,000,000	1,250,000	2,250,000
B	30,000,000	4,500,000	7,000,000
C	20,000,000	750,000	2,250,000
D	15,000,000	1,450,000	5,050,000

33. Five independent projects are available to funding by a certain public agency. The following tabulation shows the equivalent annual benefits and cost for each.

Project	Annual benefit (Rs.)	Annual cost (Rs.)
A	2,800,000	3,000,000
B	8,600,000	6,200,000
C	7,400,000	4,800,000
D	3,600,000	3,800,000
E	6,600,000	5,400,000

(a) Assume that the projects are of the types of which the benefits can be determined with considerable certainty and that the agency is willing to invest money as long as the BC ratio is least. Which alternative should be selected?
(b) What is the rank ordering of projects from best to worst?
(c) If the projects involved have intangible benefits that require considerable judgement in assigning their values, would your recommendation be affected?

34. Two projects from each of the four departments have been submitted for evaluation and they are mutually exclusive. Associated data are as follows.

Department	Project	Benefit (Rs.)	Cost (Rs.)
A	A1	200,000	80,000
	A2	110,000	90,000
B	B1	80,000	50,000
	B2	70,000	60,000
C	C1	260,000	200,000
	C2	284,000	220,000
D	D1	120,000	70,000
	D2	1,022,000	80,000

(a) Which project should be funded according to the BC ratio criterion if one project must be selected from each department?
(b) Which project should be funded if only Rs. 300,000 is available?

35. The Orissa government is planning a hydro-electric project for a river basin. In addition to the production of electric power, this project will provide flood control, irrigation and recreation benefits. The estimated benefits and costs that are expected to considerations are as follows:

	A (Rs.)	B (Rs.)	C (Rs.)
Initial cost	20,000,000	30,000,000	50,000,000
Annual benefits and costs power sales	2,000,000	1,200,000	1,800,000
Flood cost savings	200,000	350,000	400,000
Irrigation benefits	350,000	450,000	800,000
Revision benefits	100,000	200,000	950,000
Operating and maintenance costs	200,000	250,000	850,000

The interest rate is 5 per cent and the life of each project is estimated at 50 years.
(a) Using incremental benefit-cost analysis, determine which project should be selected.
(b) Calculate the benefit-cost ratio for each alternative. Is the best alternative selected of the alternative with the maximum benefit-cost ratio?
(c) If the interest rate is 8 per cent, which alternative will be chosen?

CHAPTER 7

Depreciation Analysis

7.1 INTRODUCTION

Depreciation is the decrease in the value of physical properties with the passage of time and use. Most assets, e.g. production equipment gradually become less valuable because of wear and tear or as they age. This lessening in value of machineries is recognized in accounting practices as operating expense. Instead of charging the full purchase price of a new asset as one time expense, in the accounting records the outlay is spread over the life of the asset. Annual depreciation deductions are intended to match the yearly fraction of value used by an asset in the production of income over the asset's actual economic life. However, the actual amount of depreciation can never be established until the asset is retired from service.

Depreciation can be defined in three senses: *physical depreciation*, which is caused due to physical decay; *economic depreciation*, which is the loss of value of an asset due to outdated technology, and *accounting depreciation*, which is estimated value of fall in the worth of an asset. In accounting, depreciation charge is included in the cost of production of the asset. Depreciation is a permanent, continuing and gradual shrinkage in the book value of a fixed asset.

7.2 CAUSES OF DEPRECIATION

An asset's value gets depreciated for several reasons.

Physical depreciation

Depreciation resulting because of physical impairment of an asset is known as *physical depreciation*. This type of depreciation results in the lowering of the ability of a physical asset to render its intended service. The primary causes of physical depreciation are: (a) deterioration due to action of elements including corrosion of pipes, rotting of timbers, chemical decomposition and so on, (b) wear and tear charges, (c) and physical decay.

Functional depreciation

Functional depreciation results not from deterioration in the asset's ability to serve its intended purpose, but from a change in the demand for the services it can render. The demand for the services of an asset may change. It may be more profitable to use a more efficient unit. Thus, there is no longer any work for the old asset to do, or the required work exceeds its capacity.

Technological depreciation

Due to advancements in technology, old technology becomes outdated and loses its value overtime Obsolescence of an assest also results from the invention of another asset that is sufficiently superior and which makes it uneconomical to continue using the former. An asset also becomes obsolete when it is no longer needed.

Depreciation due to accident

Sometimes due to accident or sudden failure, the asset loses its technological characteristic inherent in it.

Depreciation due to depletion

Consumption of exhaustible natural resources to produce a product or service is termed as depletion. For example, the removal of oil, timber, rock or minerals from a site decreases the value of the holding. This decrease leads to a proportionate reduction in earnings derived from the resource.

Monetary depreciation

A change in the price level also decreases the value of the owned assets. If prices rise during the life of an asset, then the comparable replacement becomes more expensive. This means that the capital recovered will be insufficient to provide an adequate substitute for the worn-out asset.

Depreciation due to time factor

There are some assets which lose their values after a particular time period. Particularly, the assets having lease, copyrights and patent rights lose their value after the expiration of the time limit.

Depreciation due to deferred maintenance

Sometimes the loss of value of an asset begins very quickly due to deferred maintenance. If proper materials are not used or instructions to operate the machine are not properly followed, the loss of value starts rather quickly.

7.3 DEPRECIABLE PROPERTY

Before discussing the different methods involved in the calculation of depreciation, we should have sufficient knowledge about depreciable property. It is that property which can be amortized or depreciated. Depreciable property may be tangible or intangible. Tangible property is any property that can be seen or touched. Intangible property is that which does not exist as a physical thing but still has values. Example copyrights and patent rights. Depreciable tangible property is of two types: (i) *real* and (ii) *personal*. Personal property is not real estate and includes machinery and equipment. Real property is land and anything that is built on it. Land is never depreciable.

A property is depreciable in the following cases:

1. The property must be used in business or to produce income.
2. It must be something that wears out, decays, deteriorates, becomes obsolete, or loses value from natural causes.
3. The property must have determinable life and that life must be longer than one year.

In general, if a property does not fulfill the above conditions, cannot be regarded as depreciable property.

7.4 DEPRECIATION METHODS

Various depreciation methods have evolved from time to time. However, there are three basic methods for understanding the various calculations of depreciation schedules that are presently in effect. It is first necessary to become acquainted with the three methods on which the current schedules are based. Some current depreciation schedules are based on Straight Line Depreciation (SLD) while others are based on a combination of straight line depreciation and declining balance depreciation.

Before discussing the basic methods and other methods of depreciation, we should know some additional terms for a clear understanding of the problem.

P = Purchase price (unadjusted basis) of an asset. This is the initial cost of procuring an asset (purchase price + sales taxes) including transportation expenses.

S = Salvage value or future value at the end of asset's life. It is the expected selling price of a property when the asset can no longer be used by its owner.

N = Useful (tax) life of asset. The expected period of time that a property will be used in a trade, business or to produce income.

n = Number of years of depreciation.

$Dt(n)$ = Annual depreciation charges.

$Bt(n)$ = Book value shown on accounting records at the end of the year. It is the original cost, basis of the property, including any adjustment.

7.4.1 Straight Line Depreciation Method

The straight line depreciation method is the most widely used and simplest method for the calculation of depreciation. It assumes that the value of an asset decreases at a constant rate. Thus, if an asset has an initial cost of Rs. 5000 and an estimated salvage value of Rs. 500, then the total depreciation and over its life will be Rs. 4500. If the estimated life is five years, the depreciation per year will be $4500/5 = 900$.

The general expression for calculation of depreciation and book value may be developed for the straight line depreciation method. The depreciation in any year is $Dt = (P - F)/n$. See Table 7.1.

Table 7.1   General Expression for the Straight Line Depreciation Method

End of year	Depreciation charge	Book value at the end of year
0	–	P
1	$\dfrac{P-F}{n}$	$P - \left(\dfrac{P-F}{n}\right)$
2	$\dfrac{P-F}{n}$	$P - 2\left(\dfrac{P-F}{n}\right)$
3	$\dfrac{P-F}{n}$	$P - 3\left(\dfrac{P-F}{n}\right)$
N	$\dfrac{P-F}{n}$	$P - t\left(\dfrac{P-F}{n}\right)$
N	$\dfrac{P-F}{n}$	$P - n\left(\dfrac{P-F}{n}\right)$

The book value is $Bt = P = t[(P - F)/n]$ and the depreciation rate per year is $1/n$.

EXAMPLE 7.1

From the following data, find out

1. the depreciation charge during year 1;
2. the depreciation charge during year 2;
3. the depreciation reserve accumulated by the end of year 3; and
4. the book value at the end of year 3.

Initial cost of the asset = Rs. 5000
Life time   = 5 years
Salvage value   = 0
The cost of capital 5 per cent

Solution

1. and 2. In the case of straight line depreciation method, as the depreciation charge is constant, the depreciation charges for year 1 and 2 are also constant.

$$Dt(1) = Dt(2) = \frac{P - F}{n} = \frac{5000}{5} = 1000 \text{ per year}$$

3. The depreciation reserve at the end of the third year is the sum of the annual depreciation charges for the first three years and is equal to $3(1000) =$ Rs. 3000
4. The book value at the end of the third year is $= 5000 - 3(5000/5) = 2000$

$$Bt(3) = 5000 - 3000 = \text{Rs. } 2000$$

7.4.2 Declining Balance Method

The value of an asset diminishes at a decreasing rate. The declining balance depreciation assumes that an asset decreases in value—faster initially rather than in the latter portion of its service life. The book value at the end of the life of the asset may not be exactly equal to the salvage value of the asset.

For example: First cost = Rs. 5000, salvage value = Rs. 1000
Life of the asset five year, depreciation rate 30 per cent per year. See Table 7.2.

Table 7.2 Declining Balance Method

End of year	Depreciation charge during year	Book value at the end of year (Rs.)
0	–	5000
1	(0.30) (50,000) = 1500	3500
2	(0.30) (3500) = 1050	2450
3	(0.30) (2450) = 735	1715
4	(0.30) (17, 115) = 515	1200
5	(0.30) (1200) = 360	840

For a depreciation rate (a) the general relationship expressing the depreciation charge in any year for declining balance depreciation is

$$D_{(t)} = aBV_{(t-1)}$$

We know, book value

$$BV_{(t)} = B_{t-1} - D_{(t)}$$

Therefore, the declining balance depreciation is

$$B_{(t)} = B_{t-1} - aB_{t-1}$$

Using this recursive expression, we can determine the general expression for the depreciation charge and the book value for any point of time. These calculations are shown in Table 7.3.

$$D_{(t)} = a(1 - a)^{t-1}P$$

and the book value

$$BV_{(t)} = (1 - R)P$$

$$BV_{(t)} = P(1 - a)^t$$

Table 7.3   General Expression for the Declining Balance Method of Depreciation

End of year	Depreciation charge during the year	Book value at the end of year
0	–	P
1	$a \times B_0 = a(P)$	$(1 - a)B_0 = (1 - a)P$
2	$a \times B_1 = a(1 - R)P$	$(1 - a)B_1 = (1 - a)^2P$
3	$a \times B_2 = a(1 - R)^2P$	$(1 - a)B_2 = (1 - a)^3P$
T	$a \times B_{t-1} = a(1 - R)^{t-1}P$	$(1 - a)B_{t-1} = (1 - a)^tP$
N	$a \times B_{t-1} = a(1 - R)^{n-1}P$	$(1 - a)B_{n-1} = (1 - a)^nP$

If the declining balance method of depreciation is used for income tax purposes, then the maximum rate that may be used is double the straight line rate which would be allowed to a particular asset, a group of assets being depreciated. Thus, for an asset with an estimated life of N years, the maximum rate that may be used with this method is $R = 2/N$. Many firms and individuals choose to depreciate their assets using declining balance depreciation with the maximum allowable rate. Such a depreciation method is commonly known as the *double declining balance* (DDB) *method of depreciation.*

EXAMPLE 7.2

Initial cost = 5000, N = 5 years, S = 0. Find $Dt(1)$, $Dt(2)$ depreciation reserve at the end of year 3, and $Bt(3)$.

1. Given that depreciation rate max = $a = (2/N) = 2/5 = 0.4$

$$D(1) = [Bt(0)](0.4)$$

$$Dt(1) = 5000(0.4) = 2000$$

2. $Dt(2) = [Bt(1)](0.4)$

$$(5000 - 2000)(0.4) = 1200$$

3. The depreciation reserve at the end of year 3 is

$$Dt(1) + Dt(2) + [Bt(2)(0.4)]$$

$$2000 + 1200 + 720 = 3920$$

4.
$$Bt(3) = P - \text{Depreciation reserve}$$
$$5000 - 3920 = 1080$$

or

$$Bt(3) = P(1 - R)^3$$
$$= 5000(1 - 0.4)^3$$
$$= 5000(0.6)^3 = 1080$$

Declining balance to straight line depreciation

A difficulty may arise with the use of declining balance depreciation because in the above example the salvage value is zero. After the end of the life time or at the end of year 5, we find that

$$Bt_{(5)} = P(1 - R)^N = 5000(0.6)^5 = 388.88$$

It is not uncommon for the book value calculated by double declining balance depreciation to exceed the asset's value at the end of its life. This situation always occurs when $S = 0$. So it is allowable under the tax law to depreciate an asset over the early portion of its life using declining balance and then switch to straight line depreciation for the remainder of the asset's life.

$$\text{Declining balance depreciation} < \left(\begin{array}{c} \text{Straight line depreciation} \\ \text{On undepriciated balance} \end{array} \right)$$

EXAMPLE 7.3

Switch from double declining balance to straight line depreciation (see Table 7.4). An asset has first a cost of 5000, a five year useful life and no salvage value. Determine an accelerated depreciation schedule in $Bt(N) = 0$.

Table 7.4 Double Declining to Straight Line Depreciation

End of year	DDB charges	Book value with DDB	SL depreciation on undepreciated balance	Book value DDB SL
0		5000		5000
1	2000	3000	5000/5 = 1000	3000
2	1200	1800	3000/4 = 750	18,000
3	720	1080	1800/3 = 600	1080
4	432	648	1080/2 = 540	540
5	259.2	388.8	540	0

Apply the double declining balance method as was done for Rs. 5000 and N values. We know book value $Bt(5) = 388.8$ is higher than the zero salvage value.

Therefore, to make the book value zero, we have to switch to straight line method.

At the end of year 2, the book value resulting from DDB depreciation is 1800 which is equal the undepreciated balance because $S = 0$. Then, the SL charges for the last three years would be $= (1800 - 0)/3 = 600$. Since this annual charge is less than DDB charge for 3 (720), the accelerated depreciation is continued another year. Thus, $Bt(3) = 1080$ and the SL depreciation charge for each of the last two years is $1080/2 = 540$. This is larger than the DDB depreciation charge for the year four (432) and signals the time to switch.

7.4.3 Modified Accelerated Cost Recovery System

Modified Accelerated Cost Recovery System (MACRS) was created by Tax Reform Act of 1986. It consists of two systems to depreciate property. The primary system is called *General Depreciated System* (GDS) while the secondary system is *Alternative Depreciation System* (ADS).

Most tangible depreciation property is handled by MACRS (GDS) system because it permits the use of declining balance with switching to the straight line method over a shorter recovery period.

Property classes

To determine the depreciation schedule appropriate for depreciable property, MACRS has defined six recovery period classes for personal property and two classes for real property.

Three year property includes special material handling devices and special tools for manufacturing.

Class life ≤ four years.

Depreciation method: 200 per cent declining balance switching to straight line with half-year convention.

Five year property includes automobiles, legal, and heavy trucks, computers, copiers, semiconductor, etc.

4 year ≤ class life < 10 year

Depreciation method: 200 per cent declining balance switching to straight line with half year convention.

Seven year property includes those not assigned to another class, such as office furnitures, fixtures.

10 year ≤class life < 16 years

Depreciation method: 200 per cent declining balance switching to straight line with half-year convention.

Ten year property class includes assets used in petroleum refining, manufacturing of castings, forging.

16 years ≤ class life < 20 years

Depreciation method: 200 per cent declining balance switching to straight line with a half-year convention.

Fifteen year property includes service station buildings, telephone distribution equipment, and municipal water and sewage treatment plants.

20 years ≤ class life < 25 years

Depreciation method: 150 per cent declining balance switching to straight line with half-year convention.

Twenty year property includes buildings and municipal water.

25 years ≤ class life

Depreciation Method: 150 per cent declining balance switching to straight line with half year convention.

For real property, the classes are described as follows. Residential property includes apartment buildings and rental houses.

Depreciation method: Straight line depreciation with half-year convention over 27.5 years. Non-residential property includes office buildings, warehouses, manufacturing facilities, refineries roads, etc.

Depreciation method: Straight line depreciation with half-year convention as 39 years.

Methods for the calculation of MACRS dealing balance depreciation

The Internal Revenue Service prescribes the following order of computation:

1. Divide the appropriate percentage (either 200 or 150 per cent) by the number of years in the recovery period.
2. Determine the annual MACRS declining balance rate by rounding the result.
3. Divide the result from step 2 by two to convert the percentage to the half-year convention for the first year of services.
4. Calculate the percentage for the second year of service by multiplying the remaining basis (the current book value) by the base rate just calculated in step 2.
5. Continue the procedure until a switch to the straight line method is allowed in order to reach the terminal salvage value. Practically, the switching from declining balance to straight line depreciation occurs when the straight line depreciation charge on the undepreciated portion of an asset value exceeds the declining balance allowance.

Since the mid-year convention is used in MACRS, the remaining life at the end of the year is determined by $N - K + 0.5$ for $K = 1, 2 \ldots N$ the straight line depreciation for the remaining year is calculated as $D(k) = BV(k)/N - k + 0.5)$.

EXAMPLE 7.4

Switch from declining balance to straight line depreciation in MACRS. The value of the asset is 10,000. The expected salvage value = 0. It is a seven year property.

Determine the appropriate depreciation table.

Solution

As it is a seven year property, it should be discounted at 200%/7. The base is 28.57.
The first year deduction will be $10,000/[28.5]/2] = 14.29$
After the first year, $Bt(1) = 10,000 - 1429 = 8571$
The second year depreciation amount will be $8571 \times 28.57\% = 2449$
Bt is $8571 - 2449 = 6122$
Book value (start of year 2) = Book value (end of year 1)
In the case of MACRS depreciation, the straight line deduction will be made by the formula

$$Dt(1) = \frac{Bt(0)}{N - k + 0.5} = \frac{10,000}{7 - 0 + 0.5} = 1333$$

$$Dt(1) = \frac{Bt(1)}{N - k + 0.5} = \frac{10,000}{7 - 1 + 0.5} = 1319$$

See Table 7.5.

Table 7.5   MACRS to Straight Line

End of year	Declining balance deduction (Rs.)	Straight line deduction (Rs.)	Book value optimal deduction (Rs.)	Depreciation charge stated as percentage of original basis
0			10,000	
1	1429	1333	8571	14.29
2	2429	1319	6122	24.29
3	1749	1113	4373	17.49
4	1249	972	3124	12.49
5	893	893	2231	8.93
6	637	893	1338	8.93
7	455	893	445	8.93
8	325	445	0	4.45

In the above table, upto fourth year the straight line depreciation is less than the declining balance deduction. In the fifth year, the straight line deduction is equal to declining balance deduction from that year we will switch over to straight line deduction. As a result at last the book value will be zero. In the last column, the depreciation charge is stated as the percentage of the asset in different years. From this percentage table, we can conveniently calculate directly the MACRS depreciation in different year. For convenience MACRS depreciation table is presented in Table 7.6.

Table 7.6   MACRS Depreciation Table

Year	Category of property					
	3 years	5 years	7 years	10 years	15 years	20 years
1	33.33	20.00	14.29	10.00	5.00	3.750
2	44.45	32.00	24.49	18.00	9.50	7.219
3	14.81	19.20	17.49	14.40	8.55	6.677
4	7.41	11.52	12.49	11.52	77.70	6.177
5		11.52	8.93	9.22	6.93	5.713
6		5.76	8.92	7.37	6.23	5.285
7			8.93	6.55	5.90	4.888
8			4.46	6.55	5.90	4.522
9				6.56	5.91	4.462
10				6.55	5.90	4.461
11				3.28	5.91	4.462
12					5.90	4.461
13					5.91	4.462
14					2.95	4.461
15						4.462
16						4.461

(Contd.)

Table 7.6 MACRS Depreciation Table (Contd.)

Table 7.6 MACRS Depreciation Table (Contd.)

	Category of property					
Year	3 years	5 years	7 years	10 years	15 years	20 years
17						4.462
18						4.461
19						462
20						9.61
21						2.231

7.5 SUM OF THE YEARS-DIGIT METHOD

To compute the depreciation deduction by Sum of the Years-Digit (SYD) method, the digits corresponding to the number for each permissible year of life are first listed in the reverse order. The sum of these digits is then determined. The depreciation factor for any year is a number from the reverse-ordered listing for that year divided by the sum of the digits. For example, for a property having a depreciable (useful) life of five years, SYD depreciate factors are given in Table 7.7.

Table 7.7 Sum of the Years-Digit Depreciation on Factor

Year	No. of the year in revenue order	SYD depreciation factor
1	5	$\dfrac{5}{15}$
2	4	$\dfrac{4}{5}$
3	3	$\dfrac{3}{15}$
4	2	$\dfrac{2}{15}$
5	1	$\dfrac{1}{15}$

The depreciation for any year is the product of SYD depreciation factor for that year, and the difference between the cost basis (B) and the estimated final SV. The general expression for the annual cost of depreciation for any year k, when N equals the depreciable life of an asset is

$$dk = Bv - SV_N \left[\frac{2(N - k + 1)}{N(N + 1)} \right]$$

The book value at the end of the year k is

$$BV_n = B - \left[\frac{2(B - SV_N)}{N} \right] + \left[\frac{(B - SV_N)}{N(N + 1)} \right] k (k + 1)$$

and the cumulative depreciation through k year is, simply,

$$dk = B - BV_k$$

EXAMPLE 7.5

A new electric saw for cutting small pieces of lumber in a lumber furniture manufacturing plant has a cost basis of 4000 and a 10-year depreciable life. The estimates *SV* of the saw is zero at the end of 10 years. Determine the annual depreciation amount of fourth year, using sum of digits method.

$$d_4 = 4000 \left[\frac{2(10-4)+1}{10(10+1)} \right] = 509.09$$

$$BV_4 = 4000 \left[\frac{2(4000)}{10} \right] 4 + \left[\frac{4000}{10(1)} \right] 4.5 = 1527.27$$

7.6 AFTER TAX ECONOMIC COMPARISONS

Till now in chapter 4–6, we have compared different alternatives by PW, FW, EAW, and IRR methods. In every economic analysis, the comparison was made by not taking tax into consideration. But we know most of the firms pay different types of taxes. One of the most important taxes is income tax which is levied on the net income of a person. But tax most of the time influences production decision and other decisions. In this section, we will compare cash flow after tax.

In many situations, before tax analysis provides adequate solutions. When the alternatives being compared are to satisfy a required function and are affected identically by taxes, the before-tax comparison gives the proper preference. Evaluation of public projects do not take taxes into consideration.

So tax effects occasionally cause the preference to switch among alternatives between before and after tax evaluations.

A simple adjustment of the rate of return calculated without regard for taxes gives a reasonable approximation to the after tax rate of return.

IRR after tax = IRR before tax (1 – Effective income tax rate)

For example, the after tax rate of return resulting from a before tax IRR of 10 per cent and an effective income tax rate of 40 per cent would be

IRR after tax = 0.10 (1 – 0.40) = 6%.

Before going for after tax comparison, we have to know how after tax cash flow tables are prepared. There are different column headings and column numbers for this purpose. See Table 7.8.

Table 7.8 After Tax Cash Flow Table

Column heading	Column number	Arithmetic computation in column
Calendar year		
Investment year	1	
Before tax operating cash flow	2	
Book value before depreciation	3	
MACRS depreciation rate	4	
Depreciation charge	5	4 × original basis
Book value after depreciation	6	(3) – (5)

(Contd.)

Table 7.8 After Tax Cash Flow Table (Contd.)

Column heading	Column number	Arithmetic computation in column
Cash flow for debt	7	
Cash flow for debt interest	8	
Taxable income	9	(2) − (5) − (8)
Cash flow for taxes	10	Tax rate × (9)
After tax cash flow	11	(2) − (7) − (10)

Thus, the after tax comparison can be made by many comparison methods, such as PW, EAW or IRR.

REVIEW QUESTIONS

1.   A truck costs 40,000 and had an estimated useful life of eight years and estimated salvage value of Rs. 4000. How much depreciation should be allocated as the new truck in each year and what is the under priceable value of the truck at the end of the fifth year, assuming the use of basic straight line depreciation?

2.   An asset was purchased for Rs. 4800. It is being depreciated in accordance with the basic straight line method for an estimated total life of 25 years and salvage value of Rs. 800. What is the difference in its book value after 10 years and the book value that would have resulted if the basic declining balance depreciation at a rate of 10 per cent had been applied for 10 years?

3.   A central air conditioning unit was purchased for Rs. 350,000 and had an expected life of 10 years. The salvage value for the unit at that time was expected to be 40,000. What will be the book value at the end of two years for the basic depreciation methods of
   (a) Straight line,
   (b) Double declining balance?

4.   An oil refinery has added a new computer to control one of its refinery units. For five-year property, what would be the depreciation percentage for the fourth year after the placement of the computer in source when using MACRS?

5.   A truck was purchased on January 1, 1994, costs Rs. 40,000 and has a MACRS tax life of five years, with an estimated salvage value of Rs. 10,000. Determine the depreciation charge for 1995 and the book value at the end of that year using the following:
   (a) MACRS straight line depreciation
   (b) MACRS accelerated depreciation.

6.   An asset for drilling was purchased and placed in service by a petroleum production company. Its cost is Rs. 50,000 and has an estimated salvage value of Rs. 12,000 at the end of an estimated useful life of 10 years. Compute the depreciation amount in the third year and the *BV* at the end of the fifth year life by each of these methods:
   (a) The straight line method
   (b) The SYD method
   (c) The 200 per cent declining balance method with switch over to straight line.

7.   A central air conditioning unit was installed in 1990 at an initial cost of Rs. 60,000 and was expected to have a salvage value of Rs. 5000 after and tax life of seven-years

(a) What amount has accumulated in MACRS straight line depreciation reserve at the end of 1993?

(b) Using MACRS accelerated depreciation, determine the book value at the end of 1994.

8. A proposed investment in a depreciable income producing an asset is expected to produce an annual net savings of Rs. 20,000. The asset has a first cost of Rs. 60,000 and estimated economic life of eight years with no salvage value. The asset qualified as a five year MACRS property, and the company has an effective income tax rate of 40 per cent and the MARR is 17 per cent.

(a) Find out the before tax rate of return for the asset described in the basic data.

(b) Determine the approximate after tax IRR from the before tax figure.

(c) Compute the after tax rate of return when MACRS based accelerate depreciation for a five-year property is applied.

CHAPTER 8

Break-Even Analysis

8.1 INTRODUCTION

Profits are the bases on which firm's health can be analysed. The sign of a healthy business is making profits consistently despite the various risks it has to face. Since profits are vital, they cannot be left to be earned by chance or luck. Proper planning and control of profits is therefore, of utmost importance for a company. Unless a firm is prepared to face the uncertainties of business, its profits would be left to chance. Hence, the firm has to plan for profits. In this regard, a thorough understanding of the relationship between cost, volume and price becomes extremely important to managers. Break-even analysis is the most important method for determining the cost-volume-profit relationship. It is also known as *cost-volume-profit* (CVP) analysis.

Break-even analysis involves the study of revenues and costs of a firm in relation to its volume of sales. It specifically involves determination of that volume at which the firm's cost and revenues will be equal. Break-even analysis captures the relation of fixed cost, variable cost, the value of output, sales mix prices, etc. to the profitability of the company.

8.1.1 Break-Even Point

Break-Even Point (BEP) is defined as that point of activity (sales volume) at which the total revenues equal the total costs, and the net income is zero. It is the point of zero profit. This is also known as *no profit no loss point*. BEP is, therefore, a point where losses cease to occur while profits have not yet begun. In case the firm produces and sells less than what is suggested by the break-even point, it would incur losses. If it produces and sells more than the level suggested by the break-even point, it would make profits. The break-even point, thus, is one indicator of the minimum level of production/ sales which the company has to achieve in order to be economically viable. It can be represented either graphically or algebraically.

8.1.2 Determination of Break-Even Point

The break-even point can be determined either in terms of physical units (products) to be produced or in terms of money (sales value in rupees). Before we get into the break-even analysis, Let us define the following symbols:

Q = Physical output of the firm

Q_{BEP} = Output at BEP

BEP   = Break-even point

P = Price per unit or average revenue

TR = Total revenue = $P \times Q$

TFC = Total fixed cost

TVC = Total variable cost = $Q \times AVC$

TC = Total cost = $TFC + TVC$

AFC = Average fixed cost (or fixed cost per unit)

AVC = Average variable cost (or variable cost per unit)

AC = Average cost = $AVC + AFC$

8.1.3 Break-Even Point in Terms of Quantity

Before deriving a formula for the BEP, we will first dfine it. We know that at BEP, $TR = TC$. Applying $TR = P \times Q_{BEP}$ and $TC = TFC + TVC$, we get

$$P \times Q_{BEP} = TFC + TVC$$
$$= TFC + (Q_{BEP} \times AVC) \text{ (since } TVC = Q_{BEP} \times AVC)$$

(We use Q_{BEP} because we are interested in the quantity of output at BEP.)

Therefore $$P \times Q_{BEP} = TFC + Q_{BEP} \times AVC$$

$$P \times Q_{BEP} - Q_{BEP} \times AVC = TFC$$

Therefore $$Q_{BEP}(P - AVC) = TFC$$

Thus $$Q_{BEP} = \frac{TFC}{P - AVC} = \frac{TFC}{ACM}$$

Hence, the break-even quantity will be

$$Q_{BEP} = \frac{\text{Total fixed cost}}{\text{Average contribution margin}}$$

or in other words,

$$Q_{BEP} = \frac{\text{Total fixed cost}}{\text{Contribution margin per unit}}$$

Derived from this process Q_{BEP} is the quantity to be produced by a firm in order to have no loss or no gain. This method is convenient for a single product firm. Q_{BEP} or break-even volume or break-even quantity is the number of units of a product which must be sold so that the firm earns enough revenue just to cover all its expenses—both fixed and variable. BEP is reached when sufficient numbers of units have been sold so that the total contribution margin of the units sold ($Q_{BEP} \times ACM$) is equal to the total fixed cost (TFC).

Thus, the break-even quantity Q_{BEP} equals to

$$\frac{\text{Total fixed cost}}{\text{Average contribution margin}}$$

We illustrate this formula with the help of an example. Assume that a hotel can have a maximum of 1000 tourists accommodated in it at a time. The daily fare is Rs. 800. The variable cost per tourist is Rs. 100 while the fixed cost is Rs. 140,000. Now we have to find the break-even quantity of tourists (i.e. the number of tourists in the hotel to attain BEP). The number of tourists to break-even is calculated as

$$Q_{BEP} = \frac{TFC}{P - AVC}$$

Here in this problem, TFC = Rs. 140,000, P = Rs. 800, AVC = Rs. 100. Hence

$$Q_{BEP} = \frac{140,000}{800 - 100} = 200 \text{ tourists}$$

Thus, if 200 tourists pay Rs. 800 and stay, the hotel will achieve the BEP.

To check the results let us find if $TR = TC$ at BEP, i.e. Q_{BEP}.

$$TR \text{ at } Q_{BEP} = P \times Q_{BEP} = 800 \times 200 = \text{Rs. } 160,000$$

$$TC = TFC + Q_{BEP}(AVC)$$

$$= 140,000 + (200 \times 100)$$

$$= \text{Rs. } 160,000$$

Therefore, $TR = TC$ at the break-even point, Q_{BEP}.

8.1.4 Break-Even Point in Terms of Sales Value

We found that the break-even point in terms of quantity can be used by a single product firm. However, this cannot be applied to a multi-product firm. Here again the BEP would be the point where fixed cost is equal to the contribution margin (sales value − variable cost). The contribution margin is expressed as a ratio to sale.

Therefore,

$$BEP(S_{BEP}) = \frac{\text{Fixed cost}}{\text{Contribution margin ratio}}$$

$$S_{BEP} = \frac{[TFC/(P - AVC)]}{P}$$

(Since contribution = $P - AVC$, i.e. price − average variable cost is the contribution.)

$$S_{BEP} = \frac{TFC}{1 - (AVC/P)}$$

$$S_{BEP} = \frac{TFC}{1 - (TVC/TR)}$$

(Applying $P = (TR/Q)$ and $AVC = (TVC/Q)$ in the original S_{BEP} formula, we get this expression.)

Both the equations for S_{BEP} yield the same result. Applying this information in the hotel problem, we will attempt to find how much money the hotel should earn to break even.

In the problem, TFC = Rs. 140,000, P = Rs. 800, AVC = Rs. 100.

$$S_{BEP} = \frac{TFC}{1-(AVC/P)} = \frac{140,000}{1-(100/800)} = Rs.\,160,000$$

Our earlier BEP in terms of quantity, Q_{BEP} = 200 at price Rs. 800 will bring in a revenue of Rs. 160,000 (800 × 200) which is the same as the BEP in terms of money value, S_{BEP} = 160,000.

8.1.5 Break-Even Point as a Percentage of Capacity

The two previous procedures found the BEP in terms of physical units of output and sales value. The full capacity of a manufacturing facility (plant) is defined as the maximum possible volume attainable with the firm's existing fixed equipment, operating policies and practices. Here the break-even point is usually expressed as a percentage of full capacity. For example, if the full capacity of a firm is 1000 units and the BEP is 500 units, then the latter can be expressed as 50 per cent of full capacity. We denote the full capacity of the firm as Q_{max}. The break-even point in terms of percentage is found as follows:

$$Per\ cent\ BEP = \frac{TFC}{(P-AVC)Q_{max}} \times 100$$

Also

$$Per\ cent\ BEP = \frac{Q_{BEP}}{Q_{max}} \times 100$$

Applying the data given in section 8.1.4 in the above formula, we get

$$Per\ cent\ BEP = \frac{140,000}{(800-100)\times 1000} \times 100 = 20\%$$

In the previous case, we found that if 200 tourists (i.e. 20 per cent) stay in the hotel, then it will attain BEP which is consistent with this equation.

8.2 BREAK-EVEN CHART

The Break-even analysis is usually presented in the form of break-even charts. It helps the managers to visualize the profit and loss implications at different levels of sales. The chart shows the extent of profit or loss to the firm at different levels of activity. Figure 8.1 illustrates a typical break-even chart.

The output is shown on the *X*-axis, and the cost and the revenue on the *Y*-axis. The Total Revenue (*TR*) curve is shown as a straight line (linear) since it is assumed that the price is constant irrespective of the output. The total revenue curve, *TR* is drawn through the origin, which says that every unit of output contributes a constant amount to the total revenue, i.e. if there is no output, then the revenue is zero and when the output increases, the revenue also increases. The total cost curve originates from the *Y*-axis at the point where the fixed cost curve meets the *Y*-axis at point *P*. The total cost is the sum of fixed cost and variable cost. In Figure 8.1, the variable cost is shown as the difference (vertical distance) between the *TC* curve and the *TFC* curve, and the fixed cost is a horizontal line all along indicating a constant *TFC*, no matter what the output is. With the same logic in mind a variation of Figure 8.1 is given in Figure 8.2.

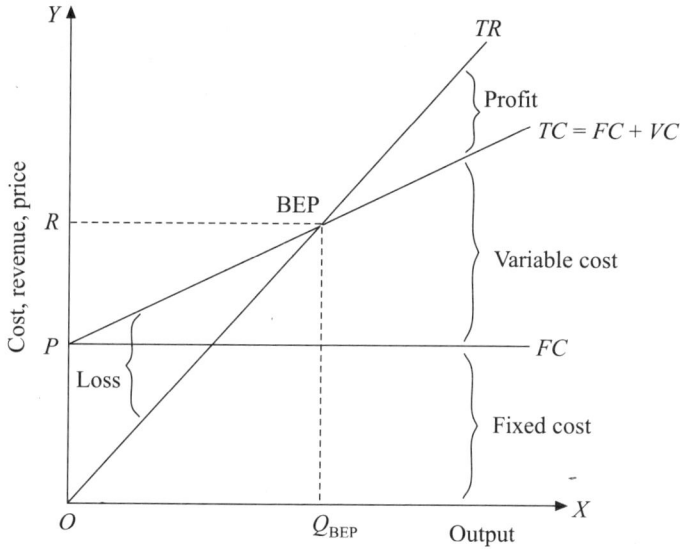

Figure 8.1 Break-even chart.

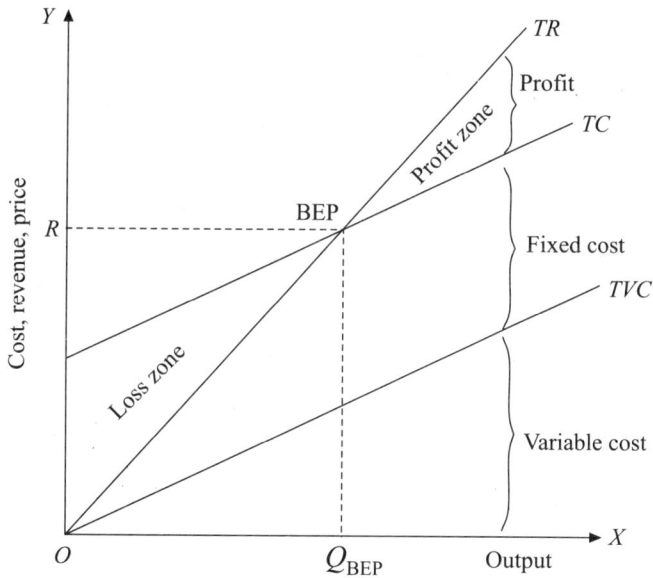

Figure 8.2 A variation of break-even chart.

The break-even point corresponds to the point of intersection of *TC* curve and *TR* curve in both the graphs. A perpendicular line to the *X*-axis from the BEP will give you break-even point in output units of the product. You will also note that below the BEP, the *TC* is greater than the *TR* and the firm is said to be in the loss zone, while above the BEP, the *TR* is greater than the *TC* and the firm is said to be in the profit zone.

8.3   BREAK-EVEN ANALYSIS ASSUMPTIONS

The following are the assumptions regarding break-even analysis:

1. The break-even analysis assumes that the costs are classified as fixed cost and variable cost, thus ignoring the semi-variable cost.
2. All revenues are perfectly variable with the physical volume of production. This assumption is not valid in all cases since price concessions may be possible for large customers.
3. The sales price of a product is assumed to be constant, thus giving linearity property to the *TR* curve.
4. It assumes constant rate of increase in variable cost.
5. The break-even analysis assumes that there will be no improvement in technology and efficiency.
6. The volume of sales and the volume of production are equal.
7. There is no change in the input price.
8. In the case of a multi-product firm, the product mix should be stable.

8.4   MANAGERIAL USES OF BREAK-EVEN ANALYSIS

To the manager or engineer of a firm, the utility of break-even analysis lies in the fact that it presents a microscopic picture of the profit structure of the business enterprise. The break-even analysis not only highlights the areas of economic strengths and weaknesses in a firm, but also sharpens the focus on certain leverages which can be operated upon to enhance its profitability. Contributions change constantly in a business setting. Through the break-even analysis, it is possible for a manager/engineer to examine the profit vulnerability of a business firm to the possible changes in the business conditions. For example, sales prospects, changes in cost structure. By the break-even analysis, it is possible to devise managerial actions to maintain and enhance the profitability of the firm. The break-even analysis can be used for the following purposes.

8.4.1   Safety Margin

The break-even chart can help the manager to get a quick idea about the profits generated at various levels of sales. But while deciding on the volume at which the firm would operate, apart from demand, the manager should also consider the 'safety margin' associated with the proposed volume. Safety margin refers to the extent to which a firm can afford a decline in sales before it starts incurring losses. The formula for determining the safety margin is

$$\text{Safety Margin} = \frac{(\text{Sales} - Q_{\text{BEP}}) \times 100}{\text{Sales}}$$

8.4.2   Volume Needed to Attain Target Profit

The break-even analysis can be utilized to determine the volume of sales necessary to achieve a target profit. The formula is

$$\text{Target Sales Volume} = \frac{\text{Fixed cost} + \text{Target profit}}{\text{Contribution margin unit}}$$

We know that Contribution Margin per unit = Selling price – Variable cost = 800 – 100 = 700.

Continuing with the previous example, if the desired profit is Rs. 6000, the target sales volume would be calculated as

$$\text{Target Sales Volume} = \frac{140,000 + 6000}{700} = 209 \text{ units}$$

That is 209 tourists should be accommodated to earn a profit of Rs. 6000.

8.4.3 Change in Price

The manager of a firm is often faced with a problem of whether to reduce the price of a product or not. Before deciding on this question, the manager must consider a number of points. A reduction in price leads to a reduction in the contribution margin. This means that the volume of sales will have to be increased even to maintain the previous level of profit. The higher the reduction in the contribution margin, the higher will be the increase in sales needed to ensure the previous profit. However, reduction in price may not always lead to a proportionate increase in the volume of sales which is often affected by elasticity of demand. Moreover, information about elasticity of demand may not be easily available. Assuming that the present conditions continue, the break-even analysis will help the manager to know the required volume of sales to maintain the previous level of profit. And on the basis of this knowledge and experience, it will be much easier for the management to analyse whether the required increase in sales will be feasible. The formula to determine the new volume of sales to maintain the same profit, given a reduction in price, is

$$Q_n = \frac{FC + P}{SP_n - VC}$$

where Q_n = New volume of sales, FC = Fixed cost, P = Profit, SP_n = New selling price, VC = Variable cost per unit (n denotes new).

Continuing with the same hotel example, if we propose a reduction of 10 per cent in price (from Rs. 800 to Rs. 720), the new sales volume needed to maintain the previous profit of Rs. 6000 would be

$$Q_n = \frac{140,000 + 6000}{920 - 100} = 236 \text{ tourists}$$

This would mean an increase of 27 tourists (from 209) or 13 per cent in sales. The manager can easily decide whether this increase is feasible or not. Alternatively, if a price increase is proposed, the question to be considered is by how much the sales volume can decline before it will wipe out the potentially profitable effect of this price increase.

8.4.4 Change in Costs

If variable cost changes

An increase in variable cost leads to a reduction in the contribution margin. Therefore, when increases in cost are expected or an unavoidable, a common question which arises is what total sales volume do we need to have to maintain our present profits without any increase in price. Alternativly, what price should be fixed for the product to maintain our present profit without any change in the sales volume. The formulas to determine the new quantity (Q_n) or the new selling price (SP_n) when there is a change in the variable cost, are

$$Q_n = \frac{FC + P}{SP_n - VC}$$

and

$$SP_n = SP + (VC_n - VC)$$

Thus in the hotel example, if the variable cost increases from Rs. 100 to Rs. 110 per unit, then

$$Q_n = \frac{140,000 + 6000}{800 - 110} = \frac{146,000}{690} = 212 \text{ tourists}$$

$$SP_n = 800 + (110 - 100) = \text{Rs. } 810$$

If fixed cost changes

An increase in the fixed cost of a firm may be caused either by external circumstances (e.g. an increase in machinery costs, taxes) or by a managerial decision (e.g. an increase in salaries). In either case, the effect is to raise the break-even point of the firm, assuming no change in price. Then the question that arises is what total sales volume do we need to maintain to have our present profits without any increase in price? Or in the alternative, what price should be set if there is no change in sales volume? The formula to determine the new quantity (Q_n) or the new price (SP_n), given a change in the fixed cost, would be

(a) $Q_n = Q + \dfrac{FC_n - FC}{SP - VC}$

(b) $SP_n = SP + \dfrac{FC_n - FC}{Q}$

8.5   LIMITATIONS OF BREAK-EVEN ANALYSIS

A few important limitations which one should keep in mind while using the break-even analysis are as follows:

1. Selling costs are especially difficult to handle in the break-even analysis. This is because the changes in selling costs are a cause and not a result of the changes in the output and sales. Besides, the relationship between output and selling expenses is unstable over time, rendering the projection of past relationship into the future inaccurate.
2. The break-even analysis is static in nature. It is based on the assumption of given relationship between costs and revenues, on the one hand, and input, on the other hand. Costs and revenues, however, may change over time making the projection based on past data wrong. As such the, break-even analysis is more useful in relatively stable and slow-moving situations rather than at volatile, erratic and widely changing ones.
3. When the break-even analysis is based on accounting data, which is usually the case, it may suffer from limitations of such data, e.g. neglect of imputed costs, arbitrary depreciation estimates, inappropriate allocation of overhead costs. Break-even analysis, therefore, can be sound and useful only if a firm maintains a good accounting system, and uses proper managerial accounting techniques and procedures.

4. Costs in a particular period may not be caused entirely by the output in that period. For example, maintenance expenses may be the result of past output or a preparation for future output. It may, therefore, be difficult to attribute them to a particular period.

5. The break-even analysis assumes that profits are a function of output ignoring the fact that they are also caused by other factors, such as technological change, improved management, changes in the scale of fixed factors of production.

6. A basic assumption in the break-even analysis is that the cost-revenue-volume relationship is linear. This is realistic only over narrow ranges of output.

7. The break-even analysis is not an effective tool for long-range use and its use should be restricted to the short run only. The analysis serves better if its use is limited to the budget period of a firm, which is usually the calendar year.

8. The scope and profile of interest included in the break-even analysis should be limited. If too many products, too many departments, or too many plants are taken together and graphed on a single break-even chart, then the performances, both good and bad, can easily be lost in the total picture of the group. However, getting useful information from the break-even chart for each brand separately can be quite different.

8.6 PROFIT-VOLUME (P/V) ANALYSIS

The profit-volume (P/V) or cost-volume-profit (CVP) analysis is the result of the attempts to apply the break-even analysis to the situations of a multi-product firm, where the break-even charts are constructed separately for different divisions or products of a firm. The individual division, department or the product is called a *sector*. The profit-volume graph will show the relationship of a firm's profit to its volume. The total profit or loss is measured on the *Y*-axis. The profit zone is above the *X*-axis and the loss zone is below the *X*-axis as shown in Figure 8.3. The volume is measured on the *X*-axis which is drawn at the point of 'zero profit'.

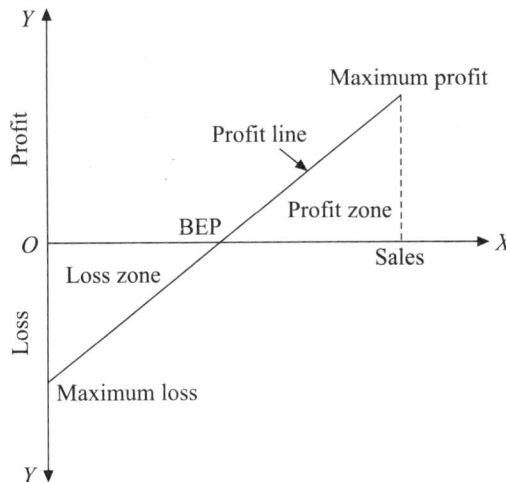

Figure 8.3 Profit-Volume analysis.

The maximum loss which occurs at zero sales volume is equal to the fixed cost and is shown below the *X*-axis, on the *Y*-axis. The maximum profit is earned when the firm works at full capacity and the maximum profit is shown on the *Y*-axis above the *X*-axis. The line joining both the points is called the profit volume line or *P/V line*. The usefulness of the graph lies in the fact that it shows at a glance the profit or loss earned by a firm by working at different levels of its capacity. The measurement of P/V ratio can be done through the following formulas.

1. P/V ratio $= \dfrac{\text{Sales} - \text{Variable cost}}{\text{Sales}} \times 100$

    $= \dfrac{\text{Contribution}}{\text{Sales}} \times 100$

    Therefore, Contribution $= P/V$ ratio $\times$ Sales

2. P/V ratio $= \dfrac{\text{Change in contribution}}{\text{Change in sales}}$

3. P/V ratio $= \dfrac{\text{Change in profit}}{\text{Change in sales}}$

4. P/V ratio $= \dfrac{\text{Profit}}{\text{Margin of safety ratio}}$

EXAMPLE 8.1

A shopkeeper plans to sell electrical switches. His purchase price of this switch is Rs 10 per piece. He can return the unsold switch to the wholesaler if the need may be. The shop is rented at Rs. 3000 which is payable in advance. The selling price of a switch is fixed at Rs. 15 per piece. Find the number of switches which must be sold to break even and also the break-even sales volume.

Solution

Break-Even Quantity,
$$Q_{\text{BEP}} = \frac{TFC}{P - AVC}$$

$$= \frac{3000}{15 - 10} = \frac{3000}{5} = 600 \text{ units}$$

Also the break-even sales volume,

$$S_{\text{BEP}} = \frac{TFC}{1 - (AVC/P)}$$

The result of break-even analysis and the sales volume selling price of the switch is Rs. 15, the break-even quantity with the price (i.e. Rs. 15 $\times$ 600 = Rs. 9000) gives us the volume.

EXAMPLE 8.2

A company's accounting department has the following data.

Sales	= Rs. 100,000
Fixed cost	= Rs. 300,000
Variable cost	= Rs. 50,000

With these given data, find the break-even point in terms of sales volume.

Solution

The break-even sales

$$S_{BEP} = \frac{TFC}{1 - (AVC/P)}$$

Since $TVC = AVC \times Q$ and Sales $= P \times Q$ we can say that
Now S_{BEP} can be rewritten as

$$\frac{TFC}{1 - (TVC/\text{Sales})} = \frac{300,000}{1 - (50,000/100,000)} = \frac{300,000}{0.5} = \text{Rs. } 600,000$$

EXAMPLE 8.3

A furniture manufacturer produces and sells cabinets, office tables and chairs. The various details regarding his business are given in the following tabular form.

Product	Selling price per unit (Rs.)	Variable cost per unit (Rs.)	% of rupee sales volume
File cabinet	1000	900	20
Office tables	500	400	30
Chairs	200	125	50

Capacity of the firm = Rs 150,000 of total sales volume
Annual fixed cost = Rs 20,000

Calculate (i) BEP_S, (ii) Profit if the firm works at 80 per cent of capacity.

Solution

The contribution towards fixed cost in each case is

1. File cabinet
   Rs. 1000 – Rs. 900 = Rs 100
2. Office tables
   Rs 500 – Rs 400 = Rs 100
3. Chairs
   Rs. 200 – Rs. 125 = Rs 75

Now these contributions are to be converted into percentages of sell prices, and the formula is

$$\frac{\text{Selling price} - \text{Variable cost}}{\text{Selling price}} \times 100$$

Therefore, the contribution percentage for individual items is

$$\text{File cabinet} = \frac{100 - 900}{1000} \times 100 = \frac{100}{1000} \times 100 = 10\%$$

$$\text{Office tables} = \frac{500 - 400}{500} \times 100 = \frac{100}{500} \times 100 = 20\%$$

$$\text{Chairs} = \frac{200 - 125}{200} \times 100 = \frac{75}{200} \times 100 = 37.5\%$$

To get the total contribution per rupee sales volume for the file cabinet, office tables and chairs, we multiply the contribution percentage of each of the products by the percentage of sales volume for that particular product and add the figures so obtained. See the following table.

Furniture (a)	Contribution % (b)	% of sales in Rs. (c)	(b × c)/100
File cabinet	10	20	2000/100 = 2.00
Office tables	20	30	600/100 = 6.00
Chairs	37.5	50	1875/100 = 18.7
			26.75 or 27%

This 27 per cent is the total contribution per rupee of overall sales given the present product sales mix

Now,

$$\text{BEP} = \frac{\text{Fixed costs}}{\text{Contribution margin ratio}} = \frac{20,000}{27\%} = \frac{20,000}{27} \times 100 = \text{Rs. } 74,074$$

and

$$\text{Profit} = \text{Total revenue} - \text{Total costs}$$

Here, Total revenue = 80 per cent of the total capacity of the firm (given data in the problem). Therefore, profit equals to

80% of Rs 150,000 – (Total fixed cost + Total variable cost) = 120,000 – (20,000 + 73% of 120,000)

$$= \text{Rs. } 12,400$$

REVIEW QUESTIONS

1. What is break-even analysis? Explain its nature.
2. Break-even analysis assumes that variable cost and revenue are linear and that fixed cost is fixed. Briefly explain it through the help of diagram.
3. How will you determine the break-even point? Derive the break-even points in terms of quantity.
4. Can there be two break-even points? Show with the help of a graph.
5. From the following information relating to a company, you are required to find out
   (a) Contribution, (b) Break-even point in units, (c) Profit

Total fixed cost	Rs. 4000
Total variable cost	Rs. 8500
Total sales	Rs. 10,000
Units sold	8000 units

6. From the following data calculate: (a) Break-even point expressed in the amount of sales in rupees, (b) Number of units that must be sold to earn a profit of as 60,000 per year.

Sales price	Rs. 20 per unit
Variable manufacturing cost	Rs. 10 per unit
Variable salary cost	Rs. 4 per unit
Fixed factory overheads	Rs. 840,000 per year
Fixed selling cost	Rs. 352,000 per year

7. A manufacturer of hand operated power tools can produce convenient attachment for use with his line of tools at an estimated annual fixed cost of Rs. 8000 and variable cost of Rs. 3.75 per attachment. He can also buy the complete attachment custom made for all units purchased beyond the 9000 unit break-even point. At what increments of sales should the manufacturer purchase the attachment?

8. From the following data calculate: (a) P/V ratio (b) profit when sales are Rs. 30,000, (c) new break-even point if selling price is reduced by 30 per cent fixed expenses, Rs. 4000 break-even point if selling price is reduced by 30 per cent.

9. The following figures are extracted from the books of manufacturing concern for the year 2007–2008.

	Rs.
Direct materials	405,000
Direct labour	70,000
Fixed overhead	60,000
Variable overhead	200,000
Sales	800,000

Calculate the break-even point. What will be the effect on BEP of an increase of 10 per cent in (a) fixed expenses, and (b) variable expenses?

Part II

FINANCIAL SYSTEM

CHAPTER 9

Commercial Banking

9.1 INTRODUCTION

A bank is an institution which deals with money and credit. It accepts deposits from the public, makes funds available to those who need them, and helps in remittance of money from one place to another. A modern bank, in fact, performs such a variety of functions that it is difficult to give a precise and general definition of it. It is because of this reason that economists define 'bank' in various ways.

According to G. Crowther, a bank "collects money from those who have it to spare or who are saving it out of their incomes, and it lends this money to those who require it". In the words of Kinley, "A bank is an establishment which makes to individuals such advances of money as may be required and safely made, and to which individuals entrust money when not required by them for use". According to John Paget, "Nobody can be a banker who does not (i) take deposit accounts, (ii) take current accounts, (iii) issue and pay cheques, and (iv) collect cheques—crossed and uncrossed—for its customers".

Professor R.S. Sayers defines the terms 'bank' and 'banking' distinctly. He defines a bank as "an institution whose debts (bank deposits) are widely accepted in settlement of other people's debts to each other". Again, according to Sayers, "Ordinary banking business consists of cash for bank deposits and bank deposits for cash; transferring bank deposits from one person or corporation to another; giving bank deposits in exchange for bills of exchange, government bonds, the secured promises of businessmen to repay and so forth". According to the Indian Companies Act, 1949, banking means "the accepting for the purpose of Indian Companies lending or investment, of deposits of money from the public, repayable on demand or otherwise, and withdrawable by cheque, draft or otherwise".

Thus, the term *bank*, in the modern times, refers to an institution having the following features:

1. **Deals with money:** The bank accepts deposits and advances loans.
2. **Handles credit:** It has the ability to create credit, i.e. the ability to expand its liabilities as a multiple of its reserves.
3. **Is a commercial institution:** It aims at earning profit.
4. **Is a unique financial institution:** It creates demand deposits which serve as a medium of exchange and, as a result, manages the payment system of the country.

9.2 FUNCTIONS OF COMMERCIAL BANKS OR MODERN BANKS

In the modern world, a bank performs such a variety of functions that it is not possible to make an all inclusive list of its operations and services. However, some basic functions performed by a bank are discussed in the following section.

9.2.1 Accepting Deposits

The *first* important function of a bank is to accept deposits from those who can save but cannot profitably utilize this saving themselves. People consider it more rational to deposit their savings in a bank because by doing so they, on the one hand, earn interest, and, on the other hand, avoid the danger of theft. To attract savings from all sorts of individuals, the bank maintains different types of accounts

1. **Fixed deposit account:**   Money in this account is deposited for a fixed period of time (e.g. one, two, or five years) and cannot be withdrawn before the expiry of that period. The rate of interest on this account is higher than that on other types of deposits. The longer the period, the higher will be the rate of interest. Fixed deposits are also called *time deposits* or *time liabilities*.

2. **Current deposit account:**   This account is generally maintained by traders and businessmen who need to make a number of payments every day. Money from this account can be withdrawn in as many times and in as much amount as desired by the depositor. Normally, no interest is paid on this account. Rather, the depositor has to pay certain incidental charges to the bank for the services rendered by it. Current deposits are also called *demand deposits* or *demand liabilities*.

3. **Saving deposit account:**   The aim of this account is to encourage and mobilize small savings of the public. Certain restrictions are imposed on the depositors regarding the number of withdrawals and the amount to be withdrawn in a given period. Cheque facility is provided to the depositors. The rate of interest paid on this deposit is low as compared to that on fixed deposit.

4. **Recurring deposit account:**   The purpose of this account is to encourage regular savings by the public, particularly by the fixed income group. Generally, money in this account is deposited in monthly instalments for a fixed period, and is repaid to the depositors along with the interest on maturity. The rate of interest on this deposit is nearly the same as that on fixed deposit.

5. **Home safe account:**   It is another scheme aiming at promoting saving habits among the people. Under this scheme, a safe is supplied to the depositor to keep it at home and put his small savings in it. Periodically, the safe is taken to the bank where the amount kept in it is credited to his account.

9.2.2 Advancing of Loans

The *second* important function of a bank is advancing of loans to the public. After keeping certain cash reserves, the bank lends its deposits to the needy borrowers. Before advancing the loans, the bank satisfies itself about the creditworthiness of the borrowers. Various types of loans granted by bank are discussed as follows:

1. **Money at call:**   This is a very short period loan and can be called back by the bank at a very short notice of one day to 14 days. This loan is generally made to other banks or financial institutions.

2. **Cash credit:**   It is a type of loan which is given to the borrower against his current assets, such as shares, stocks, bonds. This loan is not based on personal security. The bank opens the account in the name of the borrower and allows him to withdraw the money from time to time upto a certain limit as determined by the value of his current assets. Interest is charged only on the amount actually withdrawn from the account.

3. **Overdraft:**   Sometimes, the bank provides overdraft facilities to its customers through which they are allowed to withdraw more than their deposits. Interest is charged from the customers on the overdrawn amount.

4. **Discounting of bills of exchange:**   This is another popular form of lending by a modern bank. Through this method, a holder of a bill of exchange can get it discounted by the bank. In a bill of exchange, the debtor accepts the bill drawn upon him by the creditor (i.e. holder of the bill) and agrees to pay the amount mentioned on maturity. After making some marginal deductions (in the form of commission), the bank pays the value of the bill to the holder. When the bill of exchange matures, the bank gets its payment from the party which had accepted the bill. Thus, such a loan is self-liquidating.

5. **Term loans:**   Banks have also started advancing medium-term and long-term loans. The maturity period for such loans is more than one year. The amount sanctioned is either paid or credited to the account of the borrower. The interest is charged on the entire amount of the loan and it is repaid either on maturity or in instalments.

9.2.3   Credit Creation

The third function of a bank is to create credit. In fact, credit creation is the natural outcome of the process of advancing loans as adopted by banks. When a bank advances a loan to its customer, it does not lend cash but opens an account in the borrower's name and credits the amount of the loan to this account. Thus, whenever a bank grants a loan, it creates an equal amount of bank deposit. Creation of such deposits is called *credit creation* which results in a net increase in the money stock of the economy. A bank has the ability to create credit many times more than its deposits, and this ability of multiple credit creation depends on its cash-reserve ratio.

9.2.4   Promoting Cheque System

A bank also renders a very useful medium of exchange in the form of cheques. Through a cheque, the depositor directs the banker to make payment to the payee. Cheque is the most developed credit instrument in the money market. In modern business transactions, cheques have become much more convenient method of settling debts than the use of cash.

9.2.5   Agency Functions

A bank also performs certain agency functions for and on behalf of its customers. Some of them are as follows:

1. **Remittance of funds:**   A bank helps its customers in transferring funds from one place to another through cheques, drafts, etc.

2. **Collection and payment of credit instruments:**   A bank collects and pays various credit instruments, such as cheques, bills of exchange, promissory notes.

3. **Execution of standing orders:**   It executes the standing instructions of its customers for making various periodic payments. The bank pays subscriptions, rents, insurance premiums etc. on behalf of its customers.

4. **Purchasing and sale of securities:**   A bank undertakes purchase and sale of various securities, such as shares, stocks, bonds, debentures, on behalf of its customers. It neither gives any advice to its customers regarding these investments nor levies any charge on them for its services, but simply performs the function of a broker.

5. **Collection of dividends on shares:**   It collects dividends, interest on shares and debentures of its customers.

6. **Income tax consultancy:**   The bank may also employ income tax experts to prepare income tax returns for its customers and help them to get refund of income tax.

7. **Acting as trustee and executor:**   It preserves the wills of its customers and executes them after their death.

8. **Acting as representative and correspondent:**   Sometimes the bank acts as a representative and correspondents of its customers. It gets passports, traveller's tickets, books vehicles, plots for its customers and receives letters on their behalf.

9.2.6 General Utility Function

A modern bank, in addition to agency services, provides many general utility services as given here:

1. **Locker facility:**   It provides locker facility to its customers. The customers can keep their valuables and important documents in the lockers for safe custody.

2. **Traveller's cheques:**   A bank issues traveller's cheques to help its customers travel without the fear of theft or loss of money. With this facility, the customers need not take the risk of carrying cash with them during their travels.

3. **Letter of credit:**   It is issued by the bank to its customers certifying their creditworthiness. Letter of credit is very useful in foreign trade.

4. **Collection of statistics:**   A bank collects statistics giving important information relating to industry, trade and commerce, money and banking. It also publishes journals and bulletins containing research articles on economic and financial matters.

5. **Underwriting securities:**   A bank underwrites the securities issued by government, public or private bodies. Because of their full faith in a bank, the public will not hesitate in buying securities carrying the signature of a bank.

6. **Gift cheques:**   Some banks issue cheques of various denominations (say of Rs. 11, 21, 31, 51, 101) to be used by their customers on auspicious occasions.

7. **Acting as referee:**   A bank may be referred to for seeking information regarding the financial position, business reputation and respectability of its customers.

8. **Foreign exchange business:**   It also deals in the business of foreign currencies. Again, it may finance foreign trade by discounting foreign bills of exchange.

9.3   ROLE OF COMMERCIAL BANK IN DEVELOPING ECONOMY

In a modern economy, a bank should be considered not merely as dealer in money but also as leader in development. It is not only the store house of a country's wealth, but also reservoir of resources necessary for economic development. The bank plays an important role in the development of a country. It is the growth of commercial banking in the 18th and 19th centuries that led to industrial revolution in Europe. Similarly, economic progress in the present-day developing countries largely depends on the growth of sound banking system there. A commercial bank can contribute to a country's economic development in the following way:

1. **Capital formation:**   It is the most important determinant of economic development and a bank promotes capital formation which has three well-defined stages: (i) generation of saving, (ii) mobilization of saving, and (iii) canalization of saving in productive uses. A bank plays a crucial role in all the three stages of capital formation:

   (a) It stimulates savings by providing a number of incentives to the savers, such as interest on deposits, free and cheap remittance of funds, safe custody of valuables.
   (b) By expanding it branches in different areas and giving various incentives, the bank succeeds in mobilizing the savings generated in the economy.

      It not only mobilizes resources from those who have excess of them, but also makes the resources so mobilized available to those who have the opportunities of productive investment.

2. **Encouragement to entrepreneurial innovations:**   In underdeveloped countries, entre-preneurs generally hesitate to invest in new ventures and undertake innovations largely due to lack of funds. Bank loan facilities of enable the entrepreneurs to step up their investments and innovational activities, adopt new methods of production and increase productive capacity of the economy.

3. **Monetization of economy:**   This is essential for accelerating trade and economic activity in a country. A bank, which is a creator and distributor of money, allows money to play an active role in the economy. It helps the process of monetization in two ways:

   (a) A bank monetizes debts. In other words, it buys debts (i.e. securities which are not acceptable as money) and, in exchange, creates demand deposits (which are acceptable as money).
   (b) By spreading its branches in the rural and backward areas, the bank converts the non-monetized sectors of the economy into the monetized sectors.

4. **Influencing economic activity:**   A bank can directly influence economic activity, and hence, the pace of economic development through its influence on the following:

   (a) **Variations in interest rates:**   A reduction in the interest rates makes the investment more profitable and stimulates economic activity. However, an increase in the interest rate, discourages investment and economic activity. Thus, to overcome a deflationary situation, a bank can follow a cheap money policy with low interest rates. To control inflation it can adopt dear money policy with high interest rates.

   (b) **Availability of credit:**   A banker can also influence the economic activity by the availability of credit. Credit creation is an important function of the bank. Bank credit forms the major portion of money supply. Thus, through its credit creation activity the bank increases the supply of purchasing power and, hence, the aggregate demand. This, in turn, increases investment, production and trade in the economy.

5. **Implementation of monetary policy:**   Economic development needs an appropriate monetary policy. But a well-developed banking system is a necessary pre-condition for the effective implementation of the monetary policy. Control and regulation of credit by the monetary authority is not possible without the active co-operation of the banking system in the country.

6. **Promotion of trade and industry:**   Economic progress in the industrially advanced countries in the last two hundred years or so was mainly due to expansion in trade and industrialization which could not have been made possible without the development of the banking system. The use of bank cheque, bank draft and bills of exchange has revolutionized both national and international trade, which, in turn, has encouraged specialization and accelerated the pace of industrialization.

7. **Encouragement to industries:**   By granting loans (particularly medium-term and long-term), the bank can provide financial resources to industries to help them secure necessary material, machines and other inputs. In a planned economy, it is necessary that the bank should formulate it loan policies in accordance with the broad objectives and strategies of industrialization as adopted in the plan. This will promote the right type of industrialization in the economy.

8. **Regional development:**   A bank can also play an important role in achieving balanced development in the different regions of the economy. It can transfer surplus capital from the developed regions to the less developed regions where it is scarce and most needed. This reallocation of funds between regions will promote economic development in the underdeveloped areas of the economy.

9. **Improvement of agriculture and other neglected sectors:**   Underdeveloped economies are primarily agricultural economies. Majority of the population in these economies live in the rural areas. Therefore, for these economies to develop, improvement in agriculture and small-scale industries in the rural areas is essential. Till now banks in underdeveloped countries have been paying more attention to trade and commerce, and have almost neglected the agriculture and industry sector.

9.4   SOUND BANKING SYSTEM FOR UNDERDEVELOPED COUNTRIES

A sound and efficient banking system which undertakes the responsibility of promoting economic growth in underdeveloped economies must possess the following features:

1. The system of branch banking is most suitable for underdeveloped countries. More and more branches of banks should be opened in rural and backward areas to encourage savings and banking habits in these areas.

2. The system of unit banking may be developed in limited areas, particularly in big cities to meet the local financial requirements of trade and industries. This will, on the one hand, reduce the pressure on big banks, and, on the other hand, check the concentration of financial power in the hands of a few banks.

3. The banking system in the less developed countries must aim at encouraging capital formation by increasing the rates of savings and investment in these economies.

4. In the underdeveloped countries the banking system should provide easy and cheap remittance facilities to enable the movement of fund from one place to another so as to promote trade and industry.

5. The loan policy of banks in the underdeveloped countries should be rationalized in such a way that loans for productive purposes are encouraged while for conspicuous consumption and speculative activities discouraged.

6. In underdeveloped countries the loan policy should also not be restricted to short-term loans alone. The banks should provide medium-term and long-term loans to developmental activities in these countries.

7. The banks should meet the different and changing needs of the underdeveloped countries. Credit facilities should be extended to the priority sectors, such as agriculture and small-scale industries.

9.5 TYPES OF BANKS

Banks can be classified into various types on the basis of their functions. The following are the different types of banks:

1. **Commercial banks:** The institutions which organize all kinds of banking business and, generally, finance trade and commerce are called *commercial banks*. Since deposits here are for a short period, these banks normally advance short-term loans to the businessmen and traders, and avoid medium-term and long-term lending. However, recently commercial banks have also extended their areas of operation to medium-term and long-term finance. Majority of the commercial banks are in the public sector. But there are certain private sector banks operating as joint stock companies. Hence, commercial banks are also called *joint stock banks*.

2. **Industrial banks:** Industrial banks, also known as *investment banks*, mainly meet the medium-term and long-term financial needs of industries. Such long-term needs cannot be met by commercial banks because they generally deal with short-term lendings. The main functions of the industrial banks are to: (i) accept long-term deposits, (ii) grant long-term loans to the industrialists to enable them purchase land and heavy machinery, construct factory building, (iii) help sell or even underwrite the debentures and shares of industrial firms, (iv) provide information regarding the general economic position of the economy. In India, industrial banks, such as Industrial Development Bank of India, Industrial Finance Corporation of India, State Finance Corporations, are playing significant role in the industrial development of the country.

3. **Agricultural banks:** Agricultural credit needs are different from those of industry and trade. Industrial and commercial banks normally do not deal with agricultural finance. The agriculturists require: (i) short-term credit to buy seeds, fertilizers and other inputs, and (ii) long-term credit to purchase land, agricultural machinery and equipment, etc. In India, agricultural finance is generally provided by co-operative institutions. Agricultural co-operatives provide short-term loans, and Land Development Banks provide long-term credit to the agriculturists.

4. **Exchange banks:** These banks deal in foreign exchange and specialize in financing foreign trade. They facilitate international payments through the sale and purchase of bills of exchange, and, thus, play an important role in promoting foreign trade.

5. **Saving banks:** The main purpose of saving banks is to promote saving habits among the general public and mobilize their small savings. In India, postal saving banks perform this job. They open accounts and issue postal cash certificates.

6. **Central bank:** It is the apex institution which controls, regulates and supervises the monetary and credit system of the country. The important functions of the central bank are:

    (a) It has the monopoly of note issue.
    (b) The central bank acts as the banker, agent and financial adviser to the state.
    (c) It is the custodian of member banks reserves.
    (d) The central bank is the custodian of nation's reserves of international currency.
    (e) It serves as the lender of the last resort.
    (f) The central bank functions as the bank of central clearance, settlement and transfer.
    (g) It acts as the controller of credit.

Besides these functions, India's central bank, i.e. the Reserve Bank of India, also performs many developmental functions to promote economic development in the country.

9.6 BALANCE SHEET OF A BANK

The balance sheet of a bank is a statement of its liabilities and assets at a particular time. 'Liabilities' refer to all the debit items representing the obligations of the bank or others' claims on the bank. In other words, all those items because of which the bank is liable to pay to others form the liabilities. Assets, on the other hand, refer to all the credit items representing the bank's claims on others and its ownership of wealth. In other words, all those items from which the bank hopes to get an income constitute its assets. Thus, the balance sheet shows how a bank raises funds and how it invests them. It is customary that the liabilities are mentioned on the left-hand side and the assets on the right-hand side of the balance sheet. The totals on the two sides (i.e. the total liabilities and the total assets) should always be equal. Table 9.1 shows a format of a bank's balance sheet.

Table 9.1 Balance Sheet of a Bank

Liabilities	Assets
1. Share Capital	1. Cash
2. Reserve fund	(a) Cash in hand
3. Deposits:	(b) Cash with central bank
(a) Demand deposits	(c) Cash with other banks
(b) Time deposits	2. Money at call and shot notice
(c) Saving deposits	3. Bills purchased or discounted
4. Borrowings from other banks	4. Investments
5. Acceptance and endorsements	5. Loans and advances
6. Other liabilities	6. Acceptance and endorsements
	7. Buildings and other fixed assets
Total	**Total**

9.6.1 Liabilities of the Bank

The liabilities portion of the balance sheet is relatively a simple system. It consists of the following items:

1. **Share capital:** A joint stock bank initially raises its funds by issuing share capital. In other words, share capital is the contributions made by the shareholders. Share capital is in the form of: (i) authorized capital, i.e. the maximum amount of capital the bank is authorized to raise in the form of shares; (ii) issued capital, i.e. part of the authorized capital issued in the form of shares for public subscription; (iii) subscribed capital i.e. part of the issued capital actually subscribed by the public; and (iv) paid-up capital, i.e. part of the subscribed capital actually paid by the subscribers. It is the actually paid-up share capital which constitutes the liability of the bank.

2. **Reserve fund:** It is the amount accumulated over the years out of undistributed profits. Normally, all the profits of the bank are not distributed among the shareholders; some part is retained to meet contingencies. This reserve fund actually belongs to the shareholders.

3. **Deposits:** These from the public constitute the major portion of the bank's working capital. Various types of deposits accepted by a bank are: (a) *demand deposits*, i.e. deposits which can be withdrawn at any time and on which no interest is paid; (b) *time deposits*, i.e. deposits which can be withdrawn after a fixed period of time and on which a high rate of interest is paid; and (c) *saving deposits*, i.e. deposits which can be withdrawn to the limited extent in a given period and on which some interest is paid. Deposits are the liabilities of a bank towards the depositors. But they are also assets of the bank because, after keeping a certain cash reserve, it invests the balance in securities or utilizes it for advancing loans and, thus, earns income.

4. **Borrowings from banks:** Sometimes, the bank borrows loans from other banks on temporary basis to meet the increased demand for money. The central bank is the lender of the last resort and provides loan facilities to the banks in special circumstances. All these borrowings form the liability of the borrower bank.

5. **Acceptances and endorsements:** The bank also creates liabilities by accepting or endorsing the bills of exchange on behalf of its customers. Through this facility, the bank assumes the liability to pay the amount of the bill on maturity.

6. **Other liabilities:** Certain other miscellaneous liabilities are incurred by the bank. For example, by acting as an agent the bank makes collections on behalf of its customers and, thus, creates liability. Again, the profits earned by the bank represent liability because they are payable to the shareholders.

9.6.2 Assets of the Bank

The assets side of the balance sheet is both complicated and interesting. It shows the manner in which funds of a bank are utilized. Given below are various assets of a bank arranged in the ascending order of profitability and descending order of liquidity:

1. **Cash:** It is the most liquid but non-earning asset, and is considered as the first line of defence. Every bank keeps certain amount of cash in order to meet the cash requirements of its depositors. The cash of the bank includes three items: (i) cash (currency and coins) in hand, i.e. cash kept in the safe vaults of the bank; (ii) cash kept with the central bank of the country; and (iii) cash kept with other banks.

2. **Money at call and short notice:**   This refers to loans which are recoverable by the bank on demand or at a very short notice. These loans are for a maximum period of 15 days. Such loans are earning and highly liquid assets which can be converted into cash quickly and without loss. These assets are of two types: (i) call and short notice loans to the brokers in the stock market, dealers in the discount market and to other banks; (ii) short-term treasury bills, i.e. borrowing of the government for a very short period.

3. **Bills purchased or discounted:**   The bank utilizes its funds in trade bills and treasury bills which it discounts. The amount of the bills is collected by the bank on maturity. The bills discounted are short-term (normally of 90 days) self-liquidating assets. They are self-liquidating because at the end of the commercial transaction, the money will be repaid. The commercial banks generally prefer these bills because of the following reasons:

    (a) These are highly negotiable and can be easily bought and sold.
    (b) The bills are eligible for rediscounting with the central bank in case the bank needs cash before their maturity.
    (c) These bring to the bank good earning in the form of interest.

    Thus, the bills are considered ideal bank assets because they satisfy the objectives of both liquidity and profitability.

4. **Investments:**   Some funds are invested in profit-yielding assets, mainly government securities. Which are relatively safe because there is certainty of repayment after maturity. Moreover, the bank can borrow from the central bank against these securities. The bank also invests in fixed interest-yielding debentures or bonds of well-established industrial concerns. Such investments are highly shiftable and yield good income. But, at the same time, they also involve risk.

5. **Loans and advances:**   These are the most profitable and the least liquid assets of the bank. The bank provides loans and advances to businessmen either through overdraft or by discounting the bills of exchange. The difference between loans and advances is that the latter are for a short period while the former are for a relatively longer period. Loans and advances earn high rate of interest, carry greater risk and are generally non-shiftable. Thus, while loans and advances are mostly preferred by the bank because of their high yields, they are not popular from the consideration of liquidity and safety of the bank.

6. **Acceptances and endorsements:**   When a bank accepts or endorses a bill of exchange for its customer, the amount of the bill becomes the customer's liability and the bank's asset.

7. **Building and other fixed assets:**   A bank's assets also include the value of its movable and immovable properties, such as office buildings, furniture. These assets do not contribute to the income of the bank and constitute very small part of its assets.

9.6.3 Importance of Balance Sheet of a Bank

The significance of the balance sheet of a bank is clearly brought out in the following points,

1. The balance sheet represents the complete functioning of the bank and shows how the bank raises money and how it is invested.
2. It throws light on the financial position (i.e. liquidity and solvency position) of the bank because the balance sheet contains all information about its liabilities and assets.

3. The progress of the bank over time can be determined by comparing the balance sheet of different periods.

4. A comparison of the balance sheet of different banks gives comparative picture of financial position of a bank vis-a-vis that of others.

5. It brings out an important fact that the bank buys assets primarily by creating liabilities in the form of deposits. These deposits are simply debt claims against the assets of the bank.

6. The balance sheet gives an estimate of the confidence of the public in the bank. Increasing savings or time deposits in the bank reflects that the confidence of the people in it is also increasing.

7. It shows the loan and investment policy of the bank.

8. The balance sheet provides information about the interest of various persons, such as shareholders, debtors, creditors.

9.7 NEW DEVELOPMENTS IN COMMERCIAL BANKING SYSTEM

Traditional commercial loan theory has now been completely discarded and given place to the modern shiftability and anticipated income theories. All the three theories attempt to resolve the liquidity earning problem of the bank, i.e. how a bank can achieve the two conflicting objectives of liquidity and profitability simultaneously. According to the *commercial loan theory*, a bank can ensure sufficient liquidity by granting only short-term self-liquidating loans secured by goods in the process of production or goods in transit. The *shiftability theory* requires the bank to solve its liquidity problems by purchasing highly liquid assets which can be easily shifted to other banks in times of need for liquidity. According to the recent *anticipated income theory*, a bank can solve its liquidity problem even by advancing long-term loans if the borrowers repay them in series of continuous instalments. The application of shiftability theory and the anticipated income theory has enabled the commercial bank to adopt medium-term and long-term lending business along with providing sufficient liquidity. Major changes in commercial banking system are given here:

1. **Term lending:** Term loans not only increase earnings of a bank, but also improve its liquidity because such loans are almost always repaid on an instalment basis. The term loans are also beneficial to the borrowers. They are used to purchase machinery and equipment for the industries where the expected income flow from the investment will not be sufficient to repay a short-term loan. The loans are also used to supplement working capital in industries where the production process is long. Other advantages of term loans to the borrowers are:

   (a) Negotiations can be conducted privately with a lender interested in promoting a sound long-run relationship.

   (b) Maturities and conditions can be changed to fit changes in the borrowing needs and other situations.

   (c) Costs are often lower than those of alternative sources of such funds.

   (d) Funds are borrowed only when needed and can usually be repaid in advance without penalty.

2. **Hire purchase finance:** It refers to the credit facilities for the purchase of durable goods on instalment basis and is another post-war development in commercial banking. The dealers selling on hire-purchase get advances from the bank by hypotheticating their goods to it. Hire purchase facilities help the small entrepreneurs to start new businesses and the existing

small producers to purchase new tools and equipment. The commercial banks entered into this highly profitable business by acquiring the direct ownership of or a partnership in the established hire purchase finance companies. Hire purchase credit is also self-financing because the instalments paid by the buyer enable the seller to repay the bank loan regularly.

3. **Personal loans:** Another departure from the traditional banking practice is the advancing of personal loans by commercial banks. This is a direct consequence of post-war policy of redistribution of income in favour of the working class which was instrumental is stimulating consumer credit by the banks. Commercial banks started granting personal loans for meeting expenditures to purchase motor cars, household appliances, professional equipment, house repairs and decorations, etc. In Britain, the personal loan scheme was initiated by Midland Bank in 1958. Personal loans are different from hire purchase finance in that in the case of the latter, the goods are hypotheticated to the bank, whereas in the case of the former, the bank has no claim on the goods for which the loan is advanced.

4. **Declining role of commercial banks:** There has been a secular decline in the role of commercial banks. Raymond Goldsmith (1904–1988) had observed that while all financial intermediaries grew rapidly during the first half of the 20th century, the claims of non-bank intermediaries, such as co-operative credit societies, building societies, insurance companies increased much more than the demand deposit claims of the commercial banks. Besides the growth of non-bank financial intermediaries, other reasons for the decline of the role of bank finance are: (i) growth of public sector; (ii) increasing use of trade credit; (iii) changing pattern of corporate finance with greater reliance on self-finance, etc.

It is clear from the above account that commercial banks in the developing countries have undergone a period of significant change. They have left 'sound' banking principles of moving safe by advancing short-term loans only for trade purposes and entered into the more risky and so far neglected fields of industry and agriculture requiring medium-term and long-term loans. Truly, commercial banks are now playing a major role in promoting economic growth in these countries.

REVIEW QUESTIONS

1. What is a bank? What are the functions of a commercial bank in India?
2. Discuss the role of commercial banking in the economic development of a country.
3. Explain the importance of balance sheet of the bank. How far have the objectives of commercial banks been achieved?

CHAPTER 10

Reserve Bank of India

10.1 INTRODUCTION

The Reserve Bank of India (RBI) is the central bank of India. It is the apex monetary institution which supervises, regulates, controls and develops the monetary and financial system of our country. The Reserve Bank of India was established on April 1, 1935 under the Reserve Bank of India Act, 1934. Initially, it was constituted as a private shareholders' bank with a fully paid-up capital of Rs. 5 crore. However, on January 1, 1949 it was nationalized.

10.2 ORGANIZATION

The Reserve Bank operates through various organizationally, departments which are as follows:

1. **Issue department:** The main function of this department is to issue and distribute the paper currency.
2. **Banking department:** This department deals with the government transactions, manages the public debt and arranges for the transfer of government funds. It also maintains the cash reserves of the scheduled banks, provides financial assistance to the banks and functions as a clearing house.
3. **Department of banking development:** It aims at expanding banking facilities in areas which are rural and where banks are yet to play a significant rule.
4. **Department of banking operations:** The function of this department is to supervise, regulate and control the working of the banking institutions in the country. It grants licences for opening new banks or new branches of the existing banks.
5. **Agricultural credit department:** It deals with problems of agricultural credit and provides facilities of rural credit to state governments and state co-operatives.
6. **Industrial finance department:** The main objective of this department is to provide financial help to small- and medium-scale industries.
7. **Non-banking companies department:** This department supervises the activities of non-banking companies and financial institutions in the country.
8. **Exchange control department:** It conducts the business of sale and purchase of foreign exchange.

9. **Legal department:** This department provides advice to various departments on legal issues. It also gives legal advice on the implementation of banking laws in the country.
10. **Department of research and statistics:** The objective of this department is to: (i) conduct research on problems relating to money, credit, finance, production, etc., (ii) collect important statistics relating to various aspects of the economy, and (iii) publish these statistics.
11. **Department of planning and reorganization:** It deals with the formulation of new plans or reorganization of existing policies for making them more effective.
12. **Economic department:** The department is concerned with the framing of proper banking policies for better implementation of economic policies of the government.
13. **Inspection department:** It undertakes the function of inspecting various offices of commercial banks.
14. **Department of accounts and expenditure:** This department keeps proper records of all receipts and expenditures of the Reserve Bank of India.
15. **RBI services board:** It deals with the selection of new employees, for different posts in the Reserve Bank of India.

10.3 FUNCTIONS OF RESERVE BANK OF INDIA

The Reserve Bank of India performs various traditional, central banking functions and undertakes different promotional and developmental measures to meet the dynamic requirements of the country. The broad objectives of the Reserve Bank of India are: (i) regulating the issue of currency in India, (ii) keeping the foreign exchange reserves of the country, (iii) establishing the monetary stability in the country, and (iv) developing the financial structure of the country on sound lines consistent with the national socio-economic objectives and policies. The main functions of the Reserve Bank of India are described in the following paragraphs.

10.3.1 Note Issue

The Reserve Bank of India has the monopoly of note issue in the country. It has the sole right to issue currency notes of all denominations except one rupee notes. The one rupee notes are issued by Ministry of Finance of the Government of India. The Reserve Bank of India acts as the only source of legal tender because even the one rupee notes are circulated through it. It has a separate Issue Department which is entrusted with the job of issuing currency notes. The Reserve Bank has adopted minimum reserve system of note issue. Since 1957, it maintains gold and foreign exchange reserves of Rs. 200 crore, of which at least Rs. 115 crore should be in gold.

10.3.2 Banker to Government

The Reserve Bank of India acts as the banker, agent and adviser to the Government of India:

1. It maintains and operates government deposits.
2. The Reserve Bank of India collects and makes payments on behalf of the government.
3. It helps the government to float new loans and manage public debt.
4. The Reserve Bank of India sells for the Central Government treasury bills of 91 days duration.
5. It makes 'Ways and Means' advances to the Central and State Governments for periods not exceeding three months.
6. The Bank provides development finance to the government for carrying out five year plans.

7. It undertakes foreign exchange transactions on behalf of the Central Government.
8. The Reserve Bank of India acts as the agent of the Government of India in the latter's dealings with the International Monetary Fund (IMF), the World Bank, and other international financial institutions.
9. It advises the government on all financial matters, such as loan operations, investments, agricultural and industrial finance, banking, planning, economic development.

10.3.3 Banker's Bank

The Reserve Bank of India acts as the banker's bank in the following respects:

1. Every bank is under the statutory obligation to keep a certain minimum of cash reserves with the Reserve Bank of India. The purpose of these reserves is to enable the Reserve Bank of India to extend financial assistance to the scheduled banks in times of emergency, and, thus, to act as the lender of the last resort. According to the Banking Regulation Act, 1949, all scheduled banks are required to maintain with the Reserve Bank minimum cash reserves of 5 per cent of their demand liabilities and 2 per cent of their time liabilities. The Reserve Bank (Amendment) Act, 1956 empowered the Reserve Bank of India to raise the cash reserve ratio to 20 per cent in the case of demand deposits and to 8 per cent in the case of time deposits. Due to the difficulty of classifying deposits into demand and time categories, the amendment to the Banking Regulation Act in September 1972 changed the provision of reserves to 3 per cent of aggregate deposit liabilities, which can be raised to 15 per cent if the Reserve Bank considers it necessary.
2. The Reserve Bank of India provides financial assistance to the scheduled banks by discounting their eligible bills and through loans and advances against approved securities.
3. Under the Banking Regulation Act, 1949 and its various amendments, the Reserve Bank of India has been given extensive powers of supervision and control over the banking system. These regulatory powers relate to the licensing of banks and their branch expansions, liquidity of assets of the banks, management and methods of working of the banks, amalgamation, reconstruction and liquidation of banks, inspection of banks.

10.3.4 Custodian of Exchange Reserves

The Reserve Bank of India is the custodian of India's foreign exchange reserves. It maintains and stabilizes the external value of the rupee, administers exchange controls and other restrictions imposed by the government, and manages the foreign exchange reserves. Initially, the stability of exchange rate was maintained through selling and purchasing sterling at fixed rates. But after India became a member of International Monetary Fund (IMF) in 1947, the rupee was delinked with sterling and it became a multi-laterally convertible currency. Therefore, the Reserve Bank of India now sells and buys foreign currencies, and not sterling alone, in order to achieve the objective of exchange stability. The Reserve Bank of India fixes the selling and buying rates of foreign currencies. All Indian remittances to foreign countries and foreign remittances to India are made through the Reserve Bank of India.

10.3.5 Controller of Credit

As the central bank of the country, the Reserve Bank undertakes the responsibility of controlling credit in order to ensure internal price stability and promote economic growth. Through this function, the Reserve Bank attempts to achieve price stability and avoid inflationary and deflationary tendencies in the country. Price stability is essential for economic development. The Reserve Bank of India regulates the money supply in accordance with the changing requirements of the economy. It makes extensive use of various quantitative and qualitative techniques to effectively control and regulate credit in the country.

10.3.6 Ordinary Banking Functions

The Reserve Bank also performs various ordinary banking functions:

1. It accepts deposits from the central government, state governments and even private individuals without interest,
2. The Reserve Bank buys, sells and rediscounts the bills of exchange and promissory notees of the scheduled banks without restrictions,
3. It grants loans and advances to the central government, state governments, local authorities, scheduled banks and state cooperative banks, repayable within 90 days.
4. The Bank buys and sells securities of the Government of India and foreign securities.
5. It buys from and sells to the scheduled banks foreign exchanges for a minimum amount of Rs. 1 lakh.
6. It can borrow from any scheduled bank in India or from any foreign bank.
7. The Reserve Bank can open an account in the World Bank or in some foreign central bank.
8. It accepts valuables, securities, etc. for keeping them in safe custody,
9. The bank buys and sells gold and silver.

10.3.7 Miscellaneous Functions

In addition to central banking and ordinary banking functions, the Reserve Bank of India performs the following miscellaneous functions:

(a) Banker's Training College was set up to extend training facilities to supervisory staff of commercial banks. Arrangements are made to impart training to the co-operative personnel.
(b) The Reserve Bank of India collects and publishes statistical information relating to banking, finance, credit, currency, agricultrual and industrial production, etc. It also publishes the results of various studies and review of economic situation of the country in its monthly bulletins and periodicals.

10.3.8 Forbidden Business

Being the central bank of the country, the Reserve Bank is barred from competing with member banks, and has to keep its assets in liquid form to meet any situation of economic crisis. The Reserve Bank is forbidden to do certain types of business:

1. It can neither participate in nor directly provide financial assistance to any business, trade or industry.
2. The Reserve Bank can neither buy its own shares nor those of other banks or commercial and industrial undertakings,
3. It cannot grant unsecured loans and advances.
4. The Bank cannot give loans against mortgage security.

5. It cannot give interest on deposits.
6. The Reserve Bank cannot draw or accept bills not payable on demand.
7. It cannot purchase immovable property except for its own offices.

10.3.9 Promotional and Developmental Functions

Besides the traditional central banking functions, the Reserve Bank of India also performs a variety of promotional and developmental functions:

1. By encouraging the commercial banks to expand their branches in the semi-urban and rural areas, the Reserve Bank helps to

    (a) reduce the dependence of the people in these areas on the defective unorganized sector of indigenous bankers and money lenders, and
    (b) develop the banking habits of the people.
2. By establishing the Deposit Insurance Corporation, the Reserve Bank of India helps to develop the banking system of the country, instills confidence of the depositors and avoids bank failures.
3. Through institutions like Unit Trust of India, the Reserve Bank of India helps to mobilize savings in the country.
4. Since its inception, the Reserve Bank of India has been making efforts to promote institutional agricultural credit by developing co-operative credit institutions.
5. The Reserve Bank of India also helps to promote the process of industrialization in the country by selling up specialized institutions for industrial finance.
6. It also undertakes measures for developing the bill market in the country.

10.4 MONETARY POLICY OF RBI

Monetary policy refers to the policy of the central bank of a country to regulate and control the volume, cost and allocation of money and credit with the aim of achieving the objectives of optimum levels of output and employment, price stability, balance of payment equilibrium, or any other goals sset by the government.

Monetary and fiscal policies are closely interrelated and, therefore, should be pursued in coordination with each other. Fiscal policy generally brings about changes in the money supply through the budget deficit. An excessive budget deficit, for example, shifts the burden of control of inflation to monetary policy. This requires a restrictive credit policy. On the contrary, a fiscal policy, which keeps the budget deficit at a very low level, frees the monetary authority from the burden of adopting an anti-inflationary monetary policy. The monetary policy can then play a positive role in promoting economic growth by extending credit facilities to development programmes.

In a developing economy like India, appropriate monetary policy can play a positive role in creating conditions necessary for rapid economic growth. Moreover, since these economies are highly sensitive to inflationary pressures, the monetary policy should also serve to control inflationary tendencies by increasing savings by the people, checking credit expansion by the banking system and discouraging deficit financing by the government. In India, during the planning period, the aim of the monetary policy of the Reserve Bank of India has been to meet the needs of the planned development of the economy. With this broad aim, the monetary policy has been pursued to achieve the twin objectives of economic policy of the government:

1. Accelerate the process of economic growth with a view to raise national income.
2. Control and reduce the inflationary pressures in the economy.

Thus, the monetary policy of the Reserve Bank of India during the course of planning has been appropriately termed as that of 'controlled expansion'. It aims at adequately financing of economic growth and, at the same time, ensuring reasonable price stability in the country.

10.5 POLICY OF CREDIT EXPANSION

The overall trend in the economy during the planning period has been that of continuous expansion of currency and credit with an objective of meeting the developmental needs of the economy. This expansion has been achieved by adopting the following measures:

1. **Revision of open market operations:** The Reserve Bank of India revised its open operations policy in October 1956, according to which it started giving discriminatory support to the sale and purchase of government securities. Between 1948–1951, the Bank made large purchases of government securities. In the subsequent period, the Bank's sales of the government securities to the public exceeded its purchases. This excess sales method was discontinued between 1964 and 1969 with a purpose of expanding currency and credit in the economy.

2. **Liberalization of the bill market scheme:** Through the bill market scheme, the commercial banks receive additional funds from the Reserve Bank to meet the increasing credit requirements of their borrowers. Since 1957, the Reserve Bank of India has extended the bill market scheme to include export bills in order to help the commercial banks provide credit to exporters liberally.

3. **Facilities to priority sectors:** The Reserve Bank continues to provide credit facilities to priority sectors, such as small-scale industries and co-operatives, even though the general policy of the Bank is to control credit expansion. For instance, in October 1962, banks were allowed to borrow additional funds from the Reserve Bank of India in order to provide finance to small-scale industries and co-operatives. The Reserve Bank of India has also been providing short-term finance to the rural co-operatives.

4. **Refinance and rediscounting facilities:** In recent years, the Reserve Bank of India has been following a policy of providing selective refinance and rediscounting facilities. At present, banks are permitted to refinance equal to one per cent of the demand and lime liabilities at the rate of 10 per cent per annum. Refinance facilities are also available for food procurement credit and export credit.

5. **Credit facilities through financial institutions:** The Reserve Bank has also been instrumental in the establishment of various financial institutions such as Industrial Development Bank of India (IDBI), Industrial Finance Corporation of India (IFCI), Industrial Reconstruction Corporation of India (IRCI), Industrial Credit and Investment Corporation of India (ICICI), State Finance Corporations (SFCs), Agricultural Refinance and Development Corporation (ARDC) and National Bank for Agriculture and Rural Development (NABARD). Through these institutions, the Reserve Bank of India provides medium-term and long-term credit facilities for development.

6 **Deficit financing:** The continuous increase in money supply in the country has been caused by adopting the method of deficit financing to finance the budgetary deficit of the

government. This has been made possible through changes in the reserve requirements of the Reserve Bank. The reserve system was made more flexible by making two changes:

(a) By dropping proportional reserve system which required keeping of 40 per cent of reserves in gold (coins and bullion) and foreign securities, with the provision that the value of gold would not be less than Rs. 40 crore.

(b) Modifying the minimum reserve system so that the Reserve Bank of India need keep only gold worth Rs. 115 crore with the provision that the minimum requirement of keeping foreign securities of the value of Rs. 85 crore can be waived during extreme contingency.

7. **Anti-inflationary fiscal policy:** The Seventh Five Year Plan prefers an anti-inflationary fiscal policy to an anti-inflationary monetary policy and emphazsizes a positive, promotional and expansionary role for monetary policy. Bank credit to the government has been fixed at a level considered just sufficient to generate the additional money supply needed to meet the expected increase in the demand for money. Such an anti-inflationary fiscal policy will liberate the Reserve Bank for its anti-inflationary responsibilities and enable it to extend sufficient credit facilities for the development of industry and trade.

8. **Allocation of credit:** The pattern of allocation of credit is in accordance with the plan priorities. The major part of the total credit available goes to the public sector through statutory requirements and other means. A certain minimum of credit at concessional rates of interest is ensured for the priority sectors through selective credit control and the differential rate of interest scheme. Private industries can secure funds for investment purposes through public financial institutions.

10.6 POLICY OF CREDIT CONTROL

Apart from meeting developmental and expansionary requirements of the economy, the Reserve Bank of India has also been assigned the task of controlling the inflationary pressures in the economy. During the planning period, the large and continuous increase in the deficit financing and government expenditure has been expanding the monetary demand for goods and services.

But, on the other hand, factors, such as shortfalls in production, hoardings, have been creating inelasticities in the supply of commodities. As a result, the country has been experiencing an inflationary rise in prices ever since 1955–1956, and particularly after 1973–1974. The Reserve Bank of India has adopted a number of credit control measures to check the inflationary tendencies in the country. They are as follows:

1. **Bank rate:** It is the rate at which the Reserve Bank of India advances to its member banks against approved securities or rediscounts the eligible bills of exchange and other papers. The bank rate is considered as the tendsetter in the money market. Changes in the bank rate influence the entire interest rate structure, i.e. short-term and long-term interest rates. A rise in the bank rate leads to a rise in the other market interest rates, which implies a dear money policy increasing the cost of borrowing. Similarly, a fall in the bank rate results in a fall in the other market rates, which implies a cheap money policy reducing the cost of borrowing. The Reserve Bank of India has changed the bank rate from time to time to meet the changing conditions of the economy. The bank rate was raised from 3 per cent to 3.5 per cent in November 1951 and was further raised from 4 per cent in January 1963 to 5 per cent in September 1964, and to 6 per cent in February 1965. In March 1968, the

bank rate was reduced to 5 per cent in view of the recessionary conditions. Subsequently, it was further raised to 7 per cent in May to 9 per cent in July 1974 and to 10 per cent in July 1981. The bank rate was again raised to 11 per cent in July 1991. It was 12 per cent with effect from October 8, 1991. The increases in the bank rate were adopted to reduce the bank credit and control inflationary pressures. At present (with effect from April 29,1998), the bank rate is 9 per cent.

2. **Net liquidity ratio:**   In order to check excessive borrowings by the commercial banks from the Reserve Bank of India it has introduced the system of net liquidity ratio in September 1964. According to this system, a commercial bank can borrow from the Reserve Bank at the bank rate only if it maintains a minimum net liquidity ratio to its total demand and time liabilities. It will have to pay a penal rate of interest to the Reserve Bank, if the net liquidity ratio falls below the minimum ratio fixed by the Reserve Bank. The net liquidity of a borrowing bank comprises: (a) cash in hand and balances with the Reserve Bank plus, (b) balances in currency account with other banks, plus (c) investments in government and other approved securities, minus (d) borrowing from the Reserve Bank of India, the State Bank of India and the Industrial Development Bank of India.

3. **Open market operations:**   Through the technique of open market operations, the central bank seeks to influence the excess reserves position of the banks by purchasing and selling of government securities, commercial papers, etc. When the central bank purchases securities from the banks, it increases their cash reserve position and, hence, their credit creation capacity. On the other hand, when the central bank sells securities to the banks, it reduces their cash reserves and the credit creation capacity. In India, the open market operation policy of the Reserve Bank of India has not been so effective because: (a) open market operations are restricted to government securities, (b) gilt-edged market is narrow and (c) most of the open market operations are in the nature of switch operations, i.e. purchasing one loan against the other.

4. **Cash-reserve requirement:**   The central bank of a country can change the Cash-Reserve Requirement (CRR) of the bank in order to affect their credit creation capacity. An increase in the cash-reserve ratio reduces the excess reserve of the bank, and a decrease in the cash-reserve ratio increases their excess reserves. Originally, the Reserve Bank of India Act of 1934 required the commercial banks to keep with the Reserve Bank a minimum cash reserve of 5 per cent of their demand liabilities and 2 per cent of time liabilities.

5. **Statutory liquidity ratio:**   Under the original Banking Regulation Act 1949, banks were required to maintain liquid assets in the form of cash, gold and unencumbered approved securities equal to not less than 25 per cent of their total demand and time deposits liabilities. This minimum statutory liquidity ratio is in addition to the statutory cash-reserve ratio. The Reserve Bank of India has been empowered to change the minimum liquidity ratio.

6. **Selective credit controls:**   These are qualitative credit control measures undertaken by the central bank to divert the flow of credit from speculative and unproductive activities to productive and more urgent activities. Section 21 of the Banking Regulation Act 1949 empowers the Reserve Bank of India to issue directives to the banks regarding their advances. These directives may relate to: (a) the purpose for which advances may or may not be made; (b) the margins to be maintained on the secured loans; (c) the maximum amount of advances to any borrower; (d) the maximum amount upto which guarantees may be given by the banking company; and (e) the rate of interest to be charged. The Reserve Bank of India

has undertaken the ensuing selective credit controls to check speculative activities and inflationary pressures, and extend credit in developmental lines.

(a) Directives: Since 1956, the Reserve Bank of India has been making extensive use of the selective controls and has issued many **directives** to the banks. The first directive was issued on May 17, 1956 to restrict advances against paddy and rice. Later on, other commodities of common use were also included. At present, advances against the following categories of commodity are subject to selective credit control: (i) foodgrains; (ii) pulses; (iii) oilseeds; (iv) vegetable oils; (v) sugar; and (vi) *gur* and *khandsari*. The Reserve Bank has fixed minimum margins to be maintained by the banks regarding their advances against the commodities subject to selective controls. The Reserve Bank fixes higher minimum lending rate for advances against commodities subject to selective controls. State agencies such as the Food Corporation of India and State Trading Corporation nave, however, been exempted from the use of selective credit controls.

(b) Credit Authorization Scheme (CAS): It is a type of selective credit control introduced by the Reserve Bank of India in November 1965. Under this scheme, the commercial banks had to obtain Reserve Bank's authorization before granting any fresh credit of Rs. 1 crore or more to any single party. The limit was later raised gradually to Rs. 4 crore in November 1983, in respect of borrowers in private and public sector. The limit was further raised to Rs. 6 crore with effect from April 1986. Under this scheme, the Reserve Bank of India requires the commercial banks to collect, examine and supply detailed information regarding the borrowing concerns. They are also required to ascertain the working of the borrowing concerns on matters such as intercorporate lending and investment, excessive inventory build-up diversion of short-term funds for acquiring fixed assets, etc. The main purpose of this scheme is to keep a close watch on the flow of credit to the borrowers. It requires that the banks should lend to the large borrowing concerns on the basis of credit appraisal and actual requirements of the borrowers.

The Reserve Bank of India slashed its two key short-term interest rates by a percentage point on December 6, 2008 to stimulate the economy, hit by the global recession and shaken further by Mumbai's terrorist attacks. The central bank reduced the repo rate (at which it lends to the commercial banks) to 6.5 per cent and reserve repo rate (at which it borrows overnight) to 5 per cent. The Bank hopes that the rate reduction will stimulate investment and consumer demand, which have fallen sharply as the global downturn has weakened the domestic economy.

REVIEW QUESTIONS

1. Explain the main functions of the Reserve Bank of India.
2. How does the Reserve Bank of India regulate currency and credit in India?
3. Discuss the role of SBI in promoting industrial finance.
4. Examine the role of RBI in economic development of India.
5. Evaluate the working of the RBI since 1949.

CHAPTER 11

Indian Money Market

11.1 INTRODUCTION

Financial markets are functionally classified into: (i) money market, and (ii) capital market. This classification is on the basis of term of credit, i.e. whether the credit is supplied for a short period or a long period of time. Money market refers to institutional arrangements which deal with short-term funds. It is a short-term credit market that deals with relatively liquid and quickly marketable assets, such as short-term government securities, treasury bills, bills of exchange. According to G. Crowther, "Money market is a collective name given to the various firms and institutions that deal with various grades of near-money." The Reserve Bank of India defines money market as "the centre for dealing, mainly of a short-term character, in memory assets; it meets the short-term requirements of borrowers and provides liquidity or cash to lenders". Capital market, on the other hand, deals in long-term funds.

11.2 STRUCTURE OF INDIAN MONEY MARKET

In India the money market comprises two sectors: (i) *organized* sector and (ii) *unorganized* sector. See Figure 11.1. The organized sector consists of the Reserve Bank of India, the State Bank of India with its seven associates, 20 nationalized commercial banks, other schedule and non-scheduled commercial banks, foreign banks, and regional rural banks. It is called organized because its parts are systematically coordinated by the RBI. The non-bank financial institutions such as Life Insurance Corporation (LIC), General Insurance Corporation (GIC) and subsidiaries, UTI also operate in this market, but only indirectly through banks. Moreover, quasi-governmental bodies and large companies also make their short-term surplus funds available to the organized market through banks. The co-operative credit institutions occupy the intermediary position between the organized and the unorganized sector of the Indian money market. These institutions have a three-tier structure. At the top, there are state co-operative banks At the middle level, there are central co-operative banks. At the local level, there are primary credit societies and urban co-operative banks. Considering the size, method of operations, and dealings with the RBI and commercial banks, only the state and the central co-operative banks should be included in the organized sector.

```
                          ┌─────────────────────┐
                          │ Indian money market │
                          └──────────┬──────────┘
              ┌──────────────────────┴──────────────────────┐
    ┌──────────────────┐                          ┌──────────────────┐
    │ Organized sector │                          │ Unorganized sector│
    └──────────────────┘                          └──────────────────┘
```

Figure represented below as described:

- **Indian money market**
  - **Organized sector**
    - Reserve Bank of India
    - Commercial banks
      - Scheduled commercial banks
        - Public sector banks
          - State bank group
          - Nationalized banks
        - Indian banks
      - Non-scheduled banks
        - Foreign banks
        - Regional rural banks
    - Post office saving banks
    - Non-banking companies
    - Co-operative banks
  - **Unorganized sector**
    - Indigenous bankers
    - Money lenders

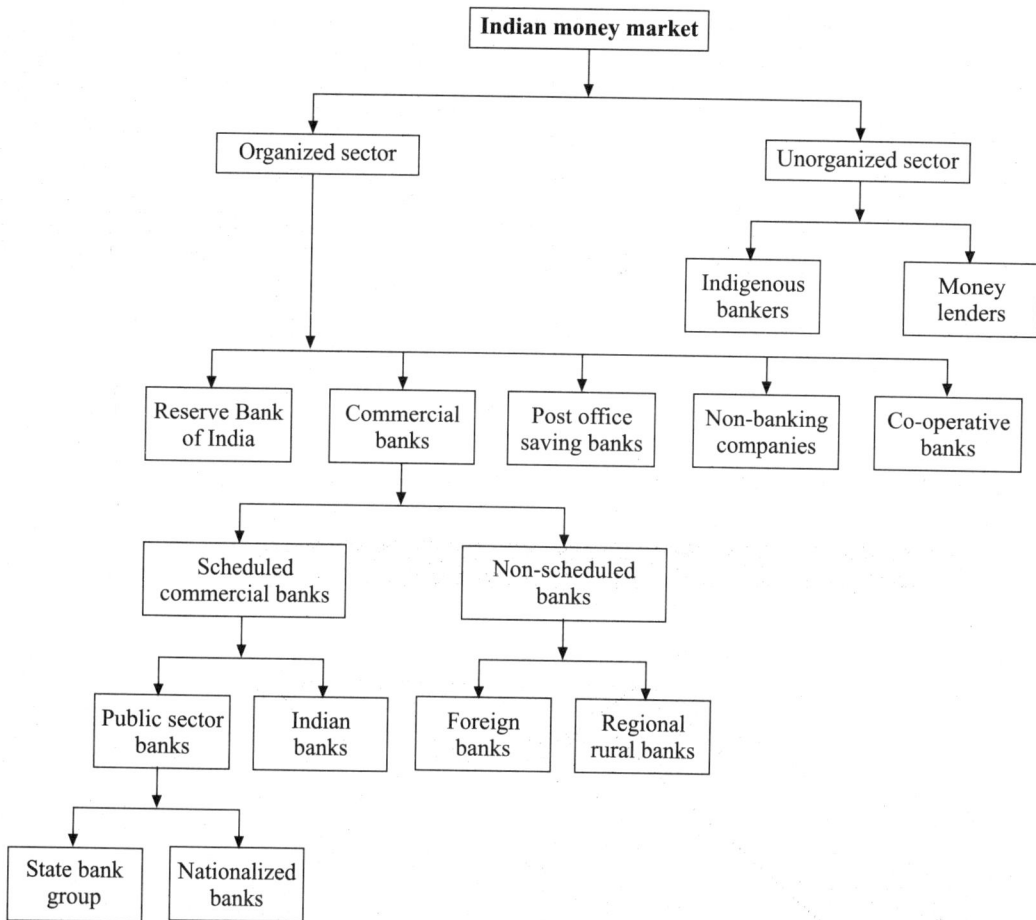

Figure 11.1 Structure of indian money market.

11.3 UNORGANIZED SECTOR OF THE INDIAN MONEY MARKET

The unorganized segment of the Indian money market is composed of unregulated non-bank financial intermediaries, indigenous bankers and money lenders which exist even in small towns and big cities. Their lending activities are mostly restricted to small towns and villages. The people who normally borrow from this unorganized sector include farmers, artisans, small traders and small-scale producers who do not have any access to modern banks. The following are some of the constituents of the unorganized money market in India:

1. **Indigenous bankers:** These include those individuals and private firms which are engaged in receiving deposits and giving loans, and, thereby, act like a mini bank. Their activities are not at all regulated. During the ancient and medieval periods, these indigenous bankers were very active. But with the growth of the modern banking, particularly after the arrival

of the British, the business of the indigenous bankers received a set back. Moreover, with the growth of commercial banks and co-operative banks, the area of operations of indigenous bankers has again contracted further. However even today, some indigenous bankers are still operating in the western and southern parts of the country and have engaged themselves in the traditional banking business.

2. **Unregulated non-bank financial intermediaries:**   There are different types of unregulated non-bank financial intermediaries in India. They are mostly constituted by loan or finance companies, chit funds and *'nidhis'*. A good number of finance companies in India are engaged in collecting substantial amount of funds in the form of deposits, borrowings and other receipts. They normally give loans to wholesale traders, retailers, artisans, and different self-employed people at a high rate of interest ranging between 36 and 48 per cent. Also there are various types of chit funds in India. These are doing business in almost all the states of the country but are majorly concentrated in Tamil Nadu and Kerala. Moreover, there are *nidhis* operating in South India which are a kind of mutual benefit funds restricted to their members.

3. **Money lenders:**   They advance loans to small borrowers, such as marginal and small farmers, agricultural labourers, artisans, factory and mine workers, low paid staffs, small traders, at a very high rate of interest. The money lenders adopt various malpractices to manipulate the loan records of these poor borrowers. There are broadly three types of money lenders: (a) professional money lenders dealing solely with money lending; (b) itinerant money lenders, such as *Kabulis* and *Pathans*, and (c) non-professional money lenders. The area of operation of these money lenders is very much localized and their method of operation also not uniform. The money lending operation of the money lenders is totally unregulated and unsupervised which leads to worst exploitation of the small borrowers. The money lenders have become a necessary evil in the absence of insufficient institutional sources of credit to the poorer section of the society. Although various measures have been introduced to control the activities of the money lenders, but due to lack of political will these are not enforced, leading to huge exploitation of small borrowers.

11.4   ORGANIZED SECTOR OF INDIAN MONEY MARKET

The organized sector of the Indian money market comprises the Reserve Bank of India (RBI), State Bank of India, Commercial banks, Co-operative banks, foreign banks, finance corporations and Discount of Finance House of India Limited. This sector of the Indian money market is quite integrated and well-organized. Mumbai, Kolkata, Chennai, Delhi, Bangalore and Ahmedabad are the leading centres of the organized sector of the Indian money market. The Mumbai money market is well organized, having the head offices of Reserve Bank of India and different commercial banks, the leading well-developed stock exchange, the bullion exchange and a fairly organized market for Government securities. All these have placed the Mumbai money market at par with the New York money market of the USA and the London money market of the UK. The main constituents of the organized sector of the Indian money market include: (i) Call Money Market, (ii) Treasury Bill Market, (iii) Commercial Bill Market, (iv) Certificates of Deposits Market, (v) Money Market for Mutual Funds, and (vi) Commercial Paper Market.

1. **Call money market:**   It is the most common form of a developed money market. Moreover, the call money market is the most sensitive segment of the financial system which reflects

clearly any change in it. The call money market in India has offices in Mumbai, Chennai and Kolkata, of which Mumbai is the most important one. In this market, the lending and borrowing operations are carried out for one day. The call money market is also termed as *inter-bank call money market*. Normally, scheduled commercial banks, co-operative banks and Discount and Finance House of India (DFHI) operate in this market. In special situations, LIC, UTI, GIC, IDBI and NABARD are permitted to operate as lenders in this call money market. In this market, the brokers play very important role.

2. **Treasury bill market:** As the name suggests, it is the market for treasury bills. In India treasury bills are short-term liabilities of the Central Government which are of 91-day and 364-day duration. Normally, the treasury bills should be issued so as to meet the temporary revenue deficit over expenditure of a government at some point of time. But, in India, nowadays the treasury bills are considered as a permanent source of funds for the Central Government. The RBI is the major holder of treasury bills, which is around 90 per cent of the total amount. Moreover since April 1, 1997, the ad-hoc treasury bills have been replaced by ways and means of advances so as to finance the temporary deficits of the Central Government.

3. **Commercial bill market:** It is a kind of sub-market which normally deals with trade bills or commercial bills. This bill normally is drawn by one merchant firm on the other and arises out of commercial transactions. The purpose for issuing a commercial bill is simply to reimburse the seller as and when the buyer delays payment. In India, however, the commercial bill market is not so well developed. This is mainly due to (i) popularity of the cash credit system in bank lending, (ii) the unwillingness on the part of the large buyer to bind himself to payment schedule related to commercial bill, and (iii) the lack of uniform approach in drawing bills.

4. **Certificate of Deposit (CD) market:** This was introduced in India by the RBI in March 1989 with the sole objective of widening the range of money market instruments and attaining higher flexibility in the development of short-term surplus funds for the investors. Initially, CDs are issued by scheduled commercial banks in multiples of Rs. 25 lakh and also to the extent of a minimum of Rs. 1 crore. The maturity of CDs varies between three months and one year. In India, in 1993, six financial institutions, viz. IDBI, ICICI, IFCI, IRBI, SIDBI and Export and Import Bank of India were permitted to issue CDs for a period varying between one and three years. Banks normally pay high rates of interest on CDs. In 1995-1996, the stringent conditions in the money market induced the bankers to mobilize a good amount of resources through CDs.

5. **Commercial Paper (CP) market:** In India, in January 1990, the CP was introduced in the money market. A listed company having working capital not less than Rs. 5 crore has the permission to issue CP. Again the CP can be issued in multiples of Rs. 25 lakh subject to a minimum of Rs. 1 crore for a maturity period varying between three and six months.

6. **Money Market Mutual Funds (MMMF):** The RBI in April 1992 introduced the MMMFs scheme. The main objective of this scheme was to arrange an additional short-term revenue for the individual investors. However, this scheme failed to receive much response as the initial guidelines were not attractive. Then, in November 1995, the RBI introduced some relaxations in order to make the scheme more attractive and flexible. As per the existing guidelines, banks, public financial institutions and private financial institutions are allowed to set up MMMFs. In the meantime, the limits of investment in individual instruments by MMMF have already been deregulated.

11.5 DRAWBACKS OF THE INDIAN MONEY MARKET

The Indian money market has distinctive drawbacks as it suffers from various defects. The following are some of its drawbacks:

1. **Lack of adequate integration:** There is a lack of adequate integration in the Indian money market. The organized and the unorganized sectors of the Indian money market are totally separate from each other and have independent financial operations of their own. Therefore, the activities of one sector have no impact on the activities of the other sector. Under such a background it is very difficult to establish a national money market. However, the Mumbai money market in recent times is fast emerging as a strong money market. Moreover, the various constituents of the Indian money market, viz. commercial banks, co-operative banks and foreign banks are competing among themselves. Particularly, the competition is stiff in the rural areas. Even the commercial banks are competing between themselves. Again, the monetary policy of the RBI is not effective to maintain adequate integration among the various constituents of the Indian money market.

2. **Shortage of funds:** Another important feature of the Indian money market is the shortage of funds. Therefore, the demand for loanable funds in the money market far exceeds their supply. This shortage of funds has mostly resulted from: (i) individuals small capacity to save because of low per capita income; (ii) inadequate banking network and poor banking habit of the people, and finally, (iii) the emergence of strong parallel economy having comprising mainly black money. In recent years, the development of rural banking structure, with the opening of rural branches of commercial banks and expansion of co-operative banks, has improved to some extent the fund position of the Indian money market.

3. **Lack of adequate banking facilities:** The Indian money market is also characterized by lack of adequate banking facilities. Th rural banking network in the country is still inadequate. The number of customers per bank office in India was 12,000 in 1993 as compared to that of only 1400 in the USA. In the rural areas, a substantial portion of the population with small saving potential have no access to the banking facilities. Under such a scenario, mobilization of the huge amount of small savings for productive uses through the expansion of banking network is not being done.

4. **Lack of rational interest rate structure:** There is a lack of rational interest structure which mostly resulted from lack of co-ordination among different banking institutions. Recently, some improvement has been made in this regard, particularly after the introduction of standardization of interest rates by the RBI to make them rational. However, the present system of administered interest rates is suffering from defects, such as (i) too many concessional rates of interest, (ii) comparatively low yield on government securities, and (iii) improper lending and deposit rates fixed by the commercial banks.

5. **Absence of organized bill market:** In India there is absence of an organized bill market although commercial banks purchase and discount both inland and foreign bills to a limited extent. Although, the RBI under its scheme of 1952 and 1970 introduced its limited bill market, but the scheme has failed to popularize bill finance in India. The popularity of the cash credit system and lack of uniformity in commercial bills are mostly responsible for the poor development of the bill market in the country.

6. **Existence of unorganized money market:** Another important feature of the Indian money market is the existence of the unorganized sector, which constitutes of indigenous bankers

and money lenders. This unorganized segment is completely separated from the organized segment of the money market. Although, the RBI has tried to bring the indigenous bankers under its direct control but such attempts have failed. Since the indigenous bankers do not form part of the organized money market, thus, RBI's control over the entire money market is quite limited.

7. **Seasonal stringency of money and fluctuations in interest rates:** Another important feature of the Indian money market is its seasonal stringency of money and the volatile fluctuation of interest rates. India, being primarily an agricultural country face every year during the period of October to June a huge demand for funds to meet the requirement for farm operations and trading in agricultural produce. But the money market not having sufficient elasticity, thus, creates seasonal stringency of funds leading to a rise in the rate of interest. However, in the rainy and slack season, the demand for fund leading to an automatic fall in the rate of interest. Such regular fluctuations in interest rates are not at all conducive for the developmental activities of the country.

11.6 SHORTCOMINGS OF INDIAN MONEY MARKET

Considering the various defects of the Indian money market, it can be observed that the money market in the country is relatively underdeveloped. Moreover, in respect of resources, organization stability and elasticity, the said market cannot be compared with the developed money markets of London and New York. But among the developing countries, India has been maintaining the most developed banking system. Even then the money market sector is still underdeveloped. The underdevelopment nature of the Indian money market is mostly because of by the following shortcomings:

1. The Indian money market fails to possess an adequate and continuous supply of short-term assets, such as treasury bills, bills of exchange, short-term government bonds.
2. This market is lacking the highly organized banking system, so important for the successful working of any money market.
3. The sub-markets, such as acceptance market and the commercial bill market are non-existent in the Indian money market.
4. The Indian money market has totally failed to develop the market for short-term assets, and, accordingly, there are no dealers of these assets who act as intermediaries between the government and the entire banking system.
5. The Indian money market is suffering from lack of co-ordination between its different constituents.
6. It fails to attract any foreign funds.

The Indian money market cannot be termed as a developed one considering its supply of fund and liquidity position. Measures to reform and strengthen the Indian money market have to be taken.

In recent years, serious efforts have been made by the Government of India and the RBI to remove the shortcomings prevalent in the Indian money market. The RBI, in the mean time, has reduced considerably the differences between the various constituents of the money market. The differences in the interest rates and the monetary stringency have been reduced by the RBI through open market operations and bill market scheme.

Even then the Indian money market is still very much dependent on the call money market which is again characterized by high volatility. At present, the RBI has introduced various measures to reform the money market as per the recommendations of Sukhamay Chakraborty Committee on "Review of the working of the monetary system" and Narasimham Committee report on the workings of the financial system in India. Some of the important reform measures introduced to strengthen the Indian money market are discussed in the following section.

11.7 MEASURES TO STRENGTHEN THE INDIAN MONEY MARKET

1. **Remission of stamp duty:** In order to remove the major administrative constraint in the use of the bill system, the Government in August 1989 remitted the stamp duty. However, experts feel that unless the cash credit system is discouraged, the government decision to remit the stamp duty is not going to favour the prevailing bill system.

2. **Deregulation of interest rates:** Another important step taken to strengthen the money market has been deregulating since May, 1989 the money market interest rates. This was to bring interest rate flexibility and transparency in the money market transactions. Again in November 1991, as per the recommendations of Narasimham Committee, the interest rates were further deregulated, and the banks and other financial institutions were advised to determine and adopt market-related rates of interest as far as practicable.

3. **Introduction of new instruments:** The RBI introduced certain money market instruments for strengthening the market conditions. These instruments are 182-day treasury bills, longer maturity treasury bills, certificates of deposits, Commercial Paper and dated Government securities. Discount and Finance House of India promoted the 182-day treasury bills systematically. These bills were the first security sold by auction for financing the fiscal deficit of the Central Government. Again, DFHI developed a secondary market in these bills and they became popular with the commercial banks. Again in 1992–1993, the Government decided to introduce the 364-day treasury bills and discontinued the 164-day treasury bills. The 364-day treasury bills can be held by commercial banks for meeting their statutory liquidity ratio.

4. **The Discount and Finance House of India (DFHI):** This institution was setup in April 25, 1988 as part of the reform package for strengthening the money market. The main function of DFHI is to bring the entire financial system consisting of the scheduled commercial banks, co-operative banks, foreign banks and all-India financial institutions, both in the public sector and in the private sector, within the fold of the Indian money market. DFHI normally buys bills and short-term papers from different banks and financial institutions in order to invest all of their idle funds for short periods. It has also started from April 1992 to buy and sell government securities in limited quantity with the necessary refinance support from the RBI.

5. **Money Market Mutual Funds (MMMFs):** The Government announced in April 1992 the establishment of MMMFs with the sole objective to bring the money market instruments within the reach of individuals. The MMMFs have been set up by different scheduled commercial banks and public financial institutions. The shares or units of MMMFs are issued only to individuals.

Thus, the aforesaid measures to reform the Indian money market have helped it to become more advanced, solvent and vibrant. With the introduction of the new instruments, the secondary market has also been developed considerably. Moreover, with the setting up of DFHI and MMMFs, a lot of considerable progress has been achieved in the Indian money market in the recent times. It is expected that there will be further progress in the Indian money market in the years to come.

11.8 INDIAN CAPITAL MARKET

By the term 'capital market' we mean a market for long-term funds, whereas the money market constitutes the market for short-term funds. The capital market includes all existing facilities and institutional arrangements developed for borrowing and lending medium- and long-term funds available in the market. However, this is not a market for capital goods. It is rather a market for raising and advancing money capital for investment purposes. In a capital market, the demand for long-term funds mostly arises from private sector manufacturing industries, agricultural sector and the Government, which are again largely utilized for the economic development of the country. Even the consumer goods industries usually need the considerable support from the capital market. Similarly, both the State and the Central Governments, which are engaged in developing infrastructural facilities, viz. transport, power, irrigation, communications, along with the development of the basic industries also need considerable support from the capital market. In a capital market, the supply of funds usually comes from individual savers, corporate savings of various banks, insurance companies, specialized financial agencies and the Government. The following are some of the institutions supplying funds to the Indian Capital market:

1. Commercial banks in India, which are interested in government securities and on debentures of companies, are considered as important investors.
2. The insurance companies, such as LIC and GIC have also attained growing importance in the Indian capital market, and are mostly investing in government securities.
3. Various special institutions, viz. IDBI, IFCI, ICICI, UTI, etc. are giving long-term capital to the private sector of the country.
4. Provident funds of employees constitute a major volume of savings. However, their investments are very much restricted in government securities.

After independence, the rapid growth and expansion of the corporate and public enterprises has necessitated the development of the capital market in India. The capital market is composed of borrowers, who demand funds and lenders, who supply funds in the market. An ideal and sound capital market always tries to offer adequate quantity of capital to any industrial and business house at a reasonable rate which are expected to result high prospective yield to make the borrowing worthwhile.

11.9 STRUCTURE OF DEVELOPMENT BANKS OF INDIA

In India the development banks (with the exception of Land Development Banks) have developed in the post-independent era. The structure of the Indian development banks can be divided into two broad categories: (i) those which promote agricultural development; and (ii) those which promote industrial development.

11.9.1 Agricultural Development Banks

The agricultural development banks in the country are further classified into three heads:

1. **At all-India level:** National Bank for Agriculture and Rural Development (NABARD)
2. **At state level:** State Land Development Banks (SLDBs).
3. **At local level:** Primary Land Development Banks (PLDBs), and branches of SLDBs.

11.9.2   Industrial Development Banks

Industrial development banks are also divided into two groups.

1. **At all-India level:**   Industrial Finance Corporation of India (IFCI), Industrial Development Bank of India (IDBI), Industrial Credit and Investment Corporation of India (ICICI), Industrial Reconstruction Bank of India (IRBI).
2. **At state level:**   State Finance Corporations (SFCs), and State Industrial Development Corporations (SIDs).

Industrial Finance Corporation of India

Industrial Finance Corporation of India (IFCI) is the first industrial development bank set up in July 1948 by the Government of India. It was established with a view to provide medium- and long-term credits to the eligible industrial units in the country. IFCI extends financial assistance to large- and medium-sized industrial units in both private and public sectors, and also to co-operatives. As a development bank, IFCI also undertakes a number of promotional activities, some on its own and some jointly with other all-India financial institutions.

Industrial Finance Corporation of India provides assistance in the following forms:

1. It grants loans and advances to industrial concerns both in rupees and in foreign currency repayable within 25 years. The limit of assistance to any single concern now is Rs. 1 crore. Under special circumstances, the limit on assistance can be raised with the permission of the government.
2. IFCI subscribes to the shares and debentures issued by the industrial concerns.
3. It underwrites the issues of stocks, shares, bonds, debentures of the industrial concerns subject to the condition that such stocks, shares, etc. are disposed of by the Corporation within a period of seven years from the time of acquisition.
4. IFCI guarantees (i) rupees loans raised from scheduled banks or state co-operative banks by the industrial concerns, (ii) foreign currency loans raised from foreign institutions, and (iii) deferred payments in respect of oil machinery imported from abroad or purchased from within the country.
5. In recent years, the Corporation has started taking interest in the promotional activities, such as organizing techno-economic surveys, setting up of technical consultancy organizations etc.

Important features of the working of IFCI are as follows:

1. The Corporation is expected to give special attention to the following categories of projects: (i) the projects promoted by new entrepreneurs and technologists; (ii) those located in the less developed areas; (iii) the projects based on indigenous technology or aimed at exploring new areas of technology; (iv) those having prospects of earning foreign exchange or import substitution; (v) the projects providing inputs for increasing agricultural production; and (vi) the projects fulfilling the increased demand for consumer goods.
2. While granting finance, greater emphasis is on setting up of new projects. Over the years new projects have accounted for about two-third of the total assistance.
3. The major beneficiaries of the financial assistance from IFCI are the private corporate sector and the co-operative sector. In the co-operative sector, the loans sanctioned to sugar industry are more significant.

4. Industry-wise distribution of the assistance shows that more than three-fourth of the aggregate assistance was sanctioned to sugar, chemicals, non-ferrous metals, engineering, fertilisers, textiles and paper industries.
5. Larger proportion of assistance has been extended to the developed regions of the country. For example, more than 50 per cent of the total financial assistance is received by the four industrially advanced states of Maharashtra, Gujarat, Tamil Nadu and West Bengal.
6. The Corporation participates in the Soft Loan Scheme introduced by Industrial Development Bank.
7. IFCI sponsored risk capital foundation in order to provide assistance to new entrepreneurs including technologists and professionals. The Foundation, which started its operations in 1976, provides loans to such entrepreneurs free of interest or at nominal interest rate.
8. The Corporation sponsored Management Development Institute which has been established to promote management education in the country.
9. The Corporation has also sponsored technical consultancy organization in Himachal Pradesh, Rajasthan and Madhya Pradesh to meet the consultancy needs of new entrepreneurs and technologists.
10. Recently, the Corporation has started four new promotional schemes: (i) interest subsidy schemes for women entrepreneurs; (ii) consultancy fee subsidy schemes for providing marketing assistance to small-scale units; (iii) encouraging modernization of tiny, small-scale and ancillary units; and (iv) controlling pollution in small- and medium-scale units.

In spite of the notable progress made by IFCI over the years, its functioning has been criticised on the following grounds:

1. IFCI has adopted a discriminatory lending policy to the disadvantage of the small- and medium-sized industrial units. Its assistance is particularly biased in favour of cotton textiles and sugar industry.
2. It has not helped much in removing regional inequalities. Less developed states are the least beneficiaries.
3. In many cases, the loans have been granted to those industrial units which could easily raise resources from the capital market.
4. The Corporation's insistence on personal guarantee of directors in addition to mortgage of property shows that it gives more importance to the status of the directors rather than to the soundness of the project.
5. IFCI has failed to exercise control over the defaulting borrowers who have not utilized loans for the purposes for which they were granted.
6. The Corporation has provided greater assistance to the consumer goods industries and only a meagre help to the basic and capital goods industries.
7. IFCI has also been criticized on the charges of indulging in nepotism and favouritism while granting loans.
8. It has been charging very high interest rates.

State Finance Corporations

Industrial Finance Corporation of India provides financial assistance to large public limited companies and co-operative societies. It does not cover the small- and medium-sized industries. In order to meet the varied financial needs of small and medium-sized industries, the Government of India in 1951 passed the State Finance Corporations Act which empowers the state governments to establish such corporations in their states. The first State Finance Corporation (SFC) was set up in 1953 in Punjab. At present, there are 18 SFCs operating in the country.

Various *functions* of and types of financial assistance provided by the SFCs are given here:

1. The SFCs have been established to provide long-term finance to small-scale and medium-sized industrial concerns organized as public or private companies, corporations, partnership or proprietary concerns.
2. They extend loans and advances to the industrial concerns repayable within a period of 20 years.
3. The corporations guarantee loans raised by the industrial concerns in the market or from scheduled or co-operative banks and repayable within 20 years.
4. The SFCs subscribe to the debentures of the industrial concerns repayable within a period of 20 years.
5. The corporations guarantee loans raised by the industrial concerns from scheduled or co-operative banks and repayable within 20 years.
6. The SFCs underwrite the issue of stocks, shares, bonds and debentures by industrial concerns.
7. They guarantee the deferred payments for the purchase of plant, machinery, etc. within the country.
8. The SFCs are prohibited from subscribing directly to the shares or stock of any company having limited liability, except for underwriting purposes, and granting any loan or advance on the security of their own shares.
9. The corporations can act as agent of the Central or State governments or some industrial financing institution for sanctioning and disbursing loans to small industries.

Important *features* of the SFCs' working are as given here:

1. The SFCs were set up with the objective of providing financial assistance to small and medium industrial concerns. Though there has been a notable rise in the overall financial assistance, the performance of individual corporations differed largely due to the attitudes and motivations of the local entrepreneurs in different states.
2. Prior to 1966, the SFCs showed preference for medium industries. But, now there has been a marked shift in their lending policies in favour of small units. In 1985–1986, the share of small units in the total loans sanctioned was 82 per cent.
3. Major beneficiaries of the financial assistance of the SFCs have been the food processing industries, services (mainly road transport), chemicals, textiles, metal products, machinery and transport equipment industries.
4. A special feature of the lending operations of SFCs has been the provision of finance to industrial concerns of backward areas. In 1985–1986, the share of the backward areas in the total assistance sanctioned by the SFCs was 53 per cent.
5. The SFCs provide concessional assistance to the industrial units located in backward areas in terms of soft loans at concessional rates, lower margins, reduced service charges, etc.
6. In order to encourage self-employment, the SFCs have formulated schemes of assistance to technician-entrepreneurs.

The actual performance of the SFCs has been criticized mainly because of the following defects and inadequacies:

1. The financial resources of the SFCs are inadequate. Moreover, they face the difficulty of finding additional funds.

2. The SFCs have not been able to provide adequate financial assistance to meet the requirements of small and medium industries.
3. They charge very high interest rates on all loans other than the soft loans. Moreover, the terms and conditions of assistance are also stringent.
4. The SFCs face the serious problem of ever increasing magnitude of overdues. The main reasons for overdues are: delay in the implementation of projects, and industrial sickness.
5. The corporations provide finance against adequate security. But many industrial units, particularly the proprietary and partnership concerns find it problematic to offer adequate security for their loans mainly because of the defects in the title to ownership and difficulties of evaluating the fixed assets.
6. The SFCs lack self-sufficient organizational set up along with adequate specialized and trained staff for ensuring their efficient functioning.
7. There is also a shortage of technical personnel for judging the soundness of the proposed schemes of the borrowing units.
8. Many difficulties are faced by the SFCs while extending financial assistance to the small industrial units.

Industrial Development Bank of India

Industrial Development Bank of India (IDBI) is the apex financial institution in the field of development banking in the country. It was established in July 1964 with the twin objectives of: (i) meeting the growing financial needs of rapid industrialization in the country, and (ii) coordinating the activities and assisting the growth of all institutions engaged in financing industries. It is an organization with sufficiently large financial resources. IDBI not only provides direct financial assistance to the large and medium-large industrial units, but also helps the small and medium industries indirectly by extending refinancing and rediscounting facilities to other industrial financing institutions. Thus, the primary aim of IDBI has been to integrate the structure of industrial financing institutions and fill the gap between demand and supply of term finance in the country. Initially, IDBI was set up as a wholly owned subsidiary of the Reserve Bank of India. However, in 1976, it was taken over by the Government of India and made an autonomous institution.

Various *functions* includes types of assistance provided by IDBI are as follows:

1. **Direct financial assistance:** IDBI provides direct financial assistance to the industrial concerns in the form of: (i) granting loans and advances; and (ii) subscribing to, purchasing or underwriting the issues of stocks, bonds or debentures.
2. **Indirect financial assistance:** It provides indirect financial assistance to the small and medium industrial concerns through other financial institution, such as State Finance Corporations, State Industrial Development Corporations, Co-operative banks, regional rural banks, commercial banks. Assistance to these institutions include: (i) refinancing of loans given by the institutions; (ii) subscribing to their shares and bonds; (iii) rediscounting of bills.
3. **Development assistance:** The creation of Development Assistance Fund is the special feature of IDBI. The Fund is used to provide assistance to those industries which are not able to obtain finance in the normal course, mainly because of heavy investment involved or low expected rate of returns. The financial sources of these Fund are mainly contributions made by the government in the form of loans, gifts, donations, etc. and from other sources. Assistance from the fund requires the prior approval of the government.

4. **Promotional function:**   Besides providing financial assistance, IDBI also undertakes various promotional activities, such as marketing and investment research, techno-economic surveys. It provides technical and administrative advice for promotion, expansion and better management of industrial concerns.

Other features of assistance extended by IDBI are as given here:

1. **Direct assistance:**   This to the industrial concerns over the years has accounted for about one third of the total assistance. In 1985–1986, IDBI sanctioned direct assistance of Rs. 1120 crore which included project loans, soft loans, underwriting of and direct subscription to shares, bonds and debentures of industrial concerns. Loans form the major portion of IDBI's direct assistance.

2. **Refinance of loans:**   IDBI has been providing refinance facilities in three ways: (i) by refinancing term loans to industry and export trade; (ii) by subscribing to the shares and bonds of the financial institutions; and (iii) by rediscounting the bills of exchange. It took over the business of the Refinance Corporation of India and started providing refinance facilities to the industrial concerns through member banks.

3. **Assistance to small-scale industries:**   IDBI has shown special interest in extending assistance to small-scale industries through its refinance schemes. In May 1986, IDBI set up a separate fund called Small Industries Development Fund (SIDF) to facilitate development, expansion, modernization, diversification and rehabilitation of small industries. It has also introduced the 'integrated term loan' facility for the new small projects. After the establishment of Small Industries Development Board of India (SIDBI), from April 1990 the entire portfolio of IDBI relating to small and tiny sector has been transferred to it.

4. **Assistance in backward areas:**   To promote industries in the backward regions of the country, IDBI has been providing financial and non-financial assistance. The financial assistance includes: (i) direct loans at concessional rates, longer initial grace period, etc.; (ii) concessional refinance facilities to industries in the backward areas; and (iii) special concessions to the projects in the north-eastern regions under the bill rediscounting scheme. The non-financial assistance is in the form of identification and formulation of variable projects, the provision of technical assistance, etc. During 1990–1991, IDBI provided 43 per cent of its total assistance to backward areas.

5. **Soft loan scheme:**   In 1976, IDBI introduced the soft loan scheme for providing concessional finance to the selected industries. This facility is available to cement, sugar, jute, cotton textiles and certain engineering industries for modernizing, replacing and renovating their plants and equipment. The concessional rate of interest is 7.5 per cent and the period of loan is 12 to 15 years.

6. **Scheme for no-industry districts:**   IDBI has introduced a special scheme for no-industry districts with a view to develop industries in these areas by providing financial, technical and administrative assistance, and arranging training for potential entrepreneurs. IDBI conducts surveys to study the industrial potential of no-industry districts.

7. **Technical consultancy organization:**   IDBI has also initiated Technical Consultancy Organization (TCO). The main objective of TCO is to organize feasibility studies, project appraisals, industrial and market potential surveys, and training programmes for new entrepreneurs.

Industrial Development Bank of India as the leading development bank, has made a significant contribution to accelerate the industrialization process in the country. The amount, range and pattern of assistance provided by IDBI has grown over the years. But, still there exist certain drawbacks because of which IDBI has not been able to develop itself as a development bank in the true sense of the term. The important criticisms of IDBI are given here:

1. It has confined itself to providing direct loans to the industrial concerns and treated the underwriting of shares and debentures of industrial concerns as a less important activity. In this way, IDBI has failed to develop the capital market in the country.
2. Similarly, in spite of repeated emphasis to assist the small-scale sector, a larger portion of IDBI's assistance has been received by the big industrial concerns.
3. IDBI has largely concentrated on providing financial assistance to industries, and given less importance to promotional and consultancy functions.
4. IDBI's lack of proper supervision of SFCs has been largely responsible for the alarming increase in overdues.

Industrial Credit and Investment Corporation of India

In 1955 Industrial Credit and Investment Corporation of India (ICICI) was registered as a private limited company. It was set up as a private sector development bank to assist and promote private industrial concerns in the country. The broad objectives of ICICI are to: (i) assist in the creation, expansion and modernization of private concerns; (ii) encourage the participation of internal and external capital in the private concerns; (iii) encourage private ownership of industrial investment.

The following *functions* are performed by ICICI:

1. Provides long-term and medium-term loans in rupees and foreign currencies.
2. Participates in the equity capital of the industrial concerns.
3. Underwrites new issues of shares and debentures.
4. Guarantees loans raised by private concerns from other sources.
5. Provides technical, managerial and administrative assistance to industrial concerns.

The important *features* of the functioning of ICICI are as given here:

1. Financial assistance as provided by ICICI includes rupee loans, foreign currency loans, guarantees, underwriting of shares and debentures, and direct subscription to shares and debentures.
2. Originally, ICICI was established to provide financial assistance to industrial concerns in the private sector. But, recently, its scope has been widened by including industrial concerns in the public, joint and co-operative sectors.
3. ICICI has been providing special attention to financing riskier and non-traditional industries, such as chemicals, petrochemicals, heavy engineering and metal products. These four categories of industries have accounted for more than half of the total assistance.
4. Lately, ICICI has also been providing assistance to small-scale industries and projects in the backward areas.
5. Along with other financial institutions, ICICI is actively participating in conducting surveys to examine industrial potential in various states.
6. In 1977, ICICI promoted the Housing Development Finance Corporation Ltd. to grant term loans for the construction and purchase of residential houses.

7. Since 1983, ICICI has been providing leasing assistance for computerization, modernization and replacement schemes for energy conservation export orientation, pollution control, balancing and expansion, etc.
8. ICICI has not contributed much to reduce regional disparities. About three-fifth of the total assistance given by ICICI has been received by the advanced states of Maharashtra, Gujarat and Tamil Nadu.
9. With effect from April 1, 1996, Shipping Credit and Investment Company of India ltd. (SCICI) was merged with ICICI.

Unit Trust of India

The Unit Trust of India (UTI) was established in 1964 as a public sector investment institution. The main objective of UTI is to mobilize the savings of the small and medium income groups, and channeling them into productive investment. It, thus, on the one hand, contributes to the industrial development and diversification of the economy, and, on the other hand, provides the small savers the opportunity for sharing the benefits of industrial development by utilizing their savings in profitable and less risky investments.

The UTI achieves its objectives by performing the following *functions:*

1. Sells its units to the investors in small and medium income groups.
2. Invests the funds so collected through the sale of units in industrial and corporate securities.
3. Distributes the annual gross income among the unit-holders in the form of dividends.

There are two main sources of capital of UTI: (i) the initial capital, and (ii) the unit capital. The initial capital of UTI was Rs. 5 crore of these, Rs. 2.5 crore were contributed by the Reserve Bank of India and the rest was subscribed by State Bank of India (Rs. 75 lakh), the Life Insurance Corporation (Rs. 75 lakh), commercial banks and other institutions (Rs. 1 crore). Unit capital is raised by the sale of units. The overall management of UTI is under the control of the Board of Trustees, comprising a Chairman and nine other trustees.

Over the years, UTI has achieved considerable *progress* in mobilizing savings through the sale of units and investing its funds profitably. During the first year of its establishment, i.e. 1964, the sales of the units were of Rs. 19.1 crore. Today, UTI has become a trust of over 4.8 crore unit holders and manages over Rs. 56,000 crore. Financial assistance sanctioned by UTI, which was Rs. 2.1 crore in 1965–1966, increased to Rs. 9.2 crore in 1970–1971 and further to Rs. 4229 crore in 1997–1998. Similarly, the assistance disbursed amounted to Rs. 1.7 crore in 1965–1966, Rs. 5.1 crore in 1970–1971 and Rs. 3449 crore in 1997–1998.

The salient *features* of the working of UTI are as given here:

1. Unit Trust of India sells the units issued by it in the denomination of Rs. 10 or Rs. 100 to the investing public.
2. It has formulated various schemes to cater the specific investment needs of different types of investors. So far, UTI has introduced 66 schemes for mobilizing savings. Its main scheme is Unit Scheme 1964. It has also started specific saving plans linked with the unit schemes; they are: Reinvestment Plan 1966, Children's Gift Plan 1970 and Unit Linked Insurance Plan 1971.
3. Unit Trust of India in association with Merrill Lynch has initiated the 'India Fund' in the UK (1986) and 'India Growth Fund' in the USA. (1988) for providing the non-resident Indians and individuals of Indian origin residing abroad and other persons resident outside India the opportunity to invest in the securities market of India through the special unit scheme.

4. In 1986, UTI also set up a 'Mutual Fund' under which 'Master Shares' were offered for public subscription. The Mutual Fund provides an outlet for small investors for investing in shares quoted in the stock exchanges.
5. It has also introduced a new scheme, i.e. Housing Development Fund Units Scheme.
6. Unit Trust of India has been paying dividend to the purchasers of the units at an progressively increasing rate.
7. It has drawn up its investment policy on the principle of maximization of earnings consistent with the safety of capital. UTI has become the single largest investor in the Indian stock markets and is the provider of large amounts of resources to the Indian Industry.
8. To encourage the small investors to purchase units, the Government of India has granted tax concessions.

Industrial Reconstruction Corporation of India

Considering the seriousness of the problem of industrial sickness, the Government of India established in April 1973 Industrial Reconstruction Corporation of India (IRCI). The main purpose of IRCI was to prevent and cure the problem of industrial sickness. It was expected to provide assistance to sick units to get rehabilitated and reconstructed. IRCI was set up with an authorized capital of Rs. 25 crore, issued capital of Rs. 10 crore and paid-up capital of Rs. 2.5 crore. The resources of the Corporation were subscribed by IDBI, IFCI, ICICI, LIC, State Bank of India and other nationalized banks. The Government of India granted an interest-free loan of Rs. 10 crore to the Corporation. Upto the end of March 1984, the IRCI sanctioned financial assistance of Rs. 266 crore and disbursed Rs. 185 crore to 242 sick or closed industrial units.

By a special Act passed in March 1985, the Government of India changed IRCI into Industrial Reconstruction Bank of India (IRBI). IRBI was set up as a statutory corporation with the objective of functioning as the principal institution for providing financial assistance needed for rehabilitation of sick industrial concerns. The authorized capital of IRBI is Rs. 200 crore and paid-up capital as on March, 31, 1989 was Rs. 112.5 crore. During 1993–1994 IRBI sanctioned financial assistance of Rs. 425.8 crore of which Rs. 188.6 crore was disbursed. At the end of June 1991, the cumulative financial assistance sanctioned and disbursed stood at Rs. 1244 and Rs. 919 crore, respectively. Industrial Reconstruction Bank of India was again changed to a full-fledged development financial institution with a new name Industrial Investment Bank of India Ltd. (IIBI) with effect from March 27, 1997.

Export-Import (EXIM) Bank of India

Export-Import (EXIM) Bank of India is the principal financial institution in India for coordinating the working of institutions engaged in financing export and import trade. It is a statutory corporation wholly owned by Government of India. EXIM bank was established on January 1, 1982 for the purpose of financing, facilitating and promoting foreign trade of India.

The authorized *capital* of EXIM Bank is Rs. 200 crore and paid up capital is Rs. 100 crore, wholly subscribed by the Central Government. The bank can raise additional resources through the following:

1. Loans/grants from Central Government and Reserve Bank of India
2. Lines of credit from institutions abroad
3. Funds raised from Euro Currency markets
4. Bonds issued in India

The main *functions* of EXIM Bank are as follows:

1. Financing of exports and imports of goods and services not only of India, but also of the third world countries.
2. Financing of exports and imports of machinery and equipment on lease basis.
3. Financing of joint ventures in foreign countries.
4. Providing loans to Indian parties to enable them to contribute to the share capital of joint ventures in foreign countries.
5 Undertaking limited merchant banking functions, such as underwriting of stocks, shares, bonds or debentures of Indian companies engaged in export or import.
6. Providing technical, administrative and financial assistance to parties in connection with export and import.

The EXIM Bank undertakes its *lending operations* under the following three broad categories:

1. Loans to commercial banks in India include:
   (a) Export bills re-discounting scheme (short-term bills).
   (b) Refinance of export capital.

2. Loan to Indian companies include:
   (a) Direct financial assistance to exporters
   (b) Technology and consultancy services
   (c) Overseas investment financing for equity participation by an Indian company in the joint ventures abroad
   (d) Pre-shipment credit in the case of export contract for capital goods

3. Loans to foreign governments, companies and financial institutions include:
   (a) Overseas buyers' credit scheme
   (b) Lines of credit to foreign governments
   (c) Relending facility to banks overseas

In order to promote export, EXIM Bank has developed the following schemes:

1. **Production equipment finance programme:** This offers rupee-term finance to eligible export-oriented units for acquisition of equipment.
2. **Export marketing finance:** This helps the Indian manufacturing companies to undertake strategic export marketing activities based on long-term and structured export plans with advanced country markets.
3. **Export vendor development finance:** This provides integrated financing packages to manufacturer-exporters and export/trading houses to prepare and implement strategic vendor development plans. The total financial **assistance** provided by EXIM Bank and outstanding at the end of March 1991 was about Rs. 2000 crore. During 1992–1993, the Bank sanctioned loans of Rs. 1590 crore registering an increase of 40 per cent over the previous year. Disbursement stood at Rs. 1296 crore, an increase of 17 per cent over the previous year. During 1997–1998, Exim Bank sanctioned loans of Rs. 1840 crore, while disbursed Rs. 1370 crore.

Small Industries Development Bank of India

Small Industries Development Bank of India (SIDBI) was established as wholly owned subsidiary of IDBI under the small Industries Development of India Act 1989. It is the principal institution for promotion, financing and development of industries in the small-scale sector. It also coordinates the functions of institutions engaged in similar activities. For this purpose, SIDBI has taken over the responsibility of administrating Small Industries Development Fund and National Equity Fund from IDBI.

The Bank provides assistance to the small-scale industries sector in the country through the existing banking and other financial institutions, such as State Financial Corporations, State Industrial Development Corporations, commercial banks, and co-operative banks. The major functions of SIDBI are given as follows:

1. Refinances loans and advances provided by the existing lending institutions to the small-scale units.
2. Discounts and rediscounts bills arising from sale of machinery to and manufactured by small-scale industrial units.
3. Extends seed capital/soft loan assistance under National Equity Fund, *Mahila Udyam Nidhi, Mahila Vikas Nidhi* and seed capital schemes.
4. Grants direct assistance and refinance loans extended by primary lending institutions for financing exports of products manufactured by small scale units.
5. Provide services such as factoring, leasing, to small units.
6. Extends financial support to State Small Industries Corporations for providing scarce raw materials to and marketing the products of the small-scale units.
7. Provides financial support to National Small Industries Corporation for providing, leasing, hire purchase and marketing help to the small-scale units.

During 1990–1991, SIDBI sanctioned financial assistance worth Rs. 2409 crore, which increased to Rs. 7482.6 crore in 1997–1998. Similarly, the assistance disbursed increased from Rs. 1839 crore in 1990–1991 to Rs. 5239.4 crore in. 1997–1998.

Life Insurance Corporation of India

Life Insurance Corporation of India (LIC) was established in 1956 to spread the message of life insurance in the country and mobilize people's savings for nation building activities. The main features of LIC are given as follows:

1. **Saving institution:** Life insurance, both promotes and mobilizes savings in the country. The income tax concession provides further incentive to higher income persons to save through LIC policies. The total volume of insurance business has also been growing with the spread of insurance-consciousness in the country. The total new business of LIC during 1995–1996 was Rs. 51,815 crore sum assured, under 10.20 lakh policies.

   The Life Insurance Corporation of India's business can grow at still faster rate if the following improvements are made by it:

   (a) The organizational and operational efficiency of LIC should be increased.
   (b) New types of insurance covers should be introduced.
   (c) The services of LIC should be extended to smaller areas of the country.
   (d) The message of life insurance should be made more popular.
   (e) The general price level should be kept stable so that the insuring public does not get cheated of a large amount of the real value of its long-term saving through inflation.

2. **Term financing institution:** LIC also functions as a large-term financing institution (or a capital market) in the country. The annual net accrual of investible funds from life insurance business (after making all kinds of payments liabilities to the policy holders) and net income

from its vast investment are quite large. During 1994–1995, LIC's total income was Rs. 18,102.92 crore, consisting of premium income of Rs 1152.80 crore, investment income of Rs. 6336.19 crore, and miscellaneous income of Rs. 238.33 crore.

3. **Investment institutions:**   It is a big investor of funds in government securities. Under the law, LIC is required to invest at least 50 per cent of its accruals in the form of premium income in government and other approved securities. LIC funds are also made available directly to the private sector through investment in shares, debentures, and loans. It also plays a significant role in developing the business of underwriting of new issues.

4. **Stabilizer in share market:**   LIC acts as a downward stabilizer in the share market. The continuous inflow of new funds enables LIC to buy shares when the market is weak. But, LIC does not usually sell shares when the market is overshot. This is partly due to the continuous pressure for investing new funds and partly due to the disincentive of the capital gains tax.

5. **Progress of LIC:**   Since its establishment, LIC has made notable progresses. With central office in Mumbai and seven zonal offices at Mumbai, Kolkata, Delhi, Chennai, Hyderabad, Kanpur and Bhopal, LIC operates through 100 divisional offices in important cities and 2021 branch offices from 1363 centres. LIC has 5.49 lakh active agents spread over the country.

General Insurance Corporation (GIC) of India

General insurance companies sell insurance against specific risks, such as loss from fire and accident to property of various kinds, such as motor vehicles, goods, machinery, buildings, and also against risk of personal accidents and sickness. The policies of these companies do not involve saving feature. The purchaser of general insurance simply buys a service and not any financial asset. In this way, the general insurance companies cannot be considered as financial intermediaries in the true sense. However, they do accumulate large amount of funds from premiums and investment income, and, thus, manage portfolios of assets like other financial institutions.

Besides the growing extent of the financial assistance by the development banks, some other important *features* regarding the functioning of these institutions are summarized here:

1. The development banks in India have been obtaining their capital resources, not directly from the public, but mainly from Government of India, the Reserve Bank of India, other financial institutions, and from foreign sources, like the World Bank, the International Finance Corporation (IFC), International Development Association (IDA).

2. The development banks provide financial assistance mainly in the form of debt lending. Investment in debentures is almost negligible.

3. The development banks cater the financial needs of large, medium and small industries, serve different regions of the country, and provide medium-term and long-term loans.

4. Some development banks (such as LDBs and NABARD) provide term-loans for the development of agriculture and rural areas.

5. A few development banks (such as IRBI) specialize in providing assistance to sick industries.

6. Institutions, such as UTI, also serve to mobilize resources from the general public.

7. The development banks also extend concessional finance to specified concerns, for specified purposes and in specified areas. The various concessions are in the form of lower interest rates, easier collateral conditions, lenient treatment of the cases of default, etc.

8. Some development banks provide other services, such as consultancy service in respect of management, administration.

REVIEW QUESTIONS

1. What are the constituents of Indian money market? Do you think that the Indian money market is a perfect market?
2. Discuss the defects of Indian money market. How can they be removed?
3. Describe the structure of development banks of India.
4. Explain the functions of EXIM Bank of India.
5. Write notes on:

    (a) Industrial Reconstruction Bank of India (IRBI)
    (b) Unit Trust of India (UTI)
    (c) EXIM Bank
    (d) Small Industries Development Bank of India (SIDBI).

Part III

COST ACCOUNTING

CHAPTER 12

Costing and Cost Concepts

12.1 INTRODUCTION

Cost accounting is being used in every sphere of modern-day business. But it has its origin in ancient times. When farmers and craftsmen used to apply the technique to ascertain the cost of their products. However, the real development in cost accounting began during the 18th and 19th century.

Cost accounting as the name suggests is accounting for cost. It consists of two words: (i) cost and (ii) accounting. *Cost* means the resources sacrificed for the production of a commodity and *accounting* refers to the financial information system. Cost accounting system can be described as measurement and reporting of resources used in monetary terms. It is the branch of accounting, dealing with classification, recording, allocation, summarization and reporting of current and prospective cost.

12.2 COSTING AND COST ACCOUNTING

Costing refers to the technique and process of ascertaining cost. The technique consists of principles and rules for determining the costs of products and services.

Cost accounting, on the other hand, is defined as the process of accounting for cost from the point at which expenditure is incurred or committed. It is that specialized branch of accounting which involves classification, accumulation, allocation, absorption and control of costs.

The concept of cost accounting is a bit wider than costing and accounting. It includes several subjects, such as costing, accounting, cost control, budgetary control, and cost audit. Cost accounting is the application of costing and accounting principles, methods and techniques to the science, art and practice of cost control. It includes presentation of information derived for the purpose of managerial decision-making.

Cost accounting has the following functions:

1. **Cost ascertainment:** Ascertaining the cost of goods produced and services rendered is the chief function of cost accounting. This purpose is sometimes referred to as product costing or cost accumulation.
2. **Cost analysis:** It is one of the important functions of cost accounting. This is because cost accounting helps in decision-making. When making a decision about running a business,

we require information about cost, revenue and other information. So we have to analyse the cost.

3. **Cost control:**   It is the chief motive of every management. Cost information shows the performance of the organization. There are two types of cost control method: (i) standard costing and (ii) Budgetary control. Actual cost is compared on the budgeted cost. This help in controlling the cost.

12.3   OBJECTIVES OF COST ACCOUNTING

Cost accounting has following objectives

1. Cost accounting helps in ascertaining the cost of production of every unit, job, operation process, department and service.
2. It indicates to management any inefficiency and the extent of various forms of waste, whether as material, time, expense or in the use of machine, equipment and tools.
3. Cost accounting discloses profitable and unprofitable activities so that steps can be taken to eliminate or reduce these from what, little or no profit is obtained or to change the method of production or incidence of cost in order to render such activities more profitable.
4. It provides actual figures of cost for comparison with estimates, and assists the management in their price fixing policy.
5. Cost accounting presents comparative cost data for different periods and volumes of production, and those that assist the management in budgetary control.
6. It records and reports to the concerned manager how actual costs compare with standard cost and the possible causes of differences between them.
7. Cost accounting indicates the exact cause of increase or decrease in profit or loss shown by the financial accounts.
8. It also provides data for comparing cost within the firm and also between similar firms.

12.4   COST CONCEPTS

Cost forms the subject matter of cost accounting. It is the resources sacrificed to achieve a specific objective. Cost is defined as the benefit sacrificed to serve some other benefit. The proper classification of cost is necessary for the clear understanding of the cost concepts.

Cost can be classified according to its common characteristics.

1. Behavioural classification
2. Direct and indirect cost
3. Product cost and period cost
4. Relevant and irrelevant cost
5. Real cost
6. Opportunity cost

12.4.1   Behavioural Classification

Behavioural classification shows how the cost behaves when production changes. According to behavioural classification, there are three types of cost: (i) fixed (ii) variable and (iii) semi-variable.

Fixed cost

Fixed cost is independent of output. Whatever may be the output, it remains constant. It is generally time based. Some typical examples of fixed cost are rent, insurance, taxes, salaries. Fixed cost is of two types: *committed fixed cost* and *discretionary fixed cost*. The shape of the fixed cost curve is presented in Figure 12.1. In the figure the output may be oq or oq_1. Whatever may be the change in the output, the fixed cost remains constant at point P.

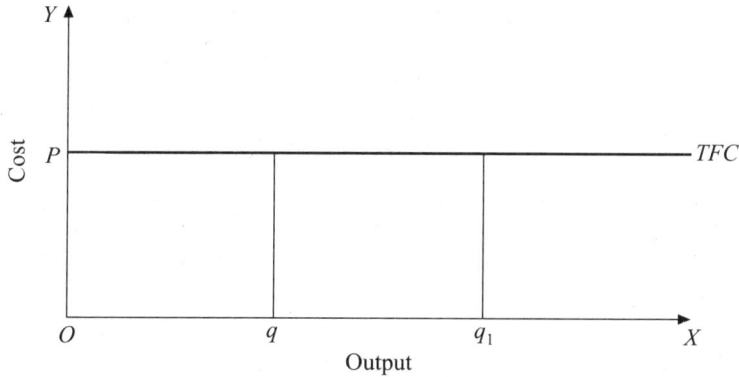

Figure 12.1   Fixed cost curve.

Variable cost

It may be defined as a cost which in the aggregate tends to vary in direct proportion to changes in the volume of output or turn-over within the relevant range for a given budget period. Examples of variable cost are material cost, direct labour cost, sales commission, power, royalty, carriage, packing cost. As output increases, variable cost increases in the same proportion. Thus, we can say that there exists a linear relationship between the output volume and the variable cost. Consequently, variable cost is constant per unit of output. Hence, the total variable cost curve is a straight line passing through the origin and the average variable cost curve is a horizontal line. The shapes of total variable cost and average variable cost curves are presented in Figures 12.2 and 12.3 respectively.

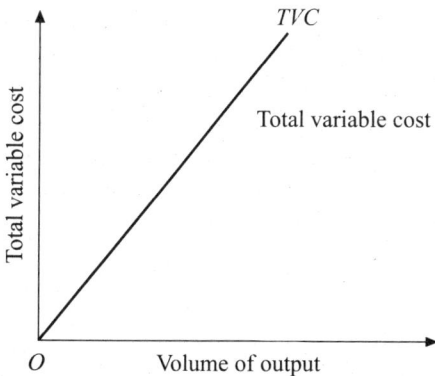

Figure 12.2   Total variable cost.

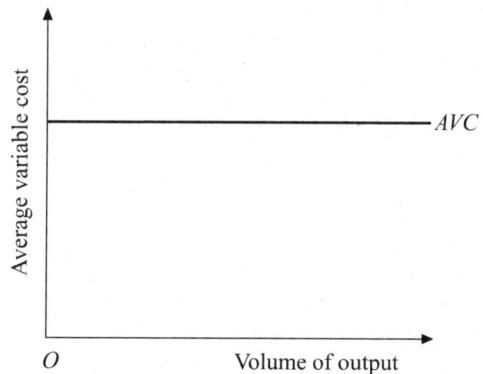

Figure 12.3   Average variable cost.

Very often, variable cost is called engineered cost because both have an explicit, specified, physical relationship with a selected measure of activity. Direct material and direct labour are prime examples of engineered cost. An engineered variable cost is said to exist when work measurement techniques (material standards with the help of production engineers, labour standards through time and motion study) have carefully established an optimum relationship between input and output. The implication for the management in planning and controlling of variable cost is that with all other factors held constant, each desired per unit expansion of productive activity triggers an incremental change in total variable cost equal to a constant amount per unit.

Semi-variable cost

The behaviour of cost cannot be expected to remain as fixed or variable under all circumstances and for all time spans. Thus, the concept of semi-variable cost arises. Semi-variable cost stands mid-way between fixed and variable costs. It is defined as a cost containing both fixed and variable elements, and which is, thus, partly affected by fluctuations in the level of activity. The fixed part of a semi-variable cost usually represents a minimum fee for making a particular item/service available. The variable portion is the cost charges for actually using the service. For example, most telephone service charges are made up of two elements:

1. A fixed charge for allowing to make a call
2. Plus an additional variable charge for each call actually made

Semi-variable cost is also known as mixed cost as it consists both of fixed cost and variable cost. Fixed cost is not affected by the changes in the volume of production, while variable cost is sensitive to changes in the volume of production. Thus, semi-variable cost changes in the same directions as volume but not in the direct proportion thereto. Hence, the shape of the semi-variable cost curve is as shown in Figure 12.4.

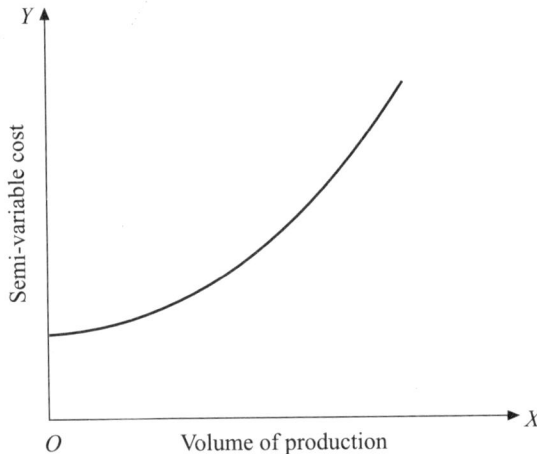

Figure 12.4   Semi-variable cost.

Marshall made a broad division of cost as fixed and variable cost. Variable cost is also known as prime cost. It includes the cost of raw materials, wages of the labourers, and wear and tear charges of machineries used for the purpose. Prime cost is called variable cost because it directly varies with the rate of production. The higher is the level of production, the more is the level of output and greater will be the amount of variable cost. The lower is the level of production, the lower is the volume of output and lower will be the variable cost. Another reason for calling it prime cost is because this is the main cost of production. In any factory, if we analyse the cost of production we find that the amount of variable cost constitutes three-fourth of the cost of production. Therefore, it is the primary or main cost of production.

The cost which is independent of output, may be more or less or even zero, is known as fixed cost. Costs of machineries, buildings, salaries of staff, maintenance of machine, telephone, wages of watch man, insurance fee or administrative expenses are examples of fixed cost. These costs are incurred whatever may be the size of the output, and are incurred before the factory starts production and after the factory closes down its production for sometime. They are payment for the fixed factors of production. Fixed cost is supplementary cost because it constitutes a small portion of the total cost of production. It is also called as of production, because it decreases per unit of output with an increase in production and increases per unit output with a decrease in production.

The difference or distinction between variable and fixed cost is not rigid. It is one of degrees, not of kind. For example, the wage paid to a typist will be fixed cost if the services of the typist is permanent. If the services of the typist can be terminated when production stops, it will be variable cost. Therefore, the distinction is of degrees and only found in the short run. In the long-run, every cost is a variable cost. See Table 12.1.

Table 12.1   Cost of Production of a Firm

Units of output	Total fixed costs	Total variable cost	Total cost (2 + 3)	Average fixed cost (2/1)	Average variable cost (3/1)	Average cost (5 + 6)	Marginal cost
(1)	(2)	(3)	(4)	(5)	(6)	(7)	(8)
1	100	100	200	100	100	200	200
2	100	150	250	50	75	125	50
3	100	200	300	33.3	66.7	100	50
4	100	260	360	25	65	90	60
5	100	320	420	20	64	84	60
6	100	410	510	16.6	86.4	85	90
7	100	503	603	14.3	71.7	86	93
8	100	652	752	12.5	81.5	94	149
9	100	827	927	11.1	91.9	103	175
10	100	1035	1135	10	103.5	113.5	208

12.4.2   Direct Cost and Indirect Cost

Direct cost is directly identified with a product, process or department. Raw materials used and labour employed in manufacturing an article are examples of direct cost.

Indirect costs is not applicable to any particular product, process or department but is common to different products. Factory manager's salary, factory rent, depreciation of machinery are typical examples of indirect cost.

12.4.3   Relevant Cost and Irrelevant Cost

Relevant cost as the name suggests is the cost which is relevant for decision-making such as differential or incremental cost, opportunity cost, out of pockets cost.

Irrelevant cost is not pertinent to a decision. It is the cost that will not be changed by a decision because irrelevant cost will not be affected it may be ignored in the decision-making process.

12.4.4   Product Cost and Period Cost

Product cost is the cost directly identified with the product. It is cost of goods produced and kept ready for sale. Product cost includes direct materials, direct labour, variable factory overheads. Period cost is that which is not directly related with the production of a commodity. It is otherwise known as fixed cost.

Direct cost

Direct cost can be of following types:

1. Direct material (e.g. Primary packing materials)
2. Direct labour (e.g. Wages paid to workers)
3. Direct expenses (e.g. Cost of special tools, patterns cost of excise duty, Hire changes of a special equipment, royalties, insurance, etc.)

Indirect cost

Indirect cost can be of following types:

1. Indirect material (e.g. fuel, lubricating oil, maintenance work, small tools)
2. Indirect labour   (e.g. wages of general supervisors, inspectors, workshop cleaners, store keeper, time keeper)
3. Indirect expenses (e.g. Rent, lighting insurance, canteen, hospital welfare expenses, it is otherwise known as overhead expenses)
   (a) Factory/work overhead (Work manager's salary, factory rent, factory insurance, salaries of clerical anu executive staff, etc.)
   (b) Office and Administrative overhead (office rent, office lighting, insurance, etc.)
   (c) Selling and distributive overhead (advertising expenses, salaries of salesman, indirect packing material)

12.4.5   Real Cost of Production

Though in our analysis, a producer is interested in the money cost of producing a commodity, another view of cost of production is known as *real cost of production*. Real cost of production refers to the sacrifices borne by the society to produce a particular commodity. According to this theory, the money cost of production is much less in comparison to the sacrifices made by the society to produce a particular commodity. To illustrate we can consider that the wage of a factory worker is not equal to the sacrifices he makes in terms of his mental and physical labour. He works under great risks. Nobody pays for it. Similarly near the factory area, the air and water get polluted. Slums come into existence which lead to spready of diseases. Nobody pays for it. Moreover, the growth of a factory brings indiscipline and conflict. Society sacrifices much. Nobody pays for this sacrifice. So from the social stand point the cost of a commodity should be calculated in terms of sacrifices. Money cost does not give the true picture of cost. Alfred Marshall defines real costs as

"the exertions of all the different kinds of labourers that are directly or indirectly involved in making it, together with the abstinence or rather the waiting's required for raising the capital used in making it, all these efforts and sacrifices together will be called the costs of production of the commodity".

Alfred Marshall conceived the cost of production in terms of pains and sacrifices. The sacrifices made by labourers to produce a commodity, the sacrifices undertaken by the savers to provide capital by reducing their consumption and all other social sacrifices made constitute the cost of production of a commodity. These real costs give the true picture of the cost of production which cannot be measured scientifically, because it involves sacrifices. Sacrifice is a subjective feeling. Its objective measurement is impossible. So people today are trying to make it objective by social cost-benefit analysis. Therefore, money costs of induction is accepted as the cost of production.

12.4.6 Opportunity Cost

Modern writers view another concept to measure the money cost. This is known as *opportunity* or *alternative costs*. Opportunity cost is the cost of alternatives foregone. If we produce one commodity, we do not produce another. Therefore, the opportunity cost of producing a commodity is equal to the cost of not producing another commodity. To take an example, if we have an acre of land and can produce potatoes on it, we get Rs. 1000. Had we not produced potatoes and instead produced rice on it we would have got Rs. 700. Therefore, the cost of producing potatoes would be equal to the alternative foregone, that is Rs. 700 from rice production. Moreover, it is not only the cost of alternatives foregone, but also the cost of the best alternative foregone. For example, a person working as a nurse becomes a nursing teacher. When she was a nurse she was getting Rs. 6000 of income per annum. But when she became a nursing teacher, she got Rs. 10,000 per annum. Then it will not be the alternative foregone as a nurse but as the best alternative foregone as a nursing teacher. Then the supply price at the cost of production will not be the Rs. 6000 per annum but Rs. 10,000 per annum. In this context, Frederil Benham defines opportunity costs as: "The opportunity cost of anything is the best alternative that could be produced by the same factor by an equivalent group of factors costing the same amount of money".

12.5 ELEMENTS OF COST

The total cost is analysed by elements of cost given in Figure 12.5.

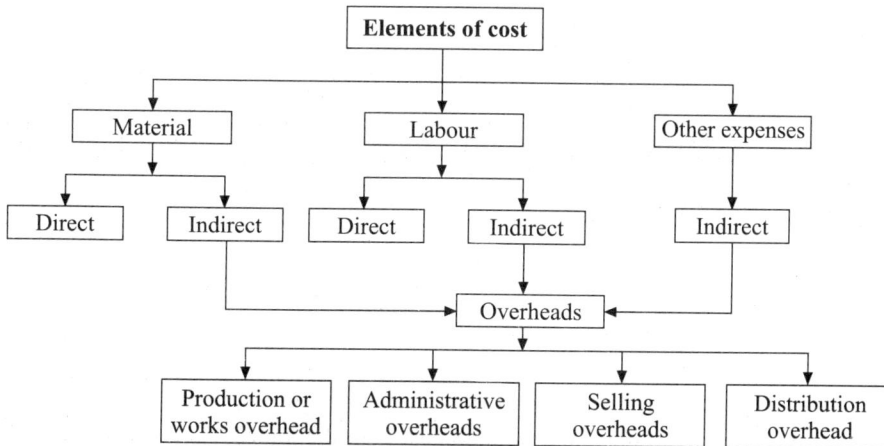

Figure 12.5 Elements of cost.

By grouping the above elements of cost, the following division of costs are obtained:

1. Prime cost: Direct material + Direct labour
2. Works or factory cost: Prime cost + Works overhead
3. Cost of production: Works cost + Administrative overhead
4. Total cost of sales: Cost of production + Selling and distribution overheads
5. Profit or loss: Sales – Total cost

EXAMPLE 12.1

Ascertain the prime cost, work cost, cost of production and total cost and profit from the following information:

Direct material	= 7000
Direct labour	= 2800
Factory expenses	= 2600
Administrative expenses	= 1000
Selling expenses	= 900
Sales	= 20,000

Solution

Prime cost	= Direct materials + Direct labour
	= Rs. 7000 + Rs. 2800
	= Rs. 9800
Work cost	= Prime cost + Factory expenses
	= Rs. 9000 + Rs. 2600
	= Rs. 12,400
Cost of production	= Works cost + Administrative expenses
	= Rs. 12,400 + Rs. 1000
	= Rs. 13,400
Total cost	= Cost of production + Selling expenses
	= Rs. 13,400 + Rs. 900
	= Rs. 14,300
Profit	= Sales – Total cost
	= Rs. 20,000 – 14,300
	= Rs. 5700

REVIEW QUESTIONS

1. Define costing. Explain the different classification of costing.
2. Distinguish between direct cost and indirect cost.
3. What is product costing? What are the different elements of costing?
4. Distinguish between fixed cost and variable cost with diagrams.
5. What do you mean by overhead? What is a cost sheet?
6. What do you mean by opportunity cost?

13

CHAPTER

Process Costing

13.1 MEANING

Process costing is a very important technique of costing. It is that form of costing which is used to ascertain the cost of a product at each process or stage of production. Thus, process costing is the method of costing employed by those industries where a product passes through different processes. In order to know the cost at each stage of production, a separate account is opened for every process. When the material is transferred from one process to another, the cost incurred upto that process is also transformed to the succeeding process. This method of costing is most suitable for mass production industries engaged in continuous production of uniform standard product, such as textiles, chemicals, paper, sugar, oil, cement, mining.

13.2 ELEMENTS OF PRODUCTION COST IN PROCESS COSTING

Following are the elements of production cost in process costing:
1. **Materials:** Typically in process costing, the material (not all) required for production is issued to the first process. Then after processing, it is passed to the next process, where extra or new materials are added, and passed to the next process and so on. Therefore, sufficient supplies of raw materials must be available to meet the production needs.
2. **Labour:** Generally, the cost of direct labour is a very small part of the total cost of production in industries adopting process costing.
3. **Production overhead:** The overhead element of total cost is generally very high in process costing.

13.3 METHODS OF PROCESS COSTING

Process costing includes the following methods of costing:

1. **Unit costing:** It is applied in industries, such as paper mills, flour mills, textile mills, and cement manufacturing. In this method, the total cost is divided by the number of units produced to ascertain the unit cost.

2. **Operating costing:** It is used to ascertain the cost of rendering services, such as railways, airways, roadways, hotels, power supply, water supply.
3. **Operation costing:** This is a further refinement of process costing and is most suitable for engineering industries, toy making, etc. where mass production is carried out in respectively.

13.4 PRINCIPLES OF PROCESS COSTING

Process costing has following principles:

1. Cost of materials, wages, and overhead expenses are collected for each process in a period.
2. Adequate records in respect of output and scrap of each process or operation during the period are kept.
3. The cost per finished output of each process is obtained by dividing the total cost incurred during a period by the number of units produced during that period, after taking into consideration the losses and amount realized from sale of scrap.
4. The finished product along with its cost is transferred from one process to the next process just like raw materials of that process.

EXAMPLE 13.1

A product passes through three distinct processes—I, II and III to completion. During the week ended 10th October, 2008, 500 units are produced. The following information is obtained:

Process I, II, III Account

	Process I	**Process II**	**Process III**
Direct materials	Rs. 3500	Rs. 1600	Rs. 1500
Direct labour	Rs. 2500	Rs. 2000	Rs. 2500

The overhead expenses for the period were Rs. 1400 apportioned to the process on the basis of wages. No work in progress existed at the beginning or at the end of the week. Prepare process cost accounts showing the unit price.

Solution

Process I Account
(Output = 500 units)

Particulars	Cost per unit (Rs.)	Total cost (Rs.)	Particulars	Cost per unit (Rs.)	Total cost (Rs.)
To direct materials	$\frac{3500}{500} = 7$	3500	Output transferred to process II	13	6500
To direct labour	$\frac{2500}{500} = 5$	2500			
To overhead charges	$\frac{500}{500} = 1$	500			
(2500/7000) × 1400					
	13	6500		13	6500

Process II Account

Particulars	Cost per unit (Rs.)	Total cost (Rs.)	Particulars	Cost per unit (Rs.)	Total cost (Rs.)
To process I A/C	13.00	6500	Output transferred to process III	21.00	10,500
To direct materials	$\frac{1600}{500} = 3.20$	1500			
To direct labour	$\frac{2000}{500} = 4.00$	2500			
To overhead charges $(2000/7000) \times 1400$	$\frac{400}{500} = 0.80$	500			
	21.00	10,500		21.00	10,500

Process III Account

Particulars	Cost per unit (Rs.)	Total cost (Rs.)	Particulars	Cost per unit (Rs.)	Total cost (Rs.)
To process I A/C	21.00	10,500	Transfer to warehouse by finished stock A/C	30.00	15,000
To direct materials	$\frac{1500}{500} = 3.00$	1500			
To direct labour	$\frac{2500}{500} = 5.00$	2500			
To overhead charges $(2500/7000) \times 1400$	$\frac{500}{500} = 1.00$	500			
	30.00	15,000		30.00	15,000

Therefore, the total cost of production is Rs. 15,000 to produce 500 units and the unit cost of production is Rs. 30.

The advantages of process costing are as follows:

1. It is possible to determine process costing periodically at short intervals.
2. Process costing is a simple and less expensive method.
3. Due to process costing it is possible to have managerial control by evaluating the performance of each process.
4. It is easy to quote the prices with standardization of process.

The disadvantages of process costing are as follows:

1. The cost is historical in nature and is not very useful for effective control.
2. There is a wide scope of error while calculating unit costs.
3. The computation of unit cost is more difficult in those cases where more than one type of product is manufactured and a division of the cost elements is necessary.

13.5 SPOILAGE

In the case of production where output passes through several stages, some wastage/spoilage of units takes place for a variety of reasons, such as breakdown of machines, use of sub-standard material, poor workmanship. The effect of wastage is that the actual units produced are less than the units introduced initially.

The wastage may be normal or abnormal. *Normal loss* may be defined as the loss of unit which is an inherent part of the production process caused by natural or unavoidable reasons, such as milling, drying, breaking, processing, loading, unloading. Any loss in excess of normal spoilage is called *abnormal loss*. It is a controllable loss. If the number of units actually lost are less than the number of units normally expected to be lost, the difference would represent an abnormal gain/effectiveness.

Normal spoilage forms part of the product cost. Therefore, the cost of production of spoiled units is recovered from the good units.

The unit cost with normal spoilage and with salvage value is computed as follows:

Cost per unit = (Total process cost – Salvage value of normal spoilage) ÷
(Total units introduced – Normal loss in unit).

The amount of loss on account of abnormal spoilage to be transferred to profit and loss account is computed as follows:

Abnormal loss = (Abnormal loss in units × Unit production cost) –
Salvage value of abnormal spoilage.

EXAMPLE 13.2

M/s. Triplex Industries produces a forged product Sunbeam after it passes through three distinct processes. The following information has been obtained from the cost accounts for the month ending December 31, 2005.

Process I, II, III Accounts

Items	Total amount (Rs.)	Process I (Rs.)	Process II (Rs.)	Process III (Rs.)
Direct materials	7542	2600	1980	2962
Direct wages	9000	2000	3000	4000
Production overhead	9000			

In process I 1000 units at Rs. 3 each were introduced. There was no stock of materials, work-in-progress and finished goods at the beginning of and at the end of the period. The output of each process passes direct to the next process and finally to the finished stock. Production overheads are recovered at 100 per cent of direct wages.

The following additional data are obtained:

Process scrap	Output during the month (units)	Percentage of normal loss to input	Value of per unit
Process I	950	5	Rs. 2
Process II	840	10	4
Process III	750	15	5

Prepare cost accounts.

Solution

Process I Account

	Units	Cost (Rs.)		Units	Cost (Rs.)
To units introduced	1000	3000	By normal loss	50	100
To direct material		2600	By output transferred		
To direct labour		2000	to process II		
To production overheads		2000	@ Rs. 10 each	950	9500
	1000	9600		1000	9600

Output valued = 9600 – 100 or 9500 + 950 = Rs. 10 per unit

Process II Account

	Units	Cost (Rs.)		Units	Cost (Rs.)
To transfer from			By normal loss	95	380
process II	950	9500	By abnormal loss		
To direct material		1980	(@ Rs. 20 per unit)	15	380
To direct labour		3000	By output transferred		
To production overheads		3000	to process III	840	16,800
	950	17,480		950	17,480

Output and abnormal loss is worked out as follows:

Cost   = 17,480 – 380 or Rs. 17,100

Units   = 950 – 95 or 855 units

Cost per unit = 17,100 ÷ 855 or Rs. 20 per unit

Process III Account

	Units	Cost (Rs.)		Units	Cost (Rs.)
To transfer from			By normal loss	126	630
process II	840	16,800	By finished stock a/c		
To direct material		2962	@ Rs. 38	750	28,500
To direct labour		4000			
To production overheads		4000			
To abnormal gain					
@ Rs. 38 each	36	1368			
	876	29,130		876	29,130

Furnished stock and abnormal gain worked out.

Cost   = Rs. 27,762 – 630 or 27,132

Units   = 840 – 126 or 714

Cost per unit = 27,132 ÷ 714 or Rs. 38 each unit

REVIEW QUESTIONS

1. Mention any three industries where process costing is applied.
2. Describe the main features of process costing.
3. Compare process costing with job costing.
4. Describe the salient features of process costing. In which industries is it relevant?
5. A product passes through two distinct processes to completion. The following information is obtained:

	Process I (Rs.)	Process II (Rs.)
Direct materials	3000	1500
Direct labour	2500	2000
Direct expenses	500	100

   Overhead expenses were Rs. 900 to be apportioned to the processes on the basis of wages. Output was 500 tonnes. Prepare process accounts showing cost per unit.

6. A product passes through three processes. Process A, Process B and Process C to completion. During the month of October 2007, 1000 units (finished) were produced and the following was the expenditure:

	Process A (Rs.)	Process B (Rs.)	Process C (Rs.)
Materials	1000	2000	1000
Labour	5000	4000	3000
Direct expenses	500	600	1000

   Indirect expenses mounted in all to Rs. 6000. These are to be allocated on the basis of direct wages. Raw materials worth Rs. 6000 were issued to process A. Ignoring the question of stock, prepare the process accounts concerned.

CHAPTER 14

Marginal Costing

14.1 INTRODUCTION

Marginal costing is the ascertainment of marginal costs. It is the effect on profit of changes in volume or type of output by differentiating between fixed cost and variable cost. Marginal costing is not a system of costing, like process costing and job costing. In fact, it is a technique concerned with the changes in cost and profit resulting from changes in the volume of output.

14.2 FEATURES OF MARGINAL COSTING

The main characteristics of marginal costing are as follows:

1. Marginal costing is a technique of costing used to ascertain marginal cost and know the impact of variable cost on the volume of output.
2. It is a technique of analysis and presentation of cost that helps the management in taking many managerial decisions.
3. All elements of cost—production, administration and selling and distribution are classified into variable and fixed components.
4. Variable cost is treated as costs of products.
5. Stocks of finished goods and work-in-process are valued at marginal cost only.
6. Profit is calculated by deducting marginal cost and fixed cost from sales.

14.3 ASSUMPTIONS

The following assumptions should be made in marginal costing:

1. All elements of cost can be segregated into fixed and variable components.
2. Variable cost remains constant per unit of output irrespective of the level of output, and, thus, fluctuates directly in proportion to the changes in the volume of output.
3. The selling price per unit remains unchanged at all levels of activity.
4. Fixed cost remains constant for the entire volume of production.
5. The volume of production or output is the only factor which influences the cost.

14.4 PROFIT UNDER MARGINAL COSTING

In marginal costing, it is assumed that the difference between the aggregate sales value and the aggregate marginal cost of the output sold provides a fund to meet the fixed cost and profit of the firm. In respect of each product, the difference between its sales value and the marginal cost is known as 'contribution' made by the product to this fund. This contribution is the difference between the sale value and the marginal cost of sales, and it contributes towards the fixed expenses and profit.

14.5 SIGNIFICANCE OF MARGINAL COSTING

Marginal costing is a technique which we get by differentiating fixed cost and variable cost. It primarily concerns with the following two aspects:

1. Ascertainment of marginal cost
2. Determination of cost-volume-profit relationship.

For example assume variable cost is Rs. 15 per unit and fixed cost for a specific period is Rs. 4000.
The present activity level is 200 units. In this case the total cost of producing 200 units will be found out as follows:

$$\text{Total Cost} = \text{Fixed cost} + (\text{Variable cost per unit} \times \text{Present production})$$
$$= \text{Rs. } 4000 + (\text{Rs. } 15 \times 200) = \text{Rs. } 7000$$

If activity level becomes 201 units, the total cost will be

$$TC = FC + (VC \text{ per unit} \times 201)$$
$$= \text{Rs. } 4000 + (\text{Rs. } 15 \times 201) = \text{Rs. } 7015$$

It means the marginal cost is Rs. 15, because change in activity level by one unit leads to a change in total cost by Rs. 15.

14.6 BREAK-EVEN POINT

The marginal costing technique is based on the idea that difference of sales and variable cost of sales provides for a fund, which is referred to as contribution. Contribution provides for fixed cost and profit. At break-even point, the contribution is just enough to provide for fixed cost. If the actual sales level is more than the BEP, the company will incur loss. Thus, in the marginal costing technique, efforts are directed to increase the total contribution only.

EXAMPLE 14.1

Cost data assumes

Sale	= Rs. 2000
Variable cost of sale	= Rs.1000

Find the contribution.

Solution

We know that

contribution   = sale – variable cost
     = Rs. 2000 – Rs. 1000 = Rs. 1000

14.7 P/V RATIO

$$\text{P/V ratio} = \frac{\text{Sales} - \text{Marginal cost of sales}}{\text{Sales}}$$

$$= \frac{\text{Sales} - \text{Price} - \text{Marginal cost}}{\text{Selling price}} = \frac{\text{Contribution}}{\text{Sales}}$$

$$= \frac{\text{Change in contribution}}{\text{Change in sales}} = \frac{\text{Change in profit}}{\text{Change in sales}}$$

Following are the main advantages of determining the P/V ratio:

1. The P/V ratio helps in determining the break-even point.
2. It helps in determining the profit at various sales levels.
3. The P/V ratio helps to find out the sales volume to earn a desired quantum of profit.
4. It helps to determine the relative profitability of different products, processes and departments.

REVIEW QUESTIONS

1. Explain marginal costing as a technique of costing.
2. Define marginal cost and marginal costing.
3. What are the advantages and disadvantages of marginal costing?
4. What do you mean by cost-volume-profit analysis? Define break-even point.
5. You are given the following information:

Fixed cost	Rs. 4000
Break-even sales	Rs. 20,000
Profit	Rs. 1000
Selling price	Rs. 20 per unit

Calculate:
(a) Sales and marginal cost of sales.
(b) New break-even point when selling price is reduced by 15 per cent.

CHAPTER 15

Standard Costing and Variance Analysis

15.1 CONCEPT OF STANDARD COSTING

Cost control, as it leads to cost reduction, should always be the objective of any firm or institution where scarce resources are used. Even if a firm can sell its goods or services at a very remunerative price, it should still try to reduce the use of factors of production without jeopardizing the quality of the product or the service. The best way of doing this would be to constantly device techniques through which cost can be further 'reduced. If this approach is adopted, i.e. an attempt is made to ascertain beforehand what the cost should be and further effort is made to ensure that the actual cost does not go beyond the predetermined level, it will be called *standard costing*. In fact, it is the philosophy of standards that means scrupulously separating all types of wastages, and losses, and not allowing them to cloud the cost of production, at least for the purpose of internal consumption which will help to bring the best results. Merely the mechanism of adopting the standard costing techniques does not ensure that optimum results will be achieved. Assume a worker normally working eight hours produces 20 units for a wage of Rs. 20. Thus, the proper labour cost of production is Re. 1 per unit. Suppose for any reason the worker produces only 12 units one day. Then the payment of Rs. 20 will be spread over 12 units and the labour cost per unit will be Rs. 1.67. But when the philosophy of standards is applied, one would say that the proper labour cost of 12 units will still remain Re. 1 per unit or Rs. 12 in all; eight units have not been produced and, therefore, at the rate of Re. 1 per unit, there is a loss of Rs. 8. This amount should be charged to a separate account and should be shown as a different item in the revenue accounts of the firm. This will help the management to know at the end of each period, the extent of losses that have been incurred unnecessarily. Moreover if the production has been able to obtain, extra efficiency its effect should also be credited to a separate account and given as a separate item in the revenue account.

This is the essence of standard costing—to set targets of cost, try to achieve those targets, compare the actual cost with the targets, ascertain the reasons and record the reasons in the books of account, or if a regular record is not maintained at least bring the monetary effects of various factors that have operated in the organization to the notice of the management. Thus, standard costing is an excellent system of controlling costs, measuring efficiency, and improving upon it.

It may be noted in passing that usually standard cost is also referred to as 'predetermined cost. This means that before a work actually starts an extremely careful estimate of cost is prepared to serve as the standard against which the actual cost incurred is to be measured. However, this term should not be confused with production cost which means the cost to be incurred actually before production commences, such as on trial runs. Further, standard cost should not be confused with estimate cost as the latter connotes rather loose forecasts of anything and the fact one thinks of actuals being correct and tends to judge the accuracy estimates on the basis of the actuals. In the case of standard cost, the emphasis is that the figures are correct and that one must explain why the actuals differ from the standards. Moreover, standards are far more exact and precise than forecasts or estimates.

15.2 DEFINITION AND MEANING

Standard cost is the scientifically predetermined cost of manufacturing a single unit or a number of units of a product, or of rendering a service during a specified future period. The Chartered Institute of Management Accountants (CIMA), London, defines standard cost as "a standard expressed in money. It is built up from an assessment of the value of cost elements. Its main uses are providing bases for performance measurement, valuing stock and establishing selling prices".

What is evident from the above-mentioned definition is that standard cost is planned cost of a product under current or anticipated operating conditions. The dictionary meaning of the word 'standard' is that it is a "thing serving as a basis for comparison", "thing recognized as model for imitation". But it should be noted that 'standard' is a relative term. Admittedly, what is standard for one may be substandard for another and vice versa. However, what is significant is that within an organization, Standard cost serves as a desirable target.

The term 'standard cost' consists of two parts, viz. 'standard' and 'cost' Standard can be established in respect of quantities and qualities life, materials and labour. Cost involves expression of standard so established in values.

Further, CIMA defines standard costing as "a control technique which compares standard costs and revenues with actual results to obtain variances which are used to stimulate improved performance". The technique of standard costing may be summarized as follows:

1. Predetermination of technical data related to production, i.e. details of materials and labour operations required for each product, the quantum of losses, level of activity.
2. Predetermination of standard cost, in full detail for each element of cost, viz. material, labour and overhead.
3. Comparison of the actual performance and cost with the standards; working out the variance, i.e. the difference between the actual and the standard cost.
4. Analysis of the variances in order to determine the reasons for deviations of actuals from the standards, and presentation of information to the appropriate level of management for suitable action.

15.3 STANDARD COSTING AND BUDGETARY CONTROL

Standard costing and budgetary control have the common objectives of controlling business operations by establishing predetermined targets, measuring the actual performances and comparing it with the targets, for the purpose of having better efficiency and reducing costs. The two systems are said to be interrelated but not inter-dependent. Standard costing is introduced primarily to ascertain the efficiency and effectiveness of cost performance. Budgetary control, on the other hand, is introduced to state in figures an approved plan of action relating to a particular period. Standard costing and budgetary control have the following common features:

1. Both have the common objective of improving managerial control.
2. The two techniques are based on the presumption that cost is controllable.
3. In both the techniques, results of comparison are analysed and reported to the management.

The distinction between standard costing and budgetary control is given in Table 15.1.

Table 15.1   Distinction between Standard Costing and Budgetary Control

Standard costing	Budgetary control
It is related with the control of expenses and, hence, is more intensive.	It is concerned with the operation of the business as a whole and, hence, is more extensive.
Standard cost is based on technical assessment.	Budgets are based on past actuals, adjusted to future trends.
To establish standard cost, some form of budgeting is essential as there is the need to forecast the level of output and prescribed set of working conditions in the periods in which the standard cost is used.	Budgetary control can be applied even without the help of standard costing.
Standard costing is set mainly for production, and production expenses.	Budget is compiled for all items of income and expenditure.
Standard cost is the protection of cost accounts.	it is a projection of financial accounts.
It sets up targets which are to be attained by actual performance.	Budget sets up maximum limits of expenses above which the actual expenditure should not normally exceed.
In standard costing, variance is analysed in detail according to its originating causes. It reveals variance through different accounts, such as material price variance, usage variance.	In budgetary control, variance is not related through the associated accounts but revealed in total.
Standard cost does not tell what the cost is expected to be, but rather what the cost should be under specific conditions of production performance. As such standard cost cannot be used for the purpose of forecasting. Standard cost is used in various management decisions, price fixing, value analysis, valuation of closing stock, etc.	Budget is anticipated or expected cost meant to be used for forecasting requirements of material, labour, cash, etc.
	It aims in policy determination, co-ordination of activities in different divisions and delegation of authority.

One must remember, however, that the two control systems are never treated as exclusive. Standard costing is a specialized system in respect of cost; budget is also concerned with cost among other things. Therefore, it would add strength to budgetary control system if it adopts standard cost in respect of cost data. The two are complimentary to each other.

15.4 STANDARD COST AND ESTIMATED COST

Both standard cost and estimated cost are predetermined cost, but their objectives are different. Important differences between the two are given in Table 15.2.

Table 15.2 Distinction between Standard Cost and Estimated Cost

Standard cost	Estimated cost
Standard cost can be applied in a business operating under standard costing system.	Estimated cost can be used in any business which is running under actual cost system.
Standards are meant for controlling future performances.	Estimates are prepared mainly for price fixing purposes.
Standard cost is determined on a scientific basis keeping in view certain factors and conditions of efficiency.	Estimated cost is calculated on the basis of past performance adjusted in the light of anticipated changes in the future.
Standard costs is used as a regular system of accounts from which variances are found out.	The use of estimated cost is for statistical data only.
Standard cost is to be fixed in respect of every element of cost and, therefore, it incorporates the whole manufacturing process.	Estimated cost can be ascertained for a part of the business and also for a particular purpose.

15.4.1 Advantages of Standard Costing

The advantages of standard costing can be fully comprehended only when one has gone through the whole chapter and studied the various implications of standard costing. However, here we give a few of the important advantages:

1. To determine standards which are at once practicable and represent efficient performance, the management will have to be fully aware of all the facilities that are available and the best way in which work can be done. For example, time and motion study, essential if labour standards, is to be fixed properly. Moreover, the management will have to gather continuous and up-to-date information about all the happening. This exercise will enable the firm to locate many sources of wastages and losses, and block them.

2. Human beings often work hard to achieve standards which are within their reach. Therefore, setting up of such standards will almost automatically mean greater efficiency in operations. Further, almost everyone will think in terms of setting the targets and of achieving them. This will be specially so if the system of rewards and punishment is also geared to the results.

3. If the standards are themselves challenged periodically on a systematic basis, then it will mean a constant improvement in efficiency.

4. Standard costing involves not only predetermined quantity standards but also standards in respect of prices and fates. This may mean that all materials issued and labour applied will be evaluated on the basis of standard price and rates. This will itself reduce clerical labour. One can say that in general standard costing is more economical than ordinary system of costing where quantities and prices vary day to day or week by week.

5. Standard costing will enable objective judgement of the people and to that extent the system of promotions, etc. will be more acceptable in the firm.

6. The managements own time can be saved to a large extent because its attention will be targetted to only those matters which are important. This will be done through the analysis of the deviation between the standard cost and the actual cost. The management needs to pay attention only to those factors which have meant efficiency or inefficiency.

7. For the purpose of fixing the prices, standard cost plays a useful role. It excludes the day to day fluctuations in cost resulting from inefficient use of resources and kind movement in prices. Standard cost represents the long-term estimates; cost and price, therefore, can be fixed on a long-term basis.

8. Even for valuation of inventory, standard cost should be the proper basis. If actual cost is high only because there has been a wastage of resources, it is not proper to capitalize those losses by including them in the value of inventory. Nothing becomes more valuable simply because of wastage and, therefore, inventory values should be better determined on the basis of standard cost.

9. If a firm practises standard costing on proper lines, i.e. standards are themselves determined in a way which will not impose too great a burden on the workers or other employees of the firm, it may infuse in the mind of the staff a desire to achieve the standards and, thus, show greater efficiency.

10. At every stage of setting the standards, simplification and standardization of products, methods and operations results and waste of time and material eliminated. This assists in managerial planning for efficient operation and benefits for all the divisions of the concern.

11. Costing procedure is simplified. There is a reduction in paper work in accounting and less number of forms and records are required. There is considerable saving in clerical time and expenditure leading to reduction in the cost of the costing system.

12. This system facilitates delegation of authority and fixation of responsibility for each department or individual.

13. When constantly reviewed, the standards provide the means for achieving the cost reduction. This is attained through improved methods, improved quality of products, better materials and men, effective selection and use of capital resources, etc.

14. Standard cost assists in performance analysis by providing ready means for preparation and interpretation of information.

15. This facilitates the integration of accounts so that reconciliation between cost accounts and financial accounts may be eliminated.

15.4.2 Limitations of Standard Costing

Standard costing has certain limitations. Which are as follows:

1. Establishment of standard cost is difficult in practice.
2. In the course of time, standards become rigid. It is not always possible to change standards to keep pace with frequent changes in the manufacturing conditions. Frequent revision of standards is costly and creates problems.
3. Inaccurate, unreliable and out-of-date standards do more harm than good.
4. Sometimes, standards create adverse psychological effects. If the standard is set at a high level, its non-achievement results in frustration and a build-up of resistance. This acts as a discouragement rather than an incentive for better efficiency.
5. Due to the play of random factors, variances cannot sometimes be properly explained, and it becomes difficult to segregate controllable and uncontrollable variances.

15.5 COMPUTATION AND ANALYSIS OF VARIANCES

The primary objective of standard costing is to reveal the difference between actual cost and standard cost. A 'variance' in standard costing refers to the divergence of actual cost from standard cost. Variances of different cost items provide the key to cost control. It indicates whether and to what extent the standards set are achieved. This enables the management to correct the adverse tendencies.

The Chartered Institute of Management Accountants, London, defines variance as "the difference between planned, budgeted, or standard cost and actual cost and similarly revenue". Variance analysis can be defined as "the analysis of performance by means of variances". It is the process of computing the amount of and isolating the cause variances between the actual cost and the standard cost. Variance analysis involves the following:

- Computation of individual variances
- Determination of the cause(s) of each variance

Actual cost which is higher than standard cost would be a sign of inefficiency, and the difference would be termed as unfavourable or adverse. A variance that reduces profit is adverse or unfavourable. A variance that increases profit is favourable. Variance is computed under each element of cost for which standards are established. Each variance is analysed to ascertain the causes so that a manager can exercise proper control. The cause is affixed to the variance. For example, material price variance will show that the variance arose due to change in the price of materials. Some of the variance are controllable while others are not. The purpose of classification is that proper emphasis can be placed on controllable variance. It follows the principle of management by exception.

Variance occurring in a period may be compared with variance on the account expressed as a percentage of the standard cost and compared with the percentage for the previous month. Comparison may be made between the standard and the actual, or between the basic standard and the current standard.

As already stated, the origin and cause of variance need to be analysed in relation to the total variances into their components parts in order to determine or isolate the causes giving rise to each variance. Equal emphasis should be laid on favourable and unfavourable variance. An unfavourable variance points out the inefficiency in use or waste of material, labour, and resources. A favourable variance may be due to improvements in effiency or production of substandard products or an incorrect standard.

A detailed probe into the variance, particularly the controllable variance, helps the management to ascertain:

1. the amount of variance;
2. its occurrence;
3. the factors responsible for it;
4. the executive responsible for the variance; and
5. corrective action which should be taken to obviate or reduce the variance.

15.5.1 Favourable and Unfavourable Variance

If the actual cost is less than the standard, the difference is known as *favourable variance*, credit variance or positive variance denoted by (F) or Cr. On the other hand, if the actual cost exceeds, the standard cost, the divergence is known as unfavourable variance, variance debit, negative variance or adverse variance denoted by (A) or Dr.

15.5.2   Controllable and Uncontrollable Variances

When the variance with respect to any cost item reflects the degree of efficiency of an individual or department, i.e. the particular individual or departmental head responsible for the variance, it is known as a *controllable variance*. Obviously, such a variance is amenable to control by suitable action. An uncontrollable variance is, on the other hand, one which is amenable to control by individual or departmental action. Such a variance is caused by external factors like change in market conditions, fluctuations in demand and supply, etc. No particular individual within the organization can be held responsible for it.

15.5.3   Material Cost Variances

Materials cost variance is the difference between the standard cost of materials specified and the actual cost of materials used.

> Material Cost Variance = Standard cost of material – Actual cost of material used.

Material cost variance arises due to variation in the price of the material or in its usage. In accordance with this, material cost variance may be analysed under two heads, viz. *materials price variance* and *materials usage variance*.

Materials price variance

This is that portion of the materials cost variance! which is due to the difference between the standard price specified and the actual price paid. Material price variance is that portion of the direct materials cost variance which is the difference between the standard prices specified and actual prices for the direct materials used. This is an incurring variance and reflects the extra price paid on the units purchased. While making this calculation standard, consumption of units should not be given any consideration. It is computed by multiplying the actual quantity by the difference between the standard price and the actual price. The formula is

> Material Price Variance = Actual quantity (Standard units price – Actual unit price)

or $= AQ(SP - AP)$

In other words, materials price variance is the difference between what it actually costs and what it would have costed if the actual usage had been paid for at the standard price.

Materials usage variance

This is that portion of materials cost variance which is due to the difference between the standard quantity of materials specified and the actual quantity used. Materials usage variance is that portion of the direct material cost variance which is the difference between the standard quantity specified for the production achieved and the actual quantity used, both valued at standard prices. The divergence of actual quantity of materials used from the standard quantity set, multiplied by standard price is known as *materials usage variance*. The formula for the calculation of this variance is:

> Materials usage variance = Standard price (Actual quantity – Standard quantity)

or $= SP(AQ - SQ).$

A favourable variance may not always be advantageous for the concern. For instance, a saving in materials usage may perhaps be affected by a reduction in the wastage, slowing down the work. But the resulting increase in labour and overhead cost may far exceed the favourable materials usage variance.

Materials usage variance may further be classified into the following:

1. **Material mixture variance:** One of the reasons for materials usage variance is change in the composition of materials mix. It results from a variation in the materials mix used in production. Thus, if a larger proportion of the more expensive material is used than that laid down in the standard mix, materials usages will reflect a higher cost than the standard. In contrast, the use of cheaper materials in large proportions will indicate a lower cost of materials usages than the standard.

2. **Material yield variance:** It is the difference between the standard yield specified and the actual yield obtained.

15.5.4 Labour Cost Variances

Labour cost variance (also termed as direct wage variance) is the difference between the standard direct wages specified for the activity and the actual direct wages paid. The formula for Labour cost variance is

$$LCV = (\text{Standard hours} \times \text{Standard rate}) - (\text{Actual hours} \times \text{Actual rate})$$

As the cost of labour is determined by labour time and wages, the labour cost variance is composed of either or both of variances relating to labour time and labour rate. As such, labour cost variance is analysed into two separate variances, viz. *wages rate variance* and *labour efficiency variance*.

Wages rate variance

This is that portion of wages variance which is due to the difference between the actual rate and the standard rate of pay specified. It is calculated like the materials price variance.

$$\text{Labour Rate Variance} = \text{Actual hours (Standard rate} - \text{Actual rate)}$$

The wage rate variance occurs due to the following causes:

1. Change in basic wage structure or change in piece work rate.
2. Overtime work in excess of that provided in the standard rate.
3. Employment of one or more workers of a different grade than the steno grade.
4. Payment of guaranteed wages to workers who are unable to earn the normal wages if such guaranteed wages form part of the direct labour cost.
5. New workers not being allowed full normal wage rates.
6. Use of different method of payment, i.e. payment of day rates while standards are based on piece work method of remuneration.
7. Higher wages paid on account of overtime for urgent work.
8. The composition of a gang as regards the skill end rate of wages being different from that laid down in the standard.

REVIEW QUESTIONS

1. Distinguish between standard costing and budgetary control.
2. Define standard costing. Explain the advantage and limitation of standard costing.
3. What do you mean by variance and discuss its significance?
4. What is the objective of variance analysis?

CHAPTER 16

Cost Control and Cost Reduction

16.1 COST CONTROL

Planning and cost control are two important functions of the management of a company with of the help cost accounting the management gets information needed in the due discharge of these two functions. By cost control we mean the regulation by executive action of the costs of operating and undertaking, particularly where the action is guided by cost accounting. According to this definition, cost control needs executive action which does not come about automatically. Cost control necessitates bringing to the notice of those who are responsible for controlling cost, the strategic points at which executive interference is demanded. Thus, cost control implies the existence of cost accounting and cost reporting, both aimed at the same goal, i.e. cost control.

The terms regulation and executive action also indicate the conscious attempt of regulating costs on the basis of predetermined ideas about what costs should be. It is only when costs are predetermined that cost control measures can give their best. Thus, cost control aims at reducing inefficiencies and wastage, and setting up predetermined cost and in achieving it.

16.2 FEATURES OF COST CONTROL

Since executive action for cost control is guided by cost accounting, it is necessary to install a system of cost accounting suited to the nature of the concern. Such a system accomplishes the function of cost ascertainment.

1. Fixation of attainable targets of performance is an essential requisite to cost control. The targets should be set scientifically, taking into consideration all practical aspects governing production and related costs. The people responsible for achieving the targets should be convinced that they are capable of achieving targets under normal circumstances.
2. Cost reporting is another feature of cost control. Particular attention should be paid to timely reporting.
3. The executive responsible for cost control should be guided by the variance reports and take the necessary corrective action to prevent the recurrence of deviations.

16.3   TECHNIQUES OF COST CONTROL

There are two important techniques of cost control, viz. *budgetary control* and *standard costing*, which are also known as *systems of cost control*.

Budgetary control is defined as the establishment of budgets relating to the responsibilities of executives to the requirements of a policy and the continuous comparison of actual budgeted results, either to secure by individual action the objectives of that policy or to provide a basis for revision.

This definition clearly lays down that budgetary control requires the establishment of budgets relating to the responsibilities of executives to the requirements of a policy. Budgetary control, thus, involves preparation of budgets and their application for control purposes. Accordingly, there cannot be budgetary control without budgets, and mere budgets do not achieve the objective of control unless actual results are compared with the targets laid down.

The followings are the steps in the process of budgetary control:

1. Laying down the objectives to be achieved by the business.
2. Formulating the necessary plans to ensure that the desired objectives are achieved.
3. Translating the plans into budgets.
4. Relating the responsibilities of executives to the budgets or particular sections of the same.
5. Continuous comparison of actual results with the budgets, and the ascertainment of deviations.
6. Investigation into the deviations to establish the causes.
7. Presentation of information to management relating the variances to individual responsibility.
8. Corrective action of management to prevent recurrence of variances.

A logical development of budgetary control is standard costing. Standard is the name given to the technique whereby standard costs are predetermined and subsequently compared with the recorded actual costs. It is, thus, a technique of cost ascertainment and cost control. This technique comprises the following steps:

1. Laying down standards of performance.
2. Measuring actual performance against the standards.
3. Computing variances, analysing them by causes, localizing and presenting timely reports.
4. Enforcing accountability of the executives concerned.
5. Taking corrective action to eliminate the variances.
6. Reviewing periodically the standards in the light of changed circumstances.

16.4   COST REDUCTION

Cost reduction is defined as the achievement of real and permanent reduction in the unit cost of goods manufactured or services rendered without impairing the suitability for the use intended.

This definition brings out the following features:

1. Cost reduction should be real. Costs should be brought down by changes in the methods of production, research, etc. within the organizational structure.
2. It should be permanent.
3. Cost reduction should not impair the suitability of goods and service for the intended use. In other words, cost reduction should not affect the quality of goods or services.

16.5   COST REDUCTION PROGRAMME

Cost reduction should not be a loose and haphazard programme which serves as a pain killer to mitigate the pain temporarily. It should be a well-thought out coordinated programme formulated at the initiative of the top managements, when they are fully convinced of the need for it and of its desirability, with the cooperation of the executives. Although the initiative might come from the top, unless the executives envince a sustained interest and play an active part in the formulation and implementation of an integrated cost reduction programme, the same might not achieve a real and permanent reduction in costs.

It is, in the light of this view, that we refer to the organization for cost reduction. The kind of organization responsible for formulating a cost reduction programme differs from concern to concern because of divergences such as the nature of the business, size of the concern, and individual requirements. However, a cost reduction committee headed by the top executive and composed of heads in charge of the various business functions, is usually set up for developing and administering the cost reduction programme. The main functions of the cost reduction committee are as follows:

1. Plan an integrated cost reduction programme.
2. Define clearly the cost reduction programme and assign responsibility amongst the executives.
3. Set targets of cost reduction and determine priorities.
4. Discuss problems arising in the course of execution of the scheme.
5. Review the progress made from time to time and to motivate the employee's to achieve the target.

16.6   AREAS OF APPLICATION

The specific areas covered by a cost reduction programme are as follows:

1. Any cost reduction programme should start with the design of the product to take advantage of the benefits accruing at every stage influenced by the design.
2. Factory organization and production methods are covered under cost reduction programme.
3. Administration is a strategic area which has cost-saving potential.
4. Possibilities of cost saving should be explored in the area of personnel management.
5. Selling and distribution channels and the methods employed should be reviewed to explore the possibility of cost reduction.

The cost reduction programme has the following advantage:

1. The concern adopting a cost reduction plan successfully gets more profit and, thus, occupies an enviable position in the industry.
2. The shareholders get higher dividends and the employees higher emoluments.
3. The organization has the capacity to build up reserves and financial stability during the period of business adversity.
4. The concern has the capacity to finance expansion or modernization programme.
5. The organization builds up goodwill.
6. The government gets more revenue due to increased taxable capacity.
7. The competitive strength of the industry gets incresed which stimulates exports.
8. The consumers get good quality products in reasonable prices.

16.7 DISTINCTION BETWEEN COST CONTROL AND COST REDUCTION

Cost control and cost reduction have following distinctions:

1. Cost control aims at achieving management objectives whereas cost reduction aims at achieving real and permanent reduction in the cost of goods and/or services.
2. Since reduction of expenditure contributes to cost improvement, cost reduction begins where cost control ends.
3. Cost control is accomplished by setting targets of performance and striving hard to achieve them by avoiding wastes and inefficiencies. Cost reduction does not concern itself with the maintenance of performance according to the targets set.
4. Cost control is essentially static in nature. When cost control is achieved, the management feels that the ultimate goal is reached. Cost reduction, on the other hand, has no such visible and ultimate goal. It is a dynamic function.
5. Cost control seeks adherence to standards whereas cost reduction is a challenge to the standards themselves.

In spite of these differences, it can be said that cost control necessarily shows the idea of cost reduction.

REVIEW QUESTIONS

1. Define cost control. Briefly discuss the salient features of cost control.
2. What do you mean by cost control?
3. Distinguish between cost control and cost reduction. What are the features of cost reduction?
4. What is a cost reduction programme? State the functions of the cost reduction committee.
5. What are the advantages of cost reduction programme?
6. State the areas covered by a cost reduction programme.

Appendix

INTEREST TABLES

Interest Table for Annual Compounding with i = 0.25%

n	$F/p,i,n$	$P/F,i,n$	$F/A,i,n$	$A/F,i,n$	$P/A,i,n$	$A/P,i,n$	$A/G,i,n$
1	1.003	0.9975	1.000	1.0000	0.9975	1.0025	0.0000
1	1.003	0.9975	1.000	1.0000	0.9975	1.0025	0.0000
2	1.005	0.9950	2.003	0.4994	1.9926	0.5019	0.5048
3	1.008	0.9925	3.008	0.3325	2.9851	0.3350	1.0020
4	1.010	0.9901	4.015	0.2491	3.9752	0.2516	1.5012
5	1.013	0.9876	5.025	0.1990	4.9628	0.2015	1.9965
6	1.015	0.9851	6.038	0.1656	5.9479	0.1681	2.4988
7	1.018	0.9827	7.053	0.1418	6.9306	0.1443	2.9938
8	1.020	0.9802	8.070	0.1239	7.9108	0.1264	3.4907
9	1.023	0.9778	9.091	0.1100	8.8886	0.1125	3.9865
10	1.025	0.9753	10.113	0.0989	9.8639	0.1014	4.4830
11	1.028	0.9729	11.139	0.0898	10.8369	0.0923	4.9779
12	1.030	0.9705	12.167	0.0822	11.8074	0.0847	5.4744
13	1.033	0.9681	13.197	0.0758	12.7754	0.0783	5.9676
14	1.036	0.9656	14.230	0.0703	13.7411	0.0728	6.4633
15	1.038	0.9632	15.266	0.0655	14.7043	0.0680	6.9569
16	1.041	0.9608	16.304	0.0613	15.6652	0.0638	7.4498
17	1.043	0.9584	17.344	0.0577	16.6237	0.0602	7.9441
18	1.046	0.9561	18.388	0.0544	17.5797	0.0569	8.4373
19	1.049	0.9537	19.434	0.0515	18.5334	0.0540	8.9293
20	1.051	0.9513	20.482	0.0488	19.4847	0.0513	9.4211
21	1.054	0.9489	21.534	0.0464	20.4336	0.0489	9.9116
22	1.056	0.9465	22.587	0.0443	21.3802	0.0468	10.4033
23	1.059	0.9442	23.644	0.0423	22.3244	0.0448	10.8944
24	1.062	0.9418	24.703	0.0405	23.2662	0.0430	11.3840
25	1.064	0.9395	25.765	0.0388	24.2057	0.0413	11.8736
26	1.067	0.9371	26.829	0.0373	25.1428	0.0398	12.3629
27	1.070	0.9348	27.896	0.0358	26.0776	0.0383	12.8520
28	1.072	0.9325	28.966	0.0345	27.0102	0.0370	13.3407
29	1.075	0.9301	30.038	0.0333	27.9403	0.0358	13.8284
30	1.078	0.9278	31.114	0.0321	28.8681	0.0346	14.3166
31	1.080	0.9255	32.191	0.0311	29.7937	0.0336	14.8043
32	1.083	0.9232	33.272	0.0301	30.7169	0.0326	15.2906
33	1.086	0.9209	34.355	0.0291	31.6378	0.0316	15.7773
34	1.089	0.9186	35.441	0.0282	32.5564	0.0307	16.2632
35	1.091	0.9163	36.530	0.0274	33.4727	0.0299	16.7491
36	1.094	0.9140	37.621	0.0266	34.3868	0.0291	17.2342
37	1.097	0.9118	38.715	0.0258	35.2985	0.0283	17.7192
38	1.100	0.9095	39.812	0.0251	36.2080	0.0276	18.2036
39	1.102	0.9072	40.911	0.0244	37.1153	0.0269	18.6878
40	1.105	0.9049	42.014	0.0238	38.0202	0.0263	19.1708
41	1.108	0.9027	43.119	0.0232	38.9229	0.0257	19.6544
42	1.111	0.9004	44.226	0.0226	39.8233	0.0251	20.1368
43	1.113	0.8982	45.337	0.0221	40.7215	0.0246	20.6187
44	1.116	0.8960	46.450	0.0215	41.6175	0.0240	21.1010
45	1.119	0.8937	47.567	0.0210	42.5112	0.0235	21.5826
46	1.122	0.8915	48.686	0.0205	43.4028	0.0230	22.0641
47	1.125	0.8893	49.807	0.0201	44.2920	0.0226	22.5441
48	1.127	0.8871	50.932	0.0196	45.1791	0.0221	23.0245
49	1.130	0.8848	52.059	0.0192	46.0640	0.0217	23.5048
50	1.133	0.8826	53.189	0.0188	46.9466	0.0213	23.9840

Interest Table for Annual Compounding with *i* = 0.25% (Contd.)

n	F/p,i,n	P/F,i,n	F/A,i,n	A/F,i,n	P/A,i,n	A/P,i,n	A/G,i,n
51	1.136	0.8804	54.322	0.0184	47.8270	0.0209	24.4631
52	1.139	0.8782	55.458	0.0180	48.7052	0.0205	24.9412
53	1.141	0.8760	56.597	0.0177	49.5813	0.0202	25.4191
54	1.144	0.8739	57.738	0.0173	50.4552	0.0198	25.8977
55	1.147	0.8717	58.883	0.0170	51.3269	0.0195	26.3752
56	1.150	0.8695	60.030	0.0167	52.1964	0.0192	26.8514
57	1.153	0.8673	61.180	0.0163	53.0637	0.0188	27.3278
58	1.156	0.8652	62.333	0.0160	53.9289	0.0185	27.8042
59	1.159	0.8630	63.489	0.0158	54.7919	0.0183	28.2795
60	1.162	0.8609	64.647	0.0155	55.6529	0.0180	28.7554
61	1.165	0.8587	65.809	0.0152	56.5115	0.0177	29.2295
62	1.167	0.8566	66.974	0.0149	57.3682	0.0174	29.7046
63	1.170	0.8544	68.141	0.0147	58.2226	0.0172	30.1784
64	1.173	0.8523	69.311	0.0144	59.0749	0.0169	30.6521
65	1.176	0.8502	70.485	0.0142	59.9251	0.0167	31.1252
66	1.179	0.8481	71.661	0.0140	60.7732	0.0165	31.5981
67	1.182	0.8460	72.840	0.0137	61.6192	0.0162	32.0704
68	1.185	0.8438	74.022	0.0135	62.4630	0.0160	32.5423
69	1.188	0.8417	75.207	0.0133	63.3048	0.0158	33.0138
70	1.191	0.8396	76.395	0.0131	64.1444	0.0156	33.4850
71	1.194	0.8375	77.586	0.0129	64.9820	0.0154	33.9556
72	1.197	0.8355	78.780	0.0127	65.8174	0.0152	34.4259
73	1.200	0.8334	79.977	0.0125	66.6508	0.0150	34.8956
74	1.203	0.8313	81.177	0.0123	67.4821	0.0148	35.3650
75	1.206	0.8292	82.380	0.0121	68.3113	0.0146	35.8342
76	1.209	0.8272	83.586	0.0120	69.1385	0.0145	36.3027
77	1.212	0.8251	84.795	0.0118	69.9636	0.0143	36.7708
78	1.215	0.8230	86.007	0.0116	70.7867	0.0141	37.2391
79	1.218	0.8210	87.222	0.0115	71.6076	0.0140	37.7061
80	1.221	0.8189	88.440	0.0113	72.4266	0.0138	38.1733
81	1.224	0.8169	89.661	0.0112	73.2435	0.0137	38.6398
82	1.227	0.8149	90.885	0.0110	74.0584	0.0135	39.1059
83	1.230	0.8128	92.113	0.0109	74.8712	0.0134	39.5717
84	1.233	0.8108	93.343	0.0107	75.6819	0.0132	40.0367
85	1.236	0.8088	94.576	0.0106	76.4907	0.0131	40.5016
86	1.240	0.8068	95.813	0.0104	77.2975	0.0129	40.9663
87	1.243	0.8047	97.052	0.0103	78.1023	0.0128	41.4305
88	1.246	0.8027	98.295	0.0102	78.9050	0.0127	41.8936
89	1.249	0.8007	99.541	0.0100	79.7057	0.0125	42.3571
90	1.252	0.7987	100.790	0.0099	80.5045	0.0124	42.8199
91	1.255	0.7967	102.041	0.0098	81.3012	0.0123	43.2824
92	1.258	0.7948	103.297	0.0097	82.0960	0.0122	43.7443
93	1.261	0.7928	104.555	0.0096	82.8888	0.0121	44.2058
94	1.265	0.7908	105.816	0.0095	83.6796	0.0120	44.6671
95	1.268	0.7888	107.081	0.0093	84.4685	0.0118	45.1280
96	1.271	0.7869	108.349	0.0092	85.2553	0.0117	45.5881
97	1.274	0.7849	109.619	0.0091	86.0402	0.0116	46.0481
98	1.277	0.7829	110.893	0.0090	86.8232	0.0115	46.5075
99	1.280	0.7810	112.171	0.0089	87.6042	0.0114	46.9667
100	1.284	0.7790	113.451	0.0088	88.3832	0.0113	47.4253

Interest Table for Annual Compounding with $i = 0.5\%$

n	$F/p, i, n$	$P/F, i, n$	$F/A, i, n$	$A/F, i, n$	$P/A, i, n$	$A/P, i, n$	$A/G, i, n$
1	1.005	0.9950	1.000	1.0000	0.9950	1.0050	0.0000
2	1.010	0.9901	2.005	0.4988	1.9851	0.5038	0.4994
3	1.015	0.9851	3.015	0.3317	2.9702	0.3367	0.9964
4	1.020	0.9802	4.030	0.2481	3.9505	0.2531	1.4944
5	1.025	0.9754	5.050	0.1980	4.9259	0.2030	1.9903
6	1.030	0.9705	6.076	0.1646	5.8964	0.1696	2.4864
7	1.036	0.9657	7.106	0.1407	6.8621	0.1457	2.9794
8	1.041	0.9609	8.141	0.1228	7.8230	0.1278	3.4743
9	1.046	0.9561	9.182	0.1089	8.7791	0.1139	3.9665
10	1.051	0.9513	10.228	0.0978	9.7304	0.1028	4.4593
11	1.056	0.9466	11.279	0.0887	10.6770	0.0937	4.9505
12	1.062	0.9419	12.336	0.0811	11.6190	0.0861	5.4411
13	1.067	0.9372	13.397	0.0746	12.5562	0.0796	5.9304
14	1.072	0.9326	14.464	0.0691	13.4887	0.0741	6.4193
15	1.078	0.9279	15.537	0.0644	14.4166	0.0694	6.9068
16	1.083	0.9233	16.614	0.0602	15.3399	0.0652	7.3941
17	1.088	0.9187	17.697	0.0565	16.2586	0.0615	7.8803
18	1.094	0.9141	18.786	0.0532	17.1728	0.0582	8.3659
19	1.099	0.9096	19.880	0.0503	18.0824	0.0553	8.8504
20	1.105	0.9051	20.979	0.0477	18.9874	0.0527	9.3344
21	1.110	0.9006	22.084	0.0453	19.8880	0.0503	9.8172
22	1.116	0.8961	23.194	0.0431	20.7841	0.0481	10.2997
23	1.122	0.8916	24.310	0.0411	21.6757	0.0461	10.7807
24	1.127	0.8872	25.432	0.0393	22.5629	0.0443	11.2613
25	1.133	0.8828	26.559	0.0377	23.4457	0.0427	11.7409
26	1.138	0.8784	27.692	0.0361	24.3240	0.0411	12.2197
27	1.144	0.8740	28.830	0.0347	25.1980	0.0397	12.6976
28	1.150	0.8697	29.975	0.0334	26.0677	0.0384	13.1749
29	1.156	0.8653	31.124	0.0321	26.9331	0.0371	13.6513
30	1.161	0.8610	32.280	0.0310	27.7941	0.0360	14.1268
31	1.167	0.8567	33.441	0.0299	28.6508	0.0349	14.6012
32	1.173	0.8525	34.609	0.0289	29.5033	0.0339	15.0752
33	1.179	0.8482	35.782	0.0279	30.3515	0.0329	15.5482
34	1.185	0.8440	36.961	0.0271	31.1956	0.0321	16.0204
35	1.191	0.8398	38.145	0.0262	32.0354	0.0312	16.4917
36	1.197	0.8356	39.336	0.0254	32.8710	0.0304	16.9622
37	1.203	0.8315	40.533	0.0247	33.7025	0.0297	17.4320
38	1.209	0.8274	41.736	0.0240	34.5299	0.0290	17.9008
39	1.215	0.8232	42.944	0.0233	35.3531	0.0283	18.3688
40	1.221	0.8191	44.159	0.0226	36.1723	0.0276	18.8360
41	1.227	0.8151	45.380	0.0220	36.9873	0.0270	19.3023
42	1.233	0.8110	46.607	0.0215	37.7983	0.0265	19.7679
43	1.239	0.8070	47.840	0.0209	38.6053	0.0259	20.2326
44	1.245	0.8030	49.079	0.0204	39.4083	0.0254	20.6966
45	1.252	0.7990	50.324	0.0199	40.2072	0.0249	21.1597
46	1.258	0.7950	51.576	0.0194	41.0022	0.0244	21.6219
47	1.264	0.7910	52.834	0.0189	41.7932	0.0239	22.0832
48	1.270	0.7871	54.098	0.0185	42.5804	0.0235	22.5439
49	1.277	0.7832	55.368	0.0181	43.3635	0.0231	23.0036
50	1.283	0.7793	56.645	0.0177	44.1428	0.0227	23.4626

Interest Table for Annual Compounding with *i* = 0.5% (Contd.)

n	*F/p,i,n*	*P/F,i,n*	*F/A,i,n*	*A/F,i,n*	*P/A,i,n*	*A/P,i,n*	*A/G,i,n*
51	1.290	0.7754	57.928	0.0173	44.9182	0.0223	23.9206
52	1.296	0.7716	59.218	0.0169	45.6898	0.0219	24.3780
53	1.303	0.7677	60.514	0.0165	46.4575	0.0215	24.8344
54	1.309	0.7639	61.817	0.0162	47.2214	0.0212	25.2902
55	1.316	0.7601	63.126	0.0158	47.9815	0.0208	25.7449
56	1.322	0.7563	64.441	0.0155	48.7378	0.0205	26.1989
57	1.329	0.7525	65.764	0.0152	49.4903	0.0202	26.6520
58	1.335	0.7488	67.092	0.0149	50.2391	0.0199	27.1044
59	1.342	0.7451	68.428	0.0146	50.9842	0.0196	27.5559
60	1.349	0.7414	69.770	0.0143	51.7256	0.0193	28.0066
61	1.356	0.7377	71.119	0.0141	52.4633	0.0191	28.4564
62	1.362	0.7340	72.475	0.0138	53.1973	0.0188	28.9054
63	1.369	0.7304	73.837	0.0135	53.9277	0.0185	29.3536
64	1.376	0.7267	75.206	0.0133	54.6544	0.0183	29.8011
65	1.383	0.7231	76.582	0.0131	55.3775	0.0181	30.2476
66	1.390	0.7195	77.965	0.0128	56.0970	0.0178	30.6933
67	1.397	0.7159	79.355	0.0126	56.8129	0.0176	31.1382
68	1.404	0.7124	80.752	0.0124	57.5253	0.0174	31.5823
69	1.411	0.7088	82.155	0.0122	58.2342	0.0172	32.0256
70	1.418	0.7053	83.566	0.0120	58.9395	0.0170	32.4681
71	1.425	0.7018	84.984	0.0118	59.6412	0.0168	32.9097
72	1.432	0.6983	86.409	0.0116	60.3395	0.0166	33.3505
73	1.439	0.6948	87.841	0.0114	61.0344	0.0164	33.7905
74	1.446	0.6914	89.280	0.0112	61.7258	0.0162	34.2297
75	1.454	0.6879	90.727	0.0110	62.4137	0.0160	34.6681
76	1.461	0.6845	92.180	0.0108	63.0982	0.0158	35.1056
77	1.468	0.6811	93.641	0.0107	63.7793	0.0157	35.5424
78	1.476	0.6777	95.109	0.0105	64.4570	0.0155	35.9783
79	1.483	0.6743	96.585	0.0104	65.1314	0.0154	36.4133
80	1.490	0.6710	98.068	0.0102	65.8024	0.0152	36.8476
81	1.498	0.6677	99.558	0.0100	66.4700	0.0150	37.2810
82	1.505	0.6643	101.056	0.0099	67.1343	0.0149	37.7136
83	1.513	0.6610	102.561	0.0098	67.7953	0.0148	38.1454
84	1.520	0.6577	104.074	0.0096	68.4531	0.0146	38.5765
85	1.528	0.6545	105.594	0.0095	69.1075	0.0145	39.0066
86	1.536	0.6512	107.122	0.0093	69.7588	0.0143	39.4360
87	1.543	0.6480	108.658	0.0092	70.4067	0.0142	39.8645
88	1.551	0.6447	110.201	0.0091	71.0515	0.0141	40.2923
89	1.559	0.6415	111.752	0.0089	71.6930	0.0139	40.7191
90	1.567	0.6383	113.311	0.0088	72.3313	0.0138	41.1452
91	1.574	0.6352	114.878	0.0087	72.9665	0.0137	41.5705
92	1.582	0.6320	116.452	0.0086	73.5985	0.0136	41.9949
93	1.590	0.6289	118.034	0.0085	74.2274	0.0135	42.4187
94	1.598	0.6257	119.624	0.0084	74.8531	0.0134	42.8415
95	1.606	0.6226	121.223	0.0082	75.4757	0.0132	43.2634
96	1.614	0.6195	122.829	0.0081	76.0953	0.0131	43.6847
97	1.622	0.6164	124.443	0.0080	76.7117	0.0130	44.1051
98	1.630	0.6134	126.065	0.0079	77.3251	0.0129	44.5246
99	1.638	0.6103	127.695	0.0078	77.9354	0.0128	44.9434
100	1.647	0.6073	129.334	0.0077	78.5427	0.0127	45.3614

Interest Table for Annual Compounding with $i = 0.75\%$

n	$F/p,i,n$	$P/F,i,n$	$F/A,i,n$	$A/F,i,n$	$P/A,i,n$	$A/P,i,n$	$A/G,i,n$
1	1.008	0.9926	1.000	1.0000	0.9926	1.0075	0.0000
2	1.015	0.9852	2.008	0.4981	1.9777	0.5056	0.4993
3	1.023	0.9778	3.023	0.3308	2.9556	0.3383	0.9956
4	1.030	0.9706	4.045	0.2472	3.9261	0.2547	1.4920
5	1.038	0.9633	5.076	0.1970	4.8895	0.2045	1.9862
6	1.046	0.9562	6.114	0.1636	5.8456	0.1711	2.4792
7	1.054	0.9490	7.160	0.1397	6.7947	0.1472	2.9710
8	1.062	0.9420	8.213	0.1218	7.7367	0.1293	3.4623
9	1.070	0.9350	9.275	0.1078	8.6717	0.1153	3.9514
10	1.078	0.9280	10.344	0.0967	9.5997	0.1042	4.4396
11	1.086	0.9211	11.422	0.0876	10.5208	0.0951	4.9265
12	1.094	0.9142	12.508	0.0800	11.4350	0.0875	5.4122
13	1.102	0.9074	13.602	0.0735	12.3425	0.0810	5.8967
14	1.110	0.9007	14.704	0.0680	13.2431	0.0755	6.3799
15	1.119	0.8940	15.814	0.0632	14.1371	0.0707	6.8618
16	1.127	0.8873	16.932	0.0591	15.0244	0.0666	7.3425
17	1.135	0.8807	18.059	0.0554	15.9052	0.0629	7.8221
18	1.144	0.8742	19.195	0.0521	16.7793	0.0596	8.3003
19	1.153	0.8676	20.339	0.0492	17.6470	0.0567	8.7771
20	1.161	0.8612	21.491	0.0465	18.5082	0.0540	9.2529
21	1.170	0.8548	22.653	0.0441	19.3630	0.0516	9.7274
22	1.179	0.8484	23.823	0.0420	20.2114	0.0495	10.2007
23	1.188	0.8421	25.001	0.0400	21.0535	0.0475	10.6726
24	1.196	0.8358	26.189	0.0382	21.8893	0.0457	11.1435
25	1.205	0.8296	27.385	0.0365	22.7190	0.0440	11.6130
26	1.214	0.8234	28.591	0.0350	23.5424	0.0425	12.0812
27	1.224	0.8173	29.805	0.0336	24.3597	0.0411	12.5483
28	1.233	0.8112	31.029	0.0322	25.1709	0.0397	13.0140
29	1.242	0.8052	32.261	0.0310	25.9761	0.0385	13.4786
30	1.251	0.7992	33.503	0.0298	26.7753	0.0373	13.9420
31	1.261	0.7932	34.755	0.0288	27.5685	0.0363	14.4040
32	1.270	0.7873	36.015	0.0278	28.3559	0.0353	14.8649
33	1.280	0.7815	37.285	0.0268	29.1374	0.0343	15.3245
34	1.289	0.7757	38.565	0.0259	29.9130	0.0334	15.7829
35	1.299	0.7699	39.854	0.0251	30.6829	0.0326	16.2400
36	1.309	0.7641	41.153	0.0243	31.4471	0.0318	16.6959
37	1.318	0.7585	42.462	0.0236	32.2055	0.0311	17.1506
38	1.328	0.7528	43.780	0.0228	32.9584	0.0303	17.6040
39	1.338	0.7472	45.109	0.0222	33.7056	0.0297	18.0561
40	1.348	0.7416	46.447	0.0215	34.4472	0.0290	18.5071
41	1.358	0.7361	47.795	0.0209	35.1834	0.0284	18.9568
42	1.369	0.7306	49.154	0.0203	35.9140	0.0278	19.4054
43	1.379	0.7252	50.523	0.0198	36.6392	0.0273	19.8526
44	1.389	0.7198	51.901	0.0193	37.3590	0.0268	20.2986
45	1.400	0.7144	53.291	0.0188	38.0735	0.0263	20.7434
46	1.410	0.7091	54.690	0.0183	38.7826	0.0258	21.1869
47	1.421	0.7039	56.101	0.0178	39.4865	0.0253	21.6292
48	1.431	0.6986	57.521	0.0174	40.1851	0.0249	22.0703
49	1.442	0.6934	58.953	0.0170	40.8785	0.0245	22.5102
50	1.453	0.6882	60.395	0.0166	41.5668	0.0241	22.9489

Interest Table for Annual Compounding with i = 0.75% (Contd.)

n	$F/p,i,n$	$P/F,i,n$	$F/A,i,n$	$A/F,i,n$	$P/A,i,n$	$A/P,i,n$	$A/G,i,n$
51	1.464	0.6831	61.848	0.0162	42.2499	0.0237	23.3862
52	1.475	0.6780	63.312	0.0158	42.9280	0.0233	23.8224
53	1.486	0.6730	64.787	0.0154	43.6010	0.0229	24.2574
54	1.497	0.6680	66.273	0.0151	44.2690	0.0226	24.6911
55	1.508	0.6630	67.770	0.0148	44.9320	0.0223	25.1236
56	1.520	0.6581	69.278	0.0144	45.5901	0.0219	25.5549
57	1.531	0.6532	70.798	0.0141	46.2432	0.0216	25.9849
58	1.542	0.6483	72.329	0.0138	46.8915	0.0213	26.4138
59	1.554	0.6435	73.871	0.0135	47.5350	0.0210	26.8414
60	1.566	0.6387	75.425	0.0133	48.1737	0.0208	27.2678
61	1.577	0.6339	76.991	0.0130	48.8077	0.0205	27.6929
62	1.589	0.6292	78.568	0.0127	49.4369	0.0202	28.1169
63	1.601	0.6245	80.157	0.0125	50.0615	0.0200	28.5396
64	1.613	0.6199	81.759	0.0122	50.6814	0.0197	28.9611
65	1.625	0.6153	83.372	0.0120	51.2966	0.0195	29.3814
66	1.637	0.6107	84.997	0.0118	51.9073	0.0193	29.8005
67	1.650	0.6061	86.635	0.0115	52.5135	0.0190	30.2183
68	1.662	0.6016	88.284	0.0113	53.1151	0.0188	30.6350
69	1.675	0.5972	89.947	0.0111	53.7123	0.0186	31.0504
70	1.687	0.5927	91.621	0.0109	54.3050	0.0184	31.4646
71	1.700	0.5883	93.308	0.0107	54.8933	0.0182	31.8776
72	1.713	0.5839	95.008	0.0105	55.4773	0.0180	32.2895
73	1.725	0.5796	96.721	0.0103	56.0568	0.0178	32.7000
74	1.738	0.5753	98.446	0.0102	56.6321	0.0177	33.1094
75	1.751	0.5710	100.185	0.0100	57.2031	0.0175	33.5176
76	1.765	0.5667	101.936	0.0098	57.7698	0.0173	33.9246
77	1.778	0.5625	103.701	0.0096	58.3323	0.0171	34.3303
78	1.791	0.5583	105.478	0.0095	58.8907	0.0170	34.7349
79	1.805	0.5542	107.269	0.0093	59.4448	0.0168	35.1382
80	1.818	0.5500	109.074	0.0092	59.9949	0.0167	35.5403
81	1.832	0.5459	110.892	0.0090	60.5408	0.0165	35.9413
82	1.845	0.5419	112.724	0.0089	61.0827	0.0164	36.3410
83	1.859	0.5378	114.569	0.0087	61.6206	0.0162	36.7396
84	1.873	0.5338	116.428	0.0086	62.1544	0.0161	37.1369
85	1.887	0.5299	118.302	0.0085	62.6843	0.0160	37.5331
86	1.901	0.5259	120.189	0.0083	63.2102	0.0158	37.9280
87	1.916	0.5220	122.090	0.0082	63.7322	0.0157	38.3218
88	1.930	0.5181	124.006	0.0081	64.2503	0.0156	38.7143
89	1.945	0.5143	125.936	0.0079	64.7646	0.0154	39.1057
90	1.959	0.5104	127.881	0.0078	65.2751	0.0153	39.4959
91	1.974	0.5066	129.840	0.0077	65.7817	0.0152	39.8849
92	1.989	0.5029	131.814	0.0076	66.2846	0.0151	40.2727
93	2.004	0.4991	133.802	0.0075	66.7837	0.0150	40.6593
94	2.019	0.4954	135.806	0.0074	67.2791	0.0149	41.0447
95	2.034	0.4917	137.824	0.0073	67.7708	0.0148	41.4289
96	2.049	0.4881	139.858	0.0072	68.2589	0.0147	41.8120
97	2.064	0.4844	141.907	0.0070	68.7433	0.0145	42.1939
98	2.080	0.4808	143.971	0.0069	69.2241	0.0144	42.5745
99	2.095	0.4772	146.051	0.0068	69.7014	0.0143	42.9541
100	2.111	0.4737	148.147	0.0068	70.1751	0.0143	43.3324

Interest Table for Annual Compounding with $i = 1\%$

n	$F/p, i, n$	$P/F, i, n$	$F/A, i, n$	$A/F, i, n$	$P/A, i, n$	$A/P, i, n$	$A/G, i, n$
1	1.010	0.9901	1.000	1.0000	0.9901	1.0100	0.0000
2	1.020	0.9803	2.010	0.4975	1.9704	0.5075	0.4976
3	1.030	0.9706	3.030	0.3300	2.9410	0.3400	0.9934
4	1.041	0.9610	4.060	0.2463	3.9020	0.2563	1.4873
5	1.051	0.9515	5.101	0.1960	4.8534	0.2060	1.9801
6	1.062	0.9420	6.152	0.1625	5.7955	0.1725	2.4710
7	1.072	0.9327	7.214	0.1386	6.7282	0.1486	2.9601
8	1.083	0.9235	8.286	0.1207	7.6517	0.1307	3.4477
9	1.094	0.9143	9.369	0.1067	8.5660	0.1167	3.9335
10	1.105	0.9053	10.462	0.0956	9.4713	0.1056	4.4179
11	1.116	0.8963	11.567	0.0865	10.3676	0.0965	4.9005
12	1.127	0.8874	12.682	0.0788	11.2551	0.0888	5.3814
13	1.138	0.8787	13.809	0.0724	12.1337	0.0824	5.8607
14	1.149	0.8700	14.947	0.0669	13.0037	0.0769	6.3383
15	1.161	0.8613	16.097	0.0621	13.8650	0.0721	6.8143
16	1.173	0.8528	17.258	0.0579	14.7179	0.0679	7.2886
17	1.184	0.8444	18.430	0.0543	15.5622	0.0643	7.7613
18	1.196	0.8360	19.615	0.0510	16.3983	0.0610	8.2323
19	1.208	0.8277	20.811	0.0481	17.2260	0.0581	8.7016
20	1.220	0.8195	22.019	0.0454	18.0455	0.0554	9.1694
21	1.232	0.8114	23.239	0.0430	18.8570	0.0530	9.6354
22	1.245	0.8034	24.472	0.0409	19.6604	0.0509	10.0997
23	1.257	0.7954	25.716	0.0389	20.4558	0.0489	10.5625
24	1.270	0.7876	26.973	0.0371	21.2434	0.0471	11.0236
25	1.282	0.7798	28.243	0.0354	22.0231	0.0454	11.4830
26	1.295	0.7720	29.526	0.0339	22.7952	0.0439	11.9409
27	1.308	0.7644	30.821	0.0324	23.5596	0.0424	12.3970
28	1.321	0.7568	32.129	0.0311	24.3164	0.0411	12.8516
29	1.335	0.7493	33.450	0.0299	25.0658	0.0399	13.3044
30	1.348	0.7419	34.785	0.0287	25.8077	0.0387	13.7556
31	1.361	0.7346	36.133	0.0277	26.5423	0.0377	14.2052
32	1.375	0.7273	37.494	0.0267	27.2696	0.0367	14.6531
33	1.389	0.7201	38.869	0.0257	27.9897	0.0357	15.0994
34	1.403	0.7130	40.258	0.0248	28.7027	0.0348	15.5441
35	1.417	0.7059	41.660	0.0240	29.4086	0.0340	15.9871
36	1.431	0.6989	43.077	0.0232	30.1075	0.0332	16.4285
37	1.445	0.6920	44.508	0.0225	30.7995	0.0325	16.8682
38	1.460	0.6852	45.953	0.0218	31.4847	0.0318	17.3063
39	1.474	0.6784	47.412	0.0211	32.1630	0.0311	17.7427
40	1.489	0.6717	48.886	0.0205	32.8347	0.0305	18.1776
41	1.504	0.6650	50.375	0.0199	33.4997	0.0299	18.6108
42	1.519	0.6584	51.879	0.0193	34.1581	0.0293	19.0424
43	1.534	0.6519	53.398	0.0187	34.8100	0.0287	19.4723
44	1.549	0.6454	54.932	0.0182	35.4554	0.0282	19.9006
45	1.565	0.6391	56.481	0.0177	36.0945	0.0277	20.3273
46	1.580	0.6327	58.046	0.0172	36.7272	0.0272	20.7523
47	1.596	0.6265	59.626	0.0168	37.3537	0.0268	21.1757
48	1.612	0.6203	61.223	0.0163	37.9740	0.0263	21.5975
49	1.628	0.6141	62.835	0.0159	38.5881	0.0259	22.0177
50	1.645	0.6080	64.463	0.0155	39.1961	0.0255	22.4363

Interest Table for Annual Compounding with $i = 1\%$ (Contd.)

n	$F/p, i, n$	$P/F, i, n$	$F/A, i, n$	$A/F, i, n$	$P/A, i, n$	$A/P, i, n$	$A/G, i, n$
51	1.661	0.6020	66.108	0.0151	39.7981	0.0251	22.8533
52	1.678	0.5961	67.769	0.0148	40.3942	0.0248	23.2686
53	1.694	0.5902	69.447	0.0144	40.9843	0.0244	23.6823
54	1.711	0.5843	71.141	0.0141	41.5687	0.0241	24.0944
55	1.729	0.5785	72.852	0.0137	42.1472	0.0237	24.5049
56	1.746	0.5728	74.581	0.0134	42.7200	0.0234	24.9138
57	1.763	0.5671	76.327	0.0131	43.2871	0.0231	25.3211
58	1.781	0.5615	78.090	0.0128	43.8486	0.0228	25.7268
59	1.799	0.5560	79.871	0.0125	44.4046	0.0225	26.1308
60	1.817	0.5504	81.670	0.0122	44.9550	0.0222	26.5333
61	1.835	0.5450	83.486	0.0120	45.5000	0.0220	26.9341
62	1.853	0.5396	85.321	0.0117	46.0396	0.0217	27.3334
63	1.872	0.5343	87.174	0.0115	46.5739	0.0215	27.7311
64	1.890	0.5290	89.046	0.0112	47.1029	0.0212	28.1272
65	1.909	0.5237	90.937	0.0110	47.6266	0.0210	28.5216
66	1.928	0.5185	92.846	0.0108	48.1451	0.0208	28.9145
67	1.948	0.5134	94.774	0.0106	48.6586	0.0206	29.3058
68	1.967	0.5083	96.722	0.0103	49.1669	0.0203	29.6955
69	1.987	0.5033	98.689	0.0101	49.6702	0.0201	30.0837
70	2.007	0.4983	100.676	0.0099	50.1685	0.0199	30.4702
71	2.027	0.4934	102.683	0.0097	50.6619	0.0197	30.8552
72	2.047	0.4885	104.710	0.0096	51.1504	0.0196	31.2386
73	2.068	0.4837	106.757	0.0094	51.6340	0.0194	31.6204
74	2.088	0.4789	108.825	0.0092	52.1129	0.0192	32.0006
75	2.109	0.4741	110.913	0.0090	52.5870	0.0190	32.3793
76	2.130	0.4694	113.022	0.0088	53.0565	0.0188	32.7564
77	2.152	0.4648	115.152	0.0087	53.5213	0.0187	33.1320
78	2.173	0.4602	117.304	0.0085	53.9815	0.0185	33.5059
79	2.195	0.4556	119.477	0.0084	54.4371	0.0184	33.8783
80	2.217	0.4511	121.671	0.0082	54.8882	0.0182	34.2492
81	2.239	0.4467	123.888	0.0081	55.3348	0.0181	34.6185
82	2.261	0.4422	126.127	0.0079	55.7771	0.0179	34.9862
83	2.284	0.4379	128.388	0.0078	56.2149	0.0178	35.3524
84	2.307	0.4335	130.672	0.0077	56.6484	0.0177	35.7170
85	2.330	0.4292	132.979	0.0075	57.0777	0.0175	36.0801
86	2.353	0.4250	135.309	0.0074	57.5026	0.0174	36.4416
87	2.377	0.4208	137.662	0.0073	57.9234	0.0173	36.8016
88	2.400	0.4166	140.038	0.0071	58.3400	0.0171	37.1601
89	2.424	0.4125	142.439	0.0070	58.7525	0.0170	37.5170
90	2.449	0.4084	144.863	0.0069	59.1609	0.0169	37.8724
91	2.473	0.4043	147.312	0.0068	59.5652	0.0168	38.2263
92	2.498	0.4003	149.785	0.0067	59.9656	0.0167	38.5786
93	2.523	0.3964	152.283	0.0066	60.3619	0.0166	38.9294
94	2.548	0.3925	154.806	0.0065	60.7544	0.0165	39.2787
95	2.574	0.3886	157.354	0.0064	61.1430	0.0164	39.6265
96	2.599	0.3847	159.927	0.0063	61.5277	0.0163	39.9727
97	2.625	0.3809	162.526	0.0062	61.9086	0.0162	40.3174
98	2.652	0.3771	165.152	0.0061	62.2858	0.0161	40.6606
99	2.678	0.3734	167.803	0.0060	62.6592	0.0160	41.0023
100	2.705	0.3697	170.481	0.0059	63.0289	0.0159	41.3425

Interest Table for Annual Compounding with i = 1.25%

n	F/p,i,n	P/F,i,n	F/A,i,n	A/F,i,n	P/A,i,n	A/P,i,n	A/G,i,n
1	1.013	0.9877	1.000	1.0000	0.9877	1.0125	0.0000
2	1.025	0.9755	2.013	0.4969	1.9631	0.5094	0.4974
3	1.038	0.9634	3.038	0.3292	2.9265	0.3417	0.9921
4	1.051	0.9515	4.076	0.2454	3.8781	0.2579	1.4848
5	1.064	0.9398	5.127	0.1951	4.8179	0.2076	1.9756
6	1.077	0.9282	6.191	0.1615	5.7460	0.1740	2.4642
7	1.091	0.9167	7.268	0.1376	6.6628	0.1501	2.9507
8	1.104	0.9054	8.359	0.1196	7.5682	0.1321	3.4352
9	1.118	0.8942	9.463	0.1057	8.4624	0.1182	3.9176
10	1.132	0.8832	10.582	0.0945	9.3456	0.1070	4.3979
11	1.146	0.8723	11.714	0.0854	10.2179	0.0979	4.8762
12	1.161	0.8615	12.860	0.0778	11.0794	0.0903	5.3525
13	1.175	0.8509	14.021	0.0713	11.9302	0.0838	5.8266
14	1.190	0.8404	15.196	0.0658	12.7706	0.0783	6.2987
15	1.205	0.8300	16.386	0.0610	13.6006	0.0735	6.7687
16	1.220	0.8197	17.591	0.0568	14.4204	0.0693	7.2366
17	1.235	0.8096	18.811	0.0532	15.2300	0.0657	7.7025
18	1.251	0.7996	20.046	0.0499	16.0296	0.0624	8.1663
19	1.266	0.7898	21.297	0.0470	16.8194	0.0595	8.6281
20	1.282	0.7800	22.563	0.0443	17.5994	0.0568	9.0878
21	1.298	0.7704	23.845	0.0419	18.3698	0.0544	9.5454
22	1.314	0.7609	25.143	0.0398	19.1307	0.0523	10.0010
23	1.331	0.7515	26.458	0.0378	19.8821	0.0503	10.4546
24	1.347	0.7422	27.788	0.0360	20.6243	0.0485	10.9061
25	1.364	0.7330	29.136	0.0343	21.3574	0.0468	11.3555
26	1.381	0.7240	30.500	0.0328	22.0813	0.0453	11.8029
27	1 399	0.7150	31.881	0.0314	22.7964	0.0439	12.2482
28	1.416	0.7062	33.280	0.0300	23.5026	0.0425	12.6915
29	1.434	0.6975	34.696	0.0288	24.2001	0.0413	13.1327
30	1.452	0.6889	36.129	0.0277	24.8890	0.0402	13.5719
31	1.470	0.6804	37.581	0.0266	25.5694	0.0391	14.0091
32	1.488	0.6720	39.051	0.0256	26.2414	0.0381	14.4442
33	1.507	0.6637	40.539	0.0247	26.9051	0.0372	14.8773
34	1.526	0.6555	42.046	0.0238	27.5606	0.0363	15.3083
35	1.545	0.6474	43.571	0.0230	28.2080	0.0355	15.7373
36	1.564	0.6394	45.116	0.0222	28.8474	0.0347	16.1643
37	1.583	0.6315	46.680	0.0214	29.4789	0.0339	16.5892
38	1.603	0.6237	48.263	0.0207	30.1026	0.0332	17.0121
39	1.623	0.6160	49.867	0.0201	30.7186	0.0326	17.4330
40	1.644	0.6084	51.490	0.0194	31.3271	0.0319	17.8519
41	1.664	0.6009	53.134	0.0188	31.9280	0.0313	18.2688
42	1.685	0.5935	54.798	0.0182	32.5214	0.0307	18.6836
43	1.706	0.5862	56.483	0.0177	33.1076	0.0302	19.0964
44	1.727	0.5789	58.189	0.0172	33.6865	0.0297	19.5072
45	1.749	0.5718	59.916	0.0167	34.2583	0.0292	19.9160
46	1.771	0.5647	61.665	0.0162	34.8230	0.0287	20.3228
47	1.793	0.5577	63.436	0.0158	35.3808	0.0283	20.7276
48	1.815	0.5509	65.229	0.0153	35.9316	0.0278	21.1303
49	1.838	0.5441	67.044	0.0149	36.4757	0.0274	21.5311
50	1.861	0.5373	68.882	0.0145	37.0130	0.0270	21.9299

Interest Table for Annual Compounding with *i* = 1.25% (Contd.)

n	F/p,i,n	P/F,i,n	F/A,i,n	A/F,i,n	P/A,i,n	A/P,i,n	A/G,i,n
51	1.884	0.5307	70.743	0.0141	37.5437	0.0266	22.3267
52	1.908	0.5242	72.628	0.0138	38.0679	0.0263	22.7215
53	1.932	0.5177	74.535	0.0134	38.5856	0.0259	23.1143
54	1.956	0.5113	76.467	0.0131	39.0969	0.0256	23.5052
55	1.980	0.5050	78.423	0.0128	39.6018	0.0253	23.8940
56	2.005	0.4987	80.403	0.0124	40.1006	0.0249	24.2809
57	2.030	0.4926	82.408	0.0121	40.5932	0.0246	24.6658
58	2.055	0.4865	84.438	0.0118	41.0797	0.0243	25.0488
59	2.081	0.4805	86.494	0.0116	41.5602	0.0241	25.4297
60	2.107	0.4746	88.575	0.0113	42.0347	0.0238	25.8088
61	2.134	0.4687	90.682	0.0110	42.5035	0.0235	26.1858
62	2.160	0.4629	92.816	0.0108	42.9664	0.0233	26.5609
63	2.187	0.4572	94.976	0.0105	43.4236	0.0230	26.9340
64	2.215	0.4516	97.163	0.0103	43.8752	0.0228	27.3052
65	2.242	0.4460	99.378	0.0101	44.3211	0.0226	27.6745
66	2.270	0.4405	101.620	0.0098	44.7616	0.0223	28.0418
67	2.299	0.4350	103.890	0.0096	45.1967	0.0221	28.4072
68	2.327	0.4297	106.189	0.0094	45.6263	0.0219	28.7706
69	2.356	0.4244	108.516	0.0092	46.0507	0.0217	29.1321
70	2.386	0.4191	110.873	0.0090	46.4698	0.0215	29.4917
71	2.416	0.4140	113.259	0.0088	46.8838	0.0213	29.8494
72	2.446	0.4088	115.675	0.0086	47.2926	0.0211	30.2051
73	2.477	0.4038	118.121	0.0085	47.6964	0.0210	30.5590
74	2.507	0.3988	120.597	0.0083	48.0952	0.0208	30.9109
75	2.539	0.3939	123.104	0.0081	48.4891	0.0206	31.2609
76	2.571	0.3890	125.643	0.0080	48.8782	0.0205	31.6091
77	2.603	0.3842	128.214	0.0078	49.2624	0.0203	31.9553
78	2.635	0.3795	130.817	0.0076	49.6419	0.0201	32.2996
79	2.668	0.3748	133.452	0.0075	50.0166	0.0200	32.6421
80	2.701	0.3702	136.120	0.0073	50.3868	0.0198	32.9826
81	2.735	0.3656	138.821	0.0072	50.7524	0.0197	33.3213
82	2.769	0.3611	141.557	0.0071	51.1135	0.0196	33.6582
83	2.804	0.3566	144.326	0.0069	51.4701	0.0194	33.9931
84	2.839	0.3522	147.130	0.0068	51.8223	0.0193	34.3262
85	2.875	0.3479	149.969	0.0067	52.1702	0.0192	34.6574
86	2.911	0.3436	152.844	0.0065	52.5138	0.0190	34.9868
87	2.947	0.3393	155.755	0.0064	52.8531	0.0189	35.3143
88	2.984	0.3351	158.702	0.0063	53.1883	0.0188	35.6400
89	3.021	0.3310	161.685	0.0062	53.5193	0.0187	35.9639
90	3.059	0.3269	164.706	0.0061	53.8462	0.0186	36.2859
91	3.097	0.3229	167.765	0.0060	54.1691	0.0185	36.6060
92	3.136	0.3189	170.862	0.0059	54.4880	0.0184	36.9244
93	3.175	0.3150	173.998	0.0057	54.8030	0.0182	37.2409
94	3.215	0.3111	177.173	0.0056	55.1141	0.0181	37.5557
95	3.255	0.3072	180.388	0.0055	55.4213	0.0180	37.8686
96	3.296	0.3034	183.643	0.0054	55.7247	0.0179	38.1797
97	3.337	0.2997	186.938	0.0053	56.0244	0.0178	38.4890
98	3.378	0.2960	190.275	0.0053	56.3204	0.0178	38.7965
99	3.421	0.2923	193.654	0.0052	56.6128	0.0177	39.1022
100	3.463	0.2887	197.074	0.0051	56.9015	0.0176	39.4061

Interest Table for Annual Compounding with *i* = 1.5%

n	F/p,i,n	P/F,i,n	F/A,i,n	A/F,i,n	P/A,i,n	A/P,i,n	A/G,i,n
1	1.015	0.9852	1.000	1.0000	0.9852	1.0150	0.0000
2	1.030	0.9707	2.015	0.4963	1.9559	0.5113	0.4962
3	1.046	0.9563	3.045	0.3284	2.9122	0.3434	0.9900
4	1.061	0.9422	4.091	0.2444	3.8544	0.2594	1.4811
5	1.077	0.9283	5.152	0.1941	4.7826	0.2091	1.9700
6	1.093	0.9145	6.230	0.1605	5.6972	0.1755	2.4563
7	1.110	0.9010	7.323	0.1366	6.5982	0.1516	2.9402
8	1.126	0.8877	8.433	0.1186	7.4859	0.1336	3.4216
9	1.143	0.8746	9.559	0.1046	8.3605	0.1196	3.9006
10	1.161	0.8617	10.703	0.0934	9.2222	0.1084	4.3770
11	1.178	0.8489	11.863	0.0843	10.0711	0.0993	4.8510
12	1.196	0.8364	13.041	0.0767	10.9075	0.0917	5.3225
13	1.214	0.8240	14.237	0.0702	11.7315	0.0852	5.7914
14	1.232	0.8118	15.450	0.0647	12.5433	0.0797	6.2580
15	1.250	0.7999	16.682	0.0599	13.3432	0.0749	6.7221
16	1.269	0.7880	17.932	0.0558	14.1312	0.0708	7.1837
17	1.288	0.7764	19.201	0.0521	14.9076	0.0671	7.6428
18	1.307	0.7649	20.489	0.0488	15.6725	0.0638	8.0995
19	1.327	0.7536	21.797	0.0459	16.4261	0.0609	8.5537
20	1.347	0.7425	23.124	0.0432	17.1686	0.0582	9.0055
21	1.367	0.7315	24.470	0.0409	17.9001	0.0559	9.4547
22	1.388	0.7207	25.837	0.0387	18.6208	0.0537	9.9016
23	1.408	0.7100	27.225	0.0367	19.3308	0.0517	10.3460
24	1.430	0.6995	28.633	0.0349	20.0304	0.0499	10.7879
25	1.451	0.6892	30.063	0.0333	20.7196	0.0483	11.2274
26	1.473	0.6790	31.514	0.0317	21.3986	0.0467	11.6644
27	1.495	0.6690	32.987	0.0303	22.0676	0.0453	12.0990
28	1.517	0.6591	34.481	0.0290	22.7267	0.0440	12.5311
29	1.540	0.6494	35.999	0.0278	23.3760	0.0428	12.9608
30	1.563	0.6398	37.539	0.0266	24.0158	0.0416	13.3881
31	1.587	0.6303	39.102	0.0256	24.6461	0.0406	13.8129
32	1.610	0.6210	40.688	0.0246	25.2671	0.0396	14.2353
33	1.634	0.6118	42.298	0.0236	25.8789	0.0386	14.6553
34	1.659	0.6028	43.933	0.0228	26.4817	0.0378	15.0728
35	1.684	0.5939	45.592	0.0219	27.0755	0.0369	15.4880
36	1.709	0.5851	47.276	0.0212	27.6606	0.0362	15.9007
37	1.735	0.5764	48.985	0.0204	28.2371	0.0354	16.3110
38	1.761	0.5679	50.720	0.0197	28.8050	0.0347	16.7189
39	1.787	0.5595	52.480	0.0191	29.3645	0.0341	17.1244
40	1.814	0.5513	54.268	0.0184	29.9158	0.0334	17.5275
41	1.841	0.5431	56.082	0.0178	30.4589	0.0328	17.9282
42	1.869	0.5351	57.923	0.0173	30.9940	0.0323	18.3265
43	1.897	0.5272	59.792	0.0167	31.5212	0.0317	18.7225
44	1.925	0.5194	61.689	0.0162	32.0405	0.0312	19.1160
45	1.954	0.5117	63.614	0.0157	32.5523	0.0307	19.5072
46	1.984	0.5042	65.568	0.0153	33.0564	0.0303	19.8960
47	2.013	0.4967	67.552	0.0148	33.5531	0.0298	20.2824
48	2.043	0.4894	69.565	0.0144	34.0425	0.0294	20.6665
49	2.074	0.4821	71.608	0.0140	34.5246	0.0290	21.0482
50	2.105	0.4750	73.682	0.0136	34.9996	0.0286	21.4275

Interest Table for Annual Compounding with $i = 1.5\%$ (Contd.)

n	$F/p,i,n$	$P/F,i,n$	$F/A,i,n$	$A/F,i,n$	$P/A,i,n$	$A/P,i,n$	$A/G,i,n$
51	2.137	0.4680	75.788	0.0132	35.4676	0.0282	21.8045
52	2.169	0.4611	77.925	0.0128	35.9287	0.0278	22.1792
53	2.201	0.4543	80.093	0.0125	36.3829	0.0275	22.5515
54	2.234	0.4475	82.295	0.0122	36.8305	0.0272	22.9215
55	2.268	0.4409	84.529	0.0118	37.2714	0.0268	23.2891
56	2.302	0.4344	86.797	0.0115	37.7058	0.0265	23.6545
57	2.336	0.4280	89.099	0.0112	38.1338	0.0262	24.0175
58	2.372	0.4217	91.436	0.0109	38.5555	0.0259	24.3782
59	2.407	0.4154	93.807	0.0107	38.9709	0.0257	24.7366
60	2.443	0.4093	96.214	0.0104	39.3802	0.0254	25.0927
61	2.480	0.4032	98.657	0.0101	39.7834	0.0251	25.4466
62	2.517	0.3973	101.137	0.0099	40.1807	0.0249	25.7981
63	2.555	0.3914	103.654	0.0096	40.5721	0.0246	26.1474
64	2.593	0.3856	106.209	0.0094	40.9578	0.0244	26.4943
65	2.632	0.3799	108.802	0.0092	41.3377	0.0242	26.8390
66	2.672	0.3743	111.434	0.0090	41.7120	0.0240	27.1815
67	2.712	0.3688	114.106	0.0088	42.0808	0.0238	27.5217
68	2.752	0.3633	116.817	0.0086	42.4441	0.0236	27.8596
69	2.794	0.3580	119.570	0.0084	42.8021	0.0234	28.1953
70	2.835	0.3527	122.363	0.0082	43.1548	0.0232	28.5288
71	2.878	0.3475	125.199	0.0080	43.5023	0.0230	28.8600
72	2.921	0.3423	128.076	0.0078	43.8446	0.0228	29.1891
73	2.965	0.3373	130.998	0.0076	44.1819	0.0226	29.5159
74	3.009	0.3323	133.963	0.0075	44.5141	0.0225	29.8405
75	3.055	0.3274	136.972	0.0073	44.8415	0.0223	30.1629
76	3.100	0.3225	140.027	0.0071	45.1641	0.0221	30.4831
77	3.147	0.3178	143.127	0.0070	45.4818	0.0220	30.8011
78	3.194	0.3131	146.274	0.0068	45.7949	0.0218	31.1169
79	3.242	0.3084	149.468	0.0067	46.1034	0.0217	31.4306
80	3.291	0.3039	152.710	0.0065	46.4072	0.0215	31.7421
81	3.340	0.2994	156.001	0.0064	46.7066	0.0214	32.0514
82	3.390	0.2950	159.341	0.0063	47.0016	0.0213	32.3586
83	3.441	0.2906	162.731	0.0061	47.2922	0.0211	32.6637
84	3.493	0.2863	166.172	0.0060	47.5786	0.0210	32.9666
85	3.545	0.2821	169.664	0.0059	47.8606	0.0209	33.2674
86	3.598	0.2779	173.209	0.0058	48.1386	0.0208	33.5660
87	3.652	0.2738	176.807	0.0057	48.4124	0.0207	33.8626
88	3.707	0.2698	180.459	0.0055	48.6822	0.0205	34.1571
89	3.762	0.2658	184.166	0.0054	48.9479	0.0204	34.4494
90	3.819	0.2619	187.929	0.0053	49.2098	0.0203	34.7397
91	3.876	0.2580	191.748	0.0052	49.4678	0.0202	35.0279
92	3.934	0.2542	195.624	0.0051	49.7219	0.0201	35.3140
93	3.993	0.2504	199.558	0.0050	49.9723	0.0200	35.5980
94	4.053	0.2467	203.552	0.0049	50.2191	0.0199	35.8800
95	4.114	0.2431	207.605	0.0048	50.4621	0.0198	36.1600
96	4.176	0.2395	211.719	0.0047	50.7016	0.0197	36.4379
97	4.238	0.2359	215.895	0.0046	50.9375	0.0196	36.7138
98	4.302	0.2325	220.133	0.0045	51.1700	0.0195	36.9877
99	4.367	0.2290	224.435	0.0045	51.3990	0.0195	37.2595
100	4.432	0.2256	228.802	0.0044	51.6246	0.0194	37.5293

Interest Table for Annual Compounding with i = 1.75%

n	$F/p,i,n$	$P/F,i,n$	$F/A,i,n$	$A/F,i,n$	$P/A,i,n$	$A/P,i,n$	$A/G,i,n$
1	1.018	0.9828	1.000	1.0000	0.9828	1.0175	0.0000
2	1.035	0.9659	2.018	0.4957	1.9487	0.5132	0.4959
3	1.053	0.9493	3.053	0.3276	2.8980	0.3451	0.9886
4	1.072	0.9330	4.106	0.2435	3.8310	0.2610	1.4784
5	1.091	0.9169	5.178	0.1931	4.7479	0.2106	1.9655
6	1.110	0.9011	6.269	0.1595	5.6490	0.1770	2.4495
7	1.129	0.8856	7.378	0.1355	6.5347	0.1530	2.9308
8	1.149	0.8704	8.508	0.1175	7.4051	0.1350	3.4091
9	1.169	0.8554	9.656	0.1036	8.2605	0.1211	3.8845
10	1.189	0.8407	10.825	0.0924	9.1012	0.1099	4.3571
11	1.210	0.8263	12.015	0.0832	9.9275	0.1007	4.8268
12	1.231	0.8121	13.225	0.0756	10.7396	0.0931	5.2936
13	1.253	0.7981	14.457	0.0692	11.5377	0.0867	5.7575
14	1.275	0.7844	15.710	0.0637	12.3220	0.0812	6.2185
15	1.297	0.7709	16.985	0.0589	13.0929	0.0764	6.6767
16	1.320	0.7576	18.282	0.0547	13.8505	0.0722	7.1320
17	1.343	0.7446	19.602	0.0510	14.5951	0.0685	7.5844
18	1.367	0.7318	20.945	0.0477	15.3269	0.0652	8.0339
19	1.390	0.7192	22.311	0.0448	16.0461	0.0623	8.4806
20	1.415	0.7068	23.702	0.0422	16.7529	0.0597	8.9245
21	1.440	0.6947	25.116	0.0398	17.4476	0.0573	9.3655
22	1.465	0.6827	26.556	0.0377	18.1303	0.0552	9.8036
23	1.490	0.6710	28.021	0.0357	18.8013	0.0532	10.2388
24	1.516	0.6594	29.511	0.0339	19.4607	0.0514	10.6713
25	1.543	0.6481	31.028	0.0322	20.1088	0.0497	11.1009
26	1.570	0.6369	32.571	0.0307	20.7458	0.0482	11.5276
27	1.597	0.6260	34.141	0.0293	21.3718	0.0468	11.9515
28	1.625	0.6152	35.738	0.0280	21.9870	0.0455	12.3726
29	1.654	0.6046	37.363	0.0268	22.5917	0.0443	12.7909
30	1.683	0.5942	39.017	0.0256	23.1859	0.0431	13.2063
31	1.712	0.5840	40.700	0.0246	23.7699	0.0421	13.6189
32	1.742	0.5740	42.412	0.0236	24.3439	0.0411	14.0287
33	1.773	0.5641	44.155	0.0226	24.9080	0.0401	14.4358
34	1.804	0.5544	45.927	0.0218	25.4624	0.0393	14.8400
35	1.835	0.5449	47.731	0.0210	26.0073	0.0385	15.2414
36	1.867	0.5355	49.566	0.0202	26.5428	0.0377	15.6400
37	1.900	0.5263	51.434	0.0194	27.0691	0.0369	16.0359
38	1.933	0.5172	53.334	0.0187	27.5863	0.0362	16.4290
39	1.967	0.5083	55.267	0.0181	28.0947	0.0356	16.8193
40	2.002	0.4996	57.234	0.0175	28.5943	0.0350	17.2068
41	2.037	0.4910	59.236	0.0169	29.0853	0.0344	17.5916
42	2.072	0.4826	61.273	0.0163	29.5679	0.0338	17.9736
43	2.109	0.4743	63.345	0.0158	30.0421	0.0333	18.3529
44	2.145	0.4661	65.453	0.0153	30.5082	0.0328	18.7295
45	2.183	0.4581	67.599	0.0148	30.9663	0.0323	19.1033
46	2.221	0.4502	69.782	0.0143	31.4165	0.0318	19.4744
47	2.260	0.4425	72.003	0.0139	31.8590	0.0314	19.8428
48	2.300	0.4349	74.263	0.0135	32.2939	0.0310	20.2085
49	2.340	0.4274	76.563	0.0131	32.7212	0.0306	20.5715
50	2.381	0.4200	78.903	0.0127	33.1413	0.0302	20.9318

Interest Table for Annual Compounding with i = 1.75% (Contd.)

n	$F/p,i,n$	$P/F,i,n$	$F/A,i,n$	$A/F,i,n$	$P/A,i,n$	$A/P,i,n$	$A/G,i,n$
51	2.422	0.4128	81.283	0.0123	33.5541	0.0298	21.2895
52	2.465	0.4057	83.706	0.0119	33.9598	0.0294	21.6444
53	2.508	0.3987	86.171	0.0116	34.3585	0.0291	21.9967
54	2.552	0.3919	88.679	0.0113	34.7504	0.0288	22.3463
55	2.597	0.3851	91.231	0.0110	35.1355	0.0285	22.6933
56	2.642	0.3785	93.827	0.0107	35.5140	0.0282	23.0376
57	2.688	0.3720	96.469	0.0104	35.8860	0.0279	23.3793
58	2.735	0.3656	99.157	0.0101	36.2516	0.0276	23.7183
59	2.783	0.3593	101.893	0.0098	36.6109	0.0273	24.0548
60	2.832	0.3531	104.676	0.0096	36.9640	0.0271	24.3886
61	2.881	0.3471	107.508	0.0093	37.3111	0.0268	24.7199
62	2.932	0.3411	110.389	0.0091	37.6522	0.0266	25.0485
63	2.983	0.3352	113.321	0.0088	37.9874	0.0263	25.3746
64	3.035	0.3295	116.304	0.0086	38.3169	0.0261	25.6981
65	3.088	0.3238	119.339	0.0084	38.6407	0.0259	26.0191
66	3.142	0.3182	122.428	0.0082	38.9589	0.0257	26.3375
67	3.197	0.3127	125.570	0.0080	39.2716	0.0255	26.6534
68	3.253	0.3074	128.768	0.0078	39.5790	0.0253	26.9667
69	3.310	0.3021	132.021	0.0076	39.8811	0.0251	27.2775
70	3.368	0.2969	135.331	0.0074	40.1780	0.0249	27.5858
71	3.427	0.2918	138.700	0.0072	40.4697	0.0247	27.8916
72	3.487	0.2868	142.127	0.0070	40.7565	0.0245	28.1949
73	3.548	0.2818	145.614	0.0069	41.0383	0.0244	28.4957
74	3.610	0.2770	149.162	0.0067	41.3153	0.0242	28.7941
75	3.674	0.2722	152.773	0.0065	41.5875	0.0240	29.0900
76	3.738	0.2675	156.446	0.0064	41.8551	0.0239	29.3835
77	3.803	0.2629	160.184	0.0062	42.1180	0.0237	29.6745
78	3.870	0.2584	163.987	0.0061	42.3764	0.0236	29.9631
79	3.938	0.2540	167.857	0.0060	42.6304	0.0235	30.2493
80	4.006	0.2496	171.795	0.0058	42.8800	0.0233	30.5330
81	4.077	0.2453	175.801	0.0057	43.1253	0.0232	30.8144
82	4.148	0.2411	179.878	0.0056	43.3664	0.0231	31.0934
83	4.220	0.2369	184.026	0.0054	43.6033	0.0229	31.3700
84	4.294	0.2329	188.246	0.0053	43.8362	0.0228	31.6443
85	4.369	0.2289	192.540	0.0052	44.0651	0.0227	31.9162
86	4.446	0.2249	196.910	0.0051	44.2900	0.0226	32.1858
87	4.524	0.2211	201.356	0.0050	44.5110	0.0225	32.4531
88	4.603	0.2173	205.880	0.0049	44.7283	0.0224	32.7180
89	4.683	0.2135	210.482	0.0048	44.9418	0.0223	32.9807
90	4.765	0.2098	215.166	0.0046	45.1517	0.0221	33.2410
91	4.849	0.2062	219.931	0.0045	45.3579	0.0220	33.4991
92	4.934	0.2027	224.780	0.0044	45.5606	0.0219	33.7549
93	5.020	0.1992	229.714	0.0044	45.7598	0.0219	34.0085
94	5.108	0.1958	234.734	0.0043	45.9556	0.0218	34.2598
95	5.197	0.1924	239.842	0.0042	46.1480	0.0217	34.5089
96	5.288	0.1891	245.039	0.0041	46.3371	0.0216	34.7557
97	5.381	0.1858	250.327	0.0040	46.5229	0.0215	35.0004
98	5.475	0.1827	255.708	0.0039	46.7056	0.0214	35.2429
99	5.571	0.1795	261.183	0.0038	46.8851	0.0213	35.4831
100	5.668	0.1764	266.753	0.0037	47.0615	0.0212	35.7213

Interest Table for Annual Compounding with $i = 2\%$

n	$F/p, i, n$	$P/F, i, n$	$F/A, i, n$	$A/F, i, n$	$P/A, i, n$	$A/P, i, n$	$A/G, i, n$
1	1.020	0.9804	1.000	1.0000	0.9804	1.0200	0.0000
2	1.040	0.9612	2.020	0.4951	1.9416	0.5151	0.4948
3	1.061	0.9423	3.060	0.3268	2.8839	0.3468	0.9867
4	1.082	0.9238	4.122	0.2426	3.8077	0.2626	1.4751
5	1.104	0.9057	5.204	0.1922	4.7135	0.2122	1.9603
6	1.126	0.8880	6.308	0.1585	5.6014	0.1785	2.4421
7	1.149	0.8706	7.434	0.1345	6.4720	0.1545	2.9207
8	1.172	0.8535	8.583	0.1165	7.3255	0.1365	3.3960
9	1.195	0.8368	9.755	0.1025	8.1622	0.1225	3.8679
10	1.219	0.8203	10.950	0.0913	8.9826	0.1113	4.3366
11	1.243	0.8043	12.169	0.0822	9.7868	0.1022	4.8020
12	1.268	0.7885	13.412	0.0746	10.5753	0.0946	5.2641
13	1.294	0.7730	14.680	0.0681	11.3484	0.0881	5.7229
14	1.319	0.7579	15.974	0.0626	12.1062	0.0826	6.1785
15	1.346	0.7430	17.293	0.0578	12.8492	0.0778	6.6308
16	1.373	0.7284	18.639	0.0537	13.5777	0.0737	7.0798
17	1.400	0.7142	20.012	0.0500	14.2918	0.0700	7.5255
18	1.428	0.7002	21.412	0.0467	14.9920	0.0667	7.9680
19	1.457	0.6864	22.840	0.0438	15.6784	0.0638	8.4072
20	1.486	0.6730	24.297	0.0412	16.3514	0.0612	8.8431
21	1.516	0.6598	25.783	0.0388	17.0112	0.0588	9.2759
22	1.546	0.6468	27.299	0.0366	17.6580	0.0566	9.7053
23	1.577	0.6342	28.845	0.0347	18.2922	0.0547	10.1316
24	1.608	0.6217	30.422	0.0329	18.9139	0.0529	10.5545
25	1.641	0.6095	32.030	0.0312	19.5234	0.0512	10.9743
26	1.673	0.5976	33.671	0.0297	20.1210	0.0497	11.3909
27	1.707	0.5859	35.344	0.0283	20.7069	0.0483	11.8042
28	1.741	0.5744	37.051	0.0270	21.2812	0.0470	12.2143
29	1.776	0.5631	38.792	0.0258	21.8443	0.0458	12.6213
30	1.811	0.5521	40.568	0.0247	22.3964	0.0447	13.0250
31	1.848	0.5412	42.379	0.0236	22.9377	0.0436	13.4255
32	1.885	0.5306	44.227	0.0226	23.4683	0.0426	13.8229
33	1.922	0.5202	46.111	0.0217	23.9885	0.0417	14.2171
34	1.961	0.5100	48.034	0.0208	24.4985	0.0408	14.6081
35	2.000	0.5000	49.994	0.0200	24.9986	0.0400	14.9960
36	2.040	0.4902	51.994	0.0192	25.4888	0.0392	15.3807
37	2.081	0.4806	54.034	0.0185	25.9694	0.0385	15.7623
38	2.122	0.4712	56.115	0.0178	26.4406	0.0378	16.1408
39	2.165	0.4619	58.237	0.0172	26.9025	0.0372	16.5161
40	2.208	0.4529	60.402	0.0166	27.3554	0.0366	16.8884
41	2.252	0.4440	62.610	0.0160	27.7994	0.0360	17.2575
42	2.297	0.4353	64.862	0.0154	28.2347	0.0354	17.6236
43	2.343	0.4268	67.159	0.0149	28.6615	0.0349	17.9865
44	2.390	0.4184	69.502	0.0144	29.0799	0.0344	18.3464
45	2.438	0.4102	71.892	0.0139	29.4901	0.0339	18.7032
46	2.487	0.4022	74.330	0.0135	29.8923	0.0335	19.0570
47	2.536	0.3943	76.817	0.0130	30.2865	0.0330	19.4077
48	2.587	0.3865	79.353	0.0126	30.6731	0.0326	19.7555
49	2.639	0.3790	81.940	0.0122	31.0520	0.0322	20.1002
50	2.692	0.3715	84.579	0.0118	31.4236	0.0318	20.4418

Interest Table for Annual Compounding with i = 2% (Contd.)

n	$F/p,i,n$	$P/F,i,n$	$F/A,i,n$	$A/F,i,n$	$P/A,i,n$	$A/P,i,n$	$A/G,i,n$
51	2.745	0.3642	87.271	0.0115	31.7878	0.0315	20.7805
52	2.800	0.3571	90.016	0.0111	32.1449	0.0311	21.1162
53	2.856	0.3501	92.816	0.0108	32.4950	0.0308	21.4490
54	2.913	0.3432	95.673	0.0105	32.8382	0.0305	21.7788
55	2.972	0.3365	98.586	0.0101	33.1747	0.0301	22.1056
56	3.031	0.3299	101.558	0.0098	33.5046	0.0298	22.4295
57	3.092	0.3234	104.589	0.0096	33.8281	0.0296	22.7505
58	3.154	0.3171	107.681	0.0093	34.1452	0.0293	23.0685
59	3.217	0.3109	110.834	0.0090	34.4561	0.0290	23.3837
60	3.281	0.3048	114.051	0.0088	34.7608	0.0288	23.6960
61	3.347	0.2988	117.332	0.0085	35.0596	0.0285	24.0054
62	3.414	0.2929	120.679	0.0083	35.3526	0.0283	24.3119
63	3.482	0.2872	124.092	0.0081	35.6398	0.0281	24.6156
64	3.551	0.2816	127.574	0.0078	35.9214	0.0278	24.9165
65	3.623	0.2761	131.126	0.0076	36.1974	0.0276	25.2146
66	3.695	0.2706	134.748	0.0074	36.4681	0.0274	25.5098
67	3.769	0.2653	138.443	0.0072	36.7334	0.0272	25.8023
68	3.844	0.2601	142.212	0.0070	36.9935	0.0270	26.0920
69	3.921	0.2550	146.056	0.0068	37.2485	0.0268	26.3789
70	4.000	0.2500	149.977	0.0067	37.4986	0.0267	26.6631
71	4.080	0.2451	153.977	0.0065	37.7437	0.0265	26.9446
72	4.161	0.2403	158.056	0.0063	37.9840	0.0263	27.2233
73	4.244	0.2356	162.217	0.0062	38.2196	0.0262	27.4993
74	4.329	0.2310	166.462	0.0060	38.4506	0.0260	27.7727
75	4.416	0.2265	170.791	0.0059	38.6771	0.0259	28.0433
76	4.504	0.2220	175.207	0.0057	38.8991	0.0257	28.3113
77	4.594	0.2177	179.711	0.0056	39.1168	0.0256	28.5767
78	4.686	0.2134	184.305	0.0054	39.3301	0.0254	28.8394
79	4.780	0.2092	188.991	0.0053	39.5394	0.0253	29.0995
80	4.875	0.2051	193.771	0.0052	39.7445	0.0252	29.3571
81	4.973	0.2011	198.646	0.0050	39.9456	0.0250	29.6120
82	5.072	0.1971	203.619	0.0049	40.1427	0.0249	29.8644
83	5.174	0.1933	208.692	0.0048	40.3360	0.0248	30.1142
84	5.277	0.1895	213.865	0.0047	40.5255	0.0247	30.3615
85	5.383	0.1858	219.143	0.0046	40.7112	0.0246	30.6062
86	5.491	0.1821	224.526	0.0045	40.8934	0.0245	30.8485
87	5.600	0.1786	230.016	0.0043	41.0719	0.0243	31.0883
88	5.712	0.1751	235.616	0.0042	41.2470	0.0242	31.3256
89	5.827	0.1716	241.329	0.0041	41.4186	0.0241	31.5604
90	5.943	0.1683	247.155	0.0040	41.5869	0.0240	31.7928
91	6.062	0.1650	253.098	0.0040	41.7519	0.0240	32.0228
92	6.183	0.1617	259.160	0.0039	41.9136	0.0239	32.2504
93	6.307	0.1586	265.343	0.0038	42.0721	0.0238	32.4755
94	6.433	0.1554	271.650	0.0037	42.2276	0.0237	32.6983
95	6.562	0.1524	278.083	0.0036	42.3800	0.0236	32.9188
96	6.693	0.1494	284.645	0.0035	42.5294	0.0235	33.1369
97	6.827	0.1465	291.338	0.0034	42.6759	0.0234	33.3527
98	6.963	0.1436	298.165	0.0034	42.8195	0.0234	33.5661
99	7.103	0.1408	305.128	0.0033	42.9603	0.0233	33.7773
100	7.245	0.1380	312.230	0.0032	43.0983	0.0232	33.9862

Interest Table for Annual Compounding with i = 3%

n	$F/p,i,n$	$P/F,i,n$	$F/A,i,n$	$A/F,i,n$	$P/A,i,n$	$A/P,i,n$	$A/G,i,n$
1	1.030	0.9709	1.000	1.0000	0.9709	1.0300	0.0000
2	1.061	0.9426	2.030	0.4926	1.9135	0.5226	0.4926
3	1.093	0.9151	3.091	0.3235	2.8286	0.3535	0.9803
4	1.126	0.8885	4.184	0.2390	3.7171	0.2690	1.4631
5	1.159	0.8626	5.309	0.1884	4.5797	0.2184	1.9409
6	1.194	0.8375	6.468	0.1546	5.4172	0.1846	2.4138
7	1.230	0.8131	7.662	0.1305	6.2303	0.1605	2.8818
8	1.267	0.7894	8.892	0.1125	7.0197	0.1425	3.3450
9	1.305	0.7664	10.159	0.0984	7.7861	0.1284	3.8032
10	1.344	0.7441	11.464	0.0872	8.5302	0.1172	4.2565
11	1.384	0.7224	12.808	0.0781	9.2526	0.1081	4.7049
12	1.426	0.7014	14.192	0.0705	9.9540	0.1005	5.1485
13	1.469	0.6810	15.618	0.0640	10.6350	0.0940	5.5872
14	1.513	0.6611	17.086	0.0585	11.2961	0.0885	6.0210
15	1.558	0.6419	18.599	0.0538	11.9379	0.0838	6.4500
16	1.605	0.6232	20.157	0.0496	12.5611	0.0796	6.8742
17	1.653	0.6050	21.762	0.0460	13.1661	0.0760	7.2936
18	1.702	0.5874	23.414	0.0427	13.7535	0.0727	7.7081
19	1.754	0.5703	25.117	0.0398	14.3238	0.0698	8.1179
20	1.806	0.5537	26.870	0.0372	14.8775	0.0672	8.5229
21	1.860	0.5375	28.676	0.0349	15.4150	0.0649	8.9231
22	1.916	0.5219	30.537	0.0327	15.9369	0.0627	9.3186
23	1.974	0.5067	32.453	0.0308	16.4436	0.0608	9.7093
24	2.033	0.4919	34.426	0.0290	16.9355	0.0590	10.0954
25	2.094	0.4776	36.459	0.0274	17.4131	0.0574	10.4768
26	2.157	0.4637	38.553	0.0259	17.8768	0.0559	10.8535
27	2.221	0.4502	40.710	0.0246	18.3270	0.0546	11.2255
28	2.288	0.4371	42.931	0.0233	18.7641	0.0533	11.5930
29	2.357	0.4243	45.219	0.0221	19.1885	0.0521	11.9558
30	2.427	0.4120	47.575	0.0210	19.6004	0.0510	12.3141
31	2.500	0.4000	50.003	0.0200	20.0004	0.0500	12.6678
32	2.575	0.3883	52.503	0.0190	20.3888	0.0490	13.0169
33	2.652	0.3770	55.078	0.0182	20.7658	0.0482	13.3616
34	2.732	0.3660	57.730	0.0173	21.1318	0.0473	13.7018
35	2.814	0.3554	60.462	0.0165	21.4872	0.0465	14.0375
36	2.898	0.3450	63.276	0.0158	21.8323	0.0458	14.3688
37	2.985	0.3350	66.174	0.0151	22.1672	0.0451	14.6957
38	3.075	0.3252	69.159	0.0145	22.4925	0.0445	15.0182
39	3.167	0.3158	72.234	0.0138	22.8082	0.0438	15.3363
40	3.262	0.3066	75.401	0.0133	23.1148	0.0433	15.6502
41	3.360	0.2976	78.663	0.0127	23.4124	0.0427	15.9597
42	3.461	0.2890	82.023	0.0122	23.7014	0.0422	16.2650
43	3.565	0.2805	85.484	0.0117	23.9819	0.0417	16.5660
44	3.671	0.2724	89.048	0.0112	24.2543	0.0412	16.8629
45	3.782	0.2644	92.720	0.0108	24.5187	0.0408	17.1556
46	3.895	0.2567	96.501	0.0104	24.7754	0.0404	17.4441
47	4.012	0.2493	100.396	0.0100	25.0247	0.0400	17.7285
48	4.132	0.2420	104.408	0.0096	25.2667	0.0396	18.0089
49	4.256	0.2350	108.541	0.0092	25.5017	0.0392	18.2852
50	4.384	0.2281	112.797	0.0089	25.7298	0.0389	18.5575

Interest Table for Annual Compounding with i = 3% (Contd.)

n	$F/p, i, n$	$P/F, i, n$	$F/A, i, n$	$A/F, i, n$	$P/A, i, n$	$A/P, i, n$	$A/G, i, n$
51	4.515	0.2215	117.181	0.0085	25.9512	0.0385	18.8258
52	4.651	0.2150	121.696	0.0082	26.1662	0.0382	19.0902
53	4.790	0.2088	126.347	0.0079	26.3750	0.0379	19.3507
54	4.934	0.2027	131.137	0.0076	26.5777	0.0376	19.6073
55	5.082	0.1968	136.072	0.0073	26.7744	0.0373	19.8600
56	5.235	0.1910	141.154	0.0071	26.9655	0.0371	20.1090
57	5.392	0.1855	146.388	0.0068	27.1509	0.0368	20.3542
58	5.553	0.1801	151.780	0.0066	27.3310	0.0366	20.5956
59	5.720	0.1748	157.333	0.0064	27.5058	0.0364	20.8333
60	5.892	0.1697	163.053	0.0061	27.6756	0.0361	21.0674
61	6.068	0.1648	168.945	0.0059	27.8404	0.0359	21.2979
62	6.250	0.1600	175.013	0.0057	28.0003	0.0357	21.5247
63	6.438	0.1553	181.264	0.0055	28.1557	0.0355	21.7480
64	6.631	0.1508	187.702	0.0053	28.3065	0.0353	21.9678
65	6.830	0.1464	194.333	0.0051	28.4529	0.0351	22.1841
66	7.035	0.1421	201.163	0.0050	28.5950	0.0350	22.3969
67	7.246	0.1380	208.198	0.0048	28.7330	0.0348	22.6063
68	7.463	0.1340	215.443	0.0046	28.8670	0.0346	22.8124
69	7.687	0.1301	222.907	0.0045	28.9971	0.0345	23.0151
70	7.918	0.1263	230.594	0.0043	29.1234	0.0343	23.2145
71	8.155	0.1226	238.512	0.0042	29.2460	0.0342	23.4107
72	8.400	0.1190	246.667	0.0041	29.3651	0.0341	23.6036
73	8.652	0.1156	255.067	0.0039	29.4807	0.0339	23.7934
74	8.912	0.1122	263.719	0.0038	29.5929	0.0338	23.9799
75	9.179	0.1089	272.631	0.0037	29.7018	0.0337	24.1634
76	9.454	0.1058	281.810	0.0035	29.8076	0.0335	24.3438
77	9.738	0.1027	291.264	0.0034	29.9103	0.0334	24.5212
78	10.030	0.0997	301.002	0.0033	30.0100	0.0333	24.6955
79	10.331	0.0968	311.032	0.0032	30.1068	0.0332	24.8669
80	10.641	0.0940	321.363	0.0031	30.2008	0.0331	25.0353
81	10.960	0.0912	332.004	0.0030	30.2920	0.0330	25.2009
82	11.289	0.0886	342.964	0.0029	30.3806	0.0329	25.3636
83	11.628	0.0860	354.253	0.0028	30.4666	0.0328	25.5235
84	11.976	0.0835	365.880	0.0027	30.5501	0.0327	25.6806
85	12.336	0.0811	377.857	0.0026	30.6312	0.0326	25.8349
86	12.706	0.0787	390.192	0.0026	30.7099	0.0326	25.9865
87	13.087	0.0764	402.898	0.0025	30.7863	0.0325	26.1355
88	13.480	0.0742	415.985	0.0024	30.8605	0.0324	26.2818
89	13.884	0.0720	429.465	0.0023	30.9325	0.0323	26.4255
90	14.300	0.0699	443.349	0.0023	31.0024	0.0323	26.5667
91	14.729	0.0679	457.649	0.0022	31.0703	0.0322	26.7053
92	15.171	0.0659	472.379	0.0021	31.!362	0.0321	26.8414
93	15.626	0.0640	487.550	0.0021	31.2002	0.0321	26.9750
94	16.095	0.0621	503.176	0.0020	31.2623	0.0320	27.1062
95	16.578	0.0603	519.272	0.0019	31.3227	0.0319	27.2350
96	17.075	0.0586	535.850	0.0019	31.3812	0.0319	27.3615
97	17.588	0.0569	552.925	0.0018	31.4381	0.0318	27.4857
98	18.115	0.0552	570.513	0.0018	31.4933	0.0318	27.6075
99	18.659	0.0536	588.629	0.0017	31.5469	0.0317	27.7271
100	19.219	0.0520	607.287	0.0016	31.5989	0.0316	27.8444

Interest   Table   for   Annual   Compounding   with i = 4%

n	$F/p,i,n$	$P/F,i,n$	$F/A,i,n$	$A/F,i,n$	$P/A,i,n$	$A/P,i,n$	$A/G,i,n$
1	1.040	0.9615	1.000	1.0000	0.9615	1.0400	0.0000
2	1.082	0.9246	2.040	0.4902	1.8861	0.5302	0.4902
3	1.125	0.8890	3.122	0.3203	2.7751	0.3603	0.9738
4	1.170	0.8548	4.246	0.2355	3.6299	0.2755	1.4510
5	1.217	0.8219	5.416	0.1846	4.4518	0.2246	1.9216
6	1.265	0.7903	6.633	0.1508	5.2421	0.1908	2.3857
7	1.316	0.7599	7.898	0.1266	6.0021	0.1666	2.8433
8	1.369	0.7307	9.214	0.1085	6.7327	0.1485	3.2944
9	1.423	0.7026	10.583	0.0945	7.4353	0.1345	3.7391
10	1.480	0.6756	12.006	0.0833	8.1109	0.1233	4.1772
11	1.539	0.6496	13.486	0.0741	8.7605	0.1141	4.6090
12	1.601	0.6246	15.026	0.0666	9.3851	0.1066	5.0343
13	1.665	0.6006	16.627	0.0601	9.9856	0.1001	5.4533
14	1.732	0.5775	18.292	0.0547	10.5631	0.0947	5.8658
15	1.801	0.5553	20.024	0.0499	11.1184	0.0899	6.2721
16	1.873	0.5339	21.825	0.0458	11.6523	0.0858	6.6720
17	1.948	0.5134	23.697	0.0422	12.1657	0.0822	7.0656
18	2.026	0.4936	25.645	0.0390	12.6593	0.0790	7.4530
19	2.107	0.4746	27.671	0.0361	13.1339	0.0761	7.8341
20	2.191	0.4564	29.778	0.0336	13.5903	0.0736	8.2091
21	2.279	0.4388	31.969	0.0313	14.0292	0.0713	8.5779
22	2.370	0.4220	34.248	0.0292	14.4511	0.0692	8.9406
23	2.465	0.4057	36.618	0.0273	14.8568	0.0673	9.2973
24	2.563	0.3901	39.083	0.0256	15.2470	0.0656	9.6479
25	2.666	0.3751	41.646	0.0240	15.6221	0.0640	9.9925
26	2.772	0.3607	44.312	0.0226	15.9828	0.0626	10.3312
27	2.883	0.3468	47.084	0.0212	16.3296	0.0612	10.6640
28	2.999	0.3335	49.968	0.0200	16.6631	0.0600	10.9909
29	3.119	0.3207	52.966	0.0189	16.9837	0.0589	11.3120
30	3.243	0.3083	56.085	0.0178	17.2920	0.0578	11.6274
31	3.373	0.2965	59.328	0.0169	17.5885	0.0569	11.9371
32	3.508	0.2851	62.701	0.0159	17.8735	0.0559	12.2411
33	3.648	0.2741	66.209	0.0151	18.1476	0.0551	12.5395
34	3.794	0.2636	69.858	0.0143	18.4112	0.0543	12.8324
35	3.946	0.2534	73.652	0.0136	18.6646	0.0536	13.1198
36	4.104	0.2437	77.598	0.0129	18.9083	0.0529	13.4018
37	4.268	0.2343	81.702	0.0122	19.1426	0.0522	13.6784
38	4.439	0.2253	85.970	0.0116	19.3679	0.0516	13.9497
39	4.616	0.2166	90.409	0.0111	19.5845	0.0511	14.2157
40	4.801	0.2083	95.025	0.0105	19.7928	0.0505	14.4765
41	4.993	0.2003	99.826	0.0100	19.9930	0.0500	14.7322
42	5.193	0.1926	104.819	0.0095	20.1856	0.0495	14.9828
43	5.400	0.1852	110.012	0.0091	20.3708	0.0491	15.2284
44	5.617	0.1780	115.413	0.0087	20.5488	0.0487	15.4690
45	5.841	0.1712	121.029	0.0083	20.7200	0.0483	15.7047
46	6.075	0.1646	126.870	0.0079	20.8846	0.0479	15.9356
47	6.318	0.1583	132.945	0.0075	21.0429	0.0475	16.1618
48	6.571	0.1522	139.263	0.0072	21.1951	0.0472	16.3832
49	6.833	0.1463	145.834	0.0069	21.3415	0.0469	16.6000
50	7.107	0.1407	152.667	0.0066	21.4822	0.0466	16.8122

Interest Table for Annual Compounding with *i* = 4% (Contd.)

n	F/p,i,n	P/F,i,n	F/A,i,n	A/F,i,n	P/A,i,n	A/P,i,n	A/G,i,n
51	7.391	0.1353	159.774	0.0063	21.6175	0.0463	17.0200
52	7.687	0.1301	167.164	0.0060	21.7476	0.0460	17.2232
53	7.994	0.1251	174.851	0.0057	21.8727	0.0457	17.4221
54	8.314	0.1203	182.845	0.0055	21.9930	0.0455	17.6167
55	8.646	0.1157	191.159	0.0052	22.1086	0.0452	17.8070
56	8.992	0.1112	199.805	0.0050	22.2198	0.0450	17.9932
57	9.352	0.1069	208.797	0.0048	22.3267	0.0448	18.1752
58	9.726	0.1028	218.149	0.0046	22.4296	0.0446	18.3532
59	10.115	0.0989	227.875	0.0044	22.5284	0.0444	18.5272
60	10.520	0.0951	237.990	0.0042	22.6235	0.0442	18.6972
61	10.940	0.0914	248.510	0.0040	22.7149	0.0440	18.8634
62	11.378	0.0879	259.450	0.0039	22.8028	0.0439	19.0258
63	11.833	0.0845	270.828	0.0037	22.8873	0.0437	19.1845
64	12.306	0.0813	282.661	0.0035	22.9685	0.0435	19.3395
65	12.799	0.0781	294.968	0.0034	23.0467	0.0434	19.4909
66	13.311	0.0751	307.767	0.0032	23.1218	0.0432	19.6388
67	13.843	0.0722	321.077	0.0031	23.1940	0.0431	19.7832
68	14.397	0.0695	334.920	0.0030	23.2635	0.0430	19.9242
69	14.973	0.0668	349.317	0.0029	23.3303	0.0429	20.0618
70	15.572	0.0642	364.290	0.0027	23.3945	0.0427	20.1961
71	16.194	0.0617	379.861	0.0026	23.4563	0.0426	20.3272
72	16.842	0.0594	396.056	0.0025	23.5156	0.0425	20.4552
73	17.516	0.0571	412.898	0.0024	23.5727	0.0424	20.5800
74	18.217	0.0549	430.414	0.0023	23.6276	0.0423	20.7018
75	18.945	0.0528	448.630	0.0022	23.6804	0.0422	20.8206
76	19.703	0.0508	467.576	0.0021	23.7312	0.0421	20.9365
77	20.491	0.0488	487.279	0.0021	23.7800	0.0421	21.0495
78	21.311	0.0469	507.770	0.0020	23.8269	0.0420	21.1597
79	22.163	0.0451	529.081	0.0019	23.8720	0.0419	21.2671
80	23.050	0.0434	551.244	0.0018	23.9154	0.0418	21.3718
81	23.972	0.0417	574.294	0.0017	23.9571	0.0417	21.4739
82	24.931	0.0401	598.265	0.0017	23.9972	0.0417	21.5734
83	25.928	0.0386	623.196	0.0016	24.0358	0.0416	21.6704
84	26.965	0.0371	649.124	0.0015	24.0729	0.0415	21.7649
85	28.044	0.0357	676.089	0.0015	24.1085	0.0415	21.8569
86	29.165	0.0343	704.132	0.0014	24.1428	0.0414	21.9466
87	30.332	0.0330	733.297	0.0014	24.1758	0.0414	22.0340
88	31.545	0.0317	763.629	0.0013	24.2075	0.0413	22.1190
89	32.807	0.0305	795.174	0.0013	24.2380	0.0413	22.2019
90	34.119	0.0293	827.981	0.0012	24.2673	0.0412	22.2825
91	35.484	0.0282	862.101	0.0012	24.2955	0.0412	22.3611
92	36.903	0.0271	897.585	0.0011	24.3226	0.0411	22.4376
93	38.380	0.0261	934.488	0.0011	24.3486	0.0411	22.5120
94	39.915	0.0251	972.868	0.0010	24.3737	0.0410	22.5845
95	41.511	0.0241	1012.782	0.0010	24.3978	0.0410	22.6550
96	43.172	0.0232	1054.294	0.0009	24.4209	0.0409	22.7236
97	44.899	0.0223	1097.465	0.0009	24.4432	0.0409	22.7904
98	46.695	0.0214	1142.364	0.0009	24.4646	0.0409	22.8553
99	48.562	0.0206	1189.058	0.0008	24.4852	0.0408	22.9185
100	50.505	0.0198	1237.621	0.0008	24.5050	0.0408	22.9800

Interest Table for Annual Compounding with $i = 5\%$

n	$F/p,i,n$	$P/F,i,n$	$F/A,i,n$	$A/F,i,n$	$P/A,i,n$	$A/P,i,n$	$A/G,i,n$
1	1.050	0.9524	1.000	1.0000	0.9524	1.0500	0.0000
2	1.102	0.9070	2.050	0.4878	1.8594	0.5378	0.4878
3	1.158	0.8638	3.152	0.3172	2.7232	0.3672	0.9675
4	1.216	0.8227	4.310	0.2320	3.5459	0.2820	1.4390
5	1.276	0.7835	5.526	0.1810	4.3295	0.2310	1.9025
6	1.340	0.7462	6.802	0.1470	5.0757	0.1970	2.3579
7	1.407	0.7107	8.142	0.1228	5.7864	0.1728	2.8052
8	1.477	0.6768	9.549	0.1047	6.4632	0.1547	3.2445
9	1.551	0.6446	11.027	0.0907	7.1078	0.1407	3.6758
10	1.629	0.6139	12.578	0.0795	7.7217	0.1295	4.0991
11	1.710	0.5847	14.207	0.0704	8.3064	0.1204	4.5144
12	1.796	0.5568	15.917	0.0628	8.8632	0.1128	4.9219
13	1.886	0.5303	17.713	0.0565	9.3936	0.1065	5.3215
14	1.980	0.5051	19.599	0.0510	9.8986	0.1010	5.7133
15	2.079	0.4810	21.579	0.0463	10.3796	0.0963	6.0973
16	2.183	0.4581	23.657	0.0423	10.8378	0.0923	6.4736
17	2.292	0.4363	25.840	0.0387	11.2741	0.0887	6.8423
18	2.407	0.4155	28.132	0.0355	11.6896	0.0855	7.2033
19	2.527	0.3957	30.539	0.0327	12.0853	0.0827	7.5569
20	2.653	0.3769	33.066	0.0302	12.4622	0.0802	7.9029
21	2.786	0.3589	35.719	0.0280	12.8211	0.0780	8.2416
22	2.925	0.3419	38.505	0.0260	13.1630	0.0760	8.5729
23	3.072	0.3256	41.430	0.0241	13.4886	0.0741	8.8970
24	3.225	0.3101	44.502	0.0225	13.7986	0.0725	9.2139
25	3.386	0.2953	47.727	0.0210	14.0939	0.0710	9.5237
26	3.556	0.2812	51.113	0.0196	14.3752	0.0696	9.8265
27	3.733	0.2678	54.669	0.0183	14.6430	0.0683	10.1224
28	3.920	0.2551	58.402	0.0171	14.8981	0.0671	10.4114
29	4.116	0.2429	62.323	0.0160	15.1411	0.0660	10.6936
30	4.322	0.2314	66.439	0.0151	15.3724	0.0651	10.9691
31	4.538	0.2204	70.761	0.0141	15.5928	0.0641	11.2381
32	4.765	0.2099	75.299	0.0133	15.8027	0.0633	11.5005
33	5.003	0.1999	80.063	0.0125	16.0025	0.0625	11.7565
34	5.253	0.1904	85.067	0.0118	16.1929	0.0618	12.0063
35	5.516	0.1813	90.320	0.0111	16.3742	0.0611	12.2498
36	5.792	0.1727	95.836	0.0104	16.5468	0.0604	12.4872
37	6.081	0.1644	101.628	0.0098	16.7113	0.0598	12.7185
38	6.385	0.1566	107.709	0.0093	16.8679	0.0593	12.9440
39	6.705	0.1491	114.095	0.0088	17.0170	0.0588	13.1636
40	7.040	0.1420	120.799	0.0083	17.1591	0.0583	13.3774
41	7.392	0.1353	127.839	0.0078	17.2944	0.0578	13.5857
42	7.762	0.1288	135.231	0.0074	17.4232	0.0574	13.7884
43	8.150	0.1227	142.993	0.0070	17.5459	0.0570	13.9857
44	8.557	0.1169	151.142	0.0066	17.6628	0.0566	14.1777
45	8.985	0.1113	159.699	0.0063	17.7741	0.0563	14.3644
46	9.434	0.1060	168.684	0.0059	17.8801	0.0559	14.5460
47	9.906	0.1009	178.119	0.0056	17.9810	0.0556	14.7226
48	10.401	0.0961	188.025	0.0053	18.0771	0.0553	14.8943
49	10.921	0.0916	198.426	0.0050	18.1687	0.0550	15.0611
50	11.467	0.0872	209.347	0.0048	18.2559	0.0548	15.2232

Interest Table for Annual Compounding with $i = 5\%$ (Contd.)

n	$F/p,i,n$	$P/F,i,n$	$F/A,i,n$	$A/F,i,n$	$P/A,i,n$	$A/P,i,n$	$A/G,i,n$
51	12.041	0.0831	220.814	0.0045	18.3390	0.0545	15.3807
52	12.643	0.0791	232.855	0.0043	18.4181	0.0543	15.5337
53	13.275	0.0753	245.498	0.0041	18.4934	0.0541	15.6822
54	13.939	0.0717	258.773	0.0039	18.5651	0.0539	15.8265
55	14.636	0.0683	272.711	0.0037	18.6335	0.0537	15.9664
56	15.367	0.0651	287.347	0.0035	18.6985	0.0535	16.1023
57	16.136	0.0620	302.714	0.0033	18.7605	0.0533	16.2341
58	16.942	0.0590	318.850	0.0031	18.8195	0.0531	16.3619
59	17.790	0.0562	335.792	0.0030	18.8758	0.0530	16.4859
60	18.679	0.0535	353.582	0.0028	18.9293	0.0528	16.6062
61	19.613	0.0510	372.261	0.0027	18.9803	0.0527	16.7227
62	20.594	0.0486	391.874	0.0026	19.0288	0.0526	16.8357
63	21.623	0.0462	412.468	0.0024	19.0751	0.0524	16.9452
64	22.705	0.0440	434.091	0.0023	19.1191	0.0523	17.0513
65	23.840	0.0419	456.795	0.0022	19.1611	0.0522	17.1541
66	25.032	0.0399	480.635	0.0021	19.2010	0.0521	17.2536
67	26.283	0.0380	505.667	0.0020	19.2391	0.0520	17.3500
68	27.598	0.0362	531.950	0.0019	19.2753	0.0519	17.4434
69	28.977	0.0345	559.548	0.0018	19.3098	0.0518	17.5337
70	30.426	0.0329	588.525	0.0017	19.3427	0.0517	17.6212
71	31.948	0.0313	618.951	0.0016	19.3740	0.0516	17.7058
72	33.545	0.0298	650.899	0.0015	19.4038	0.0515	17.7877
73	35.222	0.0284	684.443	0.0015	19.4322	0.0515	17.8669
74	36.983	0.0270	719.666	0.0014	19.4592	0.0514	17.9435
75	38.832	0.0258	756.649	0.0013	19.4850	0.0513	18.0176
76	40.774	0.0245	795.481	0.0013	19.5095	0.0513	18.0892
77	42.813	0.0234	836.255	0.0012	19.5328	0.0512	18.1585
78	44.953	0.0222	879.068	0.0011	19.5551	0.0511	18.2254
79	47.201	0.0212	924.021	0.0011	19.5763	0.0511	18.2901
80	49.561	0.0202	971.222	0.0010	19.5965	0.0510	18.3526
81	52.039	0.0192	1,020.783	0.0010	19.6157	0.0510	18.4130
82	54.641	0.0183	1,072.822	0.0009	19.6340	0.0509	18.4713
83	57.373	0.0174	1,127.463	0.0009	19.6514	0.0509	18.5277
84	60.242	0.0166	1,184.836	0.0008	19.6680	0.0508	18.5821
85	63.254	0.0158	1,245.078	0.0008	19.6838	0.0508	18.6346
86	66.417	0.0151	1,308.332	0.0008	19.6989	0.0508	18.6853
87	69.737	0.0143	1,374.748	0.0007	19.7132	0.0507	18.7343
88	73.224	0.0137	1,444.485	0.0007	19.7269	0.0507	18.7816
89	76.885	0.0130	1,517.710	0.0007	19.7399	0.0507	18.8272
90	80.730	0.0124	1,594.595	0.0006	19.7523	0.0506	18.8712
91	84.766	0.0118	1,675.324	0.0006	19.7641	0.0506	18.9136
92	89.005	0.0112	1,760.090	0.0006	19.7753	0.0506	18.9546
93	93.455	0.0107	1,849.095	0.0005	19.7860	0.0505	18.9941
94	98.127	0.0102	1,942.550	0.0005	19.7962	0.0505	19.0322
95	103.034	0.0097	2,040.677	0.0005	19.8059	0.0505	19.0689
96	108.186	0.0092	2,143.710	0.0005	19.8151	0.0505	19.1044
97	113.595	0.0088	2,251.896	0.0004	19.8239	0.0504	19.1385
98	119.275	0.0084	2,365.490	0.0004	19.8323	0.0504	19.1714
99	125.238	0.0080	2,484.765	0.0004	19.8403	0.0504	19.2031
100	131.500	0.0076	2,610.003	0.0004	19.8479	0.0504	19.2337

Interest Table for Annual Compounding with i = 6%

n	$F/p,i,n$	$P/F,i,n$	$F/A,i,n$	$A/F,i,n$	$P/A,i,n$	$A/P,i,n$	$A/G,i,n$
1	1.060	0.9434	1.000	1.0000	0.9434	1.0600	0.0000
2	1.124	0.8900	2.060	0.4854	1.8334	0.5454	0.4854
3	1.191	0.8396	3.184	0.3141	2.6730	0.3741	0.9612
4	1.262	0.7921	4.375	0.2286	3.4651	0.2886	1.4272
5	1.338	0.7473	5.637	0.1774	4.2124	0.2374	1.8836
6	1.419	0.7050	6.975	0.1434	4.9173	0.2034	2.3304
7	1.504	0.6651	8.394	0.1191	5.5824	0.1791	2.7676
8	1.594	0.6274	9.897	0.1010	6.2098	0.1610	3.1952
9	1.689	0.5919	11.491	0.0870	6.8017	0.1470	3.6133
10	1.791	0.5584	13.181	0.0759	7.3601	0.1359	4.0220
11	1.898	0.5268	14.972	0.0668	7.8869	0.1268	4.4213
12	2.012	0.4970	16.870	0.0593	8.3838	0.1193	4.8112
13	2.133	0.4688	18.882	0.0530	8.8527	0.1130	5.1920
14	2.261	0.4423	21.015	0.0476	9.2950	0.1076	5.5635
15	2.397	0.4173	23.276	0.0430	9.7122	0.1030	5.9260
16	2.540	0.3936	25.672	0.0390	10.1059	0.0990	6.2794
17	2.693	0.3714	28.213	0.0354	10.4773	0.0954	6.6240
18	2.854	0.3503	30.906	0.0324	10.8276	0.0924	6.9597
19	3.026	0.3305	33.760	0.0296	11.1581	0.0896	7.2867
20	3.207	0.3118	36.786	0.0272	11.4699	0.0872	7.6051
21	3.400	0.2942	39.993	0.0250	11.7641	0.0850	7.9151
22	3.604	0.2775	43.392	0.0230	12.0416	0.0830	8.2166
23	3.820	0.2618	46.996	0.0213	12.3034	0.0813	8.5099
24	4.049	0.2470	50.815	0.0197	12.5504	0.0797	8.7951
25	4.292	0.2330	54.864	0.0182	12.7834	0.0782	9.0722
26	4.549	0.2198	59.156	0.0169	13.0032	0.0769	9.3414
27	4.822	0.2074	63.706	0.0157	13.2105	0.0757	9.6029
28	5.112	0.1956	68.528	0.0146	13.4062	0.0746	9.8568
29	5.418	0.1846	73.640	0.0136	13.5907	0.0736	10.1032
30	5.743	0.1741	79.058	0.0126	13.7648	0.0726	10.3422
31	6.088	0.1643	84.802	0.0118	13.9291	0.0718	10.5740
32	6.453	0.1550	90.890	0.0110	14.0840	0.0710	10.7987
33	6.841	0.1462	97.343	0.0103	14.2302	0.0703	11.0165
34	7.251	0.1379	104.184	0.0096	14.3681	0.0696	11.2275
35	7.686	0.1301	111.435	0.0090	14.4982	0.0690	11.4319
36	8.147	0.1227	119.121	0.0084	14.6210	0.0684	11.6298
37	8.636	0.1158	127.268	0.0079	14.7368	0.0679	11.8212
38	9.154	0.1092	135.904	0.0074	14.8460	0.0674	12.0065
39	9.703	0.1031	145.058	0.0069	14.9491	0.0669	12.1857
40	10.286	0.0972	154.762	0.0065	15.0463	0.0665	12.3590
41	10.903	0.0917	165.047	0.0061	15.1380	0.0661	12.5264
42	11.557	0.0865	175.950	0.0057	15.2245	0.0657	12.6883
43	12.250	0.0816	187.507	0.0053	15.3062	0.0653	12.8446
44	12.985	0.0770	199.758	0.0050	15.3832	0.0650	12.9956
45	13.765	0.0727	212.743	0.0047	15.4558	0.0647	13.1413
46	14.590	0.0685	226.508	0.0044	15.5244	0.0644	13.2819
47	15.466	0.0647	241.098	0.0041	15.5890	0.0641	13.4176
48	16.394	0.0610	256.564	0.0039	15.6500	0.0639	13.5485
49	17.377	0.0575	272.958	0.0037	15.7076	0.0637	13.6748
50	18.420	0.0543	290.335	0.0034	15.7619	0.0634	13.7964

Interest Table for Annual Compounding with *i* = 6% (Contd.)

n	F/p,i,n	P/F,i,n	F/A,i,n	A/F,i,n	P/A,i,n	A/P,i,n	A/G,i,n
51	19.525	0.0512	308.755	0.0032	15.8131	0.0632	13.9137
52	20.697	0.0483	328.280	0.0030	15.8614	0.0630	14.0266
53	21.939	0.0456	348.977	0.0029	15.9070	0.0629	14.1355
54	23.255	0.0430	370.916	0.0027	15.9500	0.0627	14.2402
55	24.650	0.0406	394.171	0.0025	15.9905	0.0625	14.3411
56	26.129	0.0383	418.821	0.0024	16.0288	0.0624	14.4382
57	27.697	0.0361	444.950	0.0022	16.0649	0.0622	14.5316
58	29.359	0.0341	472.647	0.0021	16.0990	0.0621	14.6214
59	31.120	0.0321	502.006	0.0020	16.1311	0.0620	14.7079
60	32.988	0.0303	533.126	0.0019	16.1614	0.0619	14.7909
61	34.967	0.0286	566.114	0.0018	16.1900	0.0618	14.8708
62	37.065	0.0270	601.081	0.0017	16.2170	0.0617	14.9475
63	39.289	0.0255	638.146	0.0016	16.2425	0.0616	15.0213
64	41.646	0.0240	677.434	0.0015	16.2665	0.0615	15.0921
65	44.145	0.0227	719.080	0.0014	16.2891	0.0614	15.1601
66	46.794	0.0214	763.225	0.0013	16.3105	0.0613	15.2254
67	49.601	0.0202	810.019	0.0012	16.3307	0.0612	15.2881
68	52.577	0.0190	859.620	0.0012	16.3497	0.0612	15.3483
69	55.732	0.0179	912.197	0.0011	16.3676	0.0611	15.4060
70	59.076	0.0169	967.928	0.0010	16.3845	0.0610	15.4613
71	62.620	0.0160	1,027.004	0.0010	16.4005	0.0610	15.5144
72	66.377	0.0151	1,089.624	0.0009	16.4156	0.0609	15.5654
73	70.360	0.0142	1,156.002	0.0009	16.4298	0.0609	15.6142
74	74.582	0.0134	1,226.362	0.0008	16.4432	0.0608	15.6610
75	79.057	0.0126	1,300.943	0.0008	16.4558	0.0608	15.7058
76	83.800	0.0119	1,380.000	0.0007	16.4678	0.0607	15.7488
77	88.828	0.0113	1,463.800	0.0007	16.4790	0.0607	15.7900
78	94.158	0.0106	1,552.628	0.0006	16.4897	0.0606	15.8294
79	99.807	0.0100	1,646.785	0.0006	16.4997	0.0606	15.8671
80	105.796	0.0095	1,746.592	0.0006	16.5091	0.0606	15.9033
81	112.143	0.0089	1,852.388	0.0005	16.5180	0.0605	15.9379
82	118.872	0.0084	1,964.531	0.0005	16.5265	0.0605	15.9710
83	126.004	0.0079	2,083.403	0.0005	16.5344	0.0605	16.0027
84	133.564	0.0075	2,209.407	0.0005	16.5419	0.0605	16.0330
85	141.578	0.0071	2,342.971	0.0004	16.5489	0.0604	16.0620
86	150.073	0.0067	2,484.549	0.0004	16.5556	0.0604	16.0898
87	159.077	0.0063	2,634.622	0.0004	16.5619	0.0604	16.1163
88	168.622	0.0059	2,793.699	0.0004	16.5678	0.0604	16.1417
89	178.739	0.0056	2,962.321	0.0003	16.5734	0.0603	16.1659
90	189.464	0.0053	3,141.060	0.0003	16.5787	0.0603	16.1891
91	200.831	0.0050	3,330.523	0.0003	16.5837	0.0603	16.2113
92	212.881	0.0047	3,531.354	0.0003	16.5884	0.0603	16.2325
93	225.654	0.0044	3,744.235	0.0003	16.5928	0.0603	16.2527
94	239.193	0.0042	3,969.889	0.0003	16.5970	0.0603	16.2720
95	253.545	0.0039	4,209.082	0.0002	16.6009	0.0602	16.2905
96	268.758	0.0037	4,462.627	0.0002	16.6047	0.0602	16.3081
97	284.883	0.0035	4,731.385	0.0002	16.6082	0.0602	16.3250
98	301.976	0.0033	5,016.267	0.0002	16.6115	0.0602	16.3411
99	320.095	0.0031	5,318.243	0.0002	16.6146	0.0602	16.3564
100	339.300	0.0029	5,638.338	0.0002	16.6175	0.0602	16.3711

Interest Table for Annual Compounding with *i* = 7%

n	F/p,i,n	P/F,i,n	F/A,i,n	A/F,i,n	P/A,i,n	A/P,i,n	A/G,i,n
1	1.070	0.9346	1.000	1.0000	0.9346	1.0700	0.0000
2	1.145	0.8734	2.070	0.4831	1.8080	0.5531	0.4831
3	1.225	0.8163	3.215	0.3111	2.6243	0.3811	0.9549
4	1.311	0.7629	4.440	0.2252	3.3872	0.2952	1.4155
5	1.403	0.7130	5.751	0.1739	4.1002	0.2439	1.8650
6	1.501	0.6663	7.153	0.1398	4.7665	0.2098	2.3032
7	1.606	0.6227	8.654	0.1156	5.3893	0.1856	2.7304
8	1.718	0.5820	10.260	0.0975	5.9713	0.1675	3.1466
9	1.838	0.5439	11.978	0.0835	6.5152	0.1535	3.5517
10	1.967	0.5083	13.816	0.0724	7.0236	0.1424	3.9461
11	2.105	0.4751	15.784	0.0634	7.4987	0.1334	4.3296
12	2.252	0.4440	17.888	0.0559	7.9427	0.1259	4.7025
13	2.410	0.4150	20.141	0.0497	8.3577	0.1197	5.0649
14	2.579	0.3878	22.551	0.0443	8.7455	0.1143	5.4167
15	2.759	0.3624	25.129	0.0398	9.1079	0.1098	5.7583
16	2.952	0.3387	27.888	0.0359	9.4467	0.1059	6.0897
17	3.159	0.3166	30.840	0.0324	9.7632	0.1024	6.4110
18	3.380	0.2959	33.999	0.0294	10.0591	0.0994	6.7225
19	3.617	0.2765	37.379	0.0268	10.3356	0.0968	7.0242
20	3.870	0.2584	40.996	0.0244	10.5940	0.0944	7.3163
21	4.141	0.2415	44.865	0.0223	10.8355	0.0923	7.5990
22	4.430	0.2257	49.006	0.0204	11.0612	0.0904	7.8725
23	4.741	0.2109	53.436	0.0187	11.2722	0.0887	8.1369
24	5.072	0.1971	58.177	0.0172	11.4693	0.0872	8.3923
25	5.427	0.1842	63.249	0.0158	11.6536	0.0858	8.6391
26	5.807	0.1722	68.677	0.0146	11.8258	0.0846	8.8773
27	6.214	0.1609	74.484	0.0134	11.9867	0.0834	9.1072
28	6.649	0.1504	80.698	0.0124	12.1371	0.0824	9.3290
29	7.114	0.1406	87.347	0.0114	12.2777	0.0814	9.5427
30	7.612	0.1314	94.461	0.0106	12.4090	0.0806	9.7487
31	8.145	0.1228	102.073	0.0098	12.5318	0.0798	9.9471
32	8.715	0.1147	110.218	0.0091	12.6466	0.0791	10.1381
33	9.325	0.1072	118.934	0.0084	12.7538	0.0784	10.3219
34	9.978	0.1002	128.259	0.0078	12.8540	0.0778	10.4987
35	10.677	0.0937	138.237	0.0072	12.9477	0.0772	10.6687
36	11.424	0.0875	148.914	0.0067	13.0352	0.0767	10.8321
37	12.224	0.0818	160.338	0.0062	13.1170	0.0762	10.9891
38	13.079	0.0765	172.561	0.0058	13.1935	0.0758	11.1398
39	13.995	0.0715	185.641	0.0054	13.2649	0.0754	11.2845
40	14.974	0.0668	199.636	0.0050	13.3317	0.0750	11.4234
41	16.023	0.0624	214.610	0.0047	13.3941	0.0747	11.5565
42	17.144	0.0583	230.633	0.0043	13.4525	0.0743	11.6842
43	18.344	0.0545	247.777	0.0040	13.5070	0.0740	11.8065
44	19.629	0.0509	266.121	0.0038	13.5579	0.0738	11.9237
45	21.002	0.0476	285.750	0.0035	13.6055	0.0735	12.0360
46	22.473	0.0445	306.752	0.0033	13.6500	0.0733	12.1435
47	24.046	0.0416	329.225	0.0030	13.6916	0.0730	12.2463
48	25.729	0.0389	353.271	0.0028	13.7305	0.0728	12.3447
49	27.530	0.0363	379.000	0.0026	13.7668	0.0726	12.4387
50	29.457	0.0339	406.530	0.0025	13.8007	0.0725	12.5287

Interest Table for Annual Compounding with *i* = 7% (Contd.)

n	$F/p,i,n$	$P/F,i,n$	$F/A,i,n$	$A/F,i,n$	$P/A,i,n$	$A/P,i,n$	$A/G,i,n$
51	31.519	0.0317	435.987	0.0023	13.8325	0.0723	12.6146
52	33.725	0.0297	467.506	0.0021	13.8621	0.0721	12.6967
53	36.086	0.0277	501.232	0.0020	13.8898	0.0720	12.7752
54	38.612	0.0259	537.318	0.0019	13.9157	0.0719	12.8500
55	41.315	0.0242	575.930	0.0017	13.9399	0.0717	12.9215
56	44.207	0.0226	617.245	0.0016	13.9626	0.0716	12.9896
57	47.302	0.0211	661.452	0.0015	13.9837	0.0715	13.0547
58	50.613	0.0198	708.754	0.0014	14.0035	0.0714	13.1167
59	54.156	0.0185	759.367	0.0013	14.0219	0.0713	13.1758
60	57.947	0.0173	813.523	0.0012	14.0392	0.0712	13.2321
61	62.003	0.0161	871.469	0.0011	14.0553	0.0711	13.2858
62	66.343	0.0151	933.472	0.0011	14.0704	0.0711	13.3369
63	70.987	0.0141	999.816	0.0010	14.0845	0.0710	13.3856
64	75.956	0.0132	1,070.803	0.0009	14.0976	0.0709	13.4319
65	81.273	0.0123	1,146.759	0.0009	14.1099	0.0709	13.4760
66	86.962	0.0115	1,228.032	0.0008	14.1214	0.0708	13.5179
67	93.050	0.0107	1,314.994	0.0008	14.1322	0.0708	13.5578
68	99.563	0.0100	1,408.044	0.0007	14.1422	0.0707	13.5958
69	106.532	0.0094	1,507.607	0.0007	14.1516	0.0707	13.6319
70	113.990	0.0088	1,614.140	0.0006	14.1604	0.0706	13.6662
71	121.969	0.0082	1,728.130	0.0006	14.1686	0.0706	13.6988
72	130.507	0.0077	1,850.099	0.0005	14.1763	0.0705	13.7298
73	139.642	0.0072	1,980.606	0.0005	14.1834	0.0705	13.7592
74	149.417	0.0067	2,120.248	0.0005	14.1901	0.0705	13.7871
75	159.877	0.0063	2,269.666	0.0004	14.1964	0.0704	13.8136
76	171.068	0.0058	2,429.542	0.0004	14.2022	0.0704	13.8388
77	183.043	0.0055	2,600.610	0.0004	14.2077	0.0704	13.8627
78	195.856	0.0051	2,783.653	0.0004	14.2128	0.0704	13.8854
79	209.566	0.0048	2,979.509	0.0003	14.2175	0.0703	13.9069
80	224.235	0.0045	3,189.075	0.0003	14.2220	0.0703	13.9273
81	239.932	0.0042	3,413.310	0.0003	14.2262	0.0703	13.9467
82	256.727	0.0039	3,653.242	0.0003	14.2301	0.0703	13.9651
83	274.698	0.0036	3,909.969	0.0003	14.2337	0.0703	13.9825
84	293.927	0.0034	4,184.668	0.0002	14.2371	0.0702	13.9990
85	314.502	0.0032	4,478.594	0.0002	14.2403	0.0702	14.0146
86	336.517	0.0030	4,793.097	0.0002	14.2433	0.0702	14.0294
87	360.073	0.0028	5,129.614	0.0002	14.2460	0.0702	14.0434
88	385.278	0.0026	5,489.687	0.0002	14.2486	0.0702	14.0567
89	412.248	0.0024	5,874.965	0.0002	14.2511	0.0702	14.0693
90	441.105	0.0023	6,287.213	0.0002	14.2533	0.0702	14.0812
91	471.982	0.0021	6,728.318	0.0001	14.2554	0.0701	14.0925
92	505.021	0.0020	7,200.301	0.0001	14.2574	0.0701	14.1032
93	540.373	0.0019	7,705.322	0.0001	14.2593	0.0701	14.1133
94	578.199	0.0017	8,245.695	0.0001	14.2610	0.0701	14.1229
95	618.673	0.0016	8,823.894	0.0001	14.2626	0.0701	14.1319
96	661.980	0.0015	9,442.566	0.0001	14.2641	0.0701	14.1405
97	708.318	0.0014	10,104.550	0.0001	14.2655	0.0701	14.1486
98	757.901	0.0013	10,812.870	0.0001	14.2669	0.0701	14.1562
99	810.954	0.0012	11,570.770	0.0001	14.2681	0.0701	14.1635
100	867.720	0.0012	12,381.720	0.0001	14.2693	0.0701	14.1703

Interest Table for Annual Compounding with $i = 8\%$

n	$F/p,i,n$	$P/F,i,n$	$F/A,i,n$	$A/F,i,n$	$P/A,i,n$	$A/P,i,n$	$A/G,i,n$
1	1.080	0.9259	1.000	1.0000	0.9259	1.0800	0.0000
2	1.166	0.8573	2.080	0.4808	1.7833	0.5608	0.4808
3	1.260	0.7938	3.246	0.3080	2.5771	0.3880	0.9487
4	1.360	0.7350	4.506	0.2219	3.3121	0.3019	1.4040
5	1.469	0.6806	5.867	0.1705	3.9927	0.2505	1.8465
6	1.587	0.6302	7.336	0.1363	4.6229	0.2163	2.2764
7	1.714	0.5835	8.923	0.1121	5.2064	0.1921	2.6937
8	1.851	0.5403	10.637	0.0940	5.7466	0.1740	3.0985
9	1.999	0.5002	12.488	0.0801	6.2469	0.1601	3.4910
10	2.159	0.4632	14.487	0.0690	6.7101	0.1490	3.8713
11	2.332	0.4289	16.645	0.0601	7.1390	0.1401	4.2395
12	2.518	0.3971	18.977	0.0527	7.5361	0.1327	4.5958
13	2.720	0.3677	21.495	0.0465	7.9038	0.1265	4.9402
14	2.937	0.3405	24.215	0.0413	8.2442	0.1213	5.2731
15	3.172	0.3152	27.152	0.0368	8.5595	0.1168	5.5945
16	3.426	0.2919	30.324	0.0330	8.8514	0.1130	5.9046
17	3.700	0.2703	33.750	0.0296	9.1216	0.1096	6.2038
18	3.996	0.2502	37.450	0.0267	9.3719	0.1067	6.4920
19	4.316	0.2317	41.446	0.0241	9.6036	0.1041	6.7697
20	4.661	0.2145	45.762	0.0219	9.8181	0.1019	7.0370
21	5.034	0.1987	50.423	0.0198	10.0168	0.0998	7.2940
22	5.437	0.1839	55.457	0.0180	10.2007	0.0980	7.5412
23	5.871	0.1703	60.893	0.0164	10.3711	0.0964	7.7786
24	6.341	0.1577	66.765	0.0150	10.5288	0.0950	8.0066
25	6.848	0.1460	73.106	0.0137	10.6748	0.0937	8.2254
26	7.396	0.1352	79.955	0.0125	10.8100	0.0925	8.4352
27	7.988	0.1252	87.351	0.0114	10.9352	0.0914	8.6363
28	8.627	0.1159	95.339	0.0105	11.0511	0.0905	8.8289
29	9.317	0.1073	103.966	0.0096	11.1584	0.0896	9.0133
30	10.063	0.0994	113.283	0.0088	11.2578	0.0888	9.1897
31	10.868	0.0920	123.346	0.0081	11.3498	0.0881	9.3584
32	11.737	0.0852	134.214	0.0075	11.4350	0.0875	9.5197
33	12.676	0.0789	145.951	0.0069	11.5139	0.0869	9.6737
34	13.690	0.0730	158.627	0.0063	11.5869	0.0863	9.8208
35	14.785	0.0676	172.317	0.0058	11.6546	0.0858	9.9611
36	15.968	0.0626	187.102	0.0053	11.7172	0.0853	10.0949
37	17.246	0.0580	203.071	0.0049	11.7752	0.0849	10.2225
38	18.625	0.0537	220.316	0.0045	11.8289	0.0845	10.3440
39	20.115	0.0497	238.942	0.0042	11.8786	0.0842	10.4598
40	21.725	0.0460	259.057	0.0039	11.9246	0.0839	10.5699
41	23.463	0.0426	280.781	0.0036	11.9672	0.0836	10.6747
42	25.340	0.0395	304.244	0.0033	12.0067	0.0833	10.7744
43	27.367	0.0365	329.583	0.0030	12.0432	0.0830	10.8692
44	29.556	0.0338	356.950	0.0028	12.0771	0.0828	10.9592
45	31.920	0.0313	386.506	0.0026	12.1084	0.0826	11.0447
46	34.474	0.0290	418.427	0.0024	12.1374	0.0824	11.1258
47	37.232	0.0269	452.901	0.0022	12.1643	0.0822	11.2028
48	40.211	0.0249	490.133	0.0020	12.1891	0.0820	11.2758
49	43.427	0.0230	530.344	0.0019	12.2122	0.0819	11.3451
50	46.902	0.0213	573.771	0.0017	12.2335	0.0817	11.4107

Interest Table for Annual Compounding with i = 8% (Contd.)

n	$F/p,i,n$	$P/F,i,n$	$F/A,i,n$	$A/F,i,n$	$P/A,i,n$	$A/P,i,n$	$A/G,i,n$
51	50.654	0.0197	620.673	0.0016	12.2532	0.0816	11.4729
52	54.706	0.0183	671.327	0.0015	12.2715	0.0815	11.5318
53	59.083	0.0169	726.033	0.0014	12.2884	0.0814	11.5875
54	63.809	0.0157	785.115	0.0013	12.3041	0.0813	11.6403
55	68.914	0.0145	848.925	0.0012	12.3186	0.0812	11.6902
56	74.427	0.0134	917.839	0.0011	12.3321	0.0811	11.7373
57	80.381	0.0124	992.266	0.0010	12.3445	0.0810	11.7819
58	86.812	0.0115	1,072.647	0.0009	12.3560	0.0809	11.8241
59	93.757	0.0107	1,159.459	0.0009	12.3667	0.0809	11.8639
60	101.257	0.0099	1,253.216	0.0008	12.3766	0.0808	11.9015
61	109.358	0.0091	1,354.473	0.0007	12.3857	0.0807	11.9371
62	118.106	0.0085	1,463.831	0.0007	12.3942	0.0807	11.9706
63	127.555	0.0078	1,581.937	0.0006	12.4020	0.0806	12.0022
64	137.759	0.0073	1,709.493	0.0006	12.4093	0.0806	12.0320
65	148.780	0.0067	1,847.252	0.0005	12.4160	0.0805	12.0602
66	160.683	0.0062	1,996.032	0.0005	12.4222	0.0805	12.0867
67	173.537	0.0058	2,156.715	0.0005	12.4280	0.0805	12.1117
68	187.420	0.0053	2,330.252	0.0004	12.4333	0.0804	12.1352
69	202.414	0.0049	2,517.672	0.0004	12.4382	0.0804	12.1574
70	218.607	0.0046	2,720.086	0.0004	12.4428	0.0804	12.1783
71	236.095	0.0042	2,938.693	0.0003	12.4471	0.0803	12.1980
72	254.983	0.0039	3,174.789	0.0003	12.4510	0.0803	12.2165
73	275.382	0.0036	3,429.772	0.0003	12.4546	0.0803	12.2339
74	297.412	0.0034	3,705.154	0.0003	12.4580	0.0803	12.2503
75	321.205	0.0031	4,002.566	0.0002	12.4611	0.0802	12.2658
76	346.902	0.0029	4,323.772	0.0002	12.4640	0.0802	12.2803
77	374.654	0.0027	4,670.674	0.0002	12.4666	0.0802	12.2939
78	404.626	0.0025	5,045.328	0.0002	12.4691	0.0802	12.3068
79	436.996	0.0023	5,449.954	0.0002	12.4714	0.0802	12.3188
80	471.956	0.0021	5,886.950	0.0002	12.4735	0.0802	12.3301
81	509.713	0.0020	6,358.907	0.0002	12.4755	0.0802	12.3408
82	550.490	0.0018	6,868.620	0.0001	12.4773	0.0801	12.3508
83	594.529	0.0017	7,419.109	0.0001	12.4790	0.0801	12.3602
84	642.091	0.0016	8,013.639	0.0001	12.4805	0.0801	12.3690
85	693.458	0.0014	8,655.729	0.0001	12.4820	0.0801	12.3773
86	748.935	0.0013	9,349.189	0.0001	12.4833	0.0801	12.3850
87	808.850	0.0012	10,098.120	0.0001	12.4845	0.0801	12.3923
88	873.558	0.0011	10,906.980	0.0001	12.4857	0.0801	12.3991
89	943.443	0.0011	11,780.530	0.0001	12.4868	0.0801	12.4056
90	1018.918	0.0010	12,723.980	0.0001	12.4877	0.0801	12.4116
91	1100.431	0.0009	13,742.890	0.0001	12.4886	0.0801	12.4172
92	1188.466	0.0008	14,843.320	0.0001	12.4895	0.0801	12.4225
93	1283.543	0.0008	16,031.790	0.0001	12.4903	0.0801	12.4275
94	1386.227	0.0007	17,315.340	0.0001	12.4910	0.0801	12.4321
95	1497.125	0.0007	18,701.560	0.0001	12.4917	0.0801	12.4365
96	1616.895	0.0006	20,198.690	0.0000	12.4923	0.0800	12.4406
97	1746.247	0.0006	21,815.590	0.0000	12.4928	0.0800	12.4444
98	1885.947	0.0005	23,561.840	0.0000	12.4934	0.0800	12.4480
99	2036.822	0.0005	25,447.780	0.0000	12.4939	0.0800	12.4514
100	2199.768	0.0005	27,484.610	0.0000	12.4943	0.0800	12.4545

Interest Table for Annual Compounding with i = 9%

n	$F/p,i,n$	$P/F,i,n$	$F/A,i,n$	$A/F,i,n$	$P/A,i,n$	$A/P,i,n$	$A/G,i,n$
1	1.090	0.9174	1.000	1.0000	0.9174	1.0900	0.0000
2	1.188	0.8417	2.090	0.4785	1.7591	0.5685	0.4785
3	1.295	0.7722	3.278	0.3051	2.5313	0.3951	0.9426
4	1.412	0.7084	4.573	0.2187	3.2397	0.3087	1.3925
5	1.539	0.6499	5.985	0.1671	3.8897	0.2571	1.8282
6	1.677	0.5963	7.523	0.1329	4.4859	0.2229	2.2498
7	1.828	0.5470	9.200	0.1087	5.0330	0.1987	2.6574
8	1.993	0.5019	11.028	0.0907	5.5348	0.1807	3.0512
9	2.172	0.4604	13.021	0.0768	5.9952	0.1668	3.4312
10	2.367	0.4224	15.193	0.0658	6.4177	0.1558	3.7978
11	2.580	0.3875	17.560	0.0569	6.8052	0.1469	4.1510
12	2.813	0.3555	20.141	0.0497	7.1607	0.1397	4.4910
13	3.066	0.3262	22.953	0.0436	7.4869	0.1336	4.8182
14	3.342	0.2992	26.019	0.0384	7.7862	0.1284	5.1326
15	3.642	0.2745	29.361	0.0341	8.0607	0.1241	5.4346
16	3.970	0.2519	33.003	0.0303	8.3126	0.1203	5.7245
17	4.328	0.2311	36.974	0.0270	8.5436	0.1170	6.0024
18	4.717	0.2120	41.301	0.0242	8.7556	0.1142	6.2687
19	5.142	0.1945	46.019	0.0217	8.9501	0.1117	6.5236
20	5.604	0.1784	51.160	0.0195	9.1285	0.1095	6.7675
21	6.109	0.1637	56.765	0.0176	9.2922	0.1076	7.0006
22	6.659	0.1502	62.873	0.0159	9.4424	0.1059	7.2232
23	7.258	0.1378	69.532	0.0144	9.5802	0.1044	7.4357
24	7.911	0.1264	76.790	0.0130	9.7066	0.1030	7.6384
25	8.623	0.1160	84.701	0.0118	9.8226	0.1018	7.8316
26	9.399	0.1064	93.324	0.0107	9.9290	0.1007	8.0156
27	10.245	0.0976	102.723	0.0097	10.0266	0.0997	8.1906
28	11.167	0.0895	112.968	0.0089	10.1161	0.0989	8.3571
29	12.172	0.0822	124.136	0.0081	10.1983	0.0981	8.5154
30	13.268	0.0754	136.308	0.0073	10.2737	0.0973	8.6657
31	14.462	0.0691	149.575	0.0067	10.3428	0.0967	8.8083
32	15.763	0.0634	164.037	0.0061	10.4062	0.0961	8.9436
33	17.182	0.0582	179.801	0.0056	10.4644	0.0956	9.0718
34	18.728	0.0534	196.983	0.0051	10.5178	0.0951	9.1933
35	20.414	0.0490	215.711	0.0046	10.5668	0.0946	9.3083
36	22.251	0.0449	236.125	0.0042	10.6118	0.0942	9.4171
37	24.254	0.0412	258.376	0.0039	10.6530	0.0939	9.5200
38	26.437	0.0378	282.630	0.0035	10.6908	0.0935	9.6172
39	28.816	0.0347	309.067	0.0032	10.7255	0.0932	9.7090
40	31.409	0.0318	337.883	0.0030	10.7574	0.0930	9.7957
41	34.236	0.0292	369.293	0.0027	10.7866	0.0927	9.8775
42	37.318	0.0268	403.529	0.0025	10.8134	0.0925	9.9546
43	40.676	0.0246	440.847	0.0023	10.8380	0.0923	10.0273
44	44.337	0.0226	481.523	0.0021	10.8605	0.0921	10.0958
45	48.327	0.0207	525.860	0.0019	10.8812	0.0919	10.1603
46	52.677	0.0190	574.187	0.0017	10.9002	0.0917	10.2210
47	57.418	0.0174	626.864	0.0016	10.9176	0.0916	10.2780
48	62.585	0.0160	684.282	0.0015	10.9336	0.0915	10.3317
49	68.218	0.0147	746.867	0.0013	10.9482	0.0913	10.3821
50	74.358	0.0134	815.085	0.0012	10.9617	0.0912	10.4295

Interest Table for Annual Compounding with i = 9% (Contd.)

n	$F/p,i,n$	$P/F,i,n$	$F/A,i,n$	$A/F,i,n$	$P/A,i,n$	$A/P,i,n$	$A/G,i,n$
51	81.050	0.0123	889.443	0.0011	10.9740	0.0911	10.4740
52	88.344	0.0113	970.493	0.0010	10.9853	0.0910	10.5158
53	96.295	0.0104	1,058.837	0.0009	10.9957	0.0909	10.5549
54	104.962	0.0095	1,155.133	0.0009	11.0053	0.0909	10.5917
55	114.409	0.0087	1,260.095	0.0008	11.0140	0.0908	10.6261
56	124.705	0.0080	1,374.504	0.0007	11.0220	0.0907	10.6584
57	135.929	0.0074	1,499.209	0.0007	11.0294	0.0907	10.6887
58	148.162	0.0067	1,635.138	0.0006	11.0361	0.0906	10.7170
59	161.497	0.0062	1,783.300	0.0006	11.0423	0.0906	10.7435
60	176.032	0.0057	1,944.797	0.0005	11.0480	0.0905	10.7683
61	191.875	0.0052	2,120.829	0.0005	11.0532	0.0905	10.7915
62	209.143	0.0048	2,312.704	0.0004	11.0580	0.0904	10.8132
63	227.966	0.0044	2,521.848	0.0004	11.0624	0.0904	10.8335
64	248.483	0.0040	2,749.814	0.0004	11.0664	0.0904	10.8525
65	270.847	0.0037	2,998.297	0.0003	11.0701	0.0903	10.8702
66	295.223	0.0034	3,269.144	0.0003	11.0735	0.0903	10.8868
67	321.793	0.0031	3,564.367	0.0003	11.0766	0.0903	10.9023
68	350.754	0.0029	3,886.161	0.0003	11.0794	0.0903	10.9167
69	382.322	0.0026	4,236.915	0.0002	11.0820	0.0902	10.9302
70	416.731	0.0024	4,619.238	0.0002	11.0844	0.0902	10.9427
71	454.237	0.0022	5,035.969	0.0002	11.0867	0.0902	10.9545
72	495.119	0.0020	5,490.207	0.0002	11.0887	0.0902	10.9654
73	539.679	0.0019	5,985.325	0.0002	11.0905	0.0902	10.9756
74	588.250	0.0017	6,525.005	0.0002	11.0922	0.0902	10.9851
75	641.193	0.0016	7,113.256	0.0001	11.0938	0.0901	10.9940
76	698.900	0.0014	7,754.449	0.0001	11.0952	0.0901	11.0022
77	761.802	0.0013	8,453.349	0.0001	11.0965	0.0901	11.0099
78	830.364	0.0012	9,215.152	0.0001	11.0977	0.0901	11.0171
79	905.096	0.0011	10,045.520	0.0001	11.0988	0.0901	11.0237
80	986.555	0.0010	10,950.610	0.0001	11.0998	0.0901	11.0299
81	1,075.345	0.0009	11,937.170	0.0001	11.1008	0.0901	11.0357
82	1,172.126	0.0009	13,012.510	0.0001	11.1016	0.0901	11.0411
83	1,277.618	0.0008	14,184.640	0.0001	11.1024	0.0901	11.0461
84	1,392.603	0.0007	15,462.260	0.0001	11.1031	0.0901	11.0507
85	1,517.938	0.0007	16,854.860	0.0001	11.1038	0.0901	11.0551
86	1,654.552	0.0006	18,372.800	0.0001	11.1044	0.0901	11.0591
87	1,803.462	0.0006	20,027.350	0.0000	11.1049	0.0900	11.0628
88	1,965.774	0.0005	21,830.820	0.0000	11.1055	0.0900	11.0663
89	2,142.693	0.0005	23,796.590	0.0000	11.1059	0.0900	11.0696
90	2,335.536	0.0004	25,939.290	0.0000	11.1064	0.0900	11.0726
91	2,545.735	0.0004	28,274.830	0.0000	11.1067	0.0900	11.0754
92	2,774.851	0.0004	30,820.570	0.0000	11.1071	0.0900	11.0779
93	3,024.588	0.0003	33,595.420	0.0000	11.1074	0.0900	11.0804
94	3,296.800	0.0003	36,620.000	0.0000	11.1077	0.0900	11.0826
95	3,593.513	0.0003	39,916.810	0.0000	11.1080	0.0900	11.0847
96	3,916.929	0.0003	43,510.320	0.0000	11.1083	0.0900	11.0866
97	4,269.452	0.0002	47,427.250	0.0000	11.1085	0.0900	11.0884
98	4,653.703	0.0002	51,696.700	0.0000	11.1087	0.0900	11.0900
99	5,072.537	0.0002	56,350.410	0.0000	11.1089	0.0900	11.0916
100	5,529.066	0.0002	61,422.950	0.0000	11.1091	0.0900	11.0930

Interest Table for Annual Compounding with *i* = 10%

n	F/p,i,n	P/F,i,n	F/A,i,n	A/F,i,n	P/A,i,n	A/P,i,n	A/G,i,n
1	1.100	0.9091	1.000	1.0000	0.9091	1.1000	0.0000
2	1.210	0.8264	2.100	0.4762	1.7355	0.5762	0.4762
3	1.331	0.7513	3.310	0.3021	2.4869	0.4021	0.9366
4	1.464	0.6830	4.641	0.2155	3.1699	0.3155	1.3812
5	1.611	0.6209	6.105	0.1638	3.7908	0.2638	1.8101
6	1.772	0.5645	7.716	0.1296	4.3553	0.2296	2.2236
7	1.949	0.5132	9.487	0.1054	4.8684	0.2054	2.6216
8	2.144	0.4665	11.436	0.0874	5.3349	0.1874	3.0045
9	2.358	0.4241	13.579	0.0736	5.7590	0.1736	3.3724
10	2.594	0.3855	15.937	0.0627	6.1446	0.1627	3.7255
11	2.853	0.3505	18.531	0.0540	6.4951	0.1540	4.0641
12	3.138	0.3186	21.384	0.0468	6.8137	0.1468	4.3884
13	3.452	0.2897	24.523	0.0408	7.1034	0.1408	4.6988
14	3.797	0.2633	27.975	0.0357	7.3667	0.1357	4.9955
15	4.177	0.2394	31.772	0.0315	7.6061	0.1315	5.2789
16	4.595	0.2176	35.950	0.0278	7.8237	0.1278	5.5493
17	5.054	0.1978	40.545	0.0247	8.0216	0.1247	5.8071
18	5.560	0.1799	45.599	0.0219	8.2014	0.1219	6.0526
19	6.116	0.1635	51.159	0.0195	8.3649	0.1195	6.2861
20	6.728	0.1486	57.275	0.0175	8.5136	0.1175	6.5081
21	7.400	0.1351	64.003	0.0156	8.6487	0.1156	6.7189
22	8.140	0.1228	71.403	0.0140	8.7715	0.1140	6.9189
23	8.954	0.1117	79.543	0.0126	8.8832	0.1126	7.1085
24	9.850	0.1015	88.497	0.0113	8.9847	0.1113	7.2881
25	10.835	0.0923	98.347	0.0102	9.0770	0.1102	7.4580
26	11.918	0.0839	109.182	0.0092	9.1609	0.1092	7.6187
27	13.110	0.0763	121.100	0.0083	9.2372	0.1083	7.7704
28	14.421	0.0693	134.210	0.0075	9.3066	0.1075	7.9137
29	15.863	0.0630	148.631	0.0067	9.3696	0.1067	8.0489
30	17.449	0.0573	164.494	0.0061	9.4269	0.1061	8.1762
31	19.194	0.0521	181.944	0.0055	9.4790	0.1055	8.2962
32	21.114	0.0474	201.138	0.0050	9.5264	0.1050	8.4091
33	23.225	0.0431	222.252	0.0045	9.5694	0.1045	8.5152
34	25.548	0.0391	245.477	0.0041	9.6086	0.1041	8.6149
35	28.102	0.0356	271.025	0.0037	9.6442	0.1037	8.7086
36	30.913	0.0323	299.127	0.0033	9.6765	0.1033	8.7965
37	34.004	0.0294	330.040	0.0030	9.7059	0.1030	8.8789
38	37.404	0.0267	364.044	0.0027	9.7327	0.1027	8.9562
39	41.145	0.0243	401.448	0.0025	9.7570	0.1025	9.0285
40	45.259	0.0221	442.593	0.0023	9.7791	0.1023	9.0962
41	49.785	0.0201	487.852	0.0020	9.7991	0.1020	9.1596
42	54.764	0.0183	537.637	0.0019	9.8174	0.1019	9.2188
43	60.240	0.0166	592.401	0.0017	9.8340	0.1017	9.2741
44	66.264	0.0151	652.641	0.0015	9.8491	0.1015	9.3258
45	72.891	0.0137	718.905	0.0014	9.8628	0.1014	9.3740
46	80.180	0.0125	791.796	0.0013	9.8753	0.1013	9.4190
47	88.198	0.0113	871.975	0.0011	9.8866	0.1011	9.4610
48	97.017	0.0103	960.173	0.0010	9.8969	0.1010	9.5001
49	106.719	0.0094	1,057.190	0.0009	9.9063	0.1009	9.5365
50	117.391	0.0085	1,163.909	0.0009	9.9148	0.1009	9.5704

Interest Table for Annual Compounding with i = 10% (Contd.)

n	$F/p,i,n$	$P/F,i,n$	$F/A,i,n$	$A/F,i,n$	$P/A,i,n$	$A/P,i,n$	$A/G,i,n$
51	129.130	0.0077	1,281.300	0.0008	9.9226	0.1008	9.6020
52	142.043	0.0070	1,410.430	0.0007	9.9296	0.1007	9.6313
53	156.247	0.0064	1,552.473	0.0006	9.9360	0.1006	9.6586
54	171.872	0.0058	1,708.721	0.0006	9.9418	0.1006	9.6840
55	189.059	0.0053	1,880.593	0.0005	9.9471	0.1005	9.7075
56	207.965	0.0048	2,069.652	0.0005	9.9519	0.1005	9.7294
57	228.762	0.0044	2,277.617	0.0004	9.9563	0.1004	9.7497
58	251.638	0.0040	2,506.379	0.0004	9.9603	0.1004	9.7686
59	276.802	0.0036	2,758.017	0.0004	9.9639	0.1004	9.7861
60	304.482	0.0033	3,034.819	0.0003	9.9672	0.1003	9.8023
61	334.930	0.0030	3,339.301	0.0003	9.9701	0.1003	9.8173
62	368.423	0.0027	3,674.231	0.0003	9.9729	0.1003	9.8313
63	405.265	0.0025	4,042.654	0.0002	9.9753	0.1002	9.8442
64	445.792	0.0022	4,447.920	0.0002	9.9776	0.1002	9.8561
65	490.371	0.0020	4,893.712	0.0002	9.9796	0.1002	9.8672
66	539.408	0.0019	5,384.083	0.0002	9.9815	0.1002	9.8774
67	593.349	0.0017	5,923.492	0.0002	9.9831	0.1002	9.8869
68	652.684	0.0015	6,516.841	0.0002	9.9847	0.1002	9.8957
69	717.953	0.0014	7,169.525	0.0001	9.9861	0.1001	9.9038
70	789.748	0.0013	7,887.478	0.0001	9.9873	0.1001	9.9113
71	868.723	0.0012	8,677.226	0.0001	9.9885	0.1001	9.9182
72	955.595	0.0010	9,545.948	0.0001	9.9895	0.1001	9.9246
73	1,051.154	0.0010	10,501.540	0.0001	9.9905	0.1001	9.9305
74	1,156.270	0.0009	11,552.700	0.0001	9.9914	0.1001	9.9359
75	1,271.897	0.0008	12,708.970	0.0001	9.9921	0.1001	9.9410
76	1,399.086	0.0007	13,980.860	0.0001	9.9929	0.1001	9.9456
77	1,538.995	0.0006	15,379.950	0.0001	9.9935	0.1001	9.9499
78	1,692.895	0.0006	16,918.950	0.0001	9.9941	0.1001	9.9539
79	1,862.184	0.0005	18,611.840	0.0001	9.9946	0.1001	9.9576
80	2,048.403	0.0005	20,474.030	0.0000	9.9951	0.1000	9.9609
81	2,253.243	0.0004	22,522.430	0.0000	9.9956	0.1000	9.9640
82	2,478.568	0.0004	24,775.680	0.0000	9.9960	0.1000	9.9669
83	2,726.424	0.0004	27,254.240	0.0000	9.9963	0.1000	9.9695
84	2,999.067	0.0003	29,980.670	0.0000	9.9967	0.1000	9.9720
85	3,298.973	0.0003	32,979.730	0.0000	9.9970	0.1000	9.9742
86	3,628.871	0.0003	36,278.710	0.0000	9.9972	0.1000	9.9763
87	3,991.758	0.0003	39,907.580	0.0000	9.9975	0.1000	9.9782
88	4,390.934	0.0002	43,899.340	0.0000	9.9977	0.1000	9.9800
89	4,830.027	0.0002	48,290.260	0.0000	9.9979	0.1000	9.9816
90	5,313.030	0.0002	53,120.300	0.0000	9.9981	0.1000	9.9831
91	5,844.333	0.0002	58,433.330	0.0000	9.9983	0.1000	9.9844
92	6,428.766	0.0002	64,277.660	0.0000	9.9984	0.1000	9.9857
93	7,071.643	0.0001	70,706.430	0.0000	9.9986	0.1000	9.9868
94	7,778.807	0.0001	77,778.070	0.0000	9.9987	0.1000	9.9879
95	8,556.688	0.0001	85,556.880	0.0000	9.9988	0.1000	9.9889
96	9,412.358	0.0001	94,113.570	0.0000	9.9989	0.1000	9.9898
97	10,353.590	0.0001	1,03,525.900	0.0000	9.9990	0.1000	9.9906
98	11,388.950	0.0001	1,13,879.500	0.0000	9.9991	0.1000	9.9914
99	12,527.850	0.0001	1,25,268.500	0.0000	9.9992	0.1000	9.9921
100	13,780.630	0.0001	1,37,796.300	0.0000	9.9993	0.1000	9.9927

Interest Table for Annual Compounding with *i* = 11%

n	F/p,i,n	P/F,i,n	F/A,i,n	A/F,i,n	P/A,i,n	A/P,i,n	A/G,i,n
1	1.110	0.9009	1.000	1.0000	0.9009	1.1100	0.0000
2	1.232	0.8116	2.110	0.4739	1.7125	0.5839	0.4739
3	1.368	0.7312	3.342	0.2992	2.4437	0.4092	0.9306
4	1.518	0.6587	4.710	0.2123	3.1024	0.3223	1.3700
5	1.685	0.5935	6.228	0.1606	3.6959	0.2706	1.7923
6	1.870	0.5346	7.913	0.1264	4.2305	0.2364	2.1976
7	2.076	0.4817	9.783	0.1022	4.7122	0.2122	2.5863
8	2.305	0.4339	11.859	0.0843	5.1461	0.1943	2.9585
9	2.558	0.3909	14.164	0.0706	5.5370	0.1806	3.3144
10	2.839	0.3522	16.722	0.0598	5.8892	0.1698	3.6544
11	3.152	0.3173	19.561	0.0511	6.2065	0.1611	3.9788
12	3.498	0.2858	22.713	0.0440	6.4924	0.1540	4.2879
13	3.883	0.2575	26.212	0.0382	6.7499	0.1482	4.5822
14	4.310	0.2320	30.095	0.0332	6.9819	0.1432	4.8619
15	4.785	0.2090	34.405	0.0291	7.1909	0.1391	5.1275
16	5.311	0.1883	39.190	0.0255	7.3792	0.1355	5.3794
17	5.895	0.1696	44.501	0.0225	7.5488	0.1325	5.6180
18	6.544	0.1528	50.396	0.0198	7.7016	0.1298	5.8439
19	7.263	0.1377	56.939	0.0176	7.8393	0.1276	6.0574
20	8.062	0.1240	64.203	0.0156	7.9633	0.1256	6.2590
21	8.949	0.1117	72.265	0.0138	8.0751	0.1238	6.4491
22	9.934	0.1007	81.214	0.0123	8.1757	0.1223	6.6283
23	11.026	0.0907	91.148	0.0110	8.2664	0.1210	6.7969
24	12.239	0.0817	102.174	0.0098	8.3481	0.1198	6.9555
25	13.585	0.0736	114.413	0.0087	8.4217	0.1187	7.1045
26	15.080	0.0663	127.999	0.0078	8.4881	0.1178	7.2443
27	16.739	0.0597	143.079	0.0070	8.5478	0.1170	7.3754
28	18.580	0.0538	159.817	0.0063	8.6016	0.1163	7.4982
29	20.624	0.0485	178.397	0.0056	8.6501	0.1156	7.6131
30	22.892	0.0437	199.021	0.0050	8.6938	0.1150	7.7206
31	25.410	0.0394	221.913	0.0045	8.7331	0.1145	7.8210
32	28.206	0.0355	247.324	0.0040	8.7686	0.1140	7.9147
33	31.308	0.0319	275.529	0.0036	8.8005	0.1136	8.0021
34	34.752	0.0288	306.837	0.0033	8.8293	0.1133	8.0836
35	38.575	0.0259	341.590	0.0029	8.8552	0.1129	8.1594
36	42.818	0.0234	380.164	0.0026	8.8786	0.1126	8.2300
37	47.528	0.0210	422.983	0.0024	8.8996	0.1124	8.2957
38	52.756	0.0190	470.511	0.0021	8.9186	0.1121	8.3567
39	58.559	0.0171	523.267	0.0019	8.9357	0.1119	8.4133
40	65.001	0.0154	581.826	0.0017	8.9511	0.1117	8.4659
41	72.151	0.0139	646.827	0.0015	8.9649	0.1115	8.5147
42	80.088	0.0125	718.978	0.0014	8.9774	0.1114	8.5599
43	88.897	0.0112	799.066	0.0013	8.9886	0.1113	8.6017
44	98.676	0.0101	887.963	0.0011	8.9988	0.1111	8.6404
45	109.530	0.0091	986.639	0.0010	9.0079	0.1110	8.6763
46	121.579	0.0082	1,096.169	0.0009	9.0161	0.1109	8.7094
47	134.952	0.0074	1,217.748	0.0008	9.0235	0.1108	8.7400
48	149.797	0.0067	1,352.700	0.0007	9.0302	0.1107	8.7683
49	166.275	0.0060	1,502.497	0.0007	9.0362	0.1107	8.7944
50	184.565	0.0054	1,668.771	0.0006	9.0417	0.1106	8.8185

Interest Table for Annual Compounding with *i* = 11% (Contd.)

n	F/p,i,n	P/F,i,n	F/A,i,n	A/F,i,n	P/A,i,n	A/P,i,n	A/G,i,n
51	204.867	0.0049	1,853.336	0.0005	9.0465	0.1105	8.8407
52	227.402	0.0044	2,058.203	0.0005	9.0509	0.1105	8.8612
53	252.417	0.0040	2,285.606	0.0004	9.0549	0.1104	8.8801
54	280.182	0.0036	2,538.022	0.0004	9.0585	0.1104	8.8975
55	311.003	0.0032	2,818.205	0.0004	9.0617	0.1104	8.9135
56	345.213	0.0029	3,129.207	0.0003	9.0646	0.1103	8.9282
57	383.186	0.0026	3,474.420	0.0003	9.0672	0.1103	8.9418
58	425.337	0.0024	3,857.606	0.0003	9.0695	0.1103	8.9542
59	472.124	0.0021	4,282.943	0.0002	9.0717	0.1102	8.9657
60	524.057	0.0019	4,755.067	0.0002	9.0736	0.1102	8.9762
61	581.704	0.0017	5,279.124	0.0002	9.0753	0.1102	8.9859
62	645.691	0.0015	5,860.828	0.0002	9.0768	0.1102	8.9947
63	716.717	0.0014	6,506.519	0.0002	9.0782	0.1102	9.0029
64	795.556	0.0013	7,223.236	0.0001	9.0795	0.1101	9.0104
65	883.067	0.0011	8,018.792	0.0001	9.0806	0.1101	9.0172
66	980.204	0.0010	8,901.858	0.0001	9.0816	0.1101	9.0235
67	1,088.027	0.0009	9,882.062	0.0001	9.0826	0.1101	9.0293
68	1,207.710	0.0008	10,970.090	0.0001	9.0834	0.1101	9.0346
69	1,340.558	0.0007	12,177.800	0.0001	9.0841	0.1101	9.0394
70	1,488.019	0.0007	13,518.360	0.0001	9.0848	0.1101	9.0438
71	1,651.702	0.0006	15,006.380	0.0001	9.0854	0.1101	9.0479
72	1,833.389	0.0005	16,658.080	0.0001	9.0860	0.1101	9.0516
73	2,035.062	0.0005	18,491.470	0.0001	9.0864	0.1101	9.0550
74	2,258.918	0.0004	20,526.530	0.0000	9.0869	0.1100	9.0581
75	2,507.399	0.0004	22,785.450	0.0000	9.0873	0.1100	9.0610
76	2,783.213	0.0004	25,292.850	0.0000	9.0876	0.1100	9.0636
77	3,089.367	0.0003	28,076.060	0.0000	9.0880	0.1100	9.0660
78	3,429.197	0.0003	31,165.430	0.0000	9.0883	0.1100	9.0682
79	3,806.409	0.0003	34,594.630	0.0000	9.0885	0.1100	9.0701
80	4,225.114	0.0002	38,401.030	0.0000	9.0888	0.1100	9.0720
81	4,689.876	0.0002	42,626.150	0.0000	9.0890	0.1100	9.0736
82	5,205.763	0.0002	47,316.030	0.0000	9.0892	0.1100	9.0752
83	5,778.396	0.0002	52,521.780	0.0000	9.0893	0.1100	9.0765
84	6,414.020	0.0002	58,300.190	0.0000	9.0895	0.1100	9.0778
85	7,119.562	0.0001	64,714.200	0.0000	9.0896	0.1100	9.0790
86	7,902.714	0.0001	71,833.770	0.0000	9.0898	0.1100	9.0800
87	8,772.012	0.0001	79,736.480	0.0000	9.0899	0.1100	9.0810
88	9,736.934	0.0001	88,508.490	0.0000	9.0900	0.1100	9.0819
89	10,808.000	0.0001	98,245.420	0.0000	9.0901	0.1100	9.0827
90	11,996.880	0.0001	1,09,053.400	0.0000	9.0902	0.1100	9.0834
91	13,316.530	0.0001	1,21,050.300	0.0000	9.0902	0.1100	9.0841
92	14,781.350	0.0001	1,34,366.800	0.0000	9.0903	0.1100	9.0847
93	16,407.300	0.0001	1,49,148.200	0.0000	9.0904	0.1100	9.0852
94	18,212.100	0.0001	1,65,555.500	0.0000	9.0904	0.1100	9.0857
95	20,215.440	0.0000	1,83,767.600	0.0000	9.0905	0.1100	9.0862
96	22,439.130	0.0000	2,03,983.000	0.0000	9.0905	0.1100	9.0866
97	24,907.440	0.0000	2,26,422.200	0.0000	9.0905	0.1100	9.0870
98	27,647.260	0.0000	2,51,329.600	0.0000	9.0906	0.1100	9.0874
99	30,688.450	0.0000	2,78,976.900	0.0000	9.0906	0.1100	9.0877
100	34,064.180	0.0000	3,09,665.300	0.0000	9.0906	0.1100	9.0880

Interest Table for Annual Compounding with *i* = 12%

n	*F/p,i,n*	*P/F,i,n*	*F/A,i,n*	*A/F,i,n*	*P/A,i,n*	*A/P,i,n*	*A/G,i,n*
1	1.120	0.8929	1.000	1.0000	0.8929	1.1200	0.0000
2	1.254	0.7972	2.120	0.4717	1.6901	0.5917	0.4717
3	1.405	0.7118	3.374	0.2963	2.4018	0.4163	0.9246
4	1.574	0.6355	4.779	0.2092	3.0373	0.3292	1.3589
5	1.762	0.5674	6.353	0.1574	3.6048	0.2774	1.7746
6	1.974	0.5066	8.115	0.1232	4.1114	0.2432	2.1720
7	2.211	0.4523	10.089	0.0991	4.5638	0.2191	2.5515
8	2.476	0.4039	12.300	0.0813	4.9676	0.2013	2.9131
9	2.773	0.3606	14.776	0.0677	5.3283	0.1877	3.2574
10	3.106	0.3220	17.549	0.0570	5.6502	0.1770	3.5847
11	3.479	0.2875	20.655	0.0484	5.9377	0.1684	3.8953
12	3.896	0.2567	24.133	0.0414	6.1944	0.1614	4.1897
13	4.363	0.2292	28.029	0.0357	6.4235	0.1557	4.4683
14	4.887	0.2046	32.393	0.0309	6.6282	0.1509	4.7317
15	5.474	0.1827	37.280	0.0268	6.8109	0.1468	4.9803
16	6.130	0.1631	42.753	0.0234	6.9740	0.1434	5.2147
17	6.866	0.1456	48.884	0.0205	7.1196	0.1405	5.4353
18	7.690	0.1300	55.750	0.0179	7.2497	0.1379	5.6427
19	8.613	0.1161	63.440	0.0158	7.3658	0.1358	5.8375
20	9.646	0.1037	72.052	0.0139	7.4694	0.1339	6.0202
21	10.804	0.0926	81.699	0.0122	7.5620	0.1322	6.1913
22	12.100	0.0826	92.503	0.0108	7.6446	0.1308	6.3514
23	13.552	0.0738	104.603	0.0096	7.7184	0.1296	6.5010
24	15.179	0.0659	118.155	0.0085	7.7843	0.1285	6.6406
25	17.000	0.0588	133.334	0.0075	7.8431	0.1275	6.7708
26	19.040	0.0525	150.334	0.0067	7.8957	0.1267	6.8921
27	21.325	0.0469	169.374	0.0059	7.9426	0.1259	7.0049
28	23.884	0.0419	190.699	0.0052	7.9844	0.1252	7.1098
29	26.750	0.0374	214.583	0.0047	8.0218	0.1247	7.2071
30	29.960	0.0334	241.333	0.0041	8.0552	0.1241	7.2974
31	33.555	0.0298	271.293	0.0037	8.0850	0.1237	7.3811
32	37.582	0.0266	304.848	0.0033	8.1116	0.1233	7.4586
33	42.092	0.0238	342.429	0.0029	8.1354	0.1229	7.5302
34	47.143	0.0212	384.521	0.0026	8.1566	0.1226	7.5965
35	52.800	0.0189	431.664	0.0023	8.1755	0.1223	7.6577
36	59.136	0.0169	484.463	0.0021	8.1924	0.1221	7.7141
37	66.232	0.0151	543.599	0.0018	8.2075	0.1218	7.7661
38	74.180	0.0135	609.831	0.0016	8.2210	0.1216	7.8141
39	83.081	0.0120	684.010	0.0015	8.2330	0.1215	7.8582
40	93.051	0.0107	767.091	0.0013	8.2438	0.1213	7.8988
41	104.217	0.0096	860.142	0.0012	8.2534	0.1212	7.9361
42	116.723	0.0086	964.359	0.0010	8.2619	0.1210	7.9704
43	130.730	0.0076	1,081.083	0.0009	8.2696	0.1209	8.0019
44	146.418	0.0068	1,211.813	0.0008	8.2764	0.1208	8.0308
45	163.988	0.0061	1,358.230	0.0007	8.2825	0.1207	8.0572
46	183.666	0.0054	1,522.218	0.0007	8.2880	0.1207	8.0815
47	205.706	0.0049	1,705.884	0.0006	8.2928	0.1206	8.1037
48	230.391	0.0043	1,911.590	0.0005	8.2972	0.1205	8.1241
49	258.038	0.0039	2,141.981	0.0005	8.3010	0.1205	8.1427
50	289.002	0.0035	2,400.018	0.0004	8.3045	0.1204	8.1597

Interest Table for Annual Compounding with i = 12% (Contd.)

n	$F/p, i, n$	$P/F, i, n$	$F/A, i, n$	$A/F, i, n$	$P/A, i, n$	$A/P, i, n$	$A/G, i, n$
51	323.682	0.0031	2,689.020	0.0004	8.3076	0.1204	8.1753
52	362.524	0.0028	3,012.703	0.0003	8.3103	0.1203	8.1895
53	406.027	0.0025	3,375.227	0.0003	8.3128	0.1203	8.2025
54	454.751	0.0022	3,781.255	0.0003	8.3150	0.1203	8.2143
55	509.321	0.0020	4,236.005	0.0002	8.3170	0.1202	8.2251
56	570.439	0.0018	4,745.325	0.0002	8.3187	0.1202	8.2350
57	638.892	0.0016	5,315.765	0.0002	8.3203	0.1202	8.2440
58	715.559	0.0014	5,954.657	0.0002	8.3217	0.1202	8.2522
59	801.426	0.0012	6,670.215	0.0001	8.3229	0.1201	8.2596
60	897.597	0.0011	7,471.641	0.0001	8.3240	0.1201	8.2664
61	1,005.309	0.0010	8,369.238	0.0001	8.3250	0.1201	8.2726
62	1,125.946	0.0009	9,374.547	0.0001	8.3259	0.1201	8.2782
63	1,261.059	0.0008	10,500.490	0.0001	8.3267	0.1201	8.2833
64	1,412.386	0.0007	11,761.550	0.0001	8.3274	0.1201	8.2880
65	1,581.872	0.0006	13,173.940	0.0001	8.3281	0.1201	8.2922
66	1,771.697	0.0006	14,755.810	0.0001	8.3286	0.1201	8.2961
67	1,984.301	0.0005	16,527.510	0.0001	8.3291	0.1201	8.2996
68	2,222.417	0.0004	18,511.810	0.0001	8.3296	0.1201	8.3027
69	2,489.107	0.0004	20,734.230	0.0000	8.3300	0.1200	8.3056
70	2,787.800	0.0004	23,223.330	0.0000	8.3303	0.1200	8.3082
71	3,122.336	0.0003	26,011.130	0.0000	8.3307	0.1200	8.3106
72	3,497.016	0.0003	29,133.470	0.0000	8.3310	0.1200	8.3127
73	3,916.658	0.0003	32,630.480	0.0000	8.3312	0.1200	8.3147
74	4,386.657	0.0002	36,547.140	0.0000	8.3314	0.1200	8.3165
75	4,913.055	0.0002	40,933.790	0.0000	8.3316	0.1200	8.3181
76	5,502.622	0.0002	45,846.850	0.0000	8.3318	0.1200	8.3195
77	6,162.937	0.0002	51,349.480	0.0000	8.3320	0.1200	8.3208
78	6,902.490	0.0001	57,512.410	0.0000	8.3321	0.1200	8.3220
79	7,730.788	0.0001	64,414.900	0.0000	8.3323	0.1200	8.3231
80	8,658.482	0.0001	72,145.690	0.0000	8.3324	0.1200	8.3241
81	9,697.500	0.0001	80,804.180	0.0000	8.3325	0.1200	8.3250
82	10,861.200	0.0001	90,501.680	0.0000	8.3326	0.1200	8.3258
83	12,164.550	0.0001	1,01,362.900	0.0000	8.3326	0.1200	8.3265
84	13,624.290	0.0001	1,13,527.400	0.0000	8.3327	0.1200	8.3272
85	15,259.210	0.0001	1,27,151.700	0.0000	8.3328	0.1200	8.3278
86	17,090.310	0.0001	1,42,410.900	0.0000	8.3328	0.1200	8.3283
87	19,141.150	0.0001	1,59,501.200	0.0000	8.3329	0.1200	8.3288
88	21,438.090	0.0000	1,78,642.400	0.0000	8.3329	0.1200	8.3292
89	24,010.650	0.0000	2,00,080.400	0.0000	8.3330	0.1200	8.3296
90	26,891.930	0.0000	2,24,091.100	0.0000	8.3330	0.1200	8.3300
91	30,118.960	0.0000	2,50,983.000	0.0000	8.3331	0.1200	8.3303
92	33,733.240	0.0000	2,81,102.000	0.0000	8.3331	0.1200	8.3306
93	37,781.230	0.0000	3,14,835.200	0.0000	8.3331	0.1200	8.3309
94	42,314.980	0.0000	3,52,616.500	0.0000	8.3331	0.1200	8.3311
95	47,392.780	0.0000	3,94,931.500	0.0000	8.3332	0.1200	8.3313
96	53,079.910	0.0000	4,42,324.200	0.0000	8.3332	0.1200	8.3315
97	59,449.500	0.0000	4,95,404.200	0.0000	8.3332	0.1200	8.3317
98	66,583.440	0.0000	5,54,853.700	0.0000	8.3332	0.1200	8.3319
99	74,573.450	0.0000	6,21,437.100	0.0000	8.3332	0.1200	8.3320
100	83,522.270	0.0000	6,96,010.600	0.0000	8.3332	0.1200	8.3321

Interest Table for Annual Compounding with i = 13%

n	$F/p,i,n$	$P/F,i,n$	$F/A,i,n$	$A/F,i,n$	$P/A,i,n$	$A/P,i,n$	$A/G,i,n$
1	1.130	0.8850	1.000	1.0000	0.8850	1.1300	0.0000
2	1.277	0.7831	2.130	0.4695	1.6681	0.5995	0.4695
3	1.443	0.6931	3.407	0.2935	2.3612	0.4235	0.9187
4	1.630	0.6133	4.850	0.2062	2.9745	0.3362	1.3479
5	1.842	0.5428	6.480	0.1543	3.5172	0.2843	1.7571
6	2.082	0.4803	8.323	0.1202	3.9975	0.2502	2.1468
7	2.353	0.4251	10.405	0.0961	4.4226	0.2261	2.5171
8	2.658	0.3762	12.757	0.0784	4.7988	0.2084	2.8685
9	3.004	0.3329	15.416	0.0649	5.1317	0.1949	3.2014
10	3.395	0.2946	18.420	0.0543	5.4262	0.1843	3.5162
11	3.836	0.2607	21.814	0.0458	5.6869	0.1758	3.8134
12	4.335	0.2307	25.650	0.0390	5.9176	0.1690	4.0936
13	4.898	0.2042	29.985	0.0334	6.1218	0.1634	4.3573
14	5.535	0.1807	34.883	0.0287	6.3025	0.1587	4.6050
15	6.254	0.1599	40.417	0.0247	6.4624	0.1547	4.8375
16	7.067	0.1415	46.672	0.0214	6.6039	0.1514	5.0552
17	7.986	0.1252	53.739	0.0186	6.7291	0.1486	5.2589
18	9.024	0.1108	61.725	0.0162	6.8399	0.1462	5.4491
19	10.197	0.0981	70.749	0.0141	6.9380	0.1441	5.6265
20	11.523	0.0868	80.947	0.0124	7.0248	0.1424	5.7917
21	13.021	0.0768	92.470	0.0108	7.1016	0.1408	5.9454
22	14.714	0.0680	105.491	0.0095	7.1695	0.1395	6.0881
23	16.627	0.0601	120.205	0.0083	7.2297	0.1383	6.2205
24	18.788	0.0532	136.831	0.0073	7.2829	0.1373	6.3431
25	21.231	0.0471	155.619	0.0064	7.3300	0.1364	6.4566
26	23.990	0.0417	176.850	0.0057	7.3717	0.1357	6.5614
27	27.109	0.0369	200.840	0.0050	7.4086	0.1350	6.6582
28	30.633	0.0326	227.950	0.0044	7.4412	0.1344	6.7474
29	34.616	0.0289	258.583	0.0039	7.4701	0.1339	6.8296
30	39.116	0.0256	293.199	0.0034	7.4957	0.1334	6.9052
31	44.201	0.0226	332.315	0.0030	7.5183	0.1330	6.9747
32	49.947	0.0200	376.516	0.0027	7.5383	0.1327	7.0385
33	56.440	0.0177	426.463	0.0023	7.5560	0.1323	7.0971
34	63.777	0.0157	482.903	0.0021	7.5717	0.1321	7.1507
35	72.068	0.0139	546.680	0.0018	7.5856	0.1318	7.1998
36	81.437	0.0123	618.749	0.0016	7.5979	0.1316	7.2448
37	92.024	0.0109	700.186	0.0014	7.6087	0.1314	7.2858
38	103.987	0.0096	792.210	0.0013	7.6183	0.1313	7.3233
39	117.506	0.0085	896.197	0.0011	7.6268	0.1311	7.3576
40	132.781	0.0075	1,013.703	0.0010	7.6344	0.1310	7.3888
41	150.043	0.0067	1,146.484	0.0009	7.6410	0.1309	7.4172
42	169.549	0.0059	1,296.527	0.0008	7.6469	0.1308	7.4431
43	191.590	0.0052	1,466.076	0.0007	7.6522	0.1307	7.4667
44	216.497	0.0046	1,657.665	0.0006	7.6568	0.1306	7.4881
45	244.641	0.0041	1,874.162	0.0005	7.6609	0.1305	7.5076
46	276.444	0.0036	2,118.803	0.0005	7.6645	0.1305	7.5253
47	312.382	0.0032	2,395.247	0.0004	7.6677	0.1304	7.5414
48	352.992	0.0028	2,707.629	0.0004	7.6705	0.1304	7.5559
49	398.881	0.0025	3,060.621	0.0003	7.6730	0.1303	7.5692
50	450.735	0.0022	3,459.502	0.0003	7.6752	0.1303	7.5811

Interest Table for Annual Compounding with $i = 13\%$ (Contd.)

n	$F/p, i, n$	$P/F, i, n$	$F/A, i, n$	$A/F, i, n$	$P/A, i, n$	$A/P, i, n$	$A/G, i, n$
51	509.331	0.0020	3,910.237	0.0003	7.6772	0.1303	7.5920
52	575.544	0.0017	4,419.567	0.0002	7.6789	0.1302	7.6018
53	650.364	0.0015	4,995.111	0.0002	7.6805	0.1302	7.6107
54	734.912	0.0014	5,645.475	0.0002	7.6818	0.1302	7.6187
55	830.450	0.0012	6,380.387	0.0002	7.6830	0.1302	7.6260
56	938.409	0.0011	7,210.836	0.0001	7.6841	0.1301	7.6326
57	1,060.402	0.0009	8,149.245	0.0001	7.6851	0.1301	7.6385
58	1,198.254	0.0008	9,209.646	0.0001	7.6859	0.1301	7.6439
59	1,354.027	0.0007	10,407.900	0.0001	7.6866	0.1301	7.6487
60	1,530.050	0.0007	11,761.930	0.0001	7.6873	0.1301	7.6531
61	1,728.957	0.0006	13,291.980	0.0001	7.6879	0.1301	7.6570
62	1,953.721	0.0005	15,020.930	0.0001	7.6884	0.1301	7.6606
63	2,207.705	0.0005	16,974.650	0.0001	7.6888	0.1301	7.6638
64	2,494.707	0.0004	19,182.360	0.0001	7.6892	0.1301	7.6666
65	2,819.018	0.0004	21,677.070	0.0000	7.6896	0.1300	7.6692
66	3,185.491	0.0003	24,496.090	0.0000	7.6899	0.1300	7.6716
67	3,599.605	0.0003	27,681.580	0.0000	7.6902	0.1300	7.6737
68	4,067.553	0.0002	31,281.180	0.0000	7.6904	0.1300	7.6756
69	4,596.335	0.0002	35,348.730	0.0000	7.6906	0.1300	7.6773
70	5,193.858	0.0002	39,945.060	0.0000	7.6908	0.1300	7.6788
71	5,869.060	0.0002	45,138.920	0.0000	7.6910	0.1300	7.6802
72	6,632.036	0.0002	51,007.980	0.0000	7.6911	0.1300	7.6814
73	7,494.201	0.0001	57,640.010	0.0000	7.6913	0.1300	7.6826
74	8,468.446	0.0001	65,134.210	0.0000	7.6914	0.1300	7.6836
75	9,569.345	0.0001	73,602.660	0.0000	7.6915	0.1300	7.6845
76	10,813.360	0.0001	83,172.000	0.0000	7.6916	0.1300	7.6853
77	12,219.100	0.0001	93,985.340	0.0000	7.6917	0.1300	7.6860
78	13,807.580	0.0001	1,06,204.500	0.0000	7.6918	0.1300	7.6867
79	15,602.560	0.0001	1,20,012.000	0.0000	7.6918	0.1300	7.6872
80	17,630.900	0.0001	1,35,614.600	0.0000	7.6919	0.1300	7.6878
81	19,922.910	0.0001	1,53,245.500	0.0000	7.6919	0.1300	7.6882
82	22,512.890	0.0000	1,73,168.400	0.0000	7.6920	0.1300	7.6887
83	25,439.560	0.0000	1,95,681.300	0.0000	7.6920	0.1300	7.6890
84	28,746.700	0.0000	2,21,120.800	0.0000	7.6920	0.1300	7.6894
85	32,483.770	0.0000	2,49,867.500	0.0000	7.6921	0.1300	7.6897
86	36,706.670	0.0000	2,82,351.300	0.0000	7.6921	0.1300	7.6900
87	41,478.530	0.0000	3,19,058.000	0.0000	7.6921	0.1300	7.6902
88	46,870.730	0.0000	3,60,536.400	0.0000	7.6921	0.1300	7.6904
89	52,963.930	0.0000	4,07,407.200	0.0000	7.6922	0.1300	7.6906
90	59,849.240	0.0000	4,60,371.100	0.0000	7.6922	0.1300	7.6908
91	67,629.650	0.0000	5,20,220.400	0.0000	7.6922	0.1300	7.6910
92	76,421.490	0.0000	5,87,849.900	0.0000	7.6922	0.1300	7.6911
93	86,356.270	0.0000	6,64,271.300	0.0000	7.6922	0.1300	7.6912
94	97,582.590	0.0000	7,50,627.700	0.0000	7.6922	0.1300	7.6913
95	1,10,268.300	0.0000	8,48,210.200	0.0000	7.6922	0.1300	7.6914
96	1,24,603.200	0.0000	9,58,478.500	0.0000	7.6922	0.1300	7.6915
97	1,40,801.600	0.0000	10,83,082.000	0.0000	7.6923	0.1300	7.6916
98	1,59,105.800	0.0000	12,23,883.000	0.0000	7.6923	0.1300	7.6917
99	1,79,789.600	0.0000	13,82,989.000	0.0000	7.6923	0.1300	7.6918
100	2,03,162.200	0.0000	15,62,779.000	0.0000	7.6923	0.1300	7.6918

Interest Table for Annual Compounding with *i* = 14%

n	F/p,i,n	P/F,i,n	F/A,i,n	A/F,i,n	P/A,i,n	A/P,i,n	A/G,i,n
1	1.140	0.8772	1.000	1.0000	0.8772	1.1400	0.0000
2	1.300	0.7695	2.140	0.4673	1.6467	0.6073	0.4673
3	1.482	0.6750	3.440	0.2907	2.3216	0.4307	0.9129
4	1.689	0.5921	4.921	0.2032	2.9137	0.3432	1.3370
5	1.925	0.5194	6.610	0.1513	3.4331	0.2913	1.7399
6	2.195	0.4556	8.536	0.1172	3.8887	0.2572	2.1218
7	2.502	0.3996	10.730	0.0932	4.2883	0.2332	2.4832
8	2.853	0.3506	13.233	0.0756	4.6389	0.2156	2.8246
9	3.252	0.3075	16.085	0.0622	4.9464	0.2022	3.1463
10	3.707	0.2697	19.337	0.0517	5.2161	0.1917	3.4490
11	4.226	0.2366	23.045	0.0434	5.4527	0.1834	3.7333
12	4.818	0.2076	27.271	0.0367	5.6603	0.1767	3.9998
13	5.492	0.1821	32.089	0.0312	5.8424	0.1712	4.2491
14	6.261	0.1597	37.581	0.0266	6.0021	0.1666	4.4819
15	7.138	0.1401	43.842	0.0228	6.1422	0.1628	4.6990
16	8.137	0.1229	50.980	0.0196	6.2651	0.1596	4.9011
17	9.276	0.1078	59.118	0.0169	6.3729	0.1569	5.0888
18	10.575	0.0946	68.394	0.0146	6.4674	0.1546	5.2630
19	12.056	0.0829	78.969	0.0127	6.5504	0.1527	5.4243
20	13.743	0.0728	91.025	0.0110	6.6231	0.1510	5.5734
21	15.668	0.0638	104.768	0.0095	6.6870	0.1495	5.7111
22	17.861	0.0560	120.436	0.0083	6.7429	0.1483	5.8381
23	20.362	0.0491	138.297	0.0072	6.7921	0.1472	5.9549
24	23.212	0.0431	158.659	0.0063	6.8351	0.1463	6.0624
25	26.462	0.0378	181.871	0.0055	6.8729	0.1455	6.1610
26	30.167	0.0331	208.333	0.0048	6.9061	0.1448	6.2514
27	34.390	0.0291	238.499	0.0042	6.9352	0.1442	6.3342
28	39.204	0.0255	272.889	0.0037	6.9607	0.1437	6.4100
29	44.693	0.0224	312.094	0.0032	6.9830	0.1432	6.4791
30	50.950	0.0196	356.787	0.0028	7.0027	0.1428	6.5423
31	58.083	0.0172	407.737	0.0025	7.0199	0.1425	6.5998
32	66.215	0.0151	465.820	0.0021	7.0350	0.1421	6.6522
33	75.485	0.0132	532.035	0.0019	7.0482	0.1419	6.6998
34	86.053	0.0116	607.520	0.0016	7.0599	0.1416	6.7431
35	98.100	0.0102	693.573	0.0014	7.0700	0.1414	6.7824
36	111.834	0.0089	791.673	0.0013	7.0790	0.1413	6.8180
37	127.491	0.0078	903.507	0.0011	7.0868	0.1411	6.8503
38	145.340	0.0069	1,030.998	0.0010	7.0937	0.1410	6.8796
39	165.687	0.0060	1,176.338	0.0009	7.0997	0.1409	6.9060
40	188.884	0.0053	1,342.025	0.0007	7.1050	0.1407	6.9300
41	215.327	0.0046	1,530.909	0.0007	7.1097	0.1407	6.9516
42	245.473	0.0041	1,746.236	0.0006	7.1138	0.1406	6.9711
43	279.839	0.0036	1,991.709	0.0005	7.1173	0.1405	6.9886
44	319.017	0.0031	2,271.548	0.0004	7.1205	0.1404	7.0045
45	363.679	0.0027	2,590.565	0.0004	7.1232	0.1404	7.0188
46	414.594	0.0024	2,954.245	0.0003	7.1256	0.1403	7.0316
47	472.637	0.0021	3,368.839	0.0003	7.1277	0.1403	7.0432
48	538.807	0.0019	3,841.476	0.0003	7.1296	0.1403	7.0536
49	614.240	0.0016	4,380.283	0.0002	7.1312	0.1402	7.0630
50	700.233	0.0014	4,994.523	0.0002	7.1327	0.1402	7.0714

Interest Table for Annual Compounding with *i* = 14% (Contd.)

n	F/p,i,n	P/F,i,n	F/A,i,n	A/F,i,n	P/A,i,n	A/P,i,n	A/G,i,n
51	798.266	0.0013	5,694.756	0.0002	7.1339	0.1402	7.0789
52	910.023	0.0011	6,493.022	0.0002	7.1350	0.1402	7.0857
53	1,037.426	0.0010	7,403.045	0.0001	7.1360	0.1401	7.0917
54	1,182.666	0.0008	8,440.472	0.0001	7.1368	0.1401	7.0972
55	1,348.239	0.0007	9,623.137	0.0001	7.1376	0.1401	7.1020
56	1,536.993	0.0007	10,971.380	0.0001	7.1382	0.1401	7.1064
57	1,752.172	0.0006	12,508.370	0.0001	7.1388	0.1401	7.1103
58	1,997.476	0.0005	14,260.540	0.0001	7.1393	0.1401	7.1138
59	2,277.122	0.0004	16,258.020	0.0001	7.1397	0.1401	7.1169
60	2,595.920	0.0004	18,535.140	0.0001	7.1401	0.1401	7.1197
61	2,959.348	0.0003	21,131.060	0.0000	7.1404	0.1400	7.1222
62	3,373.657	0.0003	24,090.410	0.0000	7.1407	0.1400	7.1245
63	3,845.969	0.0003	27,464.060	0.0000	7.1410	0.1400	7.1265
64	4,384.405	0.0002	31,310.030	0.0000	7.1412	0.1400	7.1283
65	4,998.221	0.0002	35,694.430	0.0000	7.1414	0.1400	7.1299
66	5,697.972	0.0002	40,692.660	0.0000	7.1416	0.1400	7.1313
67	6,495.688	0.0002	46,390.630	0.0000	7.1418	0.1400	7.1325
68	7,405.085	0.0001	52,886.320	0.0000	7.1419	0.1400	7.1337
69	8,441.796	0.0001	60,291.400	0.0000	7.1420	0.1400	7.1347
70	9,623.649	0.0001	68,733.210	0.0000	7.1421	0.1400	7.1356
71	10,970.960	0.0001	78,356.850	0.0000	7.1422	0.1400	7.1364
72	12,506.890	0.0001	89,327.810	0.0000	7.1423	0.1400	7.1371
73	14,257.860	0.0001	1,01,834.700	0.0000	7.1424	0.1400	7.1377
74	16,253.960	0.0001	1,16,092.600	0.0000	7.1424	0.1400	7.1383
75	18,529.510	0.0001	1,32,346.500	0.0000	7.1425	0.1400	7.1388
76	21,123.640	0.0000	1,50,876.000	0.0000	7.1425	0.1400	7.1393
77	24,080.950	0.0000	1,71,999.700	0.0000	7.1426	0.1400	7.1397
78	27,452.290	0.0000	1,96,080.600	0.0000	7.1426	0.1400	7.1400
79	31,295.610	0.0000	2,23,532.900	0.0000	7.1426	0.1400	7.1403
80	35,676.990	0.0000	2,54,828.500	0.0000	7.1427	0.1400	7.1406
81	40,671.770	0.0000	2,90,505.500	0.0000	7.1427	0.1400	7.1409
82	46,365.830	0.0000	3,31,177.300	0.0000	7.1427	0.1400	7.1411
83	52,857.040	0.0000	3,77,543.100	0.0000	7.1427	0.1400	7.1413
84	60,257.030	0.0000	4,30,400.200	0.0000	7.1427	0.1400	7.1415
85	68,693.000	0.0000	4,90,657.200	0.0000	7.1428	0.1400	7.1416
86	78,310.030	0.0000	5,59,350.300	0.0000	7.1428	0.1400	7.1418
87	89,273.430	0.0000	6,37,660.200	0.0000	7.1428	0.1400	7.1419
88	1,01,771.700	0.0000	7,26,933.600	0.0000	7.1428	0.1400	7.1420
89	1,16,019.800	0.0000	8,28,705.400	0.0000	7.1428	0.1400	7.1421
90	1,32,262.500	0.0000	9,44,725.100	0.0000	7.1428	0.1400	7.1422
91	1,50,779.300	0.0000	10,76,988.000	0.0000	7.1428	0.1400	7.1423
92	1,71,888.400	0.0000	12,27,767.000	0.0000	7.1428	0.1400	7.1423
93	1,95,952.700	0.0000	13,99,655.000	0.0000	7.1428	0.1400	7.1424
94	2,23,386.200	0.0000	15,95,608.000	0.0000	7.1428	0.1400	7.1424
95	2,54,660.200	0.0000	18,18,994.000	0.0000	7.1428	0.1400	7.1425
96	2,90,312.600	0.0000	20,73,655.000	0.0000	7.1428	0.1400	7.1425
97	3,30,956.400	0.0000	23,63,967.000	0.0000	7.1428	0.1400	7.1426
98	3,77,290.300	0.0000	26,94,924.000	0.0000	7.1428	0.1400	7.1426
99	4,30,111.000	0.0000	30,72,214.000	0.0000	7.1428	0.1400	7.1426
100	4,90,326.500	0.0000	35,02,325.000	0.0000	7.1428	0.1400	7.1427

Interest Table for Annual Compounding with *i* = 15%

n	F/p,i,n	P/F,i,n	F/A,i,n	A/F,i,n	P/A,i,n	A/P,i,n	A/G,i,n
1	1.150	0.8696	1.000	1.0000	0.8696	1.1500	0.0000
2	1.323	0.7561	2.150	0.4651	1.6257	0.6151	0.4651
3	1.521	0.6575	3.472	0.2880	2.2832	0.4380	0.9071
4	1.749	0.5718	4.993	0.2003	2.8550	0.3503	1.3263
5	2.011	0.4972	6.742	0.1483	3.3522	0.2983	1.7228
6	2.313	0.4323	8.754	0.1142	3.7845	0.2642	2.0972
7	2.660	0.3759	11.067	0.0904	4.1604	0.2404	2.4498
8	3.059	0.3269	13.727	0.0729	4.4873	0.2229	2.7813
9	3.518	0.2843	16.786	0.0596	4.7716	0.2096	3.0922
10	4.046	0.2472	20.304	0.0493	5.0188	0.1993	3.3832
11	4.652	0.2149	24.349	0.0411	5.2337	0.1911	3.6549
12	5.350	0.1869	29.002	0.0345	5.4206	0.1845	3.9082
13	6.153	0.1625	34.352	0.0291	5.5831	0.1791	4.1438
14	7.076	0.1413	40.505	0.0247	5.7245	0.1747	4.3624
15	8.137	0.1229	47.580	0.0210	5.8474	0.1710	4.5650
16	9.358	0.1069	55.717	0.0179	5.9542	0.1679	4.7522
17	10.761	0.0929	65.075	0.0154	6.0472	0.1654	4.9251
18	12.375	0.0808	75.836	0.0132	6.1280	0.1632	5.0843
19	14.232	0.0703	88.212	0.0113	6.1982	0.1613	5.2307
20	16.367	0.0611	102.444	0.0098	6.2593	0.1598	5.3651
21	18.822	0.0531	118.810	0.0084	6.3125	0.1584	5.4883
22	21.645	0.0462	137.632	0.0073	6.3587	0.1573	5.6010
23	24.891	0.0402	159.276	0.0063	6.3988	0.1563	5.7040
24	28.625	0.0349	184.168	0.0054	6.4338	0.1554	5.7979
25	32.919	0.0304	212.793	0.0047	6.4641	0.1547	5.8834
26	37.857	0.0264	245.712	0.0041	6.4906	0.1541	5.9612
27	43.535	0.0230	283.569	0.0035	6.5135	0.1535	6.0319
28	50.066	0.0200	327.104	0.0031	6.5335	0.1531	6.0960
29	57.575	0.0174	377.170	0.0027	6.5509	0.1527	6.1541
30	66.212	0.0151	434.745	0.0023	6.5660	0.1523	6.2066
31	76.144	0.0131	500.957	0.0020	6.5791	0.1520	6.2541
32	87.565	0.0114	577.100	0.0017	6.5905	0.1517	6.2970
33	100.700	0.0099	664.666	0.0015	6.6005	0.1515	6.3357
34	115.805	0.0086	765.365	0.0013	6.6091	0.1513	6.3705
35	133.176	0.0075	881.170	0.0011	6.6166	0.1511	6.4019
36	153.152	0.0065	1,014.346	0.0010	6.6231	0.1510	6.4301
37	176.125	0.0057	1,167.497	0.0009	6.6288	0.1509	6.4554
38	202.543	0.0049	1,343.622	0.0007	6.6338	0.1507	6.4781
39	232.925	0.0043	1,546.166	0.0006	6.6380	0.1506	6.4985
40	267.864	0.0037	1,779.090	0.0006	6.6418	0.1506	6.5168
41	308.043	0.0032	2,046.954	0.0005	6.6450	0.1505	6.5331
42	354.250	0.0028	2,354.997	0.0004	6.6478	0.1504	6.5478
43	407.387	0.0025	2,709.247	0.0004	6.6503	0.1504	6.5609
44	468.495	0.0021	3,116.634	0.0003	6.6524	0.1503	6.5725
45	538.769	0.0019	3,585.128	0.0003	6.6543	0.1503	6.5830
46	619.585	0.0016	4,123.898	0.0002	6.6559	0.1502	6.5923
47	712.522	0.0014	4,743.483	0.0002	6.6573	0.1502	6.6006
48	819.401	0.0012	5,456.005	0.0002	6.6585	0.1502	6.6080
49	942.311	0.0011	6,275.406	0.0002	6.6596	0.1502	6.6146
50	1,083.658	0.0009	7,217.717	0.0001	6.6605	0.1501	6.6205

Interest Table for Annual Compounding with i = 15% (Contd.)

n	$F/p,i,n$	$P/F,i,n$	$F/A,i,n$	$A/F,i,n$	$P/A,i,n$	$A/P,i,n$	$A/G,i,n$
51	1,246.206	0.0008	8,301.373	0.0001	6.6613	0.1501	6.6257
52	1,433.137	0.0007	9,547.581	0.0001	6.6620	0.1501	6.6304
53	1,648.108	0.0006	10,980.720	0.0001	6.6626	0.1501	6.6345
54	1,895.324	0.0005	12,628.820	0.0001	6.6631	0.1501	6.6382
55	2,179.622	0.0005	14,524.150	0.0001	6.6636	0.1501	6.6414
56	2,506.566	0.0004	16,703.770	0.0001	6.6640	0.1501	6.6443
57	2,882.551	0.0003	19,210.340	0.0001	6.6644	0.1501	6.6469
58	3,314.933	0.0003	22,092.890	0.0000	6.6647	0.1500	6.6492
59	3,812.173	0.0003	25,407.820	0.0000	6.6649	0.1500	6.6512
60	4,383.999	0.0002	29,219.990	0.0000	6.6651	0.1500	6.6530
61	5,041.599	0.0002	33,603.990	0.0000	6.6653	0.1500	6.6546
62	5,797.839	0.0002	38,645.590	0.0000	6.6655	0.1500	6.6560
63	6,667.515	0.0001	44,443.440	0.0000	6.6657	0.1500	6.6572
64	7,667.642	0.0001	51,110.940	0.0000	6.6658	0.1500	6.6583
65	8,817.787	0.0001	58,778.580	0.0000	6.6659	0.1500	6.6593
66	10,140.460	0.0001	67,596.370	0.0000	6.6660	0.1500	6.6602
67	11,661.530	0.0001	77,736.830	0.0000	6.6661	0.1500	6.6609
68	13,410.750	0.0001	89,398.350	0.0000	6.6662	0.1500	6.6616
69	15,422.370	0.0001	1,02,809.100	0.0000	6.6662	0.1500	6.6622
70	17,735.720	0.0001	1,18,231.500	0.0000	6.6663	0.1500	6.6627
71	20,396.080	0.0000	1,35,967.200	0.0000	6.6663	0.1500	6.6632
72	23,455.490	0.0000	1,56,363.300	0.0000	6.6664	0.1500	6.6636
73	26,973.810	0.0000	1,79,818.800	0.0000	6.6664	0.1500	6.6640
74	31,019.890	0.0000	2,06,792.600	0.0000	6.6665	0.1500	6.6643
75	35,672.870	0.0000	2,37,812.500	0.0000	6.6665	0.1500	6.6646
76	41,023.800	0.0000	2,73,485.300	0.0000	6.6665	0.1500	6.6648
77	47,177.370	0.0000	3,14,509.100	0.0000	6.6665	0.1500	6.6650
78	54,253.980	0.0000	3,61,686.500	0.0000	6.6665	0.1500	6.6652
79	62,392.080	0.0000	4,15,940.500	0.0000	6.6666	0.1500	6.6654
80	71,750.880	0.0000	4,78,332.600	0.0000	6.6666	0.1500	6.6656
81	82,513.520	0.0000	5,50,083.500	0.0000	6.6666	0.1500	6.6657
82	94,890.550	0.0000	6,32,597.000	0.0000	6.6666	0.1500	6.6658
83	1,09,124.100	0.0000	7,27,487.500	0.0000	6.6666	0.1500	6.6659
84	1,25,492.800	0.0000	8,36,611.700	0.0000	6.6666	0.1500	6.6660
85	1,44,316.700	0.0000	9,62,104.300	0.0000	6.6666	0.1500	6.6661
86	1,65,964.200	0.0000	11,06,421.000	0.0000	6.6666	0.1500	6.6661
87	1,90,858.800	0.0000	12,72,385.000	0.0000	6.6666	0.1500	6.6662
88	2,19,487.600	0.0000	14,63,244.000	0.0000	6.6666	0.1500	6.6663
89	2,52,410.700	0.0000	16,82,732.000	0.0000	6.6666	0.1500	6.6663
90	2,90,272.400	0.0000	19,35,142.000	0.0000	6.6666	0.1500	6.6664
91	3,33,813.200	0.0000	22,25,415.000	0.0000	6.6666	0.1500	6.6664
92	3,83,885.200	0.0000	25,59,228.000	0.0000	6.6666	0.1500	6.6664
93	4,41,468.000	0.0000	29,43,113.000	0.0000	6.6667	0.1500	6.6665
94	5,07,688.200	0.0000	33,84,581.000	0.0000	6.6667	0.1500	6.6665
95	5,83,841.500	0.0000	38,92,270.000	0.0000	6.6667	0.1500	6.6665
96	6,71,417.600	0.0000	44,76,110.000	0.0000	6.6667	0.1500	6.6665
97	7,72,130.200	0.0000	51,47,528.000	0.0000	6.6667	0.1500	6.6665
98	8,87,949.700	0.0000	59,19,658.000	0.0000	6.6667	0.1500	6.6666
99	10,21,142.000	0.0000	68,07,608.000	0.0000	6.6667	0.1500	6.6666
100	11,74,314.000	0.0000	78,28,750.000	0.0000	6.6667	0.1500	6.6666

Interest Table for Annual Compounding with $i = 16\%$

n	$F/p,i,n$	$P/F,i,n$	$F/A,i,n$	$A/F,i,n$	$P/A,i,n$	$A/P,i,n$	$A/G,i,n$
1	1.160	0.8621	1.000	1.0000	0.8621	1.1600	0.0000
2	1.346	0.7432	2.160	0.4630	1.6052	0.6230	0.4630
3	1.561	0.6407	3.506	0.2853	2.2459	0.4453	0.9014
4	1.811	0.5523	5.066	0.1974	2.7982	0.3574	1.3156
5	2.100	0.4761	6.877	0.1454	3.2743	0.3054	1.7060
6	2.436	0.4104	8.977	0.1114	3.6847	0.2714	2.0729
7	2.826	0.3538	11.414	0.0876	4.0386	0.2476	2.4169
8	3.278	0.3050	14.240	0.0702	4.3436	0.2302	2.7388
9	3.803	0.2630	17.518	0.0571	4.6065	0.2171	3.0391
10	4.411	0.2267	21.321	0.0469	4.8332	0.2069	3.3187
11	5.117	0.1954	25.733	0.0389	5.0286	0.1989	3.5783
12	5.936	0.1685	30.850	0.0324	5.1971	0.1924	3.8189
13	6.886	0.1452	36.786	0.0272	5.3423	0.1872	4.0413
14	7.988	0.1252	43.672	0.0229	5.4675	0.1829	4.2464
15	9.266	0.1079	51.659	0.0194	5.5755	0.1794	4.4352
16	10.748	0.0930	60.925	0.0164	5.6685	0.1764	4.6086
17	12.468	0.0802	71.673	0.0140	5.7487	0.1740	4.7676
18	14.463	0.0691	84.141	0.0119	5.8178	0.1719	4.9130
19	16.777	0.0596	98.603	0.0101	5.8775	0.1701	5.0457
20	19.461	0.0514	115.380	0.0087	5.9288	0.1687	5.1666
21	22.574	0.0443	134.840	0.0074	5.9731	0.1674	5.2766
22	26.186	0.0382	157.415	0.0064	6.0113	0.1664	5.3765
23	30.376	0.0329	183.601	0.0054	6.0442	0.1654	5.4671
24	35.236	0.0284	213.977	0.0047	6.0726	0.1647	5.5490
25	40.874	0.0245	249.214	0.0040	6.0971	0.1640	5.6230
26	47.414	0.0211	290.088	0.0034	6.1182	0.1634	5.6898
27	55.000	0.0182	337.502	0.0030	6.1364	0.1630	5.7500
28	63.800	0.0157	392.502	0.0025	6.1520	0.1625	5.8041
29	74.008	0.0135	456.303	0.0022	6.1656	0.1622	5.8528
30	85.850	0.0116	530.311	0.0019	6.1772	0.1619	5.8964
31	99.586	0.0100	616.161	0.0016	6.1872	0.1616	5.9356
32	115.519	0.0087	715.747	0.0014	6.1959	0.1614	5.9706
33	134.003	0.0075	831.266	0.0012	6.2034	0.1612	6.0019
34	155.443	0.0064	965.269	0.0010	6.2098	0.1610	6.0299
35	180.314	0.0055	1,120.711	0.0009	6.2153	0.1609	6.0548
36	209.164	0.0048	1,301.025	0.0008	6.2201	0.1608	6.0771
37	242.630	0.0041	1,510.189	0.0007	6.2242	0.1607	6.0969
38	281.451	0.0036	1,752.819	0.0006	6.2278	0.1606	6.1145
39	326.483	0.0031	2,034.270	0.0005	6.2309	0.1605	6.1302
40	378.721	0.0026	2,360.754	0.0004	6.2335	0.1604	6.1441
41	439.316	0.0023	2,739.474	0.0004	6.2358	0.1604	6.1565
42	509.606	0.0020	3,178.790	0.0003	6.2377	0.1603	6.1674
43	591.143	0.0017	3,688.396	0.0003	6.2394	0.1603	6.1771
44	685.726	0.0015	4,279.539	0.0002	6.2409	0.1602	6.1857
45	795.442	0.0013	4,965.265	0.0002	6.2421	0.1602	6.1934
46	922.713	0.0011	5,760.707	0.0002	6.2432	0.1602	6.2001
47	1,070.347	0.0009	6,683.419	0.0001	6.2442	0.1601	6.2060
48	1,241.603	0.0008	7,753.767	0.0001	6.2450	0.1601	6.2113
49	1,440.259	0.0007	8,995.369	0.0001	6.2457	0.1601	6.2160
50	1,670.701	0.0006	10,435.630	0.0001	6.2463	0.1601	6.2201

Interest Table for Annual Compounding with *i* = 16% (Contd.)

n	$F/p, i, n$	$P/F, i, n$	$F/A, i, n$	$A/F, i, n$	$P/A, i, n$	$A/P, i, n$	$A/G, i, n$
51	1,938.013	0.0005	12,106.330	0.0001	6.2468	0.1601	6.2237
52	2,248.094	0.0004	14,044.340	0.0001	6.2472	0.1601	6.2269
53	2,607.790	0.0004	16,292.440	0.0001	6.2476	0.1601	6.2297
54	3,025.036	0.0003	18,900.220	0.0001	6.2479	0.1601	6.2321
55	3,509.041	0.0003	21,925.260	0.0000	6.2482	0.1600	6.2343
56	4,070.487	0.0002	25,434.300	0.0000	6.2485	0.1600	6.2362
57	4,721.765	0.0002	29,504.780	0.0000	6.2487	0.1600	6.2379
58	5,477.247	0.0002	34,226.550	0.0000	6.2489	0.1600	6.2394
59	6,353.607	0.0002	39,703.790	0.0000	6.2490	0.1600	6.2407
60	7,370.183	0.0001	46,057.400	0.0000	6.2492	0.1600	6.2419
61	8,549.413	0.0001	53,427.580	0.0000	6.2493	0.1600	6.2429
62	9,917.318	0.0001	61,976.990	0.0000	6.2494	0.1600	6.2437
63	11,504.090	0.0001	71,894.310	0.0000	6.2495	0.1600	6.2445
64	13,344.740	0.0001	83,398.400	0.0000	6.2495	0.1600	6.2452
65	15,479.900	0.0001	96,743.130	0.0000	6.2496	0.1600	6.2458
66	17,956.680	0.0001	1,12,223.000	0.0000	6.2497	0.1600	6.2463
67	20,829.750	0.0000	1,30,179.700	0.0000	6.2497	0.1600	6.2468
68	24,162.510	0.0000	1,51,009.500	0.0000	6.2497	0.1600	6.2472
69	28,028.510	0.0000	1,75,172.000	0.0000	6.2498	0.1600	6.2475
70	32,513.070	0.0000	2,03,200.500	0.0000	6.2498	0.1600	6.2478
71	37,715.160	0.0000	2,35,713.500	0.0000	6.2498	0.1600	6.2481
72	43,749.590	0.0000	2,73,428.700	0.0000	6.2499	0.1600	6.2484
73	50,749.520	0.0000	3,17,178.300	0.0000	6.2499	0.1600	6.2486
74	58,869.440	0.0000	3,67,927.800	0.0000	6.2499	0.1600	6.2487
75	68,288.550	0.0000	4,26,797.200	0.0000	6.2499	0.1600	6.2489
76	79,214.710	0.0000	4,95,085.700	0.0000	6.2499	0.1600	6.2490
77	91,889.060	0.0000	5,74,300.400	0.0000	6.2499	0.1600	6.2492
78	1,06,591.300	0.0000	6,66,189.500	0.0000	6.2499	0.1600	6.2493
79	1,23,645.900	0.0000	7,72,780.600	0.0000	6.2499	0.1600	6.2494
80	1,43,429.300	0.0000	8,96,426.600	0.0000	6.2500	0.1600	6.2494
81	1,66,377.900	0.0000	10,39,856.000	0.0000	6.2500	0.1600	6.2495
82	1,92,998.400	0.0000	12,06,234.000	0.0000	6.2500	0.1600	6.2496
83	2,23,878.100	0.0000	13,99,232.000	0.0000	6.2500	0.1600	6.2496
84	2,59,698.600	0.0000	16,23,110.000	0.0000	6.2500	0.1600	6.2497
85	3,01,250.400	0.0000	18,82,809.000	0.0000	6.2500	0.1600	6.2497
86	3,49,450.400	0.0000	21,84,059.000	0.0000	6.2500	0.1600	6.2498
87	4,05,362.500	0.0000	25,33,509.000	0.0000	6.2500	0.1600	6.2498
88	4,70,220.500	0.0000	29,38,872.000	0.0000	6.2500	0.1600	6.2498
89	5,45,455.700	0.0000	34,09,092.000	0.0000	6.2500	0.1600	6.2498
90	6,32,728.600	0.0000	39,54,547.000	0.0000	6.2500	0.1600	6.2499
91	7,33,965.100	0.0000	45,87,276.000	0.0000	6.2500	0.1600	6.2499
92	8,51,399.400	0.0000	53,21,241.000	0.0000	6.2500	0.1600	6.2499
93	9,87,623.400	0.0000	61,72,641.000	0.0000	6.2500	0.1600	6.2499
94	11,45,643.000	0.0000	71,60,263.000	0.0000	6.2500	0.1600	6.2499
95	13,28,946.000	0.0000	83,05,905.000	0.0000	6.2500	0.1600	6.2499
96	15,41,577.000	0.0000	96,34,852.000	0.0000	6.2500	0.1600	6.2499
97	17,88,230.000	0.0000	1,11,76,430.000	0.0000	6.2500	0.1600	6.2499
98	20,74,346.000	0.0000	1,29,64,660.000	0.0000	6.2500	0.1600	6.2500
99	24,06,241.000	0.0000	1,50,39,000.000	0.0000	6.2500	0.1600	6.2500
100	27,91,240.000	0.0000	1,74,45,240.000	0.0000	6.2500	0.1600	6.2500

Interest Table for Annual Compounding with *i* = 17%

n	F/p,i,n	P/F,i,n	F/A,i,n	A/F,i,n	P/A,i,n	A/P,i,n	A/G,i,n
1	1.170	0.8547	1.000	1.0000	0.8547	1.1700	0.0000
2	1.369	0.7305	2.170	0.4608	1.5852	0.6308	0.4608
3	1.602	0.6244	3.539	0.2826	2.2096	0.4526	0.8958
4	1.874	0.5337	5.141	0.1945	2.7432	0.3645	1.3051
5	2.192	0.4561	7.014	0.1426	3.1993	0.3126	1.6893
6	2.565	0.3898	9.207	0.1086	3.5892	0.2786	2.0489
7	3.001	0.3332	11.772	0.0849	3.9224	0.2549	2.3845
8	3.511	0.2848	14.773	0.0677	4.2072	0.2377	2.6969
9	4.108	0.2434	18.285	0.0547	4.4506	0.2247	2.9870
10	4.807	0.2080	22.393	0.0447	4.6586	0.2147	3.2555
11	5.624	0.1778	27.200	0.0368	4.8364	0.2068	3.5035
12	6.580	0.1520	32.824	0.0305	4.9884	0.2005	3.7318
13	7.699	0.1299	39.404	0.0254	5.1183	0.1954	3.9417
14	9.007	0.1110	47.103	0.0212	5.2293	0.1912	4.1340
15	10.539	0.0949	56.110	0.0178	5.3242	0.1878	4.3098
16	12.330	0.0811	66.649	0.0150	5.4053	0.1850	4.4702
17	14.426	0.0693	78.979	0.0127	5.4746	0.1827	4.6162
18	16.879	0.0592	93.406	0.0107	5.5339	0.1807	4.7488
19	19.748	0.0506	110.285	0.0091	5.5845	0.1791	4.8689
20	23.106	0.0433	130.033	0.0077	5.6278	0.1777	4.9776
21	27.034	0.0370	153.138	0.0065	5.6648	0.1765	5.0757
22	31.629	0.0316	180.172	0.0056	5.6964	0.1756	5.1641
23	37.006	0.0270	211.801	0.0047	5.7234	0.1747	5.2436
24	43.297	0.0231	248.807	0.0040	5.7465	0.1740	5.3149
25	50.658	0.0197	292.105	0.0034	5.7662	0.1734	5.3789
26	59.270	0.0169	342.762	0.0029	5.7831	0.1729	5.4362
27	69.345	0.0144	402.032	0.0025	5.7975	0.1725	5.4873
28	81.134	0.0123	471.378	0.0021	5.8099	0.1721	5.5329
29	94.927	0.0105	552.512	0.0018	5.8204	0.1718	5.5736
30	111.065	0.0090	647.439	0.0015	5.8294	0.1715	5.6098
31	129.946	0.0077	758.503	0.0013	5.8371	0.1713	5.6419
32	152.036	0.0066	888.449	0.0011	5.8437	0.1711	5.6705
33	177.882	0.0056	1,040.485	0.0010	5.8493	0.1710	5.6958
34	208.122	0.0048	1,218.367	0.0008	5.8541	0.1708	5.7182
35	243.503	0.0041	1,426.490	0.0007	5.8582	0.1707	5.7380
36	284.899	0.0035	1,669.993	0.0006	5.8617	0.1706	5.7555
37	333.332	0.0030	1,954.892	0.0005	5.8647	0.1705	5.7710
38	389.998	0.0026	2,288.224	0.0004	5.8673	0.1704	5.7847
39	456.298	0.0022	2,678.221	0.0004	5.8695	0.1704	5.7967
40	533.868	0.0019	3,134.519	0.0003	5.8713	0.1703	5.8073
41	624.626	0.0016	3,668.387	0.0003	5.8729	0.1703	5.8166
42	730.812	0.0014	4,293.013	0.0002	5.8743	0.1702	5.8248
43	855.050	0.0012	5,023.825	0.0002	5.8755	0.1702	5.8320
44	1,000.409	0.0010	5,878.875	0.0002	5.8765	0.1702	5.8383
45	1,170.478	0.0009	6,879.283	0.0001	5.8773	0.1701	5.8439
46	1,369.459	0.0007	8,049.761	0.0001	5.8781	0.1701	5.8487
47	1,602.268	0.0006	9,419.221	0.0001	5.8787	0.1701	5.8530
48	1,874.653	0.0005	11,021.490	0.0001	5.8792	0.1701	5.8567
49	2,193.344	0.0005	12,896.140	0.0001	5.8797	0.1701	5.8600
50	2,566.213	0.0004	15,089.490	0.0001	5.8801	0.1701	5.8629

Interest Table for Annual Compounding with *i* = 17% (Contd.)

n	F/p,i,n	P/F,i,n	F/A,i,n	A/F,i,n	P/A,i,n	A/P,i,n	A/G,i,n
51	3,002.468	0.0003	17,655.690	0.0001	5.8804	0.1701	5.8654
52	3,512.888	0.0003	20,658.160	0.0000	5.8807	0.1700	5.8675
53	4,110.078	0.0002	24,171.050	0.0000	5.8809	0.1700	5.8695
54	4,808.792	0.0002	28,281.130	0.0000	5.8811	0.1700	5.8711
55	5,626.286	0.0002	33,089.920	0.0000	5.8813	0.1700	5.8726
56	6,582.756	0.0002	38,716.210	0.0000	5.8815	0.1700	5.8738
57	7,701.823	0.0001	45,298.960	0.0000	5.8816	0.1700	5.8750
58	9,011.133	0.0001	53,000.780	0.0000	5.8817	0.1700	5.8759
59	10,543.030	0.0001	62,011.910	0.0000	5.8818	0.1700	5.8768
60	12,335.340	0.0001	72,554.940	0.0000	5.8819	0.1700	5.8775
61	14,432.350	0.0001	84,890.270	0.0000	5.8819	0.1700	5.8781
62	16,885.840	0.0001	99,322.610	0.0000	5.8820	0.1700	5.8787
63	19,756.440	0.0001	1,16,208.500	0.0000	5.8821	0.1700	5.8792
64	23,115.030	0.0000	1,35,964.900	0.0000	5.8821	0.1700	5.8796
65	27,044.590	0.0000	1,59,079.900	0.0000	5.8821	0.1700	5.8799
66	31,642.170	0.0000	1,86,124.500	0.0000	5.8822	0.1700	5.8803
67	37,021.330	0.0000	2,17,766.700	0.0000	5.8822	0.1700	5.8805
68	43,314.960	0.0000	2,54,788.000	0.0000	5.8822	0.1700	5.8808
69	50,678.500	0.0000	2,98,102.900	0.0000	5.8822	0.1700	5.8810
70	59,293.850	0.0000	3,48,781.500	0.0000	5.8823	0.1700	5.8812
71	69,373.790	0.0000	4,08,075.200	0.0000	5.8823	0.1700	5.8813
72	81,167.340	0.0000	4,77,449.100	0.0000	5.8823	0.1700	5.8815
73	94,965.780	0.0000	5,58,616.400	0.0000	5.8823	0.1700	5.8816
74	1,11,110.000	0.0000	6,53,582.200	0.0000	5.8823	0.1700	5.8817
75	1,29,998.700	0.0000	7,64,692.100	0.0000	5.8823	0.1700	5.8818
76	1,52,098.400	0.0000	8,94,690.700	0.0000	5.8823	0.1700	5.8819
77	1,77,955.100	0.0000	10,46,789.000	0.0000	5.8823	0.1700	5.8819
78	2,08,207.500	0.0000	12,24,744.000	0.0000	5.8823	0.1700	5.8820
79	2,43,602.800	0.0000	14,32,952.000	0.0000	5.8823	0.1700	5.8820
80	2,85,015.300	0.0000	16,76,554.000	0.0000	5.8823	0.1700	5.8821
81	3,33,467.900	0.0000	19,61,570.000	0.0000	5.8823	0.1700	5.8821
82	3,90,157.400	0.0000	22,95,038.000	0.0000	5.8823	0.1700	5.8821
83	4,56,484.100	0.0000	26,85,195.000	0.0000	5.8823	0.1700	5.8822
84	5,34,086.400	0.0000	31,41,679.000	0.0000	5.8823	0.1700	5.8822
85	6,24,881.000	0.0000	36,75,765.000	0.0000	5.8823	0.1700	5.8822
86	7,31,110.800	0.0000	43,00,646.000	0.0000	5.8823	0.1700	5.8822
87	8,55,399.600	0.0000	50,31,757.000	0.0000	5.8823	0.1700	5.8823
88	10,00,818.000	0.0000	58,87,157.000	0.0000	5.8823	0.1700	5.8823
89	11,70,957.000	0.0000	68,87,974.000	0.0000	5.8823	0.1700	5.8823
90	13,70,019.000	0.0000	80,58,930.000	0.0000	5.8823	0.1700	5.8823
91	16,02,922.000	0.0000	94,28,948.000	0.0000	5.8823	0.1700	5.8823
92	18,75,419.000	0.0000	1,10,31,870.000	0.0000	5.8824	0.1700	5.8823
93	21,94,240.000	0.0000	1,29,07,290.000	0.0000	5.8824	0.1700	5.8823
94	25,67,261.000	0.0000	1,51,01,530.000	0.0000	5.8824	0.1700	5.8823
95	30,03,695.000	0.0000	1,76,68,790.000	0.0000	5.8824	0.1700	5.8823
96	35,14,324.000	0.0000	2,06,72,490.000	0.0000	5.8824	0.1700	5.8823
97	41,11,758.000	0.0000	2,41,86,810.000	0.0000	5.8824	0.1700	5.8823
98	48,10,758.000	0.0000	2,82,98,570.000	0.0000	5.8824	0.1700	5.8823
99	56,28,586.000	0.0000	3,31,09,320.000	0.0000	5.8824	0.1700	5.8823
100	65,85,446.000	0.0000	3,87,37,910.000	0.0000	5.8824	0.1700	5.8823

Interest Table for Annual Compounding with $i = 18\%$

n	F/p,i,n	P/F,i,n	F/A,i,n	A/F,i,n	P/A,i,n	A/P,i,n	A/G,i,n
1	1.180	0.8475	1.000	1.0000	0.8475	1.1800	0.0000
2	1.392	0.7182	2.180	0.4587	1.5656	0.6387	0.4587
3	1.643	0.6086	3.572	0.2799	2.1743	0.4599	0.8902
4	1.939	0.5158	5.215	0.1917	2.6901	0.3717	1.2947
5	2.288	0.4371	7.154	0.1398	3.1272	0.3198	1.6728
6	2.700	0.3704	9.442	0.1059	3.4976	0.2859	2.0252
7	3.185	0.3139	12.142	0.0824	3.8115	0.2624	2.3526
8	3.759	0.2660	15.327	0.0652	4.0776	0.2452	2.6558
9	4.435	0.2255	19.086	0.0524	4.3030	0.2324	2.9358
10	5.234	0.1911	23.521	0.0425	4.4941	0.2225	3.1936
11	6.176	0.1619	28.755	0.0348	4.6560	0.2148	3.4303
12	7.288	0.1372	34.931	0.0286	4.7932	0.2086	3.6470
13	8.599	0.1163	42.219	0.0237	4.9095	0.2037	3.8449
14	10.147	0.0985	50.818	0.0197	5.0081	0.1997	4.0250
15	11.974	0.0835	60.965	0.0164	5.0916	0.1964	4.1887
16	14.129	0.0708	72.939	0.0137	5.1624	0.1937	4.3369
17	16.672	0.0600	87.068	0.0115	5.2223	0.1915	4.4708
18	19.673	0.0508	103.740	0.0096	5.2732	0.1896	4.5916
19	23.214	0.0431	123.414	0.0081	5.3162	0.1881	4.7003
20	27.393	0.0365	146.628	0.0068	5.3527	0.1868	4.7978
21	32.324	0.0309	174.021	0.0057	5.3837	0.1857	4.8851
22	38.142	0.0262	206.345	0.0048	5.4099	0.1848	4.9632
23	45.008	0.0222	244.487	0.0041	5.4321	0.1841	5.0329
24	53.109	0.0188	289.495	0.0035	5.4509	0.1835	5.0950
25	62.669	0.0160	342.604	0.0029	5.4669	0.1829	5.1502
26	73.949	0.0135	405.273	0.0025	5.4804	0.1825	5.1991
27	87.260	0.0115	479.222	0.0021	5.4919	0.1821	5.2425
28	102.967	0.0097	566.482	0.0018	5.5016	0.1818	5.2810
29	121.501	0.0082	669.449	0.0015	5.5098	0.1815	5.3149
30	143.371	0.0070	790.949	0.0013	5.5168	0.1813	5.3448
31	169.178	0.0059	934.320	0.0011	5.5227	0.1811	5.3712
32	199.630	0.0050	1,103.498	0.0009	5.5277	0.1809	5.3945
33	235.563	0.0042	1,303.128	0.0008	5.5320	0.1808	5.4149
34	277.964	0.0036	1,538.691	0.0006	5.5356	0.1806	5.4328
35	327.998	0.0030	1,816.655	0.0006	5.5386	0.1806	5.4485
36	387.038	0.0026	2,144.653	0.0005	5.5412	0.1805	5.4623
37	456.704	0.0022	2,531.691	0.0004	5.5434	0.1804	5.4744
38	538.911	0.0019	2,988.395	0.0003	5.5452	0.1803	5.4849
39	635.915	0.0016	3,527.307	0.0003	5.5468	0.1803	5.4941
40	750.380	0.0013	4,163.222	0.0002	5.5482	0.1802	5.5022
41	885.448	0.0011	4,913.602	0.0002	5.5493	0.1802	5.5092
42	1,044.829	0.0010	5,799.051	0.0002	5.5502	0.1802	5.5153
43	1,232.899	0.0008	6,843.881	0.0001	5.5510	0.1801	5.5206
44	1,454.820	0.0007	8,076.780	0.0001	5.5517	0.1801	5.5253
45	1,716.688	0.0006	9,531.599	0.0001	5.5523	0.1801	5.5293
46	2,025.692	0.0005	11,248.290	0.0001	5.5528	0.1801	5.5328
47	2,390.317	0.0004	13,273.980	0.0001	5.5532	0.1801	5.5359
48	2,820.574	0.0004	15,664.300	0.0001	5.5536	0.1801	5.5385
49	3,328.277	0.0003	18,484.870	0.0001	5.5539	0.1801	5.5408
50	3,927.368	0.0003	21,813.150	0.0000	5.5541	0.1800	5.5428

Interest Table for Annual Compounding with *i* = 18% (Contd.)

n	F/p, i, n	P/F, i, n	F/A, i, n	A/F, i, n	P/A, i, n	A/P, i, n	A/G, i, n
51	4,634.294	0.0002	25,740.520	0.0000	5.5544	0.1800	5.5445
52	5,468.468	0.0002	30,374.820	0.0000	5.5545	0.1800	5.5460
53	6,452.792	0.0002	35,843.290	0.0000	5.5547	0.1800	5.5473
54	7,614.294	0.0001	42,296.080	0.0000	5.5548	0.1800	5.5485
55	8,984.868	0.0001	49,910.380	0.0000	5.5549	0.1800	5.5494
56	10,602.150	0.0001	58,895.250	0.0000	5.5550	0.1800	5.5503
57	12,510.530	0.0001	69,497.400	0.0000	5.5551	0.1800	5.5510
58	14,762.430	0.0001	82,007.930	0.0000	5.5552	0.1800	5.5516
59	17,419.670	0.0001	96,770.380	0.0000	5.5552	0.1800	5.5522
60	20,555.210	0.0000	1,14,190.000	0.0000	5.5553	0.1800	5.5526
61	24,255.150	0.0000	1,34,745.200	0.0000	5.5553	0.1800	5.5530
62	28,621.070	0.0000	1,59,000.400	0.0000	5.5554	0.1800	5.5534
63	33,772.870	0.0000	1,87,621.500	0.0000	5.5554	0.1800	5.5537
64	39,851.990	0.0000	2,21,394.400	0.0000	5.5554	0.1800	5.5539
65	47,025.350	0.0000	2,61,246.400	0.0000	5.5554	0.1800	5.5542
66	55,489.910	0.0000	3,08,271.700	0.0000	5.5555	0.1800	5.5544
67	65,478.100	0.0000	3,63,761.600	0.0000	5.5555	0.1800	5.5545
68	77,264.160	0.0000	4,29,239.800	0.0000	5.5555	0.1800	5.5547
69	91,171.710	0.0000	5,06,504.000	0.0000	5.5555	0.1800	5.5548
70	1,07,582.600	0.0000	5,97,675.600	0.0000	5.5555	0.1800	5.5549
71	1,26,947.500	0.0000	7,05,258.300	0.0000	5.5555	0.1800	5.5550
72	1,49,798.100	0.0000	8,32,205.900	0.0000	5.5555	0.1800	5.5551
73	1,76,761.700	0.0000	9,82,003.900	0.0000	5.5555	0.1800	5.5551
74	2,08,578.800	0.0000	11,58,766.000	0.0000	5.5555	0.1800	5.5552
75	2,46,123.100	0.0000	13,67,345.000	0.0000	5.5555	0.1800	5.5553
76	2,90,425.200	0.0000	16,13,468.000	0.0000	5.5555	0.1800	5.5553
77	3,42,701.800	0.0000	19,03,893.000	0.0000	5.5555	0.1800	5.5553
78	4,04,388.100	0.0000	22,46,595.000	0.0000	5.5555	0.1800	5.5554
79	4,77,178.000	0.0000	26,50,983.000	0.0000	5.5555	0.1800	5.5554
80	5,63,070.100	0.0000	31,28,161.000	0.0000	5.5555	0.1800	5.5554
81	6,64,422.800	0.0000	36,91,232.000	0.0000	5.5555	0.1800	5.5554
82	7,84,018.900	0.0000	43,55,655.000	0.0000	5.5555	0.1800	5.5555
83	9,25,142.300	0.0000	51,39,674.000	0.0000	5.5555	0.1800	5.5555
84	10,91,668.000	0.0000	60,64,817.000	0.0000	5.5556	0.1800	5.5555
85	12,88,168.000	0.0000	71,56,485.000	0.0000	5.5556	0.1800	5.5555
86	15,20,039.000	0.0000	84,44,652.000	0.0000	5.5556	0.1800	5.5555
87	17,93,646.000	0.0000	99,64,693.000	0.0000	5.5556	0.1800	5.5555
88	21,16,502.000	0.0000	1,17,58,340.000	0.0000	5.5556	0.1800	5.5555
89	24,97,473.000	0.0000	1,38,74,840.000	0.0000	5.5556	0.1800	5.5555
90	29,47,018.000	0.0000	1,63,72,310.000	0.0000	5.5556	0.1800	5.5555
91	34,77,482.000	0.0000	1,93,19,340.000	0.0000	5.5556	0.1800	5.5555
92	41,03,428.000	0.0000	2,27,96,820.000	0.0000	5.5556	0.1800	5.5555
93	48,42,045.000	0.0000	2,69,00,250.000	0.0000	5.5556	0.1800	5.5555
94	57,13,614.000	0.0000	3,17,42,290.000	0.0000	5.5556	0.1800	5.5555
95	67,42,065.000	0.0000	3,74,55,910.000	0.0000	5.5556	0.1800	5.5555
96	79,55,637.000	0.0000	4,41,97,970.000	0.0000	5.5556	0.1800	5.5555
97	93,87,652.000	0.0000	5,21,53,620.000	0.0000	5.5556	0.1800	5.5555
98	1,10,77,430.000	0.0000	6,15,41,270.000	0.0000	5.5556	0.1800	5.5555
99	1,30,71,370.000	0.0000	7,26,18,710.000	0.0000	5.5556	0.1800	5.5555
100	1,54,24,210.000	0.0000	8,56,90,080.000	0.0000	5.5556	0.1800	5.5555

Interest Table for Annual Compounding with $i = 19\%$

n	F/p,i,n	P/F,i,n	F/A,i,n	A/F,i,n	P/A,i,n	A/P,i,n	A/G,i,n
1	1.190	0.8403	1.000	1.0000	0.8403	1.1900	0.0000
2	1.416	0.7062	2.190	0.4566	1.5465	0.6466	0.4566
3	1.685	0.5934	3.606	0.2773	2.1399	0.4673	0.8846
4	2.005	0.4987	5.291	0.1890	2.6386	0.3790	1.2844
5	2.386	0.4190	7.297	0.1371	3.0576	0.3271	1.6566
6	2.840	0.3521	9.683	0.1033	3.4098	0.2933	2.0019
7	3.379	0.2959	12.523	0.0799	3.7057	0.2699	2.3211
8	4.021	0.2487	15.902	0.0629	3.9544	0.2529	2.6154
9	4.785	0.2090	19.923	0.0502	4.1633	0.2402	2.8856
10	5.695	0.1756	24.709	0.0405	4.3389	0.2305	3.1331
11	6.777	0.1476	.30.404	0.0329	4.4865	0.2229	3.3589
12	8.064	0.1240	37.180	0.0269	4.6105	0.2169	3.5645
13	9.596	0.1042	45.244	0.0221	4.7147	0.2121	3.7509
14	11.420	0.0876	54.841	0.0182	4.8023	0.2082	3.9196
15	13.590	0.0736	66.261	0.0151	4.8759	0.2051	4.0717
16	16.172	0.0618	79.850	0.0125	4.9377	0.2025	4.2086
17	19.244	0.0520	96.022	0.0104	4.9897	0.2004	4.3314
18	22.901	0.0437	115.266	0.0087	5.0333	0.1987	4.4413
19	27.252	0.0367	138.167	0.0072	5.0700	0.1972	4.5394
20	32.429	0.0308	165.418	0.0060	5.1009	0.1960	4.6268
21	38.591	0.0259	197.848	0.0051	5.1268	0.1951	4.7045
22	45.923	0.0218	236.439	0.0042	5.1486	0.1942	4.7734
23	54.649	0.0183	282.362	0.0035	5.1668	0.1935	4.8344
24	65.032	0.0154	337.011	0.0030	5.1822	0.1930	4.8883
25	77.388	0.0129	402.043	0.0025	5.1951	0.1925	4.9359
26	92.092	0.0109	479.431	0.0021	5.2060	0.1921	4.9777
27	109.589	0.0091	571.523	0.0017	5.2151	0.1917	5.0145
28	130.411	0.0077	681.113	0.0015	5.2228	0.1915	5.0468
29	155.190	0.0064	811.524	0.0012	5.2292	0.1912	5.0751
30	184.676	0.0054	966.714	0.0010	5.2347	0.1910	5.0998
31	219.764	0.0046	1,151.389	0.0009	5.2392	0.1909	5.1215
32	261.519	0.0038	1,371.154	0.0007	5.2430	0.1907	5.1403
33	311.208	0.0032	1,632.673	0.0006	5.2462	0.1906	5.1568
34	370.337	0.0027	1,943.881	0.0005	5.2489	0.1905	5.1711
35	440.701	0.0023	2,314.218	0.0004	5.2512	0.1904	5.1836
36	524.435	0.0019	2,754.920	0.0004	5.2531	0.1904	5.1944
37	624.077	0.0016	3,279.355	0.0003	5.2547	0.1903	5.2038
38	742.652	0.0013	3,903.432	0.0003	5.2561	0.1903	5.2119
39	883.756	0.0011	4,646.085	0.0002	5.2572	0.1902	5.2190
40	1,051.670	0.0010	5,529.842	0.0002	5.2582	0.1902	5.2251
41	1,251.487	0.0008	6,581.511	0.0002	5.2590	0.1902	5.2304
42	1,489.270	0.0007	7,832.999	0.0001	5.2596	0.1901	5.2349
43	1,772.231	0.0006	9,322.269	0.0001	5.2602	0.1901	5.2389
44	2,108.955	0.0005	11,094.500	0.0001	5.2607	0.1901	5.2423
45	2,509.657	0.0004	13,203.460	0.0001	5.2611	0.1901	5.2452
46	2,986.492	0.0003	15,713.110	0.0001	5.2614	0.1901	5.2478
47	3,553.925	0.0003	18,699.610	0.0001	5.2617	0.1901	5.2499
48	4,229.172	0.0002	22,253.530	0.0000	5.2619	0.1900	5.2518
49	5,032.714	0.0002	26,482.710	0.0000	5.2621	0.1900	5.2534
50	5,988.931	0.0002	31,515.430	0.0000	5.2623	0.1900	5.2548

Interest Table for Annual Compounding with i = 19% (Contd.)

n	$F/p, i, n$	$P/F, i, n$	$F/A, i, n$	$A/F, i, n$	$P/A, i, n$	$A/P, i, n$	$A/G, i, n$
51	7,126.827	0.0001	37,504.360	0.0000	5.2624	0.1900	5.2560
52	8,480.925	0.0001	44,631.190	0.0000	5.2625	0.1900	5.2570
53	10,092.300	0.0001	53,112.110	0.0000	5.2626	0.1900	5.2579
54	12,009.840	0.0001	63,204.420	0.0000	5.2627	0.1900	5.2587
55	14,291.710	0.0001	75,214.260	0.0000	5.2628	0.1900	5.2593
56	17,007.140	0.0001	89,505.980	0.0000	5.2628	0.1900	5.2599
57	20,238.490	0.0000	1,06,513.100	0.0000	5.2629	0.1900	5.2603
58	24,083.810	0.0000	1,26,751.600	0.0000	5.2629	0.1900	5.2608
59	28,659.730	0.0000	1,50,835.400	0.0000	5.2630	0.1900	5.2611
60	34,105.080	0.0000	1,79,495.200	0.0000	5.2630	0.1900	5.2614
61	40,585.050	0.0000	2,13,600.300	0.0000	5.2630	0.1900	5.2617
62	48,296.210	0.0000	2,54,185.300	0.0000	5.2630	0.1900	5.2619
63	57,472.500	0.0000	3,02,481.600	0.0000	5.2631	0.1900	5.2621
64	68,392.280	0.0000	3,59,954.100	0.0000	5.2631	0.1900	5.2622
65	81,386.810	0.0000	4,28,346.400	0.0000	5.2631	0.1900	5.2624
66	96,850.310	0.0000	5,09,733.200	0.0000	5.2631	0.1900	5.2625
67	1,15,251.900	0.0000	6,06,583.500	0.0000	5.2631	0.1900	5.2626
68	1,37,149.700	0.0000	7,21,835.500	0.0000	5.2631	0.1900	5.2627
69	1,63,208.200	0.0000	8,58,985.200	0.0000	5.2631	0.1900	5.2627
70	1,94,217.800	0.0000	10,22,194.000	0.0000	5.2631	0.1900	5.2628
71	2,31,119.200	0.0000	12,16,411.000	0.0000	5.2631	0.1900	5.2629
72	2,75,031.800	0.0000	14,47,531.000	0.0000	5.2631	0.1900	5.2629
73	3,27,287.900	0.0000	17,22,563.000	0.0000	5.2631	0.1900	5.2629
74	3,89,472.600	0.0000	20,49,851.000	0.0000	5.2631	0.1900	5.2630
75	4,63,472.400	0.0000	24,39,323.000	0.0000	5.2631	0.1900	5.2630
76	5,51,532.200	0.0000	29,02,796.000	0.0000	5.2631	0.1900	5.2630
77	6,56,323.300	0.0000	34,54,328.000	0.0000	5.2632	0.1900	5.2630
78	7,81,024.800	0.0000	41,10,651.000	0.0000	5.2632	0.1900	5.2631
79	9,29,419.600	0.0000	48,91,677.000	0.0000	5.2632	0.1900	5.2631
80	11,06,009.000	0.0000	58,21,097.000	0.0000	5.2632	0.1900	5.2631
81	13,16,151.000	0.0000	69,27,106.000	0.0000	5.2632	0.1900	5.2631
82	15,66,220.000	0.0000	82,43,259.000	0.0000	5.2632	0.1900	5.2631
83	18,63,802.000	0.0000	98,09,478.000	0.0000	5.2632	0.1900	5.2631
84	22,17,925.000	0.0000	1,16,73,280.000	0.0000	5.2632	0.1900	5.2631
85	26,39,330.000	0.0000	1,38,91,210.000	0.0000	5.2632	0.1900	5.2631
86	31,40,803.000	0.0000	1,65,30,540.000	0.0000	5.2632	0.1900	5.2631
87	37,37,556.000	0.0000	1,96,71,340.000	0.0000	5.2632	0.1900	5.2631
88	44,47,692.000	0.0000	2,34,08,900.000	0.0000	5.2632	0.1900	5.2631
89	52,92,754.000	0.0000	2,78,56,600.000	0.0000	5.2632	0.1900	5.2631
90	62,98,377.000	0.0000	3,31,49,350.000	0.0000	5.2632	0.1900	5.2631
91	74,95,069.000	0.0000	3,94,47,730.000	0.0000	5.2632	0.1900	5.2631
92	89,19,133.000	0.0000	4,69,42,800.000	0.0000	5.2632	0.1900	5.2631
93	1,06,13,770.000	0.0000	5,58,61,930.000	0.0000	5.2632	0.1900	5.2631
94	1,26,30,380.000	0.0000	6,64,75,700.000	0.0000	5.2632	0.1900	5.2632
95	1,50,30,160.000	0.0000	7,91,06,100.000	0.0000	5.2632	0.1900	5.2632
96	1,78,85,890.000	0.0000	9,41,36,260.000	0.0000	5.2632	0.1900	5.2632
97	2,12,84,210.000	0.0000	11,20,22,200.000	0.0000	5.2632	0.1900	5.2632
98	2,53,28,210.000	0.0000	13,33,06,400.000	0.0000	5.2632	0.1900	5.2632
99	3,01,40,570.000	0.0000	15,86,34,600.000	0.0000	5.2632	0.1900	5.2632
100	3,58,67,290.000	0.0000	18,87,75,200.000	0.0000	5.2632	0.1900	5.2632

Interest Table for Annual Compounding with i = 20%

n	$F/p,i,n$	$P/F,i,n$	$F/A,i,n$	$A/F,i,n$	$P/A,i,n$	$A/P,i,n$	$A/G,i,n$
1	1.200	0.8333	1.000	1.0000	0.8333	1.2000	0.0000
2	1.440	0.6944	2.200	0.4545	1.5278	0.6545	0.4545
3	1.728	0.5787	3.640	0.2747	2.1065	0.4747	0.8791
4	2.074	0.4823	5.368	0.1863	2.5887	0.3863	1.2742
5	2.488	0.4019	7.442	0.1344	2.9906	0.3344	1.6405
6	2.986	0.3349	9.930	0.1007	3.3255	0.3007	1.9788
7	3.583	0.2791	12.916	0.0774	3.6046	0.2774	2.2902
8	4.300	0.2326	16.499	0.0606	3.8372	0.2606	2.5756
9	5.160	0.1938	20.799	0.0481	4.0310	0.2481	2.8364
10	6.192	0.1615	25.959	0.0385	4.1925	0.2385	3.0739
11	7.430	0.1346	32.150	0.0311	4.3271	0.2311	3.2893
12	8.916	0.1122	39.581	0.0253	4.4392	0.2253	3.4841
13	10.699	0.0935	48.497	0.0206	4.5327	0.2206	3.6597
14	12.839	0.0779	59.196	0.0169	4.6106	0.2169	3.8175
15	15.407	0.0649	72.035	0.0139	4.6755	0.2139	3.9588
16	18.488	0.0541	87.442	0.0114	4.7296	0.2114	4.0851
17	22.186	0.0451	105.931	0.0094	4.7746	0.2094	4.1976
18	26.623	0.0376	128.117	0.0078	4.8122	0.2078	4.2975
19	31.948	0.0313	154.740	0.0065	4.8435	0.2065	4.3861
20	38.338	0.0261	186.688	0.0054	4.8696	0.2054	4.4643
21	46.005	0.0217	225.026	0.0044	4.8913	0.2044	4.5334
22	55.206	0.0181	271.031	0.0037	4.9094	0.2037	4.5941
23	66.247	0.0151	326.237	0.0031	4.9245	0.2031	4.6475
24	79.497	0.0126	392.484	0.0025	4.9371	0.2025	4.6943
25	95.396	0.0105	471.981	0.0021	4.9476	0.2021	4.7352
26	114.475	0.0087	567.377	0.0018	4.9563	0.2018	4.7709
27	137.371	0.0073	681.853	0.0015	4.9636	0.2015	4.8020
28	164.845	0.0061	819.223	0.0012	4.9697	0.2012	4.8291
29	197.814	0.0051	984.068	0.0010	4.9747	0.2010	4.8527
30	237.376	0.0042	1,181.882	0.0008	4.9789	0.2008	4.8731
31	284.852	0.0035	1,419.258	0.0007	4.9824	0.2007	4.8908
32	341.822	0.0029	1,704.110	0.0006	4.9854	0.2006	4.9061
33	410.186	0.0024	2,045.931	0.0005	4.9878	0.2005	4.9194
34	492.224	0.0020	2,456.118	0.0004	4.9898	0.2004	4.9308
35	590.668	0.0017	2,948.341	0.0003	4.9915	0.2003	4.9406
36	708.802	0.0014	3,539.009	0.0003	4.9929	0.2003	4.9491
37	850.562	0.0012	4,247.812	0.0002	4.9941	0.2002	4.9564
38	1,020.675	0.0010	5,098.374	0.0002	4.9951	0.2002	4.9627
39	1,224.810	0.0008	6,119.049	0.0002	4.9959	0.2002	4.9681
40	1,469.772	0.0007	7,343.858	0.0001	4.9966	0.2001	4.9728
41	1,763.726	0.0006	8,813.630	0.0001	4.9972	0.2001	4.9767
42	2,116.471	0.0005	10,577.360	0.0001	4.9976	0.2001	4.9801
43	2,539.766	0.0004	12,693.830	0.0001	4.9980	0.2001	4.9831
44	3,047.718	0.0003	15,233.590	0.0001	4.9984	0.2001	4.9856
45	3,657.263	0.0003	18,281.310	0.0001	4.9986	0.2001	4.9877
46	4,388.715	0.0002	21,938.580	0.0000	4.9989	0.2000	4.9895
47	5,266.458	0.0002	26,327.290	0.0000	4.9991	0.2000	4.9911
48	6,319.749	0.0002	31,593.750	0.0000	4.9992	0.2000	4.9924
49	7,583.699	0.0001	37,913.490	0.0000	4.9993	0.2000	4.9935
50	9,100.439	0.0001	45,497.190	0.0000	4.9995	0.2000	4.9945

Interest Table for Annual Compounding with $i = 20\%$ (Contd.)

n	$F/p,i,n$	$P/F,i,n$	$F/A,i,n$	$A/F,i,n$	$P/A,i,n$	$A/P,i,n$	$A/G,i,n$
51	10,920.530	0.0001	54,597.640	0.0000	4.9995	0.2000	4.9953
52	13,104.630	0.0001	65,518.160	0.0000	4.9996	0.2000	4.9960
53	15,725.560	0.0001	78,622.790	0.0000	4.9997	0.2000	4.9966
54	18,870.670	0.0001	94,348.350	0.0000	4.9997	0.2000	4.9971
55	22,644.810	0.0000	1,13,219.000	0.0000	4.9998	0.2000	4.9976
56	27,173.760	0.0000	1,35,863.800	0.0000	4.9998	0.2000	4.9979
57	32,608.520	0.0000	1,63,037.600	0.0000	4.9998	0.2000	4.9983
58	39,130.220	0.0000	1,95,646.100	0.0000	4.9999	0.2000	4.9985
59	46,956.270	0.0000	2,34,776.400	0.0000	4.9999	0.2000	4.9987
60	56,347.520	0.0000	2,81,732.600	0.0000	4.9999	0.2000	4.9989
61	67,617.030	0.0000	3,38,080.100	0.0000	4.9999	0.2000	4.9991
62	81,140.430	0.0000	4,05,697.200	0.0000	4.9999	0.2000	4.9992
63	97,368.520	0.0000	4,86,837.700	0.0000	4.9999	0.2000	4.9994
64	1,16,842.200	0.0000	5,84,206.100	0.0000	5.0000	0.2000	4.9995
65	1,40,210.700	0.0000	7,01,048.300	0.0000	5.0000	0.2000	4.9995
66	1,68,252.800	0.0000	8,41,258.900	0.0000	5.0000	0.2000	4.9996
67	2,01,903.400	0.0000	10,09,512.000	0.0000	5.0000	0.2000	4.9997
68	2,42,284.000	0.0000	12,11,415.000	0.0000	5.0000	0.2000	4.9997
69	2,90,740.800	0.0000	14,53,699.000	0.0000	5.0000	0.2000	4.9998
70	3,48,889.000	0.0000	17,44,440.000	0.0000	5.0000	0.2000	4.9998
71	4,18,666.800	0.0000	20,93,329.000	0.0000	5.0000	0.2000	4.9998
72	5,02,400.200	0.0000	25,11,996.000	0.0000	5.0000	0.2000	4.9999
73	6,02,880.100	0.0000	30,14,396.000	0.0000	5.0000	0.2000	4.9999
74	7,23,456.200	0.0000	36,17,276.000	0.0000	5.0000	0.2000	4.9999
75	8,68,147.500	0.0000	43,40,733.000	0.0000	5.0000	0.2000	4.9999
76	10,41,777.000	0.0000	52,08,880.000	0.0000	5.0000	0.2000	4.9999
77	12,50,132.000	0.0000	62,50,657.000	0.0000	5.0000	0.2000	4.9999
78	15,00,159.000	0.0000	75,00,790.000	0.0000	5.0000	0.2000	4.9999
79	18,00,191.000	0.0000	90,00,948.000	0.0000	5.0000	0.2000	5.0000
80	21,60,229.000	0.0000	1,08,01,140.000	0.0000	5.0000	0.2000	5.0000
81	25,92,274.000	0.0000	1,29,61,370.000	0.0000	5.0000	0.2000	5.0000
82	31,10,729.000	0.0000	1,55,53,640.000	0.0000	5.0000	0.2000	5.0000
83	37,32,876.000	0.0000	1,86,64,370.000	0.0000	5.0000	0.2000	5.0000
84	44,79,450.000	0.0000	2,23,97,250.000	0.0000	5.0000	0.2000	5.0000
85	53,75,340.000	0.0000	2,68,76,700.000	0.0000	5.0000	0.2000	5.0000
86	64,50,408.000	0.0000	3,22,52,040.000	0.0000	5.0000	0.2000	5.0000
87	77,40,490.000	0.0000	3,87,02,450.000	0.0000	5.0000	0.2000	5.0000
88	92,88,588.000	0.0000	4,64,42,940.000	0.0000	5.0000	0.2000	5.0000
89	1,11,46,310.000	0.0000	5,57,31,520.000	0.0000	5.0000	0.2000	5.0000
90	1,33,75,570.000	0.0000	6,68,77,830.000	0.0000	5.0000	0.2000	5.0000
91	1,60,50,680.000	0.0000	8,02,53,400.000	0.0000	5.0000	0.2000	5.0000
92	1,92,60,820.000	0.0000	9,63,04,080.000	0.0000	5.0000	0.2000	5.0000
93	2,31,12,980.000	0.0000	11,55,64,900.000	0.0000	5.0000	0.2000	5.0000
94	2,77,35,580.000	0.0000	13,86,77,900.000	0.0000	5.0000	0.2000	5.0000
95	3,32,82,700.000	0.0000	16,64,13,500.000	0.0000	5.0000	0.2000	5.0000
96	3,99,39,230.000	0.0000	19,96,96,100.000	0.0000	5.0000	0.2000	5.0000
97	4,79,27,070.000	0.0000	23,96,35,400.000	0.0000	5.0000	0.2000	5.0000
98	5,75,12,490.000	0.0000	28,75,62,400.000	0.0000	5.0000	0.2000	5.0000
99	6,90,14,980.000	0.0000	34,50,74,900.000	0.0000	5.0000	0.2000	5.0000
100	8,28,17,980.000	0.0000	41,40,89,900.000	0.0000	5.0000	0.2000	5.0000

Interest Table for Annual Compounding with $i = 21\%$

n	$F/p, i, n$	$P/F, i, n$	$F/A, i, n$	$A/F, i, n$	$P/A, i, n$	$A/P, i, n$	$A/G, i, n$
1	1.210	0.8264	1.000	1.0000	0.8264	1.2100	0.0000
2	1.464	0.6830	2.210	0.4525	1.5095	0.6625	0.4525
3	1.772	0.5645	3.674	0.2722	2.0739	0.4822	0.8737
4	2.144	0.4665	5.446	0.1836	2.5404	0.3936	1.2641
5	2.594	0.3855	7.589	0.1318	2.9260	0.3418	1.6246
6	3.138	0.3186	10.183	0.0982	3.2446	0.3082	1.9561
7	3.797	0.2633	13.321	0.0751	3.5079	0.2851	2.2597
8	4.595	0.2176	17.119	0.0584	3.7256	0.2684	2.5366
9	5.560	0.1799	21.714	0.0461	3.9054	0.2561	2.7882
10	6.728	0.1486	27.274	0.0367	4.0541	0.2467	3.0159
11	8.140	0.1228	34.001	0.0294	4.1769	0.2394	3.2213
12	9.850	0.1015	42.142	0.0237	4.2785	0.2337	3.4059
13	11.918	0.0839	51.991	0.0192	4.3624	0.2292	3.5712
14	14.421	0.0693	63.910	0.0156	4.4317	0.2256	3.7188
15	17.449	0.0573	78.331	0.0128	4.4890	0.2228	3.8500
16	21.114	0.0474	95.780	0.0104	4.5364	0.2204	3.9664
17	25.548	0.0391	116.894	0.0086	4.5755	0.2186	4.0694
18	30.913	0.0323	142.441	0.0070	4.6079	0.2170	4.1602
19	37.404	0.0267	173.354	0.0058	4.6346	0.2158	4.2400
20	45.259	0.0221	210.758	0.0047	4.6567	0.2147	4.3100
21	54.764	0.0183	256.018	0.0039	4.6750	0.2139	4.3713
22	66.264	0.0151	310.782	0.0032	4.6900	0.2132	4.4248
23	80.180	0.0125	377.046	0.0027	4.7025	0.2127	4.4714
24	97.017	0.0103	457.225	0.0022	4.7128	0.2122	4.5120
25	117.391	0.0085	554.243	0.0018	4.7213	0.2118	4.5471
26	142.043	0.0070	671.634	0.0015	4.7284	0.2115	4.5776
27	171.872	0.0058	813.677	0.0012	4.7342	0.2112	4.6039
28	207.965	0.0048	985.549	0.0010	4.7390	0.2110	4.6266
29	251.638	0.0040	1,193.514	0.0008	4.7430	0.2108	4.6462
30	304.482	0.0033	1,445.152	0.0007	4.7463	0.2107	4.6631
31	368.423	0.0027	1,749.634	0.0006	4.7490	0.2106	4.6775
32	445.792	0.0022	2,118.057	0.0005	4.7512	0.2105	4.6900
33	539.408	0.0019	2,563.849	0.0004	4.7531	0.2104	4.7006
34	652.684	0.0015	3,103.258	0.0003	4.7546	0.2103	4.7097
35	789.748	0.0013	3,755.942	0.0003	4.7559	0.2103	4.7175
36	955.595	0.0010	4,545.690	0.0002	4.7569	0.2102	4.7242
37	1,156.270	0.0009	5,501.285	0.0002	4.7578	0.2102	4.7299
38	1,399.086	0.0007	6,657.555	0.0002	4.7585	0.2102	4.7347
39	1,692.895	0.0006	8,056.642	0.0001	4.7591	0.2101	4.7389
40	2,048.403	0.0005	9,749.536	0.0001	4.7596	0.2101	4.7424
41	2,478.568	0.0004	11,797.940	0.0001	4.7600	0.2101	4.7454
42	2,999.067	0.0003	14,276.510	0.0001	4.7603	0.2101	4.7479
43	3,628.871	0.0003	17,275.570	0.0001	4.7606	0.2101	4.7501
44	4,390.934	0.0002	20,904.450	0.0000	4.7608	0.2100	4.7519
45	5,313.030	0.0002	25,295.380	0.0000	4.7610	0.2100	4.7534
46	6,428.766	0.0002	30,608.410	0.0000	4.7612	0.2100	4.7547
47	7,778.807	0.0001	37,037.180	0.0000	4.7613	0.2100	4.7559
48	9,412.358	0.0001	44,815.990	0.0000	4.7614	0.2100	4.7568
49	11,388.950	0.0001	54,228.350	0.0000	4.7615	0.2100	4.7576
50	13,780.630	0.0001	65,617.310	0.0000	4.7616	0.2100	4.7583

Interest Table for Annual Compounding with *i* = 21% (Contd.)

n	F/p,i,n	P/F,i,n	F/A,i,n	A/F,i,n	P/A,i,n	A/P,i,n	A/G,i,n
51	16,674.570	0.0001	79,397.940	0.0000	4.7616	0.2100	4.7588
52	20,176.230	0.0000	96,072.500	0.0000	4.7617	0.2100	4.7593
53	24,413.240	0.0000	1,16,248.700	0.0000	4.7617	0.2100	4.7597
54	29,540.010	0.0000	1,40,662.000	0.0000	4.7617	0.2100	4.7601
55	35,743.420	0.0000	1,70,202.000	0.0000	4.7618	0.2100	4.7604
56	43,249.540	0.0000	2,05,945.400	0.0000	4.7618	0.2100	4.7606
57	52,331.940	0.0000	2,49,195.000	0.0000	4.7618	0.2100	4.7608
58	63,321.650	0.0000	3,01,527.000	0.0000	4.7618	0.2100	4.7610
59	76,619.210	0.0000	3,64,848.600	0.0000	4.7618	0.2100	4.7611
60	92,709.240	0.0000	4,41,467.800	0.0000	4.7619	0.2100	4.7613
61	1,12,178.200	0.0000	5,34,177.000	0.0000	4.7619	0.2100	4.7614
62	1,35,735.600	0.0000	6,46,355.300	0.0000	4.7619	0.2100	4.7614
63	1,64,240.100	0.0000	7,82,090.800	0.0000	4.7619	0.2100	4.7615
64	1,98,730.500	0.0000	9,46,331.000	0.0000	4.7619	0.2100	4.7616
65	2,40,463.900	0.0000	11,45,062.000	0.0000	4.7619	0.2100	4.7616
66	2,90,961.400	0.0000	13,85,526.000	0.0000	4.7619	0.2100	4.7617
67	3,52,063.200	0.0000	16,76,487.000	0.0000	4.7619	0.2100	4.7617
68	4,25,996.500	0.0000	20,28,550.000	0.0000	4.7619	0.2100	4.7617
69	5,15,455.800	0.0000	24,54,547.000	0.0000	4.7619	0.2100	4.7618
70	6,23,701.600	0.0000	29,70,003.000	0.0000	4.7619	0.2100	4.7618
71	7,54,678.900	0.0000	35,93,704.000	0.0000	4.7619	0.2100	4.7618
72	9,13,161.500	0.0000	43,48,384.000	0.0000	4.7619	0.2100	4.7618
73	11,04,926.000	0.0000	52,61,546.000	0.0000	4.7619	0.2100	4.7618
74	13,36,960.000	0.0000	63,66,471.000	0.0000	4.7619	0.2100	4.7619
75	16,17,722.000	0.0000	77,03,431.000	0.0000	4.7619	0.2100	4.7619
76	19,57,443.000	0.0000	93,21,153.000	0.0000	4.7619	0.2100	4.7619
77	23,68,506.000	0.0000	1,12,78,600.000	0.0000	4.7619	0.2100	4.7619
78	28,65,893.000	0.0000	1,36,47,100.000	0.0000	4.7619	0.2100	4.7619
79	34,67,730.000	0.0000	1,65,13,000.000	0.0000	4.7619	0.2100	4.7619
80	41,95,954.000	0.0000	1,99,80,730.000	0.0000	4.7619	0.2100	4.7619
81	50,77,104.000	0.0000	2,41,76,680.000	0.0000	4.7619	0.2100	4.7619
82	61,43,296.000	0.0000	2,92,53,790.000	0.0000	4.7619	0.2100	4.7619
83	74,33,388.000	0.0000	3,53,97,090.000	0.0000	4.7619	0.2100	4.7619
84	89,94,400.000	0.0000	4,28,30,470.000	0.0000	4.7619	0.2100	4.7619
85	1,08,83,220.000	0.0000	5,18,24,870.000	0.0000	4.7619	0.2100	4.7619
86	1,31,68,700.000	0.0000	6,27,08,090.000	0.0000	4.7619	0.2100	4.7619
87	1,59,34,130.000	0.0000	7,58,76,800.000	0.0000	4.7619	0.2100	4.7619
88	1,92,80,300.000	0.0000	9,18,10,940.000	0.0000	4.7619	0.2100	4.7619
89	2,33,29,160.000	0.0000	11,10,91,200.000	0.0000	4.7619	0.2100	4.7619
90	2,82,28,290.000	0.0000	13,44,20,400.000	0.0000	4.7619	0.2100	4.7619
91	3,41,56,230.000	0.0000	16,26,48,700.000	0.0000	4.7619	0.2100	4.7619
92	4,13,29,030.000	0.0000	19,68,04,900.000	0.0000	4.7619	0.2100	4.7619
93	5,00,08,130.000	0.0000	23,81,34,000.000	0.0000	4.7619	0.2100	4.7619
94	6,05,09,840.000	0.0000	28,81,42,100.000	0.0000	4.7619	0.2100	4.7619
95	7,32,16,910.000	0.0000	34,86,51,900.000	0.0000	4.7619	0.2100	4.7619
96	8,85,92,460.000	0.0000	42,18,68,900.000	0.0000	4.7619	0.2100	4.7619
97	10,71,96,900.000	0.0000	51,04,61,400.000	0.0000	4.7619	0.2100	4.7619
98	12,97,08,200.000	0.0000	61,76,58,300.000	0.0000	4.7619	0.2100	4.7619
99	15,69,47,000.000	0.0000	74,73,66,600.000	0.0000	4.7619	0.2100	4.7619
100	18,99,05,800.000	0.0000	90,43,13,600.000	0.0000	4.7619	0.2100	4.7619

Interest Table for Annual Compounding with i = 22%

n	$F/p,i,n$	$P/F,i,n$	$F/A,i,n$	$A/F,i,n$	$P/A,i,n$	$A/P,i,n$	$A/G,i,n$
1	1.220	0.8197	1.000	1.0000	0.8197	1.2200	0.0000
2	1.488	0.6719	2.220	0.4505	1.4915	0.6705	0.4505
3	1.816	0.5507	3.708	0.2697	2.0422	0.4897	0.8683
4	2.215	0.4514	5.524	0.1810	2.4936	0.4010	1.2542
5	2.703	0.3700	7.740	0.1292	2.8636	0.3492	1.6090
6	3.297	0.3033	10.442	0.0958	3.1669	0.3158	1.9337
7	4.023	0.2486	13.740	0.0728	3.4155	0.2928	2.2297
8	4.908	0.2038	17.762	0.0563	3.6193	0.2763	2.4982
9	5.987	0.1670	22.670	0.0441	3.7863	0.2641	2.7409
10	7.305	0.1369	28.657	0.0349	3.9232	0.2549	2.9593
11	8.912	0.1122	35.962	0.0278	4.0354	0.2478	3.1551
12	10.872	0.0920	44.874	0.0223	4.1274	0.2423	3.3299
13	13.264	0.0754	55.746	0.0179	4.2028	0.2379	3.4855
14	16.182	0.0618	69.010	0.0145	4.2646	0.2345	3.6233
15	19.742	0.0507	85.192	0.0117	4.3152	0.2317	3.7451
16	24.086	0.0415	104.935	0.0095	4.3567	0.2295	3.8524
17	29.384	0.0340	129.020	0.0078	4.3908	0.2278	3.9465
18	35.849	0.0279	158.405	0.0063	4.4187	0.2263	4.0289
19	43.736	0.0229	194.254	0.0051	4.4415	0.2251	4.1009
20	53.358	0.0187	237.989	0.0042	4.4603	0.2242	4.1635
21	65.096	0.0154	291.347	0.0034	4.4756	0.2234	4.2178
22	79.418	0.0126	356.444	0.0028	4.4882	0.2228	4.2649
23	96.889	0.0103	435.861	0.0023	4.4985	0.2223	4.3056
24	118.205	0.0085	532.751	0.0019	4.5070	0.2219	4.3407
25	144.210	0.0069	650.956	0.0015	4.5139	0.2215	4.3709
26	175.937	0.0057	795.166	0.0013	4.5196	0.2213	4.3968
27	214.643	0.0047	971.103	0.0010	4.5243	0.2210	4.4191
28	261.864	0.0038	1,185.745	0.0008	4.5281	0.2208	4.4381
29	319.474	0.0031	1,447.609	0.0007	4.5312	0.2207	4.4544
30	389.758	0.0026	1,767.083	0.0006	4.5338	0.2206	4.4683
31	475.505	0.0021	2,156.842	0.0005	4.5359	0.2205	4.4801
32	580.116	0.0017	2,632.347	0.0004	4.5376	0.2204	4.4902
33	707.742	0.0014	3,212.464	0.0003	4.5390	0.2203	4.4988
34	863.445	0.0012	3,920.205	0.0003	4.5402	0.2203	4.5060
35	1,053.403	0.0009	4,783.651	0.0002	4.5411	0.2202	4.5122
36	1,285.152	0.0008	5,837.055	0.0002	4.5419	0.2202	4.5174
37	1,567.886	0.0006	7,122.207	0.0001	4.5426	0.2201	4.5218
38	1,912.820	0.0005	8,690.092	0.0001	4.5431	0.2201	4.5256
39	2,333.641	0.0004	10,602.910	0.0001	4.5435	0.2201	4.5287
40	2,847.042	0.0004	12,936.560	0.0001	4.5439	0.2201	4.5314
41	3,473.391	0.0003	15,783.600	0.0001	4.5441	0.2201	4.5336
42	4,237.538	0.0002	19,256.990	0.0001	4.5444	0.2201	4.5355
43	5,169.796	0.0002	23,494.530	0.0000	4.5446	0.2200	4.5371
44	6,307.152	0.0002	28,664.330	0.0000	4.5447	0.2200	4.5385
45	7,694.725	0.0001	34,971.480	0.0000	4.5449	0.2200	4.5396
46	9,387.564	0.0001	42,666.210	0.0000	4.5450	0.2200	4.5406
47	11,452.830	0.0001	52,053.780	0.0000	4.5451	0.2200	4.5414
48	13,972.450	0.0001	63,506.600	0.0000	4.5451	0.2200	4.5420
49	17,046.390	0.0001	77,479.060	0.0000	4.5452	0.2200	4.5426
50	20,796.600	0.0000	94,525.440	0.0000	4.5452	0.2200	4.5431

Interest Table for Annual Compounding with i = 22% **(Contd.)**

n	$F/p, i, n$	$P/F, i, n$	$F/A, i, n$	$A/F, i, n$	$P/A, i, n$	$A/P, i, n$	$A/G, i, n$
51	25,371.850	0.0000	1,15,322.100	0.0000	4.5453	0.2200	4.5434
52	30,953.660	0.0000	1,40,693.900	0.0000	4.5453	0.2200	4.5438
53	37,763.470	0.0000	1,71,647.600	0.0000	4.5453	0.2200	4.5441
54	46,071.430	0.0000	2,09,411.100	0.0000	4.5454	0.2200	4.5443
55	56,207.150	0.0000	2,55,482.500	0.0000	4.5454	0.2200	4.5445
56	68,572.720	0.0000	3,11,689.600	0.0000	4.5454	0.2200	4.5446
57	83,658.740	0.0000	3,80,262.500	0.0000	4.5454	0.2200	4.5448
58	1,02,063.700	0.0000	4,63,921.200	0.0000	4.5454	0.2200	4.5449
59	1,24,517.700	0.0000	5,65,984.800	0.0000	4.5454	0.2200	4.5450
60	1,51,911.600	0.0000	6,90,502.600	0.0000	4.5454	0.2200	4.5451
61	1,85,332.100	0.0000	8,42,414.100	0.0000	4.5454	0.2200	4.5451
62	2,26,105.200	0.0000	10,27,746.000	0.0000	4.5454	0.2200	4.5452
63	2,75,848.300	0.0000	12,53,851.000	0.0000	4.5454	0.2200	4.5452
64	3,36,535.000	0.0000	15,29,700.000	0.0000	4.5454	0.2200	4.5453
65	4,10,572.700	0.0000	18,66,235.000	0.0000	4.5454	0.2200	4.5453
66	5,00,898.700	0.0000	22,76,808.000	0.0000	4.5454	0.2200	4.5453
67	6,11,096.400	0.0000	27,77,706.000	0.0000	4.5454	0.2200	4.5453
68	7,45,537.600	0.0000	33,88,803.000	0.0000	4.5454	0.2200	4.5454
69	9,09,556.000	0.0000	41,34,341.000	0.0000	4.5454	0.2200	4.5454
70	11,09,658.000	0.0000	50,43,897.000	0.0000	4.5455	0.2200	4.5454
71	13,53,783.000	0.0000	61,53,555.000	0.0000	4.5455	0.2200	4.5454
72	16,51,616.000	0.0000	75,07,339.000	0.0000	4.5455	0.2200	4.5454
73	20,14,971.000	0.0000	91,58,955.000	0.0000	4.5455	0.2200	4.5454
74	24,58,265.000	0.0000	1,11,73,930.000	0.0000	4.5455	0.2200	4.5454
75	29,99,083.000	0.0000	1,36,32,190.000	0.0000	4.5455	0.2200	4.5454
76	36,58,882.000	0.0000	1,66,31,280.000	0.0000	4.5455	0.2200	4.5454
77	44,63,836.000	0.0000	2,02,90,160.000	0.0000	4.5455	0.2200	4.5454
78	54,45,880.000	0.0000	2,47,54,000.000	0.0000	4.5455	0.2200	4.5454
79	66,43,974.000	0.0000	3,01,99,880.000	0.0000	4.5455	0.2200	4.5454
80	81,05,648.000	0.0000	3,68,43,850.000	0.0000	4.5455	0.2200	4.5454
81	98,88,891.000	0.0000	4,49,49,500.000	0.0000	4.5455	0.2200	4.5454
82	1,20,64,450.000	0.0000	5,48,38,390.000	0.0000	4.5455	0.2200	4.5454
83	1,47,18,630.000	0.0000	6,69,02,840.000	0.0000	4.5455	0.2200	4.5454
84	1,79,56,720.000	0.0000	8,16,21,480.000	0.0000	4.5455	0.2200	4.5454
85	2,19,07,210.000	0.0000	9,95,78,200.000	0.0000	4.5455	0.2200	4.5455
86	2,67,26,790.000	0.0000	12,14,85,400.000	0.0000	4.5455	0.2200	4.5455
87	3,26,06,690.000	0.0000	14,82,12,200.000	0.0000	4.5455	0.2200	4.5455
88	3,97,80,160.000	0.0000	18,08,18,900.000	0.0000	4.5455	0.2200	4.5455
89	4,85,31,800.000	0.0000	22,05,99,100.000	0.0000	4.5455	0.2200	4.5455
90	5,92,08,790.000	0.0000	26,91,30,900.000	0.0000	4.5455	0.2200	4.5455
91	7,22,34,720.000	0.0000	32,83,39,700.000	0.0000	4.5455	0.2200	4.5455
92	8,81,26,380.000	0.0000	40,05,74,400.000	0.0000	4.5455	0.2200	4.5455
93	10,75,14,200.000	0.0000	48,87,00,900.000	0.0000	4.5455	0.2200	4.5455
94	13,11,67,300.000	0.0000	59,62,15,000.000	0.0000	4.5455	0.2200	4.5455
95	16,00,24,100.000	0.0000	72,73,82,300.000	0.0000	4.5455	0.2200	4.5455
96	19,52,29,400.000	0.0000	88,74,06,500.000	0.0000	4.5455	0.2200	4.5455
97	23,81,79,900.000	0.0000	1,08,26,36,000.000	0.0000	4.5455	0.2200	4.5455
98	29,05,79,500.000	0.0000	1,32,08,16,000.000	0.0000	4.5455	0.2200	4.5455
99	35,45,07,000.000	0.0000	1,61,13,95,000.000	0.0000	4.5455	0.2200	4.5455
100	43,24,98,600.000	0.0000	1,96,59,03,000.000	0.0000	4.5455	0.2200	4.5455

Interest Table for Annual Compounding with i = 23%

n	$F/p,i,n$	$P/F,i,n$	$F/A,i,n$	$A/F,i,n$	$P/A,i,n$	$A/P,i,n$	$A/G,i,n$
1	1.230	0.8130	1.000	1.0000	0.8130	1.2300	0.0000
2	1.513	0.6610	2.230	0.4484	1.4740	0.6784	0.4484
3	1.861	0.5374	3.743	0.2672	2.0114	0.4972	0.8630
4	2.289	0.4369	5.604	0.1785	2.4483	0.4085	1.2443
5	2.815	0.3552	7.893	0.1267	2.8035	0.3567	1.5935
6	3.463	0.2888	10.708	0.0934	3.0923	0.3234	1.9116
7	4.259	0.2348	14.171	0.0706	3.3270	0.3006	2.2001
8	5.239	0.1909	18.430	0.0543	3.5179	0.2843	2.4605
9	6.444	0.1552	23.669	0.0422	3.6731	0.2722	2.6946
10	7.926	0.1262	30.113	0.0332	3.7993	0.2632	2.9040
11	9.749	0.1026	38.039	0.0263	3.9018	0.2563	3.0905
12	11.991	0.0834	47.788	0.0209	3.9852	0.2509	3.2560
13	14.749	0.0678	59.779	0.0167	4.0530	0.2467	3.4023
14	18.141	0.0551	74.528	0.0134	4.1082	0.2434	3.5311
15	22.314	0.0448	92.669	0.0108	4.1530	0.2408	3.6441
16	27.446	0.0364	114.983	0.0087	4.1894	0.2387	3.7428
17	33.759	0.0296	142.429	0.0070	4.2190	0.2370	3.8289
18	41.523	0.0241	176.188	0.0057	4.2431	0.2357	3.9036
19	51.074	0.0196	217.712	0.0046	4.2627	0.2346	3.9684
20	62.821	0.0159	268.785	0.0037	4.2786	0.2337	4.0243
21	77.269	0.0129	331.606	0.0030	4.2916	0.2330	4.0725
22	95.041	0.0105	408.875	0.0024	4.3021	0.2324	4.1139
23	116.901	0.0086	503.916	0.0020	4.3106	0.2320	4.1494
24	143.788	0.0070	620.817	0.0016	4.3176	0.2316	4.1797
25	176.859	0.0057	764.605	0.0013	4.3232	0.2313	4.2057
26	217.537	0.0046	941.464	0.0011	4.3278	0.2311	4.2278
27	267.570	0.0037	1,159.001	0.0009	4.3316	0.2309	4.2465
28	329.111	0.0030	1,426.571	0.0007	4.3346	0.2307	4.2625
29	404.807	0.0025	1,755.683	0.0006	4.3371	0.2306	4.2760
30	497.913	0.0020	2,160.490	0.0005	4.3391	0.2305	4.2875
31	612.433	0.0016	2,658.402	0.0004	4.3407	0.2304	4.2971
32	753.292	0.0013	3,270.835	0.0003	4.3421	0.2303	4.3053
33	926.549	0.0011	4,024.127	0.0002	4.3431	0.2302	4.3122
34	1,139.655	0.0009	4,950.676	0.0002	4.3440	0.2302	4.3180
35	1,401.776	0.0007	6,090.332	0.0002	4.3447	0.2302	4.3228
36	1,724.185	0.0006	7,492.107	0.0001	4.3453	0.2301	4.3269
37	2,120.747	0.0005	9,216.291	0.0001	4.3458	0.2301	4.3304
38	2,608.519	0.0004	11,337.040	0.0001	4.3462	0.2301	4.3333
39	3,208.479	0.0003	13,945.560	0.0001	4.3465	0.2301	4.3357
40	3,946.428	0.0003	17,154.040	0.0001	4.3467	0.2301	4.3377
41	4,854.107	0.0002	21,100.460	0.0000	4.3469	0.2300	4.3394
42	5,970.552	0.0002	25,954.570	0.0000	4.3471	0.2300	4.3408
43	7,343.778	0.0001	31,925.120	0.0000	4.3472	0.2300	4.3420
44	9,032.846	0.0001	39,268.900	0.0000	4.3473	0.2300	4.3430
45	11,110.400	0.0001	48,301.740	0.0000	4.3474	0.2300	4.3438
46	13,665.790	0.0001	59,412.140	0.0000	4.3475	0.2300	4.3445
47	16,808.930	0.0001	73,077.940	0.0000	4.3476	0.2300	4.3450
48	20,674.980	0.0000	89,886.850	0.0000	4.3476	0.2300	4.3455
49	25,430.220	0.0000	1,10,561.800	0.0000	4.3477	0.2300	4.3459
50	31,279.170	0.0000	1,35,992.100	0.0000	4.3477	0.2300	4.3462

Interest Table for Annual Compounding with *i* = 23% (Contd.)

n	F/p,i,n	P/F,i,n	F/A,i,n	A/F,i,n	P/A,i,n	A/P,i,n	A/G,i,n
51	38,473.380	0.0000	1,67,271.200	0.0000	4.3477	0.2300	4.3465
52	47,322.260	0.0000	2,05,744.600	0.0000	4.3477	0.2300	4.3467
53	58,206.380	0.0000	2,53,066.900	0.0000	4.3478	0.2300	4.3469
54	71,593.850	0.0000	3,11,273.200	0.0000	4.3478	0.2300	4.3471
55	88,060.430	0.0000	3,82,867.100	0.0000	4.3478	0.2300	4.3472
56	1,08,314.300	0.0000	4,70,927.500	0.0000	4.3478	0.2300	4.3473
57	1,33,226.600	0.0000	5,79,241.700	0.0000	4.3478	0.2300	4.3474
58	1,63,868.700	0.0000	7,12,468.400	0.0000	4.3478	0.2300	4.3475
59	2,01,558.500	0.0000	8,76,337.100	0.0000	4.3478	0.2300	4.3475
60	2,47,917.000	0.0000	10,77,896.000	0.0000	4.3478	0.2300	4.3476
61	3,04,937.900	0.0000	13,25,813.000	0.0000	4.3478	0.2300	4.3476
62	3,75,073.600	0.0000	16,30,750.000	0.0000	4.3478	0.2300	4.3477
63	4,61,340.600	0.0000	20,05,824.000	0.0000	4.3478	0.2300	4.3477
64	5,67,448.800	0.0000	24,67,164.000	0.0000	4.3478	0.2300	4.3477
65	6,97,962.100	0.0000	30,34,613.000	0.0000	4.3478	0.2300	4.3477
66	8,58,493.300	0.0000	37,32,575.000	0.0000	4.3478	0.2300	4.3477
67	10,55,947.000	0.0000	45,91,069.000	0.0000	4.3478	0.2300	4.3478
68	12,98,815.000	0.0000	56,47,015.000	0.0000	4.3478	0.2300	4.3478
69	15,97,542.000	0.0000	69,45,829.000	0.0000	4.3478	0.2300	4.3478
70	19,64,976.000	0.0000	85,43,371.000	0.0000	4.3478	0.2300	4.3478
71	24,16,921.000	0.0000	1,05,08,350.000	0.0000	4.3478	0.2300	4.3478
72	29,72,813.000	0.0000	1,29,25,270.000	0.0000	4.3478	0.2300	4.3478
73	36,56,560.000	0.0000	1,58,98,080.000	0.0000	4.3478	0.2300	4.3478
74	44,97,568.000	0.0000	1,95,54,640.000	0.0000	4.3478	0.2300	4.3478
75	55,32,009.000	0.0000	2,40,52,210.000	0.0000	4.3478	0.2300	4.3478
76	68,04,370.000	0.0000	2,95,84,210.000	0.0000	4.3478	0.2300	4.3478
77	83,69,376.000	0.0000	3,63,88,590.000	0.0000	4.3478	0.2300	4.3478
78	1,02,94,330.000	0.0000	4,47,57,960.000	0.0000	4.3478	0.2300	4.3478
79	1,26,62,030.000	0.0000	5,50,52,290.000	0.0000	4.3478	0.2300	4.3478
80	1,55,74,290.000	0.0000	6,77,14,320.000	0.0000	4.3478	0.2300	4.3478
81	1,91,56,380.000	0.0000	8,32,88,610.000	0.0000	4.3478	0.2300	4.3478
82	2,35,62,350.000	0.0000	10,24,45,000.000	0.0000	4.3478	0.2300	4.3478
83	2,89,81,690.000	0.0000	12,60,07,300.000	0.0000	4.3478	0.2300	4.3478
84	3,56,47,480.000	0.0000	15,49,89,000.000	0.0000	4.3478	0.2300	4.3478
85	4,38,46,400.000	0.0000	19,06,36,500.000	0.0000	4.3478	0.2300	4.3478
86	5,39,31,070.000	0.0000	23,44,82,900.000	0.0000	4.3478	0.2300	4.3478
87	6,63,35,210.000	0.0000	28,84,14,000.000	0.0000	4.3478	0.2300	4.3478
88	8,15,92,310.000	0.0000	35,47,49,200.000	0.0000	4.3478	0.2300	4.3478
89	10,03,58,500.000	0.0000	43,63,41,400.000	0.0000	4.3478	0.2300	4.3478
90	12,34,41,000.000	0.0000	53,67,00,000.000	0.0000	4.3478	0.2300	4.3478
91	15,18,32,400.000	0.0000	66,01,41,000.000	0.0000	4.3478	0.2300	4.3478
92	18,67,53,900.000	0.0000	81,19,73,300.000	0.0000	4.3478	0.2300	4.3478
93	22,97,07,300.000	0.0000	99,87,27,200.000	0.0000	4.3478	0.2300	4.3478
94	28,25,39,900.000	0.0000	1,22,84,34,000.000	0.0000	4.3478	0.2300	4.3478
95	34,75,24,100.000	0.0000	1,51,09,75,000.000	0.0000	4.3478	0.2300	4.3478
96	42,74,54,700.000	0.0000	1,85,84,98,000.000	0.0000	4.3478	0.2300	4.3478
97	52,57,69,300.000	0.0000	2,28,59,53,000.000	0.0000	4.3478	0.2300	4.3478
98	64,66,96,100.000	0.0000	2,81,17,22,000.000	0.0000	4.3478	0.2300	4.3478
99	79,54,36,300.000	0.0000	3,45,84,19,000.000	0.0000	4.3478	0.2300	4.3478
100	97,83,86,500.000	0.0000	4,25,38,54,000.000	0.0000	4.3478	0.2300	4.3478

Interest Table for Annual Compounding with $i = 24\%$

n	$F/p,i,n$	$P/F,i,n$	$F/A,i,n$	$A/F,i,n$	$P/A,i,n$	$A/P,i,n$	$A/G,i,n$
1	1.240	0.8065	1.000	1.0000	0.8065	1.2400	0.0000
2	1.538	0.6504	2.240	0.4464	1.4568	0.6864	0.4464
3	1.907	0.5245	3.778	0.2647	1.9813	0.5047	0.8577
4	2.364	0.4230	5.684	0.1759	2.4043	0.4159	1.2346
5	2.932	0.3411	8.048	0.1242	2.7454	0.3642	1.5782
6	3.635	0.2751	10.980	0.0911	3.0205	0.3311	1.8898
7	4.508	0.2218	14.615	0.0684	3.2423	0.3084	2.1710
8	5.590	0.1789	19.123	0.0523	3.4212	0.2923	2.4236
9	6.931	0.1443	24.712	0.0405	3.5655	0.2805	2.6492
10	8.594	0.1164	31.643	0.0316	3.6819	0.2716	2.8499
11	10.657	0.0938	40.238	0.0249	3.7757	0.2649	3.0276
12	13.215	0.0757	50.895	0.0196	3.8514	0.2596	3.1843
13	16.386	0.0610	64.110	0.0156	3.9124	0.2556	3.3218
14	20.319	0.0492	80.496	0.0124	3.9616	0.2524	3.4420
15	25.196	0.0397	100.815	0.0099	4.0013	0.2499	3.5467
16	31.243	0.0320	126.011	0.0079	4.0333	0.2479	3.6376
17	38.741	0.0258	157.253	0.0064	4.0591	0.2464	3.7162
18	48.039	0.0208	195.994	0.0051	4.0799	0.2451	3.7840
19	59.568	0.0168	244.033	0.0041	4.0967	0.2441	3.8423
20	73.864	0.0135	303.601	0.0033	4.1103	0.2433	3.8922
21	91.592	0.0109	377.465	0.0026	4.1212	0.2426	3.9349
22	113.574	0.0088	469.057	0.0021	4.1300	0.2421	3.9712
23	140.831	0.0071	582.630	0.0017	4.1371	0.2417	4.0022
24	174.631	0.0057	723.461	0.0014	4.1428	0.2414	4.0284
25	216.542	0.0046	898.092	0.0011	4.1474	0.2411	4.0507
26	268.512	0.0037	1,114.634	0.0009	4.1511	0.2409	4.0695
27	332.955	0.0030	1,383.147	0.0007	4.1542	0.2407	4.0853
28	412.864	0.0024	1,716.102	0.0006	4.1566	0.2406	4.0987
29	511.952	0.0020	2,128.966	0.0005	4.1585	0.2405	4.1099
30	634.820	0.0016	2,640.918	0.0004	4.1601	0.2404	4.1193
31	787.177	0.0013	3,275.738	0.0003	4.1614	0.2403	4.1272
32	976.100	0.0010	4,062.916	0.0002	4.1624	0.2402	4.1338
33	1,210.364	0.0008	5,039.016	0.0002	4.1632	0.2402	4.1394
34	1,500.851	0.0007	6,249.380	0.0002	4.1639	0.2402	4.1440
35	1,861.055	0.0005	7,750.231	0.0001	4.1644	0.2401	4.1479
36	2,307.709	0.0004	9,611.287	0.0001	4.1649	0.2401	4.1511
37	2,861.559	0.0003	11,919.000	0.0001	4.1652	0.2401	4.1537
38	3,548.333	0.0003	14,780.560	0.0001	4.1655	0.2401	4.1560
39	4,399.933	0.0002	18,328.890	0.0001	4.1657	0.2401	4.1578
40	5,455.917	0.0002	22,728.820	0.0000	4.1659	0.2400	4.1593
41	6,765.337	0.0001	28,184.740	0.0000	4.1661	0.2400	4.1606
42	8,389.019	0.0001	34,950.080	0.0000	4.1662	0.2400	4.1617
43	10,402.380	0.0001	43,339.100	0.0000	4.1663	0.2400	4.1625
44	12,898.960	0.0001	53,741.480	0.0000	4.1663	0.2400	4.1633
45	15,994.700	0.0001	66,640.440	0.0000	4.1664	0.2400	4.1639
46	19,833.440	0.0001	82,635.150	0.0000	4.1665	0.2400	4.1643
47	24,593.460	0.0000	1,02,468.600	0.0000	4.1665	0.2400	4.1648
48	30,495.890	0.0000	1,27,062.100	0.0000	4.1665	0.2400	4.1651
49	37,814.910	0.0000	1,57,558.000	0.0000	4.1666	0.2400	4.1654
50	46,890.490	0.0000	1,95,372.900	0.0000	4.1666	0.2400	4.1656

Interest Table for Annual Compounding with i = 24% (Contd.)

n	$F/p,i,n$	$P/F,i,n$	$F/A,i,n$	$A/F,i,n$	$P/A,i,n$	$A/P,i,n$	$A/G,i,n$
51	58,144.210	0.0000	2,42,263.400	0.0000	4.1666	0.2400	4.1658
52	72,098.810	0.0000	3,00,407.600	0.0000	4.1666	0.2400	4.1659
53	89,402.520	0.0000	3,72,506.400	0.0000	4.1666	0.2400	4.1661
54	1,10,859.100	0.0000	4,61,909.000	0.0000	4.1666	0.2400	4.1662
55	1,37,465.300	0.0000	5,72,768.100	0.0000	4.1666	0.2400	4.1663
56	1,70,457.000	0.0000	7,10,233.500	0.0000	4.1666	0.2400	4.1663
57	2,11,366.700	0.0000	8,80,690.400	0.0000	4.1666	0.2400	4.1664
58	2,62,094.700	0.0000	10,92,057.000	0.0000	4.1667	0.2400	4.1664
59	3,24,997.500	0.0000	13,54,152.000	0.0000	4.1667	0.2400	4.1665
60	4,02,996.900	0.0000	16,79,149.000	0.0000	4.1667	0.2400	4.1665
61	4,99,716.100	0.0000	20,82,146.000	0.0000	4.1667	0.2400	4.1665
62	6,19,648.000	0.0000	25,81,863.000	0.0000	4.1667	0.2400	4.1666
63	7,68,363.500	0.0000	32,01,510.000	0.0000	4.1667	0.2400	4.1666
64	9,52,770.800	0.0000	39,69,874.000	0.0000	4.1667	0.2400	4.1666
65	11,81,436.000	0.0000	49,22,645.000	0.0000	4.1667	0.2400	4.1666
66	14,64,981.000	0.0000	61,04,082.000	0.0000	4.1667	0.2400	4.1666
67	18,16,576.000	0.0000	75,69,062.000	0.0000	4.1667	0.2400	4.1666
68	22,52,554.000	0.0000	93,85,638.000	0.0000	4.1667	0.2400	4.1666
69	27,93,167.000	0.0000	1,16,38,190.000	0.0000	4.1667	0.2400	4.1666
70	34,63,527.000	0.0000	1,44,31,360.000	0.0000	4.1667	0.2400	4.1666
71	42,94,774.000	0.0000	1,78,94,890.000	0.0000	4.1667	0.2400	4.1667
72	53,25,520.000	0.0000	2,21,89,660.000	0.0000	4.1667	0.2400	4.1667
73	66,03,644.000	0.0000	2,75,15,180.000	0.0000	4.1667	0.2400	4.1667
74	81,88,519.000	0.0000	3,41,18,830.000	0.0000	4.1667	0.2400	4.1667
75	1,01,53,760.000	0.0000	4,23,07,350.000	0.0000	4.1667	0.2400	4.1667
76	1,25,90,670.000	0.0000	5,24,61,110.000	0.0000	4.1667	0.2400	4.1667
77	1,56,12,430.000	0.0000	6,50,51,780.000	0.0000	4.1667	0.2400	4.1667
78	1,93,59,410.000	0.0000	8,06,64,220.000	0.0000	4.1667	0.2400	4.1667
79	2,40,05,670.000	0.0000	10,00,23,600.000	0.0000	4.1667	0.2400	4.1667
80	2,97,67,040.000	0.0000	12,40,29,300.000	0.0000	4.1667	0.2400	4.1667
81	3,69,11,120.000	0.0000	15,37,96,300.000	0.0000	4.1667	0.2400	4.1667
82	4,57,69,790.000	0.0000	19,07,07,500.000	0.0000	4.1667	0.2400	4.1667
83	5,67,54,550.000	0.0000	23,64,77,300.000	0.0000	4.1667	0.2400	4.1667
84	7,03,75,630.000	0.0000	29,32,31,800.000	0.0000	4.1667	0.2400	4.1667
85	8,72,65,780.000	0.0000	36,36,07,500.000	0.0000	4.1667	0.2400	4.1667
86	10,82,09,600.000	0.0000	45,08,73,300.000	0.0000	4.1667	0.2400	4.1667
87	13,41,79,900.000	0.0000	55,90,82,800.000	0.0000	4.1667	0.2400	4.1667
88	16,63,83,100.000	0.0000	69,32,62,800.000	0.0000	4.1667	0.2400	4.1667
89	20,63,15,000.000	0.0000	85,96,45,800.000	0.0000	4.1667	0.2400	4.1667
90	25,58,30,600.000	0.0000	1,06,59,61,000.000	0.0000	4.1667	0.2400	4.1667
91	31,72,30,000.000	0.0000	1,32,17,92,000.000	0.0000	4.1667	0.2400	4.1667
92	39,33,65,100.000	0.0000	1,63,90,21,000.000	0.0000	4.1667	0.2400	4.1667
93	48,77,72,800.000	0.0000	2,03,23,87,000.000	0.0000	4.1667	0.2400	4.1667
94	60,48,38,300.000	0.0000	2,52,01,60,000.000	0.0000	4.1667	0.2400	4.1667
95	74,99,99,400.000	0.0000	3,12,49,98,000.000	0.0000	4.1667	0.2400	4.1667
96	92,99,99,400.000	0.0000	3,87,49,98,000.000	0.0000	4.1667	0.2400	4.1667
97	1,15,31,99,000.000	0.0000	4,80,49,97,000.000	0.0000	4.1667	0.2400	4.1667
98	1,42,99,67,000.000	0.0000	5,95,81,96,000.000	0.0000	4.1667	0.2400	4.1667
99	1,77,31,59,000.000	0.0000	7,38,81,64,000.000	0.0000	4.1667	0.2400	4.1667
100	2,19,87,18,000.000	0.0000	9,16,13,22,000.000	0.0000	4.1667	0.2400	4.1667

Interest Table for Annual Compounding with $i = 25\%$

n	$F/p,i,n$	$P/F,i,n$	$F/A,i,n$	$A/F,i,n$	$P/A,i,n$	$A/P,i,n$	$A/G,i,n$
1	1.250	0.8000	1.000	1.0000	0.8000	1.2500	0.0000
2	1.563	0.6400	2.250	0.4444	1.4400	0.6944	0.4444
3	1.953	0.5120	3.813	0.2623	1.9520	0.5123	0.8525
4	2.441	0.4096	5.766	0.1734	2.3616	0.4234	1.2249
5	3.052	0.3277	8.207	0.1218	2.6893	0.3718	1.5631
6	3.815	0.2621	11.259	0.0888	2.9514	0.3388	1.8683
7	4.768	0.2097	15.073	0.0663	3.1611	0.3163	2.1424
8	5.960	0.1678	19.842	0.0504	3.3289	0.3004	2.3872
9	7.451	0.1342	25.802	0.0388	3.4631	0.2888	2.6048
10	9.313	0.1074	33.253	0.0301	3.5705	0.2801	2.7971
11	11.642	0.0859	42.566	0.0235	3.6564	0.2735	2.9663
12	14.552	0.0687	54.208	0.0184	3.7251	0.2684	3.1145
13	18.190	0.0550	68.760	0.0145	3.7801	0.2645	3.2437
14	22.737	0.0440	86.949	0.0115	3.8241	0.2615	3.3559
15	28.422	0.0352	109.687	0.0091	3.8593	0.2591	3.4530
16	35.527	0.0281	138.109	0.0072	3.8874	0.2572	3.5366
17	44.409	0.0225	173.636	0.0058	3.9099	0.2558	3.6084
18	55.511	0.0180	218.045	0.0046	3.9279	0.2546	3.6698
19	69.389	0.0144	273.556	0.0037	3.9424	0.2537	3.7222
20	86.736	0.0115	342.945	0.0029	3.9539	0.2529	3.7667
21	108.420	0.0092	429.681	0.0023	3.9631	0.2523	3.8045
22	135.525	0.0074	538.101	0.0019	3.9705	0.2519	3.8365
23	169.407	0.0059	673.626	0.0015	3.9764	0.2515	3.8634
24	211.758	0.0047	843.033	0.0012	3.9811	0.2512	3.8861
25	264.698	0.0038	1,054.791	0.0009	3.9849	0.2509	3.9052
26	330.872	0.0030	1,319.489	0.0008	3.9879	0.2508	3.9212
27	413.590	0.0024	1,650.361	0.0006	3.9903	0.2506	3.9346
28	516.988	0.0019	2,063.952	0.0005	3.9923	0.2505	3.9457
29	646.235	0.0015	2,580.940	0.0004	3.9938	0.2504	3.9551
30	807.794	0.0012	3,227.174	0.0003	3.9950	0.2503	3.9628
31	1,009.742	0.0010	4,034.968	0.0002	3.9960	0.2502	3.9693
32	1,262.178	0.0008	5,044.710	0.0002	3.9968	0.2502	3.9746
33	1,577.722	0.0006	6,306.888	0.0002	3.9975	0.2502	3.9791
34	1,972.152	0.0005	7,884.610	0.0001	3.9980	0.2501	3.9828
35	2,465.191	0.0004	9,856.762	0.0001	3.9984	0.2501	3.9858
36	3,081.488	0.0003	12,321.950	0.0001	3.9987	0.2501	3.9883
37	3,851.860	0.0003	15,403.440	0.0001	3.9990	0.2501	3.9904
38	4,814.825	0.0002	19,255.300	0.0001	3.9992	0.2501	3.9921
39	6,018.532	0.0002	24,070.130	0.0000	3.9993	0.2500	3.9935
40	7,523.164	0.0001	30,088.660	0.0000	3.9995	0.2500	3.9947
41	9,403.955	0.0001	37,611.820	0.0000	3.9996	0.2500	3.9956
42	11,754.940	0.0001	47,015.780	0.0000	3.9997	0.2500	3.9964
43	14,693.680	0.0001	58,770.720	0.0000	3.9997	0.2500	3.9971
44	18,367.100	0.0001	73,464.400	0.0000	3.9998	0.2500	3.9976
45	22,958.880	0.0000	91,831.500	0.0000	3.9998	0.2500	3.9980
46	28,698.600	0.0000	1,14,790 400	0.0000	3.9999	0.2500	3.9984
47	35,873.240	0.0000	1,43,489.000	0.0000	3.9999	0.2500	3.9987
48	44,841.560	0.0000	1,79,362.200	0.0000	3.9999	0.2500	3.9989
49	56,051.940	0.0000	2,24,203.800	0.0000	3.9999	0.2500	3.9991
50	70,064.930	0.0000	2,80,255.700	0.0000	3.9999	0.2500	3.9993

Interest Table for Annual Compounding with *i* = 25% (Contd.)

n	*F/p, i, n*	*P/F, i, n*	*F/A, i, n*	*A/F, i, n*	*P/A, i, n*	*A/P, i, n*	*A/G, i, n*
51	87,581.160	0.0000	3,50,320.600	0.0000	4.0000	0.2500	3.9994
52	1,09,476.500	0.0000	4,37,901.800	0.0000	4.0000	0.2500	3.9995
53	1,36,845.600	0.0000	5,47,378.300	0.0000	4.0000	0.2500	3.9996
54	1,71,056.900	0.0000	6,84,223.800	0.0000	4.0000	0.2500	3.9997
55	2,13,821.200	0.0000	8,55,280.700	0.0000	4.0000	0.2500	3.9997
56	2,67,276.500	0.0000	10,69,102.000	0.0000	4.0000	0.2500	3.9998
57	3,34,095.600	0.0000	13,36,379.000	0.0000	4.0000	0.2500	3.9998
58	4,17,619.500	0.0000	16,70,474.000	0.0000	4.0000	0.2500	3.9999
59	5,22,024.400	0.0000	20,88,094.000	0.0000	4.0000	0.2500	3.9999
60	6,52,530.500	0.0000	26,10,118.000	0.0000	4.0000	0.2500	3.9999
61	8,15,663.100	0.0000	32,62,649.000	0.0000	4.0000	0.2500	3.9999
62	10,19,579.000	0.0000	40,78,312.000	0.0000	4.0000	0.2500	3.9999
63	12,74,474.000	0.0000	50,97,890.000	0.0000	4.0000	0.2500	4.0000
64	15,93,092.000	0.0000	63,72,364.000	0.0000	4.0000	0.2500	4.0000
65	19,91,365.000	0.0000	79,65,456.000	0.0000	4.0000	0.2500	4.0000
66	24,89,206.000	0.0000	99,56,821.000	0.0000	4.0000	0.2500	4.0000
67	31,11,508.000	0.0000	1,24,46,030.000	0.0000	4.0000	0.2500	4.0000
68	38,89,385.000	0.0000	1,55,57,540.000	0.0000	4.0000	0.2500	4.0000
69	48,61,731.000	0.0000	1,94,46,920.000	0.0000	4.0000	0.2500	4.0000
70	60,77,164.000	0.0000	2,43,08,650.000	0.0000	4.0000	0.2500	4.0000
71	75,96,455.000	0.0000	3,03,85,820.000	0.0000	4.0000	0.2500	4.0000
72	94,95,568.000	0.0000	3,79,82,270.000	0.0000	4.0000	0.2500	4.0000
73	1,18,69,460.000	0.0000	4,74,77,840.000	0.0000	4.0000	0.2500	4.0000
74	1,48,36,830.000	0.0000	5,93,47,300.000	0.0000	4.0000	0.2500	4.0000
75	1,85,46,030.000	0.0000	7,41,84,130.000	0.0000	4.0000	0.2500	4.0000
76	2,31,82,540.000	0.0000	9,27,30,160.000	0.0000	4.0000	0.2500	4.0000
77	2,89,78,180.000	0.0000	11,59,12,700.000	0.0000	4.0000	0.2500	4.0000
78	3,62,22,720.000	0.0000	14,48,90,900.000	0.0000	4.0000	0.2500	4.0000
79	4,52,78,400.000	0.0000	18,11,13,600.000	0.0000	4.0000	0.2500	4.0000
80	5,65,98,000.000	0.0000	22,63,92,000.000	0.0000	4.0000	0.2500	4.0000
81	7,07,47,500.000	0.0000	28,29,90,000.000	0.0000	4.0000	0.2500	4.0000
82	8,84,34,380.000	0.0000	35,37,37,500.000	0.0000	4.0000	0.2500	4.0000
83	11,05,43,000.000	0.0000	44,21,71,900.000	0.0000	4.0000	0.2500	4.0000
84	13,81,78,700.000	0.0000	55,27,14,800.000	0.0000	4.0000	0.2500	4.0000
85	17,27,23,400.000	0.0000	69,08,93,600.000	0.0000	4.0000	0.2500	4.0000
86	21,59,04,200.000	0.0000	86,36,16,900.000	0.0000	4.0000	0.2500	4.0000
87	26,98,80,300.000	0.0000	1,07,95,21,000.000	0.0000	4.0000	0.2500	4.0000
88	33,73,50,400.000	0.0000	1,34,94,02,000.000	0.0000	4.0000	0.2500	4.0000
89	42,16,88,000.000	0.0000	1,68,67,52,000.000	0.0000	4.0000	0.2500	4.0000
90	52,71,10,000.000	0.0000	2,10,84,40,000.000	0.0000	4.0000	0.2500	4.0000
91	65,88,87,500.000	0.0000	2,63,55,50,000.000	0.0000	4.0000	0.2500	4.0000
92	82,36,09,300.000	0.0000	3,29,44,37,000.000	0.0000	4.0000	0.2500	4.0000
93	1,02,95,12,000.000	0.0000	4,11,80,46,000.000	0.0000	4.0000	0.2500	4.0000
94	1,28,68,90,000.000	0.0000	5,14,75,58,000.000	0.0000	4.0000	0.2500	4.0000
95	1,60,86,12,000.000	0.0000	6,43,44,48,000.000	0.0000	4.0000	0.2500	4.0000
96	2,01,07,65,000.000	0.0000	8,04,30,59,000.000	0.0000	4.0000	0.2500	4.0000
97	2,51,34,56,000.000	0.0000	10,05,38,20,000.000	0.0000	4.0000	0.2500	4.0000
98	3,14,18,20,000.000	0.0000	12,56,72,80,000.000	0.0000	4.0000	0.2500	4.0000
99	3,92,72,75,000.000	0.0000	15,70,91,00,000.000	0.0000	4.0000	0.2500	4.0000
100	4,90,90,94,000.000	0.0000	19,63,63,80,000.000	0.0000	4.0000	0.2500	4.0000

Interest Table for Annual Compounding with $i = 26\%$

n	$F/p,i,n$	$P/F,i,n$	$F/A,i,n$	$A/F,i,n$	$P/A,i,n$	$A/P,i,n$	$A/G,i,n$
1	1.260	0.7937	1.000	1.0000	0.7937	1.2600	0.0000
2	1.588	0.6299	2.260	0.4425	1.4235	0.7025	0.4425
3	2.000	0.4999	3.848	0.2599	1.9234	0.5199	0.8473
4	2.520	0.3968	5.848	0.1710	2.3202	0.4310	1.2154
5	3.176	0.3149	8.368	0.1195	2.6351	0.3795	1.5481
6	4.002	0.2499	11.544	0.0866	2.8850	0.3466	1.8472
7	5.042	0.1983	15.546	0.0643	3.0833	0.3243	2.1143
8	6.353	0.1574	20.588	0.0486	3.2407	0.3086	2.3516
9	8.005	0.1249	26.940	0.0371	3.3657	0.2971	2.5613
10	10.086	0.0992	34.945	0.0286	3.4648	0.2886	2.7455
11	12.708	0.0787	45.031	0.0222	3.5435	0.2822	2.9066
12	16.012	0.0625	57.739	0.0173	3.6060	0.2773	3.0468
13	20.175	0.0496	73.751	0.0136	3.6555	0.2736	3.1682
14	25.421	0.0393	93.926	0.0106	3.6949	0.2706	3.2729
15	32.030	0.0312	119.347	0.0084	3.7261	0.2684	3.3628
16	40.358	0.0248	151.377	0.0066	3.7509	0.2666	3.4396
17	50.851	0.0197	191.735	0.0052	3.7705	0.2652	3.5051
18	64.072	0.0156	242.585	0.0041	3.7861	0.2641	3.5608
19	80.731	0.0124	306.658	0.0033	3.7985	0.2633	3.6079
20	101.721	0.0098	387.389	0.0026	3.8083	0.2626	3.6476
21	128.169	0.0078	489.110	0.0020	3.8161	0.2620	3.6810
22	161.492	0.0062	617.278	0.0016	3.8223	0.2616	3.7091
23	203.480	0.0049	778.771	0.0013	3.8273	0.2613	3.7326
24	256.385	0.0039	982.251	0.0010	3.8312	0.2610	3.7522
25	323.045	0.0031	1,238.636	0.0008	3.8342	0.2608	3.7685
26	407.037	0.0025	1,561.682	0.0006	3.8367	0.2606	3.7821
27	512.867	0.0019	1,968.719	0.0005	3.8387	0.2605	3.7934
28	646.212	0.0015	2,481.586	0.0004	3.8402	0.2604	3.8028
29	814.228	0.0012	3,127.798	0.0003	3.8414	0.2603	3.8105
30	1,025.927	0.0010	3,942.026	0.0003	3.8424	0.2603	3.8169
31	1,292.668	0.0008	4,967.953	0.0002	3.8432	0.2602	3.8222
32	1,628.761	0.0006	6,260.620	0.0002	3.8438	0.2602	3.8265
33	2,052.239	0.0005	7,889.382	0.0001	3.8443	0.2601	3.8301
34	2,585.821	0.0004	9,941.621	0.0001	3.8447	0.2601	3.8330
35	3,258.135	0.0003	12,527.440	0.0001	3.8450	0.2601	3.8354
36	4,105.250	0.0002	15,785.580	0.0001	3.8452	0.2601	3.8374
37	5,172.615	0.0002	19,890.830	0.0001	3.8454	0.2601	3.8390
38	6,517.495	0.0002	25,063.440	0.0000	3.8456	0.2600	3.8403
39	8,212.043	0.0001	31,580.940	0.0000	3.8457	0.2600	3.8414
40	10,347.180	0.0001	39,792.980	0.0000	3.8458	0.2600	3.8423
41	13,037.440	0.0001	50,140.160	0.0000	3.8459	0.2600	3.8430
42	16,427.170	0.0001	63,177.600	0.0000	3.8459	0.2600	3.8436
43	20,698.240	0.0000	79,604.770	0.0000	3.8460	0.2600	3.8441
44	26,079.780	0.0000	1,00,303.000	0.0000	3.8460	0.2600	3.8445
45	32,860.520	0.0000	1,26,382.800	0.0000	3.8460	0.2600	3.8448
46	41,404.260	0.0000	1,59,243.300	0.0000	3.8461	0.2600	3.8450
47	52,169.370	0.0000	2,00,647.600	0.0000	3.8461	0.2600	3.8453
48	65,733.410	0.0000	2,52,817.000	0.0000	3.8461	0.2600	3.8454
49	82,824.100	0.0000	3,18,550.400	0.0000	3.8461	0.2600	3.8456
50	1,04,358.300	0.0000	4,01,374.400	0.0000	3.8461	0.2600	3.8457

Interest Table for Annual Compounding with i = 27%

n	$F/p,i,n$	$P/F,i,n$	$F/A,i,n$	$A/F,i,n$	$P/A,i,n$	$A/P,i,n$	$A/G,i,n$
1	1.270	0.7874	1.000	1.0000	0.7874	1.2700	0.0000
2	1.613	0.6200	2.270	0.4405	1.4074	0.7105	0.4405
3	2.048	0.4882	3.883	0.2575	1.8956	0.5275	0.8422
4	2.601	0.3844	5.931	0.1686	2.2800	0.4386	1.2060
5	3.304	0.3027	8.533	0.1172	2.5827	0.3872	1.5334
6	4.196	0.2383	11.837	0.0845	2.8210	0.3545	1.8263
7	5.329	0.1877	16.032	0.0624	3.0087	0.3324	2.0866
8	6.768	0.1478	21.361	0.0468	3.1564	0.3168	2.3166
9	8.595	0.1164	28.129	0.0356	3.2728	0.3056	2.5187
10	10.915	0.0916	36.723	0.0272	3.3644	0.2972	2.6952
11	13.862	0.0721	47.639	0.0210	3.4365	0.2910	2.8485
12	17.605	0.0568	61.501	0.0163	3.4933	0.2863	2.9810
13	22.359	0.0447	79.107	0.0126	3.5381	0.2826	3.0951
14	28.396	0.0352	101.465	0.0099	3.5733	0.2799	3.1927
15	36.062	0.0277	129.861	0.0077	3.6010	0.2777	3.2759
16	45.799	0.0218	165.924	0.0060	3.6228	0.2760	3.3466
17	58.165	0.0172	211.723	0.0047	3.6400	0.2747	3.4063
18	73.870	0.0135	269.888	0.0037	3.6536	0.2737	3.4567
19	93.815	0.0107	343.758	0.0029	3.6642	0.2729	3.4990
20	119.145	0.0084	437.572	0.0023	3.6726	0.2723	3.5344
21	151.314	0.0066	556.717	0.0018	3.6792	0.2718	3.5640
22	192.168	0.0052	708.030	0.0014	3.6844	0.2714	3.5886
23	244.054	0.0041	900.199	0.0011	3.6885	0.2711	3.6091
24	309.948	0.0032	1,144.252	0.0009	3.6918	0.2709	3.6260
25	393.634	0.0025	1,454.200	0.0007	3.6943	0.2707	3.6400
26	499.915	0.0020	1.847.834	0.0005	3.6963	0.2705	3.6516
27	634.892	0.0016	2,347.750	0.0004	3.6979	0.2704	3.6611
28	806.313	0.0012	2,982.642	0.0003	3.6991	0.2703	3.6689
29	1,024.018	0.0010	3,788.955	0.0003	3.7001	0.2703	3.6754
30	1,300.503	0.0008	4,812.973	0.0002	3.7009	0.2702	3.6806
31	1,651.638	0.0006	6,113.475	0.0002	3.7015	0.2702	3.6849
32	2,097.581	0.0005	7,765.113	0.0001	3.7019	0.2701	3.6884
33	2,663.927	0.0004	9,862.693	0.0001	3.7023	0.2701	3.6913
34	3,383.188	0.0003	12,526.620	0.0001	3.7026	0.2701	3.6937
35	4,296.648	0.0002	15,909.810	0.0001	3.7028	0.2701	3.6956
36	5,456.743	0.0002	20,206.450	0.0000	3.7030	0.2700	3.6971
37	6,930.064	0.0001	25,663.200	0.0000	3.7032	0.2700	3.6984
38	8,801.180	0.0001	32,593.260	0.0000	3.7033	0.2700	3.6994
39	11,177.500	0.0001	41,394.440	0.0000	3.7034	0.2700	3.7002
40	14,195.420	0.0001	52,571.930	0.0000	3.7034	0.2700	3.7009
41	18,028.190	0.0001	66,767.350	0.0000	3.7035	0.2700	3.7014
42	22,895.800	0.0000	84,795.540	1.0000	3.7035	0.2700	3.7019
43	29,077.660	0.0000	1,07,691.300	0.0000	3.7036	0.2700	3.7022
44	36,928.630	0.0000	1,36,769.000	0.0000	3.7036	0.2700	3.7025
45	46,899.360	0.0000	1,73,697.600	0.0000	3.7036	0.2700	3.7027
46	59,562.180	0.0000	2,20,597.000	0.0000	3.7036	0.2700	3.7029
47	75,643.960	0.0000	2,80,159.100	0.0000	3.7037	0.2700	3.7031
48	96,067.830	0.0000	3,55,803.100	0.0000	3.7037	0.2700	3.7032
49	1,22,006.100	0.0000	4,51,870.900	0.0000	3.7037	0.2700	3.7033
50	1,54,947.800	0.0000	5,73,877.000	0.0000	3.7037	0.2700	3.7034

Interest Table for Annual Compounding with $i = 28\%$

n	$F/p,i,n$	$P/F,i,n$	$F/A,i,n$	$A/F,i,n$	$P/A,i,n$	$A/P,i,n$	$A/G,i,n$
1	1.280	0.7813	1.000	1.0000	0.7812	1.2800	0.0000
2	1.638	0.6104	2.280	0.4386	1.3916	0.7186	0.4386
3	2.097	0.4768	3.918	0.2552	1.8684	0.5352	0.8371
4	2.684	0.3725	6.016	0.1662	2.2410	0.4462	1.1966
5	3.436	0.2910	8.700	0.1149	2.5320	0.3949	1.5189
6	4.398	0.2274	12.136	0.0824	2.7594	0.3624	1.8057
7	5.629	0.1776	16.534	0.0605	2.9370	0.3405	2.0594
8	7.206	0.1388	22.163	0.0451	3.0758	0.3251	2.2823
9	9.223	0.1084	29.369	0.0340	3.1842	0.3140	2.4770
10	11.806	0.0847	38.593	0.0259	3.2689	0.3059	2.6460
11	15.112	0.0662	50.398	0.0198	3.3351	0.2998	2.7919
12	19.343	0.0517	65.510	0.0153	3.3868	0.2953	2.9172
13	24.759	0.0404	84.853	0.0118	3.4272	0.2918	3.0243
14	31.691	0.0316	109.612	0.0091	3.4587	0.2891	3.1153
15	40.565	0.0247	141.303	0.0071	3.4834	0.2871	3.1923
16	51.923	0.0193	181.868	0.0055	3.5026	0.2855	3.2572
17	66.461	0.0150	233.791	0.0043	3.5177	0.2843	3.3117
18	85.071	0.0118	300.252	0.0033	3.5294	0.2833	3.3573
19	108.890	0.0092	385.323	0.0026	3.5386	0.2826	3.3953
20	139.380	0.0072	494.213	0.0020	3.5458	0.2820	3.4269
21	178.406	0.0056	633.592	0.0016	3.5514	0.2816	3.4531
22	228.360	0.0044	811.998	0.0012	3.5558	0.2812	3.4747
23	292.300	0.0034	1,040.358	0.0010	3.5592	0.2810	3.4925
24	374.144	0.0027	1,332.658	0.0008	3.5619	0.2808	3.5071
25	478.905	0.0021	1,706.802	0.0006	3.5640	0.2806	3.5191
26	612.998	0.0016	2,185.707	0.0005	3.5656	0.2805	3.5289
27	784.637	0.0013	2,798.704	0.0004	3.5669	0.2804	3.5370
28	1,004.336	0.0010	3,583.342	0.0003	3.5679	0.2803	3.5435
29	1,285.550	0.0008	4,587.677	0.0002	3.5687	0.2802	3.5489
30	1,645.504	0.0006	5,873.227	0.0002	3.5693	0.2802	3.5532
31	2,106.245	0.0005	7,518.730	0.0001	3.5697	0.2801	3.5567
32	2,695.993	0.0004	9,624.974	0.0001	3.5701	0.2801	3.5596
33	3,450.871	0.0003	12,320.970	0.0001	3.5704	0.2801	3.5619
34	4,417.115	0.0002	15,771.840	0.0001	3.5706	0.2801	3.5637
35	5,653.906	0.0002	20,188.950	0.0000	3.5708	0.2800	3.5652
36	7,237.000	0.0001	25,842.860	0.0000	3.5709	0.2800	3.5665
37	9,263.359	0.0001	33,079.860	0.0000	3.5710	0.2800	3.5674
38	11,857.100	0.0001	42,343.210	0.0000	3.5711	0.2800	3.5682
39	15,177.090	0.0001	54,200.310	0.0000	3.5712	0.2800	3.5689
40	19,426.670	0.0001	69,377.400	0.0000	3.5712	0.2800	3.5694
41	24,866.140	0.0000	88,804.060	0.0000	3.5713	0.2800	3.5698
42	31,828.660	0.0000	1,13,670.200	0.0000	3.5713	0.2800	3.5701
43	40,740.680	0.0000	1,45,498.900	0.0000	3.5713	0.2800	3.5704
44	52,148.070	0.0000	1,86,239.500	0.0000	3.5714	0.2800	3.5706
45	66,749.530	0.0000	2,38,387.600	0.0000	3.5714	0.2800	3.5708
46	85,439.390	0.0000	3,05,137.100	0.0000	3.5714	0.2800	3.5709
47	1,09,362.400	0.0000	3,90,576.500	0.0000	3.5714	0.2800	3.5710
48	1,39,983.900	0.0000	4,99,938.900	0.0000	3.5714	0.2800	3.5711
49	1,79,179.400	0.0000	6,39,922.800	0.0000	3.5714	0.2800	3.5712
50	2,29,349.600	0.0000	8,19,102.100	0.0000	3.5714	0.2800	3.5712

Interest Table for Annual Compounding with i = 29%

n	$F/p,i,n$	$P/F,i,n$	$F/A,i,n$	$A/F,i,n$	$P/A,i,n$	$A/P,i,n$	$A/G,i,n$
1	1.290	0.7752	1.000	1.0000	0.7752	1.2900	0.0000
2	1.664	0.6009	2.290	0.4367	1.3761	0.7267	0.4367
3	2.147	0.4658	3.954	0.2529	1.8420	0.5429	0.8320
4	2.769	0.3611	6.101	0.1639	2.2031	0.4539	1.1874
5	3.572	0.2799	8.870	0.1127	2.4830	0.4027	1.5045
6	4.608	0.2170	12.442	0.0804	2.7000	0.3704	1.7854
7	5.945	0.1682	17.051	0.0586	2.8682	0.3486	2.0326
8	7.669	0.1304	22.995	0.0435	2.9986	0.3335	2.2486
9	9.893	0.1011	30.664	0.0326	3.0997	0.3226	2.4362
10	12.761	0.0784	40.556	0.0247	3.1781	0.3147	2.5980
11	16.462	0.0607	53.318	0.0188	3.2388	0.3088	2.7369
12	21.236	0.0471	69.780	0.0143	3.2859	0.3043	2.8553
13	27.395	0.0365	91.016	0.0110	3.3224	0.3010	2.9558
14	35.339	0.0283	118.411	0.0084	3.3507	0.2984	3.0406
15	45.587	0.0219	153.750	0.0065	3.3726	0.2965	3.1119
16	58.808	0.0170	199.337	0.0050	3.3896	0.2950	3.1715
17	75.862	0.0132	258.145	0.0039	3.4028	0.2939	3.2212
18	97.862	0.0102	334.007	0.0030	3.4130	0.2930	3.2624
19	126.242	0.0079	431.869	0.0023	3.4210	0.2923	3.2966
20	162.852	0.0061	558.112	0.0018	3.4271	0.2918	3.3247
21	210.079	0.0048	720.964	0.0014	3.4319	0.2914	3.3478
22	271.003	0.0037	931.043	0.0011	3.4356	0.2911	3.3668
23	349.593	0.0029	1,202.046	0.0008	3.4384	0.2908	3.3823
24	450.975	0.0022	1,551.639	0.0006	3.4406	0.2906	3.3949
25	581.758	0.0017	2,002.614	0.0005	3.4423	0.2905	3.4052
26	750.468	0.0013	2,584.372	0.0004	3.4437	0.2904	3.4136
27	968.104	0.0010	3,334.840	0.0003	3.4447	0.2903	3.4204
28	1,248.854	0.0008	4,302.944	0.0002	3.4455	0.2902	3.4258
29	1,611.021	0.0006	5,551.797	0.0002	3.4461	0.2902	3.4303
30	2.078.217	0.0005	7,162.818	0.0001	3.4466	0.2901	3.4338
31	2,680.900	0.0004	9,241.035	0.0001	3.4470	0.2901	3.4367
32	3,458.361	0.0003	11,921.940	0.0001	3.4473	0.2901	3.4390
33	4,461.285	0.0002	15,380.290	0.0001	3.4475	0.2901	3.4409
34	5,755.058	0.0002	19,841.580	0.0001	3.4477	0.2901	3.4424
35	7,424.025	0.0001	25,596.640	0.0000	3.4478	0.2900	3.4436
36	9,576.991	0.0001	33,020.660	0.0000	3.4479	0.2900	3.4445
37	12,354.320	0.0001	42,597.650	0.0000	3.4480	0.2900	3.4453
38	15,937.070	0.0001	54,951.980	0.0000	3.4481	0.2900	3.4459
39	20,558.820	0.0000	70,889.040	0.0000	3.4481	0.2900	3.4464
40	26,520.880	0.0000	91,447.850	0.0000	3.4481	0.2900	3.4468
41	34,211.930	0.0000	1,17,968.700	0.0000	3.4482	0.2900	3.4471
42	44,133.390	0.0000	1,52,180.600	0.0000	3.4482	0.2900	3.4473
43	56,932.070	0.0000	1,96,314.100	0.0000	3.4482	0.2900	3.4475
44	73,442.370	0.0000	2,53,246.100	0.0000	3.4482	0.2900	3.4477
45	94,740.650	0.0000	3,26,688.500	0.0000	3.4482	0.2900	3.4478
46	1,22,215.400	0.0000	4,21,429.100	0.0000	3.4482	0.2900	3.4479
47	1,57,657.900	0.0000	5,43,644.500	0.0000	3.4483	0.2900	3.4480
48	2,03,378.700	0.0000	7,01,302.500	0.0000	3.4483	0.2900	3.4480
49	2,62,358.500	0.0000	9,04,681.100	0.0000	3.4483	0.2900	3.4481
50	3,38,442.500	0.0000	11,67,040.000	0.0000	3.4483	0.2900	3.4481

Interest Table for Annual Compounding with $i = 30\%$

n	$F/p,i,n$	$P/F,i,n$	$F/A,i,n$	$A/F,i,n$	$P/A,i,n$	$A/P,i,n$	$A/G,i,n$
1	1.300	0.7692	1.000	1.0000	0.7692	1.3000	0.0000
2	1.690	0.5917	2.300	0.4348	1.3609	0.7348	0.4348
3	2.197	0.4552	3.990	0.2506	1.8161	0.5506	0.8271
4	2.856	0.3501	6.187	0.1616	2.1662	0.4616	1.1783
5	3.713	0.2693	9.043	0.1106	2.4356	0.4106	1.4903
6	4.827	0.2072	12.756	0.0784	2.6427	0.3784	1.7654
7	6.275	0.1594	17.583	0.0569	2.8021	0.3569	2.0063
8	8.157	0.1226	23.858	0.0419	2.9247	0.3419	2.2156
9	10.604	0.0943	32.015	0.0312	3.0190	0.3312	2.3963
10	13.786	0.0725	42.619	0.0235	3.0915	0.3235	2.5512
11	17.922	0.0558	56.405	0.0177	3.1473	0.3177	2.6833
12	23.298	0.0429	74.327	0.0135	3.1903	0.3135	2.7952
13	30.287	0.0330	97.625	0.0102	3.2233	0.3102	2.8895
14	39.374	0.0254	127.912	0.0078	3.2487	0.3078	2.9685
15	51.186	0.0195	167.286	0.0060	3.2682	0.3060	3.0344
16	66.542	0.0150	218.472	0.0046	3.2832	0.3046	3.0892
17	86.504	0.0116	285.014	0.0035	3.2948	0.3035	3.1345
18	112.455	0.0089	371.518	0.0027	3.3037	0.3027	3.1718
19	146.192	0.0068	483.973	0.0021	3.3105	0.3021	3.2025
20	190.049	0.0053	630.165	0.0016	3.3158	0.3016	3.2275
21	247.064	0.0040	820.214	0.0012	3.3198	0.3012	3.2480
22	321.184	0.0031	1,067.278	0.0009	3.3230	0.3009	3.2646
23	417.539	0.0024	1,388.462	0.0007	3.3253	0.3007	3.2781
24	542.800	0.0018	1,806.000	0.0006	3.3272	0.3006	3.2890
25	705.640	0.0014	2,348.800	0.0004	3.3286	0.3004	3.2979
26	917.332	0.0011	3,054.440	0.0003	3.3297	0.3003	3.3050
27	1,192.532	0.0008	3,971.772	0.0003	3.3305	0.3003	3.3107
28	1,550.291	0.0006	5,164.303	0.0002	3.3312	0.3002	3.3153
29	2,015.378	0.0005	6,714.594	0.0001	3.3317	0.3001	3.3189
30	2,619.991	0.0004	8,729.971	0.0001	3.3321	0.3001	3.3219
31	3,405.988	0.0003	11,349.960	0.0001	3.3324	0.3001	3.3242
32	4,427.785	0.0002	14,755.950	0.0001	3.3326	0.3001	3.3261
33	5,756.121	0.0002	19,183.740	0.0001	3.3328	0.3001	3.3276
34	7,482.956	0.0001	24,939.850	0.0000	3.3329	0.3000	3.3288
35	9,727.842	0.0001	32,422.810	0.0000	3.3330	0.3000	3.3297
36	12,646.190	0.0001	42,150.650	0.0000	3.3331	0.3000	3.3305
37	16,440.050	0.0001	54,796.830	0.0000	3.3331	0.3000	3.3311
38	21,372.070	0.0000	71,236.880	0.0000	3.3332	0.3000	3.3316
39	27,783.680	0.0000	92,608.940	0.0000	3.3332	0.3000	3.3319
40	36,118.790	0.0000	1,20,392.600	0.0000	3.3332	0.3000	3.3322
41	46,954.420	0.0000	1,56,511.400	0.0000	3.3333	0.3000	3.3325
42	61,040.750	0.0000	2,03,465.800	0.0000	3.3333	0.3000	3.3326
43	79,352.960	0.0000	2,64,506.500	0.0000	3.3333	0.3000	3.3328
44	1,03,158.900	0.0000	3,43,859.500	0.0000	3.3333	0.3000	3.3329
45	1,34,106.500	0.0000	4,47,018.300	0.0000	3.3333	0.3000	3.3330
46	1,74,338.400	0.0000	5,81,124.800	0.0000	3.3333	0.3000	3.3331
47	2,26,640.000	0.0000	7,55,463.100	0.0000	3.3333	0.3000	3.3331
48	2,94,632.000	0.0000	9,82,103.100	0.0000	3.3333	0.3000	3.3332
49	3,83,021.500	0.0000	12,76,735.000	0.0000	3.3333	0.3000	3.3332
50	4,97,927.900	0.0000	16,59,756.000	0.0000	3.3333	0.3000	3.3332

Interest Table for Annual Compounding with *i* = 35%

n	F/p, i, n	P/F, i, n	F/A, i, n	A/F, i, n	P/A, i, n	A/P, i, n	A/G, i, n
1	1.350	0.7407	1.000	1.0000	0.7407	1.3500	0.0000
2	1.823	0.5487	2.350	0.4255	1.2894	0.7755	0.4255
3	2.460	0.4064	4.173	0.2397	1.6959	0.5897	0.8029
4	3.322	0.3011	6.633	0.1508	1.9969	0.5008	1.1341
5	4.484	0.2230	9.954	0.1005	2.2200	0.4505	1.4220
6	6.053	0.1652	14.438	0.0693	2.3852	0.4193	1.6698
7	8.172	0.1224	20.492	0.0488	2.5075	0.3988	1.8811
8	11.032	0.0906	28.664	0.0349	2.5982	0.3849	2.0597
9	14.894	0.0671	39.696	0.0252	2.6653	0.3752	2.2094
10	20.107	0.0497	54.590	0.0183	2.7150	0.3683	2.3338
11	27.144	0.0368	74.697	0.0134	2.7519	0.3634	2.4364
12	36.644	0.0273	101.841	0.0098	2.7792	0.3598	2.5205
13	49.470	0.0202	138.485	0.0072	2.7994	0.3572	2.5889
14	66.784	0.0150	187.954	0.0053	2.8144	0.3553	2.6443
15	90.158	0.0111	254.739	0.0039	2.8255	0.3539	2.6889
16	121.714	0.0082	344.897	0.0029	2.8337	0.3529	2.7246
17	164.314	0.0061	466.611	0.0021	2.8398	0.3521	2.7530
18	221.824	0.0045	630.925	0.0016	2.8443	0.3516	2.7756
19	299.462	0.0033	852.748	0.0012	2.8476	0.3512	2.7935
20	404.274	0.0025	1,152.210	0.0009	2.8501	0.3509	2.8075
21	545.769	0.0018	1,556.484	0.0006	2.8519	0.3506	2.8186
22	736.789	0.0014	2,102.253	0.0005	2.8533	0.3505	2.8272
23	994.665	0.0010	2,839.042	0.0004	2.8543	0.3504	2.8340
24	1,342.797	0.0007	3,833.707	0.0003	2.8550	0.3503	2.8393
25	1,812.776	0.0006	5,176.504	0.0002	2.8556	0.3502	2.8433
26	2,447.248	0.0004	6,989.281	0.0001	2.8560	0.3501	2.8465
27	3,303.785	0.0003	9,436.529	0.0001	2.8563	0.3501	2.8490
28	4,460.110	0.0002	12,740.320	0.0001	2.8565	0.3501	2.8509
29	6,021.148	0.0002	17,200.420	0.0001	2.8567	0.3501	2.8523
30	8,128.550	0.0001	23,221.570	0.0000	2.8568	0.3500	2.8535
31	10,973.540	0.0001	31,350.120	0.0000	2.8569	0.3500	2.8543
32	14,814.280	0.0001	42,323.670	0.0000	2.8570	0.3500	2.8550
33	19,999.280	0.0001	57,137.950	0.0000	2.8570	0.3500	2.8555
34	26,999.030	0.0000	77,137.230	0.0000	2.8570	0.3500	2.8559
35	36,448.690	0.0000	1,04,136.300	0.0000	2.8571	0.3500	2.8562
36	49,205.730	0.0000	1,40,585.000	0.0000	2.8571	0.3500	2.8564
37	66,427.740	0.0000	1,89,790.700	0.0000	2.8571	0.3500	2.8566
38	89,677.440	0.0000	2,56,218.400	0.0000	2.8571	0.3500	2.8567
39	1,21,064.600	0.0000	3,45,895.900	0.0000	2.8571	0.3500	2.8568
40	1,63,437.100	0.0000	4,66,960.400	0.0000	2.8571	0.3500	2.8569
41	2,20,640.200	0.0000	6,30,397.600	0.0000	2.8571	0.3500	2.8570
42	2,97,864.200	0.0000	8,51,037.700	0.0000	2.8571	0.3500	2.8570
43	4,02,116.700	0.0000	11,48,902.000	0.0000	2.8571	0.3500	2.8570
44	5,42,857.500	0.0000	15,51,019.000	0.0000	2.8571	0.3500	2.8571
45	7,32,857.600	0.0000	20,93,876.000	0.0000	2.8571	0.3500	2.8571
46	9,89,357.800	0.0000	28,26,734.000	0.0000	2.8571	0.3500	2.8571
47	13,35,633.000	0.0000	38,16,092.000	0.0000	2.8571	0.3500	2.8571
48	18,03,105.000	0.0000	51,51,725.000	0.0000	2.8571	0.3500	2.8571
49	24,34,191.000	0.0000	69,54,830.000	0.0000	2.8571	0.3500	2.8571
50	32,86,158.000	0.0000	93,89,020.000	0.0000	2.8571	0.3500	2.8571

Interest Table for Annual Compounding with $i = 40\%$

n	$F/p, i, n$	$P/F, i, n$	$F/A, i, n$	$A/F, i, n$	$P/A, i, n$	$A/P, i, n$	$A/G, i, n$
1	1.400	0.7143	1.000	1.0000	0.7143	1.4000	0.0000
2	1.960	0.5102	2.400	0.4167	1.2245	0.8167	0.4167
3	2.744	0.3644	4.360	0.2294	1.5889	0.6294	0.7798
4	3.842	0.2603	7.104	0.1408	1.8492	0.5408	1.0923
5	5.378	0.1859	10.946	0.0914	2.0352	0.4914	1.3580
6	7.530	0.1328	16.324	0.0613	2.1680	0.4613	1.5811
7	10.541	0.0949	23.853	0.0419	2.2628	0.4419	1.7664
8	14.758	0.0678	34.395	0.0291	2.3306	0.4291	1.9185
9	20.661	0.0484	49.153	0.0203	2.3790	0.4203	2.0422
10	28.925	0.0346	69.814	0.0143	2.4136	0.4143	2.1419
11	40.496	0.0247	98.739	0.0101	2.4383	0.4101	2.2215
12	56.694	0.0176	139.235	0.0072	2.4559	0.4072	2.2845
13	79.371	0.0126	195.929	0.0051	2.4685	0.4051	2.3341
14	111.120	0.0090	275.300	0.0036	2.4775	0.4036	2.3729
15	155.568	0.0064	386.420	0.0026	2.4839	0.4026	2.4030
16	217.795	0.0046	541.988	0.0018	2.4885	0.4018	2.4262
17	304.913	0.0033	759.783	0.0013	2.4918	0.4013	2.4441
18	426.879	0.0023	1,064.697	0.0009	2.4941	0.4009	2.4577
19	597.630	0.0017	1,491.576	0.0007	2.4958	0.4007	2.4682
20	836.682	0.0012	2,089.205	0.0005	2.4970	0.4005	2.4761
21	1,171.355	0.0009	2,925.888	0.0003	2.4979	0.4003	2.4821
22	1,639.897	0.0006	4,097.243	0.0002	2.4985	0.4002	2.4866
23	2,295.856	0.0004	5,737.140	0.0002	2.4989	0.4002	2.4900
24	3,214.198	0.0003	8,032.995	0.0001	2.4992	0.4001	2.4925
25	4,499.877	0.0002	11,247.190	0.0001	2.4994	0.4001	2.4944
26	6299.828	0.0002	15,747.070	0.0001	2.4996	0.4001	2.4959
27	8,819.759	0.0001	22,046.900	0.0000	2.4997	0.4000	2.4969
28	12,347.660	0.0001	30,866.660	0.0000	2.4998	0.4000	2.4977
29	17,286.730	0.0001	43,214.320	0.0000	2.4999	0.4000	2.4983
30	24,201.420	0.0000	60,501.050	0.0000	2.4999	0.4000	2.4988
31	33,881.990	0.0000	84,702.460	0.0000	2.4999	0.4000	2.4991
32	47,434.780	0.0000	1,18,584.400	0.0000	2.4999	0.4000	2.4993
33	66,408.680	0.0000	1,66,019.200	0.0000	2.5000	0.4000˙	2.4995
34	92,972.150	0.0000	2,32,427.900	0.0000	2.5000	0.4000	2.4996
35	1,30,161.000	0.0000	3,25,400.000	0.0000	2.5000	0.4000	2.4997
36	1,82,225.400	0.0000	4,55,561.000	0.0000	2.5000	0.4000	2.4998
37	2,55,115.600	0.0000	6,37,786.500	0.0000	2.5000	0.4000	2.4999
38	3,57,161.800	0.0000	8,92,902.000	0.0000	2.5000	0.4000	2.4999
39	5,00,026.600	0.0000	12,50,064.000	0.0000	2.5000	0.4000	2.4999
40	7,00,037.100	0.0000	17,50,090.000	0.0000	2.5000	0.4000	2.4999
41	9,80,051.900	0.0000	24,50,127.000	0.0000	2.5000	0.4000	2.5000
42	13,72,073.000	0.0000	34,30,179.000	0.0000	2.5000	0.4000	2.5000
43	19,20,902.000	0.0000	48,02,252.000	0.0000	2.5000	0.4000	2.5000
44	26,89,262.000	0.0000	67,23,153.000	0.0000	2.5000	0.4000	2.5000
45	37,64,967.000	0.0000	94,12,415.000	0.0000	2.5000	0.4000	2.5000
46	52,70,954.000	0.0000	1,31,77,380.000	0.0000	2.5000	0.4000	2.5000
47	73,79,336.000	0.0000	1,84,48,340.000	0.0000	2.5000	0.4000	2.5000
48	1,03,31,070.000	0.0000	2,58,27,670.000	0.0000	2.5000	0.4000	2.5000
49	1,44,63,500.000	0.0000	3,61,58,740.000	0.0000	2.5000	0.4000	2.5000
50	2,02,48,890.000	0.0000	5,06,22,230.000	0.0000	2.5000	0.4000	2.5000

Interest Table for Annual Compounding with $i = 45\%$

n	$F/p,i,n$	$P/F,i,n$	$F/A,i,n$	$A/F,i,n$	$P/A,i,n$	$A/P,i,n$	$A/G,i,n$
1	1.450	0.6897	1.000	1.0000	0.6897	1.4500	0.0000
2	2.103	0.4756	2.450	0.4082	1.1653	0.8582	0.4082
3	3.049	0.3280	4.553	0.2197	1.4933	0.6697	0.7578
4	4.421	0.2262	7.601	0.1316	1.7195	0.5816	1.0528
5	6.410	0.1560	12.022	0.0832	1.8755	0.5332	1.2980
6	9.294	0.1076	18.431	0.0543	1.9831	0.5043	1.4988
7	13.476	0.0742	27.725	0.0361	2.0573	0.4861	1.6612
8	19.541	0.0512	41.202	0.0243	2.1085	0.4743	1.7907
9	28.334	0.0353	60.743	0.0165	2.1438	0.4665	1.8930
10	41.085	0.0243	89.077	0.0112	2.1681	0.4612	1.9728
11	59.573	0.0168	130.162	0.0077	2.1849	0.4577	2.0344
12	86.381	0.0116	189.735	0.0053	2.1965	0.4553	2.0817
13	125.252	0.0080	276.115	0.0036	2.2045	0.4536	2.1176
14	181.615	0.0055	401.367	0.0025	2.2100	0.4525	2.1447
15	263.342	0.0038	582.983	0.0017	2.2138	0.4517	2.1650
16	381.846	0.0026	846.325	0.0012	2.2164	0.4512	2.1802
17	553.677	0.0018	1,228.171	0.0008	2.2182	0.4508	2.1915
18	802.831	0.0012	1,781.848	0.0006	2.2195	0.4506	2.1998
19	1,164.106	0.0009	2,584.680	0.0004	2.2203	0.4504	2.2059
20	1,687.953	0.0006	3,748.785	0.0003	2.2209	0.4503	2.2104
21	2,447.532	0.0004	5,436.739	0.0002	2.2213	0.4502	2.2136
22	3,548.922	0.0003	7,884.272	0.0001	2.2216	0.4501	2.2160
23	5,145.937	0.0002	11,433.190	0.0001	2.2218	0.4501	2.2178
24	7,461.609	0.0001	16,579.130	0.0001	2.2219	0.4501	2.2190
25	10,819.330	0.0001	24,040.740	0.0000	2.2220	0.4500	2.2199
26	15,688.040	0.0001	34,860.080	0.0000	2.2221	0.4500	2.2206
27	22,747.650	0.0000	50,548.120	0.0000	2.2221	0.4500	2.2210
28	32,984.100	0.0000	73,295.770	0.0000	2.2222	0.4500	2.2214
29	47,826.940	0.0000	1,06,279.900	0.0000	2.2222	0.4500	2.2216
30	69,349.070	0.0000	1,54,106.800	0.0000	2.2222	0.4500	2.2218
31	1,00,556.200	0.0000	2,23,455.900	0.0000	2.2222	0.4500	2.2219
32	1,45,806.400	0.0000	3,24,012.100	0.0000	2.2222	0.4500	2.2220
33	2,11,419.300	0.0000	4,69,818.500	0.0000	2.2222	0.4500	2.2221
34	3,06,558.000	0.0000	6,81,237.900	0.0000	2.2222	0.4500	2.2221
35	4,44,509.200	0.0000	9,87,795.900	0.0000	2.2222	0.4500	2.2221
36	6,44,538.300	0.0000	14,32,305.000	0.0000	2.2222	0.4500	2.2222
37	9,34,580.600	0.0000	20,76,844.000	0.0000	2.2222	0.4500	2.2222
38	13,55,142.000	0.0000	30,11,425.000	0.0000	2.2222	0.4500	2.2222
39	19,64,956.000	0.0000	43,66,567.000	0.0000	2.2222	0.4500	2.2222
40	28,49,186.000	0.0000	63,31,523.000	0.0000	2.2222	0.4500	2.2222
41	41,31,320.000	0.0000	91,80,709.000	0.0000	2.2222	0.4500	2.2222
42	59,90,415.000	0.0000	1,33,12,030.000	0.0000	2.2222	0.4500	2.2222
43	86,86,101.000	0.0000	1,93,02,440.000	0.0000	2.2222	0.4500	2.2222
44	1,25,94,850.000	0.0000	2,79,88,550.000	0.0000	2.2222	0.4500	2.2222
45	1,82,62,530.000	0.0000	4,05,83,400.000	0.0000	2.2222	0.4500	2.2222
46	2,64,80,670.000	0.0000	5,88,45,930.000	0.0000	2.2222	0.4500	2.2222
47	3,83,96,970.000	0.0000	8,53,26,600.000	0.0000	2.2222	0.4500	2.2222
48	5,56,75,610.000	0.0000	12,37,23,600.000	0.0000	2.2222	0.4500	2.2222
49	8,07,29,630.000	0.0000	17,93,99,200.000	0.0000	2.2222	0.4500	2.2222
50	11,70,58,000.000	0.0000	26,01,28,900.000	0.0000	2.2222	0.4500	2.2222

Interest Table for Annual Compounding with i = **50%**

n	$F/p, i, n$	$P/F, i, n$	$F/A, i, n$	$A/F, i, n$	$P/A, i, n$	$A/P, i, n$	$A/G, i, n$
1	1.500	0.6667	1.000	1.0000	0.6667	1.5000	0.0000
2	2.250	0.4444	2.500	0.4000	1.1111	0.9000	0.4000
3	3.375	0.2963	4.750	0.2105	1.4074	0.7105	0.7368
4	5.063	0.1975	8.125	0.1231	1.6049	0.6231	1.0154
5	7.594	0.1317	13.188	0.0758	1.7366	0.5758	1.2417
6	11.391	0.0878	20.781	0.0481	1.8244	0.5481	1.4226
7	17.086	0.0585	32.172	0.0311	1.8829	0.5311	1.5648
8	25.629	0.0390	49.258	0.0203	1.9220	0.5203	1.6752
9	38.443	0.0260	74.887	0.0134	1.9480	0.5134	1.7596
10	57.665	0.0173	113.330	0.0088	1.9653	0.5088	1.8235
11	86.498	0.0116	170.995	0.0058	1.9769	0.5058	1.8713
12	129.746	0.0077	257.493	0.0039	1.9846	0.5039	1.9068
13	194.620	0.0051	387.239	0.0026	1.9897	0.5026	1.9329
14	291.929	0.0034	581.859	0.0017	1.9931	0.5017	1.9519
15	437.894	0.0023	873.788	0.0011	1.9954	0.5011	1.9657
16	656.841	0.0015	1,311.682	0.0008	1.9970	0.5008	1.9756
17	985.261	0.0010	1,968.523	0.0005	1.9980	0.5005	1.9827
18	1,477.892	0.0007	2,953.784	0.0003	1.9986	0.5003	1.9878
19	2,216.838	0.0005	4,431.676	0.0002	1.9991	0.5002	1.9914
20	3,325.257	0.0003	6,648.513	0.0002	1.9994	0.5002	1.9940
21	4,987.885	0.0002	9,973.769	0.0001	1.9996	0.5001	1.9958
22	7,481.828	0.0001	14,961.660	0.0001	1.9997	0.5001	1.9971
23	11,222.740	0.0001	22,443.480	0.0000	1.9998	0.5000	1.9980
24	16,834.110	0.0001	33,666.220	0.0000	1.9999	0.5000	1.9986
25	25,251.170	0.0000	50,500.340	0.0000	1.9999	0.5000	1.9990
26	37,876.750	0.0000	75,751.500	0.0000	1.9999	0.5000	1.9993
27	56,815.130	0.0000	1,13,628.300	0.0000	2.0000	0.5000	1.9995
28	85,222.690	0.0000	1,70,443.400	0.0000	2.0000	0.5000	1.9997
29	1,27,834.000	0.0000	2,55,666.100	0.0000	2.0000	0.5000	1.9998
30	1,91,751.100	0.0000	3,83,500.100	0.0000	2.0000	0.5000	1.9998
31	2,87,626.600	0.0000	5,75,251.200	0.0000	2.0000	0.5000	1.9999
32	4,31,439.900	0.0000	8,62,877.800	0.0000	2.0000	0.5000	1.9999
33	6,47,159.800	0.0000	12,94,318.000	0.0000	2.0000	0.5000	1.9999
34	9,70,739.800	0.0000	19,41,478.000	0.0000	2.0000	0.5000	2.0000
35	14,56,110.000	0.0000	29,12,217.000	0.0000	2.0000	0.5000	2.0000
36	21,84,164.000	0.0000	43,68,327.000	0.0000	2.0000	0.5000	2.0000
37	32,76,247.000	0.0000	65,52,491.000	0.0000	2.0000	0.5000	2.0000
38	49,14,370.000	0.0000	98,28,738.000	0.0000	2.0000	0.5000	2.0000
39	73,71,555.000	0.0000	1,47,43,110.000	0.0000	2.0000	0.5000	2.0000
40	1,10,57,330.000	0.0000	2,21,14,660.000	0.0000	2.0000	0.5000	2.0000
41	1,65,86,000.000	0.0000	3,31,72,000.000	0.0000	2.0000	0.5000	2.0000
42	2,48,79,000.000	0.0000	4,97,57,990.000	0.0000	2.0000	0.5000	2.0000
43	3,73,18,500.000	0.0000	7,46,37,000.000	0.0000	2.0000	0.5000	2.0000
44	5,59,77,750.000	0.0000	11,19,55,500.000	0.0000	2.0000	0.5000	2.0000
45	8,39,66,620.000	0.0000	16,79,33,200.000	0.0000	2.0000	0.5000	2.0000
46	12,59,49,900.000	0.0000	25,18,99,900.000	0.0000	2.0000	0.5000	2.0000
47	18,89,24,900.000	0.0000	37,78,49,800.000	0.0000	2.0000	0.5000	2.0000
48	28,33,87,300.000	0.0000	56,67,74,600.000	0.0000	2.0000	0.5000	2.0000
49	42,50,81,000.000	0.0000	85,01,62,000.000	0.0000	2.0000	0.5000	2.0000
50	63,76,21,500.000	0.0000	1,27,52,43,000.000	0.0000	2.0000	0.5000	2.0000

Bibliography

Agasty, M.P., *Engineering Economics and Costing*, Scitech Publication, Hyderabad, 2006.

Ahuja, H.L., *The Theory of Demand*, S. Chand and Company Ltd., New Delhi, 1982.

Arasu, B.S. and Paul, J.P., *Break-Even Analysis*, Scitech Publication, Hyderabad, 2004.

Blank, L.T. and Tarquin, A.J., *Engineering Economy*, McGraw-Hill, New York, 1989.

Collier, C.A., *Engineering Cost Analysis*, Harper and Row, New York, 1982.

Fleisher, G.A., *Introduction to Engineering Economy*, PWS Publishing Company, Boston, 1994.

Frost, M.J., *How to Use Cost Benefit Analysis in Project Appraisal*, John Wiley and Sons, New York, 1975.

Grant, E.L., Ireson, W.G. and Leavenworth, R.S., *Principle of Engineering Economy*, Ronald Press, New York, 1996.

Horn Green, C.T., *Cost Accounting,* Prentice Hall of India, New Delhi 2000.

Jelen, F.C. and Black, J.H., *Cost and Optimization Engineering*, McGraw-Hill New Delhi, 1983.

Lang, H.J., *Cost Analysis for Capital Investment Decisions*, Marcel Dekker, Inc. New York, 1989.

Mishra, P.K., *Process Costing*, Alok Publication, 2004.

Pail, R.R., *Money Banking and International Trade*, Kalyani Publisher, New Delhi, 1999.

Panneerselvam, R, '*Evaluation of public activities*', *Indian Economic Panorama*, Vol. 2, No. 4, pp. 21–22, 1992.

Riggs, J.L., *Engineering Economics*, McGraw-Hill, New York, 1982.

Steiner, H.M., *Engineering Economic Principles*, McGraw-Hill Book, New York, 1992.

Index

Agricultural development banks, 181
Annuity, 71
Annuity due, 72
Arc elasticity of demand, 30

Banks
    assets of, 161
    balance sheet of, 160
    liabilities of, 161
Banks, types of, 159
    agricultural, 159
    central, 160
    commercial, 159
    exchange, 160
    industrial, 159
    saving, 160
Break-even analysis, 137
Break-even chart, 140
Break-even point, 137
    as a percentage of capacity, 140
    in terms of quantity, 138
    in terms of sales value, 139

Call money market, 176
Cash flow diagrams, 76
Cash flows, types of, 75
    initial investment, 75
    operating, 76
    terminal, 76
Certificate of deposit market, 177
Change in costs, 143
Change in price, 143

Commercial banking, 153
Commercial banks, functions of, 154–155
Commercial bill market, 177
Commercial paper market, 177
Cost accounting, 197
    objectives of, 198
Cost-benefit analysis, 110–111
Cost control, 222
    features of, 222
    techniques of, 223
Cost curves, 44
Costing, 197
Cost reduction, 223
Costs, elements of, 203
Credit authorization scheme, 173
Current deposit account, 154

Das Kapital, 5
Deferred annuity, 72
Demand schedule, 19
    individual, 19
    market, 20
Depreciable property, 125
Depreciation analysis, 124
Depreciation, causes of, 124–125
Depreciation methods, 126
    declining balance, 127
    modified accelerated cost recovery system, 130
    straight line, 126
Diminishing marginal rate of technical substitution, 37
Diminishing marginal utility analysis, 13

Direct cost, 201
Discount and finance house of India, 180

Economic activities, 8
    consumption, 8
    exchange and distribution, 8
    international trade, 8
    money and banking, 8
    production, 8
Economics, 3
Elasticity of demand, 24
Elasticity of supply, 54
Engineering economics, 3
    definition of, 6
    principles of, 10
    scope of, 6
Equal-payment series
    capital recovery amount, 69
    compound amount, 65
    present worth amount, 68
    sinking fund, 66
Equal product curves, 35
    properties of, 38
Equi-marginal utility, 14
Equivalence, principles of, 78
Equivalent annual worth comparison, 94
Estimated cost, 217
Export-import bank of India, 189
External rate of return, 101

Fixed cost, 199
Fixed deposit account, 154
Future worth method, 89

General insurance corporation of India, 192
Giffen goods, 24

Hire purchase finance, 163
Home safe account, 154

Income effect, 23
Indian capital market, 181
Indian money market, 174
    organized sector of, 176
    structure of, 174
    unorganized sector of, 175
Indirect cost, 201

Industrial credit and investment corporation of India, 187
Industrial development bank of India, 185
Industrial development banks, 182
Industrial finance corporation of India, 182
Industrial reconstruction corporation of India, 189
Internal rate of return, 101
Introspective method, 13
Irrelevant cost, 202

Law of demand, 16, 22
    limitations of, 24
Law of supply, 54
Law of variable proportions, 38
Life insurance corporation of India, 191
Long-run average cost curves, 51

Macroeconomics, 6
Marginal costing, 211
Marginal rate of technical substitution, 36
Marginal utility analysis, 12
Minimum acceptable rate of return, 101
Money market mutual funds, 177

Opportunity cost, 203

Period cost, 202
Philosopher's stone, 3
Population, principles of, 5
Present worth method, 82
Price elasticity of demand, 25
Price elasticity, types of, 26
    perfectly elastic demand, 26
    perfectly inelastic demand, 26
    relatively elastic demand, 27
    relatively inelastic demand, 28
    unit elasticity demand, 26
Principles of engineering economy, 6
Process costing, 205
Product cost, 202
Profit-volume (P/V)
    analysis, 145
    ratio, 213

Rate of return method, 100
Real cost of production, 202
Recurring deposit account, 154

Relevant cost, 201
Reserve bank of India, 165
    functions of, 166–169
    monetary policy of, 169
    organization of, 165
Returns to scale, 41
    constant, 42
    decreasing, 43
    increasing, 43

Safety margin, 142
Saving deposit account, 154
Semi-variable cost, 200
Short-run average cost curves, 47
Short-run total costs, 45
Single-payment compound amount, 64
Single-payment present worth amount, 64
Small industries development bank of India, 190
Spoilage, 208
Standard costing, 214
    advantages of, 217
    and budgetry control, 215
    definition of, 215
    limitation of, 218

State finance corporations, 183
Substitution effect, 23
Sum of the years-digit method, 133

Term lending, 163
Time value of money, 63
Treasury bill market, 177

Uniform gradient series factor, 70
Unit trust of India, 188
Utility analysis, 12

Variable cost, 199
Variance analysis, 214
Variances,
    computation and analysis of, 219
    controllable, 220
    favourable, 219
    labour cost, 221
    material cost, 220
    uncontrollable, 220
    unfavourable, 219